THE CHRISTIAN MONITORS

THE LEWIS WALPOLE SERIES IN EIGHTEENTH-CENTURY CULTURE AND HISTORY

The Lewis Walpole Series, published by Yale University Press with the aid of the Annie Burr Lewis Fund, is dedicated to the culture and history of the long eighteenth century (from the Glorious Revolution to the accession of Queen Victoria). It welcomes work in a variety of fields, including literature and history, the visual arts, political philosophy, music, legal history, and the history of science. In addition to original scholarly work, the series publishes new editions and translations of writing from the period, as well as reprints of major books that are currently unavailable. Though the majority of books in the series will probably concentrate on Great Britain and the Continent, the range of our geographical interests is as wide as Horace Walpole's.

THE CHRISTIAN MONITORS

The Church of England and the
Age of Benevolence, 1680–1730

Brent S. Sirota

Yale UNIVERSITY PRESS

NEW HAVEN AND LONDON

Published with assistance from the Annie Burr Lewis Fund.

Yale University Press books may be purchased in quantity for educational, business, or
promotional use. For information, please e-mail sales.press@yale.edu (U.S. office) or
sales@yaleup.co.uk (U.K. office).

Designed by James J. Johnson.
Set in Minion type by IDS Infotech, Ltd.
Printed in the United States of America.

Library of Congress Cataloging-in-Publication Data

Sirota, Brent S., 1976–
The Christian monitors : the Church of England and the age of benevolence, 1680–1730 /
Brent S. Sirota.
pages cm.—(The Lewis Walpole series in eighteenth-century culture and history)
Includes bibliographical references and index.

ISBN 978-0-300-16710-8 (cloth : alk. paper) 1. Church of England—History—17th century.
2. Anglican Communion—England—History—17th century. 3. England—Church
history—17th century. 4. Church of England—History—18th century. 5. Anglican
Communion—England—History—18th century. 6. England—Church history—18th
century. I. Title.
BX5081.S57 2014
283'.4209033—dc23
2013018588

A catalogue record for this book is available from the British Library.

This paper meets the requirements of ANSI/NISO Z39.48-1992 (Permanence of Paper).

10 9 8 7 6 5 4 3 2 1

To Alexandra Armitage, still sacred

As a matter of fact, in England, at least, it is these smaller associations which have always counted for most in the life of the individual. His school or college, his parish or country, his union or regiment, his wife or family is the most vitally important part in the life of most men; and in so far as England has anything worthy in civic life to show to the world, it is the spectacle of individuals bred up or living within the small associations which mold the life of men more immediately than does the great collectivity we call the State.

—JOHN NEVILLE FIGGIS, *Churches in the Modern State* (1914)

The Anglo-Saxons display a capacity for diluting their religion, probably in excess of that of any other race.

—T. S. ELIOT, "The Idea of a Christian Society" (1939)

Contents

Acknowledgments

When the present study was in its infancy, it took its title not from John Rawlet's 1686 devotional tract *The Christian Monitor*, but from a 1691 spital sermon preached by John Tillotson, just before he was named archbishop of Canterbury, titled "On Doing Good." This was the title the project bore in the letter of introduction with which the University of Chicago equipped me for my earliest research trips to the United Kingdom. On one such occasion, I presented this letter with my passport to the Border Force officer at Heathrow airport to explain the reason for my visit. He chortled audibly and asked, "Have we done any good?" before waving me through. He wasn't waiting for an answer. Even if he had been, the present study would not serve.

A decade later, I can only say that I have been the recipient of a great deal of benevolence during the completion of this book. I sincerely thank the staff members of the Manuscript and Rare Books Rooms of the British Library, Lambeth Palace Library, the Bodleian Library at Oxford University, Cambridge University Library, Regenstein Library at the University of Chicago, the Beinecke Library at Yale University, and the Harry Ransom Center at the University of Texas at Austin for their guidanc e and assistance. My very special thanks to Pamela Hunter, the archivist at C. Hoare & Co. Bank on Fleet Street, who was an invaluable guide to mapping the philanthropic networks of late-seventeenth-century London. Thanks also to the good folks at the D. H. Hill Library at North Carolina State University: daily walks over to the circulation desk there, I can confess, have always been as much about head-clearing and pleasant conversation as they have been about resource procurement.

Acknowledgments

I am also grateful for the opportunities I have had to present various aspects and permutations of the arguments in this book at numerous conferences and symposia over the past few years at the University of Chicago, Yale University, Princeton University, Roger Williams University, Ohio University, Bangor University, the Huntington Library, Haverford College, and the Triangle Intellectual History Seminar in North Carolina, as well as at meetings of the North American Conference on British Studies, the British Scholar Society, and the Southeastern American Conference on Eighteenth Century Studies. I am indebted to the organizers and attendants of all these meetings for their collegiality, critical engagement, and conversation. Research for this study has been generously funded by the Nicholson Center on British Studies at the University of Chicago and the North Carolina State University Department of History. Much of this work was researched and written during my year as a postdoctoral fellow at the Institute for Historical Studies at the University of Texas at Austin. My warmest thanks to Julie Hardwick, Bob Olwell, Brian Levack, Neil Kamil, Courtney Meador, and the other IHS fellows for making my family and me feel at home in Texas.

I have benefited from the kindness and wisdom of many professors and mentors over the years. My dissertation advisor Steve Pincus gave this religion student from the Divinity School a seat in his British History seminar and eventually a place in the doctoral program in history. He has been a gracious mentor, a rigorous supervisor, a convivial dining companion, and a good friend. Steve has been involved with every step of this project from proposal to press, and whatever merits it may possess owe much to his tireless engagement. As a graduate student, I was tasked with picking up both Rachel Weil and Margaret Hunt from O'Hare airport for a conference, and I somehow managed to parlay that debacle of lost luggage and mixed connections into enduring friendships with both of these incredibly generous scholars. They have read and commented on nearly every incarnation of this project. The wise and affable John Spurr of Swansea University taught me, through advice and example, how to do rich, painstaking, politically sophisticated ecclesiastical history. Every day I discover new intellectual debts to his work. Chicago gained an honorary citizen when Allan Macinnes served as visiting professor for a semester at the University of Chicago; and we students who had the good fortune to study with him gained a virtual second advisor, who to this day can always be counted on for advice, political opinions, and the next round anywhere in the world. Stephen Taylor,

Dan Szechi, and Alan Houston have also been unstinting in their help and counsel.

My colleagues here in the department of history at North Carolina State University have also been instrumental in helping me bring this book to fruition. Our leaders Jonathan Ocko and David Zonderman have steered the department through dire economic times. My colleagues Holly Brewer, Julia Rudolph, Tony La Vopa, Mimi Kim, and Chad Luddington have all kindly read over and commented on various parts of the manuscript. I wish to express my particular gratitude to my colleague Steven Vincent, who has read and thoughtfully engaged with every chapter of the present work. David Ambaras, Megan Cherry, Haydon Cherry, Nick Robbins, Judy Kertész, and Noah Strote have helped me in innumerable ways through countless lunches, hallway exchanges, book recommendations, and various other nameless acts of charity and beneficence. My dear friend and colleague Kat Charron has been my infallible guide to southern living, southern history, and the perfect Old Fashioned. I also thank my students here at NC State, particularly my graduate students Brad Dixon, Linda Wendling, Zach Ferguson, and Rob Super with whom many of these arguments received their first airing and discussion.

Thanks to Chris Rogers and Christina Tucker at Yale University Press for helping bring this project to completion. I am grateful to the readers for the press, whose invaluable feedback and incisive criticism helped shape the book into its final form. My sincere gratitude to the book's copy editor, Jessie Dolch, my lively correspondent for the past few months on subjects ranging from English usage to proper manuscript citation to the disputed spelling of the names of English clergymen.

I have benefited from the friendship and camaraderie of many kind souls. My friend James Vaughn, it is safe to say, has been more familiar with the intellectual evolution of this project than anyone outside my immediate family. I cannot thank him enough for the visits, arguments, email exchanges, and readthroughs graciously on offer since around the third week of graduate school. I also offer my hearty thanks for the support, company, and boundless hospitality of Abby Swingen, Bill Bulman, Phil Stern, Robert Ingram, Michael Brillman, Raven Glidden, Isaac Zaur, Nick Popper, Amy Haley, Lyman Stebbins, Craig Hargett, Chris Dudley, Fredrik Jonsson, Sarah Ellenzweig, Glenn Calderwood, Scott and Amber Richard, John and Susan Worth, Jason Sloat, Paul Smith and Michelle Mills, Ben Helphand, Geoff Bucknum, and Rosali Middleman. All of them have been good enough to share their thoughts, time, tables, libraries, record collections, and homes with me on various occasions. Peter and Mariolina Freeth opened up their beautiful Muswell Hill home to my wife and me when we were living in London, and we will always look back fondly on the days we spent with them there.

My family has been a source of endless love, support, laughter, and, yes, patience these past years. My father and mother, Robert and Carol Sirota, have never flagged in their encouragement and generosity. Their love has made this life and this book possible, and they have watched with mounting excitement and, I hope, pride as this project has coalesced. I simply cannot thank them enough for everything they have given me—starting with a love not just for books, but for the stories and lives of other people. To them I owe, above all, the sympathetic imagination that is the first impulse toward the writing of history. I also thank my father-in-law and mother-in-law, Rodman and Elsa Forter, lovers of history and late-night conversation; they have been a second set of parents to me. My thanks also to my sister Wendy and her husband Ricky Kleinsmith and my brother-in-law Rod Forter and his wife Rebecca, purveyors of good cheer, fierce argument, and well-mixed cocktails. My four-year-old son, Ezra, is one of the absolute joys of my life. He has acquired a clipboard and proclaimed himself a teacher. Perhaps it's as simple as that. Beautiful little Simone arrived just about a week after the submission of this manuscript to the press. May all her days proceed with such impeccable timing.

This book is dedicated to my wife, partner, and best friend Alexandra Armitage Forter Sirota. Her work in relief agencies, settlement houses, and public policy first got me thinking about the intersection of government, religious entities, and voluntary associations in the making of civil society. I'm not sure she would recognize her career in twenty-first-century antipoverty and employment policy in a book about the eighteenth-century British age of benevolence. Nevertheless, those efforts inspired this book and continue to inspire its author. She finds a way to do good every day.

Notes on Style

All quotations from historical sources have been rendered in modern English orthography. All dates before 1752 are given in Old Style, according to the Julian calendar in use in England throughout the period considered here. However, the year is presumed to have begun on 1 January, rather than 25 March as some contemporaries reckoned. All information concerning sources is available in the endnotes.

THE CHRISTIAN MONITORS

Introduction

On a Thursday in Whitsun week 1715, William Wake, bishop of Lincoln, delivered the annual sermon before the pupils, teachers, and trustees of the London charity schools assembled at St. Sepulchre, Holborn, a few short blocks from St. Paul's Cathedral. Established in 1704, the anniversary sermons were founded to promote the Anglican education of poor children throughout the metropolis. In the intervening decade, the sermons had become something more: testimonials to a great revival unfolding within the Church of England. Wake hailed the "improvements which have been made within these few years last past" to public worship and devotion—frequent communions, daily prayers, public catechizing—"[a]nd all these carefully attended upon by the greatest number of pious and well-disposed Christians that perhaps has ever been known in any age." With these must be listed the "public provision which has been made for the better support of the established ministry at home, and for the planting of churches and ministers . . . abroad," corporate institutions such as the Sons of the Clergy, Queen Anne's Bounty, and the Society for the Propagation of the Gospel in Foreign Parts (SPG). Wake could not refrain from mentioning the proliferation of "voluntary societies," such as the Society for Promoting Christian Knowledge (SPCK), and the multiplying societies for the reformation of manners, all of which, though operating without official mandate, were "approved of and countenanced by public authority." Everywhere was evidence of an established church in the flush of revival, one characterized not only by a new diligence in pastoral engagement, but, more remarkably, by a wave of new Anglican institutions permeating civic life in England.[1]

The Anglican revival of the late seventeenth and early eighteenth centuries is the subject of this book.[2] The Church of England in this period, as William Wake so ably delineated in a sermon delivered mere months before his elevation to the primacy, was engaged in a multifaceted program of confessional revitalization, characterized by augmented pastoral initiative, heightened popular devotion, public and private institution-building, and efforts at liturgical and ecclesiastical reform. As such, the Anglican revival intersected with nearly every plane of social and political life in rapidly modernizing England and its commercial and territorial empire of the late seventeenth and early eighteenth centuries. The Anglican revival was not, as the late Victorian secretary of the SPCK Edmund McClure put it, merely "a chapter in English church history," but a development of enormous social, political, and cultural resonance that shaped the contours of English church, state, and civil society in the eighteenth century and beyond. The institutions born of the Anglican revival served as the Church of England's primary instruments of modernization and adaptation throughout the first half of the eighteenth century. And indeed, the revival's cherished ideals of "national reformation" and moral renewal loomed large in the construction of British national and imperial identity throughout the postrevolutionary era.[3] The "golden age" of Victorian philanthropy is inconceivable without the institutional foundations of the Augustan period.[4] And in the twenty-first century, those in the United Kingdom who call for the building of a "big society," characterized by voluntary associations, religious philanthropy, and mutual aid, are (usually unwittingly) speaking a language of social action first adumbrated in the Anglican revival of the turn of the eighteenth century.[5] That such voluntarism is often presumed to draw upon a virtually transhistorical feature of British public life is, in and of itself, a testimony to the success of that revival in implanting its ideological and institutional imperatives into the national character. The Anglican revival did not create civil society in England, but it consecrated it to the social and philanthropic purposes to which it has, for good or ill, perennially aspired throughout modern British history.

This book traces the Anglican revival from its origins in the late Restoration period through its climax in the so-called Glorious Revolution of 1688–1689, its centrality to the reformist agendas that informed the ensuing civil and ecclesiastical settlement, and the permeation by its various social and institutional forms of postrevolutionary civic life in England. The revival was born of a period of religious and political reconstruction, acquired a pronounced political character during an era of revolutionary crisis and partisan struggle, and ultimately achieved normative status in the "age of benevolence" that by the mid-eighteenth century had come to define English public life. Through the social and political vicissitudes of the revolutionary era, the Anglican revival evolved from a program of religious renewal into a fundamental component of the English national culture.

The Anglican revival thus must be restored to the history of revolutionary England, where contemporaries had long located it. William Wake, for one, had no doubt that an awakening Church of England comprised the vanguard of opposition to the religious policies of James II during the 1680s. In his 1715 sermon, he explicitly dated the origins of the Anglican revival to the final years of the Restoration, specifically, the end of the reign of Charles II and that of his brother and successor James II, when the nation was beset by "fears of popery, and of that ruin of our laws and liberties as well as our religion, with which we were at that time eminently threatened."[6] Churchmen then responded with a widespread program of Protestant devotion, pastoral engagement, and religious education on behalf of their vulnerable flocks. The success of the Revolution, he preached, "was almost entirely owing to our people being taught of God." Wake thus placed the Revolution at the climax of the Anglican revival. Credit belonged in large part to the "zeal and diligence of our clergy in those days," not only for "setting the nation in a true knowledge and just esteem of their reformed religion and worship," but for raising "that noble spirit which then showed itself in all orders of men among us." God then rewarded the nation's piety and steadfastness with deliverance at home and victory abroad. The dialectic that Wake and many of his contemporaries outlined was astonishingly clear. The Anglican revival not only had preceded the Revolution of 1688–1689, it had to a large extent nursed the revolutionary spirit and ensured its ultimate triumph. The Revolution had, in turn, rendered England safe for moral and religious renewal.[7]

Situating the Anglican revival on either side of the political and ecclesiastical crisis of the reign of James II and its revolutionary dénouement permits a productive reconsideration of the effect of the Revolution of 1688–1689 on the social and religious life of eighteenth-century England. The Revolution must neither be conceived as an absolute rupture dividing a Restoration Church of England deeply invested in coercion from a postrevolutionary Church of England resigned to persuasion, nor be elided in the interest of a seamless transition in the genealogy of the English confessional state. The periodization employed in this book eschews both of these frameworks. Taking account of the late Restoration milieu of the Anglican revival permits the consideration of broad continuities between the pastoral and confessional agendas of late-seventeenth-century Anglicanism and its eighteenth-century successor, while underscoring certain consequences of the Revolution that made the objectives of late Restoration Anglicanism either undesirable or unrealizable.

Anglican revival and ecclesiastical reform were from the outset deeply intertwined with the revolutionary program of 1688–1689 and its legacy. What remains puzzling, however, is just why moral and religious renewal assumed the peculiar form that it did during the postrevolutionary era. The Church of England suddenly found itself at the vanguard of what historians deem "the society-making age in religion and philanthropy."[8] Anglican hierarchy, clergy, and laity in this period collaborated in the conception, cultivation, and promotion of an array of new institutions, many of them with little or no precedent within the ecclesiastical constitution, devoted to moral and religious oversight, confessional expansion, and charitable relief. The late seventeenth and early eighteenth centuries witnessed the emergence of a panoply of well-known Anglican and Protestant ecumenical institutions—the Sons of the Clergy, the Welsh Trust, the SPCK, the SPG, the societies for the reformation of manners, the charity school movement, the Poor Proselytes Society, the Bray Associates, and the Georgia Trust—not to mention a host of ad hoc relief agencies addressing the lives of seamen, soldiers, merchants, and religious refugees. Many of these organizations have individually received attention from historians (often celebratory chronicles by their own members), but few scholars have attempted to account broadly for the explosion of Anglican institution-building during this period. As a result, contemporary historians know a good deal about the personnel and logistics of many of these institutions but have shockingly little to say about the social, political, and ideological circumstances that permitted their proliferation.

This myopia is even more curious given the fact that historians have long singled out the extraordinary vogue for new modes of public association as the distinguishing characteristic of the Anglican revival of the late seventeenth and early eighteenth centuries. Before this period, Canon Frederick Bullock argues, "there is not too much expression in England of the idea of an inner circle, loyal to the main body, but trying also to stimulate it to fresh life and quickened enthusiasm."[9] The final years of the seventeenth century broke decisively with the past.

"The island," writes Dudley Bahlmann, "seemed to be swept by a fever that led men to join groups."[10] Mark Pattison's pioneering essay on religious societies details the "vigorous moral reaction" that accompanied the "exterior dynastic revolution" of 1688 and made the ensuing decades "a time of fruitful schemes of charitable cooperation."[11] John Overton considers the multiplication of religious societies within the established church at this time "a sure symptom of its vigour."[12] John Wickham Legg credits the end of the seventeenth century with a rediscovery of the religious ideal of the common life, expressed in the spread of societies devoted to prayer, study, charity, and moral reform.[13] The Edwardian historian of philanthropy Benjamin Kirkman Gray similarly hails the "feeling for the power of association" as the prevailing principle of social life in this period.[14] More recent overviews of the eighteenth-century Church of England similarly note the unprecedented "willingness of some Churchmen to countenance, even to encourage, more voluntaristic approaches to pastoral problems."[15]

While such observations are commonplace in the historiography, they fail to address what must be considered one of the great puzzles of Anglican political and ecclesiastical history during the late seventeenth and early eighteenth centuries: why did the agenda of Anglican renewal largely proceed on this associational footing? Paradoxically, the Church of England in this period was characterized by both constitutional inertia and institutional fecundity.[16] The revivalist imperatives that seized the church in the decades surrounding the Revolution of 1688–1689 yielded virtually no substantive reform of the doctrine, liturgy, or governance of the established church but rather an extraordinary wave of organizational experimentation and institution-building on the margins, as it were, of the ecclesiastical constitution. The established church, the institutional conservatism of which comprised perhaps its most celebrated link to the pre-Reformation past in England and to primitive Christianity in general, gloried in unleashing a host of anomalous new organizations upon the face of English national life. And though the various societies and enterprises possessed distinct origins, forms, objectives, and even political complexions, enthusiastic supporters such as William Wake were quite happy to invoke them all in a single breath as collective evidence of the vitality of Anglicanism and the moral renewal of England.

Interestingly, observers had as yet no name to signify the culture of moral, religious, and philanthropic enterprise that emerged at the interstices of Anglican revival and English revolution. But they were nevertheless palpably aware of its recent dramatic emergence and generally inclined to see it as a singular phenomenon. Public life in postrevolutionary England was suddenly illuminated by what one observer hailed as a "constellation of noble designs," an array of voluntary associations, chartered bodies, and charitable trusts pursuing religious and charitable work at home and abroad.[17] Observers were no less struck by this new spirit of moral and religious engagement than by the elaborate and unprecedented institutional infrastructure erected at its behest. In 1707, the London curate White Kennett considered it "the singular glory to our present times, that there be set up of late many offices of doing good, worthy men formed into societies for several noble and excellent ends."[18] Samuel Bradford, rector of St. Mary-le-Bow, spoke heartily, if clumsily, of "the several excellent designs which have begun by several pious and serious persons forming themselves into societies for the mutual assistance of each other."[19] Similarly, the physician Francis Lee wrote of "the several of ways and means which are carrying on in this age, to relieve either the spiritual or the temporal necessities of men, and to promote Christian knowledge and practice both at home and abroad."[20] These witnesses were grasping at a novel set of cultural and religious imperatives and institutional arrangements avant la lettre. It was not until the middle decades of the eighteenth century that such tributes began coalescing into the conceit of the postrevolutionary period as a uniquely charitable age, or an age of benevolence.

By the mid-eighteenth century, the notion of an age of benevolence had been enshrined in the mythos of British national life.[21] "It is certain," proclaimed Jonathan Swift in 1733, "that the genius of the people of England is strongly turned to public charities."[22] The schoolmaster James Welton marveled in 1759 that "the benevolence of this age has been such . . . that there is hardly a natural evil, for which some degree of consolation has not been provided." According to the Baptist minister Thomas Llewelyn, the century was characterized above all by an "exuberance of charity," manifest in the "millions of sterling [that] have been expended on works of benevolence in this country since the year 1700."[23] Over the course of the century, the collective benevolence of Britons, and the multiplying organizations and institutions in which it was lodged, occupied an ever larger place in the British national consciousness. Like the Enlightenment, with which it is sometimes compared (or conflated), the notion of an age of benevolence at once comprised a social and cultural program, an array of new institutions and practices, and an epochal identity.[24] Public life in Britain, related the popular *London Magazine* in 1767, now proceeded amidst "the numerous plans, proposals and schemes offered to the public for relieving distress, encouraging merit, promoting virtue, and propagating religion."[25] In 1778, when the bishop of Chester Beilby Porteus sought to console the public over the worsening crisis of the American empire, he reminded his auditors in the House of Lords of the national blessings of civil liberty, Protestantism, and toleration as well as the "boundless munificence" with which the kingdom's poor and distressed were relieved "both by private charity and public institutions."[26] Charity was now numbered among the "Revolution principles" that comprised the touchstone of British national identity throughout the eighteenth century. Indeed, for some, benevolence functioned as the cynosure of Revolution principles, the end to which liberty, property, and Protestantism were ideally consecrated. "True liberty," wrote the celebrated Anglican philanthropist Jonas Hanway, "consists in doing well."[27] Accompanying Great Britain's rise to national greatness in the century following the Glorious Revolution was, it seems, a self-confessed rise to national goodness.[28]

The history of the Anglican revival, its political commitments and ideological presuppositions, not to mention its institutional innovations, thus offers a novel approach to the making of modern Britain. From the crucible of the Revolution of 1688–1689—and particularly, from the Revolution as an ecclesiastical crisis—emerged what we would today recognize as a peculiarly English conception of "civil society," comprising not only the space of purposive association, but the privileged site of social action.[29] At the end of the seventeenth century, the noisome Restoration domain of coffeehouses, conventicles, and combinations underwent a dramatic moral valorization as a sphere of public life uniquely hospitable to the organized pursuit of the common good.[30] During this period, English men and women embraced a new conception of social engagement in civil society—a pursuit of virtue, it should be added, utterly foreign to the prevailing political languages of the preceding age, republicanism and absolutism. The Revolution, it might be said, did not so much mark the birth of the "associational world" of civil society in England as its baptism, its consecration to higher moral and spiritual purpose.[31] The Church of England, of course, administered this great societal sacrament. The established church's cultivation of a vast array of new associations and organizations, and its willingness to invest them with even a portion of its sacred function, imbued English civil society with an unprecedented moral legitimacy. As the historian Paul Slack notes, it was during the period after the Glorious Revolution that England embraced the "public advantage of competing and overlapping societies within societies."[32] His sometime collaborator Peter Clark adds that in the eighteenth century, "the image and the concept of the voluntary society increasingly penetrated every nook and cranny of British social and cultural life."[33] The Anglican revival, then, effectively created the conditions for an eighteenth-century age of benevolence rooted not in the British state, but in the manifold associations and enterprises of civil society. Even as it outstripped the confessional purposes to which it was once consecrated, English civil society long bore the trace of its revivalist origins in the highly moralized nationalist mythologies of patriotism and benevolence. Indeed, the moral ascendancy of civil society achieved in the eighteenth century no doubt contributed to the long-term occlusion of the state in the British social imaginary.[34]

The present investigation of the Anglican revival and its contribution to the eighteenth-century age of benevolence, it must be stipulated, is not intended to contribute to a burgeoning corpus of historical apologetics for an oft-maligned period in English religious history. The objective here is not to posit a narrative of Anglican renewal in the place of the long-prevailing account of the "church in danger" from Catholicism, Nonconformity, irreligion, and enlightenment. Intimations of Anglican revival in the late seventeenth and early eighteenth centuries were not in any meaningful sense more substantive or more accurate than the widespread apprehensions of religious decline. Indeed, this book proceeds from the fact that contemporaries found both narratives ready to hand for assessing the state of English Christianity during this time, and various audiences were willing to attribute no small amount of plausibility to each. Why, then, was the Church of England perceived as simultaneously exultant and embattled? Which developments in particular underpinned and justified such competing assessments? Rather than passing judgment on the spiritual life of an age, this book shows how the opposition and interaction of these competing tropes comprised the framework of ecclesiastical politics in this period. Together, the alternative rhetorics of renewal and decline mapped the place of the Church of England within the broader discourse of "Revolution politics," the continuously contested meaning and legacy of the Revolution of 1688–1689 in the making of postrevolutionary state and society.[35] The Anglican revival was thus never simply an event occurring within the church; it also provided an ideological key by which late-seventeenth- and early-eighteenth-century English men and women could decipher contemporary events during a period of revolutionary upheaval. Like the contemporaneous rhetoric of the "church in danger," the discourse and program of the Anglican revival lent a particular meaning and moral valence to the events of the Revolution of 1688–1689 and the ensuing ecclesiastical settlement, which was in turn used to fashion and legitimate an Anglican establishmentarianism for the postrevolutionary era.

One way of approaching the paradox of these contradictory discourses is by situating the Anglican revival and the ensuing age of benevolence at the nexus of the two (seemingly) countervailing social processes of confessionalization and secularization. The eighteenth century began with a flurry of Anglican aggrandizement and institution-building at home and abroad of which churchmen were never fully in control; and these energies diffused into a more generalized British civic investment, still possessed of a strong moral content but markedly diminished confessional identity.[36] The soteriological imperatives that accompanied the initial burst of dynamic Anglican establishmentarianism became increasingly confined within a framework of immanence.[37] Projects and institutions that might have expressly embodied a salvation agenda at the beginning of the century increasingly articulated their objectives in the language of improvement and social utility, or at the very least, a more denominationally inclusive language of virtue and benevolence, even when their identity with the established church and its sacred functions remained pronounced.[38] Endeavors once vigorously expressive of Anglicanism over time became broadly expressive of Britishness; the works of *societas Christiana* diffused out into a more generalized civil society. Observers could thus exult in the national reformation that seemed to be unfolding in postrevolutionary Britain while fretting as the salvific agenda of such enterprises waned.

Arguably the most influential paradigm in the recent historiography of Protestant and Catholic reformations in continental Europe, the concept of confessionalization has long been conspicuous by its absence from the historiography of early modern England and Scotland. The term "confessionalization" generally denotes the collaboration of early modern civil and ecclesiastical authorities in the processes of societal integration, religious acculturation, and social disciplining in a given territory. In this paradigm Catholic, Lutheran, and Calvinist territories alike were conceived as sites of mutually reinforcing processes of confessional homogenization (and along with it, differentiation from and marginalization of competing faiths), ecclesiastical institutionalization, and political centralization. In other words, early modern European polities were supposed to have sponsored equivalent programs of "politico-religious integration of society" based on emerging confessional identities, irrespective of their doctrinal content.[39] The classic confessionalization paradigm has, however, gained little purchase in the historiography of the English Reformation, where scholars believe that the herky-jerky nature of the Reformation during the Tudor period bred both a high degree of religious and doctrinal pluralism among the populace and a real skepticism about the prospects for confessional uniformity at the level of the English state. In the interests of political security and stability, state-building in England advanced without the investments in confessional uniformity character-istic of the territorial states on the Continent.[40]

Recently, however, certain recognizable elements of the confessionalization paradigm have appeared in English historiography under the guise of England's so-called long reformation. This approach suggests that the "Protestant nation" was an exceedingly long time in the making. The framework of an English Reformation spanning Tudor, Stuart, and Hanoverian ages has allowed histo-rians to place the social and pastoral agendas of the late-seventeenth- and eighteenth-century Church of England on a long continuum with the Protestant acculturation efforts of the earliest reformers as well as their Puritan and Laudian heirs. "The achievement of a Christian society," Eamon Duffy announced in his pioneering Neale Lecture in 1996, "is, or was, an ongoing project which those charged with its attainment have never believed to be complete."[41] From the premise of what Duffy called "a long-term preoccupation with the conversion of the nation," historians have detected enduring continuities (though punctuated by political crisis) in English Protestant efforts at Christian education and cate-chesis, professionalization of the clergy, inculcation of popular piety, reformation of manners, and corporal disciplining through institutions such as workhouses and hospitals—many of the objectives associated with the Anglican revival of the late seventeenth and early eighteenth centuries.[42]

Such an approach, it should be said, puts some pressure on Jonathan Clark's provocative construction of the English ancien régime in the long eighteenth century as a "confessional state" underpinned by an orthodox political theology of which the established church was the sole custodian.[43] At the very least, it invites historians to rethink the processes by which a "confessional state" was installed at the apex of a very slowly confessionalizing society, and whether such a status really deserves the character of hegemony. Moreover, there is little reason to assume that the "confessional state" of the long eighteenth century was any more invested in confessionalization efforts than either of its Tudor or Stuart forebears. "Royal supremacy and monarchical interests," Patrick Collinson reminds us, "frustrated more than they furthered the cause of Reformation."[44] Clark's account requires that the "hegemonic set of ideas" that he believes comprised the English ancien régime were somehow in and of themselves instrumental in the work of Anglican confessionalization. In Clark's vision of the long eighteenth century, Jeremy Gregory points out, the tenets of Anglicanism seem "almost magically to have percolated down the social scale." Against Clark, Gregory suggests that the "confessional state" in the eighteenth century was for most churchmen largely aspirational, "something to work for; it had not yet been achieved."[45]

This, of course, returns us to the matter of instrumentation. What were the means of Anglican confessionalization? When and under what circumstances did they alter? The "long reformation" framework, on the one hand, proves useful for identifying and understanding long-term continuities in Anglican pastoral, educational, and disciplinary objectives. The concept of the "confessional state," on the other, highlights the idealization of outcomes in the mutually reinforcing languages of civil and ecclesiastical order throughout the long eighteenth century. But neither adequately accounts for the morphology of the Anglican revival of the late seventeenth and early eighteenth centuries, the voluntaristic, associational, and entrepreneurial dimensions that seemed to strike all observers as its signal features. Moreover, neither model offers much insight into the *politicization of tactics* by which the Anglican revival was interjected into the heart of "Revolution politics." As we shall see, it was not incidental that some observers saw the SPCK as a potential rival to the convocation of the province of Canterbury; that Thomas Bray's parochial libraries were conceived as substitutes for the decayed rural deaneries; that certain kinds of ecumenical engagement with the wider Protestant world were viewed more favorably than others; and that Daniel Defoe could mock Mary Astell's famed academy for women as a "Protestant nunnery" while promoting his own friendly society for widows. Such controversies rarely turned on mere logistics. The agents and instruments of revival—lay or clerical, associational or ecclesiastical, novel or traditional, confessional or ecumenical—mattered, and their significance was always evaluated in light of the changing configurations of church, state, and civil society in the postrevolutionary era.

From this perspective one can discern the ways in which Anglican confessionalization was haunted by the prospect of secularization in the later seventeenth and early eighteenth centuries. Here I would like to use the term "secularization" sensu stricto, meaning the movement, transfer, or relocation out of the ecclesiastical sphere and into the world, or the *saeculum*—the sense in which it was used to describe a monk's departure from the cloister or the political expropriation of church lands or wealth.[46] The Anglican revival of this period was characterized by the established church routinely going beyond itself: cultivating institutions foreign to its constitution, mobilizing resources alien to its patrimony, and delegating aspects of its monitory or meliorative functions to personnel outside of its hierarchy. Simply put, a program of ecclesiastical renewal continually enlisted what many considered nonecclesiastical instruments and agents in furtherance of Anglican confessionalization, social discipline, and charitable engagement. Moreover, the peculiarly associational, entrepreneurial, and frankly improvisational character of the Anglican revival routinely precluded the maintenance of ecclesiastical supervision and control. The fact that an avowedly "religious" agenda may have been embraced by all participants in the Anglican revival should not obscure the ever-present prospect of secularization in this strictly *ecclesial* sense.

The Anglican revival unfolded on the fault line between church and civil society. Secularization, understood as the movement toward the latter, was thus not only a structural feature of the revival, but a central element in its politicization. Moreover, one cannot discount the legitimating force that Anglican promotion and cultivation of voluntary associations had on rival denominations, commercial projectors, and other public-minded citizens. For instance, it is well known that the SPCK inspired the founding of a Scottish counterpart devoted to Presbyterian establishmentarianism shortly after the Union. William Whiston's proposal for anti-Trinitarian societies for promoting primitive Christianity followed shortly thereafter. This is a perfect example of secularization in the ecclesial sense: there need be no diminution of the religious identity or objectives of any of these entities, but the movement beyond the traditional demarcations of the (Anglican) ecclesiastical sphere is unmistakable. In legitimating the form and operations of such associations, the Church of England reinforced the sense of civil society as a forum uniquely hospitable to such religious, moral, or philanthropic agendas, while effectively guaranteeing its institutional and ideological heterogeneity.

The end result may well have been an eighteenth-century age of benevolence comprehended in highly moralistic and nationalistic terms, but rarely in exclusively confessional ones. The age of benevolence was relatively open to all comers. And thus, secularization in the ecclesial sense used here may well have ultimately contributed to the process of secularization in the more familiarly sociological sense, that is, referring to the declining social significance of religion.[47] Certainly, this was the way in which the age of benevolence was increasingly understood by pious critics around the turn of the nineteenth century. With philanthropy unmoored from its original confessional berth, the conservative evangelical Hannah More wondered whether "to consider benevolence as a substitute for Christianity, [rather] than as evidence of it." The age was one, the evangelical Isaac Crouch caustically remarked in 1786, "in which benevolence is the fashionable, and the only virtue." From a different end of the political and ecclesiological spectrum, the populist William Cobbett used his vituperative *History of the Reformation in England and Ireland* to launch a vicious assault on the culture of eighteenth-century British philanthropy, in which the established church (through the Anglican societies) endlessly solicited contributions from civil society to perform the basic religious and social services for which its vast patrimony was allegedly inadequate. Cobbett blamed the Reformation for replacing the "old English hospitality" and charity of the traditional church with the "wild schemes and cruel projects" of the so-called age of benevolence.[48]

The title of this book, *The Christian Monitors*, is intended to pose precisely these questions about the agency, location, and tactics of Anglican confessionalization in the late seventeenth and early eighteenth centuries. Cribbed from the name of John Rawlet's immensely popular 1686 devotional tract and the rash of specialized "monitors" for seamen, soldiers, gentlemen, debtors, and others that followed in its train, the book's title invites consideration of who exactly comprised the "Christian monitors" of national life in late-seventeenth- and early-eighteenth-century England. With whom or what lay that pastoral function "to constantly ensure, sustain, and improve the lives of each and every one" that the philosopher Michel Foucault famously diagnosed to be at the heart of modern governance?[49]

This book may thus be thought of as a political history of the Anglican revival, one that attempts to excavate the fault line between church and civil society in the decades surrounding the Revolution of 1688–1689. The Anglican investment in civil society was first undertaken during the crisis of the late Restoration and its revolutionary climax and settlement. Far from occurring quietly and without controversy, the revival occupied the very center of Anglican life and ecclesiastical politics during this period. Chapter 1 examines the Anglican revival of the later seventeenth century—the popular preaching, devotional writing, pastoral care, and charitable outreach that sought to restore the Church of England not simply to the English constitution, but to the hearts of the English populace. This chapter examines the ways in which the broad-based and highly establishmentarian Anglican revival of the late Restoration period acquired a markedly oppositional character during the reign of James II. The threat of Catholic absolutism and religious pluralism lent notions of ecclesiastical renewal and reform a newfound urgency that would carry through the collapse of the Stuart monarchy and the Revolution settlement that followed. Chapter 2 considers the imperatives of Anglican reform in the ensuing settlement of the established church. Against prevailing historiographical accounts that place the court of William and Mary at the vanguard of a moral and religious reform movement, this chapter demonstrates that the limitations and failures of royal efforts impelled the migration of initiative away from the court toward a new culture of projecting and association. Chapter 3 examines the origins and ideals of the greatest product of the postrevolutionary culture of moral and religious association and activism, the Society for Promoting Christian Knowledge. This chapter highlights the ideological and political contradictions that exercised the SPCK during its first two decades, most importantly, its dual fidelity to Anglican hegemony and "Revolution principles," demonstrating that the antinomies at the heart of the organization transformed an ostensibly bipartisan entity into a pillar of "church Whiggery." Chapters 4 and 5 reconsider the origins and program of the postrevolutionary Anglican high-church movement in light of the contemporaneous culture of Anglican voluntarism. One of the central, albeit heretofore largely unrecognized features of Anglican high churchmanship in this period was its fervent desire to demarcate and police the increasingly blurry line between church and civil society. Chapter 4 examines the contribution of the nonjurors to the social thought of postrevolutionary Anglican high churchmanship, specifically their central notion of the Church of England as a "distinct society" irreducible to either state or voluntary association. The burgeoning influence of nonjuring ecclesiological principles infused the broader Anglican high-church movement with visions of religious renewal markedly different from those pursued by the Anglican voluntary sector. Chapter 5 treats the Anglican high-church campaign to restore the convocation and enact a comprehensive program of ecclesiastical reform as an alternative to Anglican voluntarism. Mistrustful of the projects and societies of the associational world, Anglican high churchmen sought to refurbish the traditional instruments of ecclesiastical discipline. Chapter 6 considers the role of the Anglican voluntary sector in the work of ecclesiastical expansion abroad. The efforts of Anglican activists and associations were not only essential to the exporting of the Church of England, but to importing, as it were, a benevolence of global scope into the domestic British public sphere. The chapter concludes by suggesting that such efforts must be considered among the foundations of British humanitarianism. The book's conclusion considers the effect of postrevolutionary Anglican benevolence on the structure and character of British national life in the mid-eighteenth century.

For too long, the politics of the Anglican revival have been considered epiphenomenal, mere accretions on the preexisting processes of political and ecclesiastical polarization that comprised the politics of church and state in postrevolutionary England. This book finds this view untenable. Anglican renewal was not ancillary to the postrevolutionary "rage of party," a series of afterthoughts occurring to fully formed, ideologically mature political or ecclesiastical parties already engaged in ferocious struggle. On the contrary, irreconcilable visions of Anglican confessionalization contributed in large part to the processes of political and religious polarization that characterized the era. The Anglican revival was not passively politicized; it was an engine of politicization in its own right. To align with one faction or another in the civil and ecclesiastical politics of this period was, in most cases, to *already* possess a set of convictions regarding the place of the Church of England in public life and the proper means to secure its function there.

This book takes great pains not to deploy party labels carelessly or anachronistically to explain the various reform agendas under consideration. In the first place, it will eschew the anachronistic use of the postrevolutionary ecclesiastical party denominations "high church" and "low church" to navigate Restoration Anglicanism. As we will see, Anglican renewal was championed by various sectors of the Restoration Church of England during the reigns of Charles II and James II. Political proclivities were no real indication of reformist sentiments in this period, and many initiatives were embraced as warmly by the "Yorkist" circles that had rallied to James during the exclusion crisis as by the city divines in London, many of whom retained some residual sympathies to Whiggery. One must not forget that when James II pressed his brother-in-law, the leading Tory

Anglican peer Laurence Hyde, Earl of Rochester, to convert to Roman Catholicism, Rochester sought to enlist the counsel of those renowned "latitudinarians" John Tillotson and Edward Stillingfleet. The Anglican defense against Catholic incursion at this time readily traversed political lines. Only with the Revolution and its immediate aftermath will this study begin to speak of "Williamites" in the Church of England, those churchmen who enthusiastically embraced the new regime of William and Mary and whose careers were advanced under it. Unfortunately, this term has no clear opposite in this period. Most conformist Anglican churchmen who warily accepted the Revolution, usually with real reservations, were neither Jacobites (active supporters of the House of Stuart) nor nonjurors (those churchmen who deliberately withheld their allegiance from the new regime and generally suffered for their scruples). They were simply conservatives, committed on the whole to limiting the transformative effect of the Revolution settlement. It would not be until the end of the reign of William that the vague disaffection of conservative Anglican churchmen coalesced into the postrevolutionary Anglican high-church movement, which was actively committed to reconstructing the social power of the Church of England. This book will, as much as possible, limit the use of the term "high church" to both juring and nonjuring proponents of this particular movement. By the reign of Queen Anne, it is also possible to speak of a "low-church" or "church Whig" party committed to the Revolution settlement in church and state and the Hanoverian succession as the surest means of its conservation. This book hopes to show the various ways in which the imperatives of Anglican renewal contributed to the formulation and articulation of these various stances within the body of the Church of England.

It must again be stressed that this book is not intended as an assessment of the successes and failures of the Anglican revival, measured either quantitatively or qualitatively. I will not be enlisting in the ranks of historians who, for nearly a century now, have been rising to defend the honor of the eighteenth-century Church of England against the quarrelsome shades of long dead Victorians. Though admittedly productive of some extraordinary research into the ecclesiastical history of the early modern period, this effort generally concedes the premise to its long departed evangelical and Tractarian antagonists that it is the obligation of historians to grade the religious vitality of previous ages on an absolute scale, not to mention the mistaken assumption (successfully challenged by revisionist historians of the English Reformation) that religious change is explicable only in terms of some defect in the prevailing faith which it is the task of historians to identify. Such an approach to the eighteenth-century Church of England has long outgrown the confessional agenda for which it was first adopted and has become something like a vestigial appendage to contemporary ecclesiastical historiography, bereft of any function or vitality of its own. Readers are now as a matter of course inducted into moldering controversies over the reputation of the Georgian Church of England in which they can hardly be expected to have any enduring stake. It is worth noting that Jonathan Clark's path-breaking, albeit controversial, study *English Society 1660–1832* has perhaps been so productive of new research agendas largely because it sidestepped these debates altogether, making its case for the vitality of the eighteenth-century Church of England against the liberal and Marxist proponents of secularization and modernization, rather than the Victorian devotees of more salubrious Christianities. Nevertheless, this book concerns itself not with the degree of religious vitality in the late-seventeenth- and early-eighteenth-century Church of England, but with the forms such piety and devotion took. As we will see, it was above all as an organizational revolution that the Anglican revival had its primary effect on the social life of Georgian Britain.

CHAPTER 1

Revival and Revolution

On 7 October 1688, Thomas Tenison celebrated the communion service according to the Book of Common Prayer in the bustling Westminster parish of St. Martin's-in-the-Fields. Less than half a mile from Whitehall, St. Martin's stood, as it were, upon the fault line of the widening breach between the established Church of England and its supreme governor, the Roman Catholic monarch James II. Its chancel that day was permeated by the revolutionary crisis that had since the previous summer engulfed the kingdom. The incumbent Tenison was one of the leading anti-Catholic controversialists among the London clergy and an architect of the clerical opposition to the ecclesiastical policies of the king.[1] His wealthy Westminster parish was a popular resort for men seeking sacramental qualification for public service under the terms of the Test Act, the repeal of which had become the king's primary domestic policy objective.[2] That Sunday, Tenison's sermon on 2 Timothy 3:16 comprised another sally in the ongoing controversy over the Protestant rule of faith.[3] Against the disparagements of the Jesuit Charles Petre at mass the previous Sunday, Tenison affirmed "the Scriptures to be our only rule of faith, and its perfection above all traditions." Sporadic anti-Catholic rioting in anticipation of the imminent invasion of the Prince of Orange was already afoot throughout London, and Petre's remarks had provoked an angry crowd to pull the Jesuit bodily from the pulpit, causing "a great disturbance in the City." Amidst the incipient popular violence in the metropolis, Tenison's anti-Catholic obloquy from the pulpit bordered on incendiary. The following prayer for "the whole state of Christ's Church militant here in earth" might have struck his parishioners as unusually resonant amidst the deepening crisis of national Protestantism. Tenison then consecrated the elements and administered the sacrament of the Lord's Supper to nearly one thousand communicants.[4]

The Church of England seemed to be rising up against its supreme governor while kneeling. Such was the paradox of revolutionary Anglicanism, that is, the manner in which the church participated in the events of the Revolution of 1688–1689. Ecclesiastical engagement in the Revolution was of decisive political import, even as the church frequently seemed to eschew politics. Revolutionary Anglicanism routinely took the form of a pious "antipolitics," generally expressed as strict conformity, dexterous controversy, and diligent ministry of care. What, then, was the nature of ecclesiastical participation in the Revolution of 1688–1689? This chapter traces the origins of the various methods by which the Church of England sought to secure its flock from Roman Catholic aggrandizement. How did a set of ostensibly nonpolitical pastoral practices acquire revolutionary force during the political and ecclesiastical crisis of the reign of James? And how did the adoption of these instruments determine the character of the postrevolutionary Anglicanism of the eighteenth century?

The centrality of the established Church of England to the crisis that consumed the monarchy of James II is exceedingly well known, and yet little consensus exists on the nature of revolutionary Anglicanism. Indeed, for many historians, the term verges on oxymoron. Scholars of the period are routinely confronted with a vision of the established church standing at the center of revolutionary turmoil, yet to which no revolutionary politics or ideology may be ascribed. How are we to make sense of this seeming contradiction? After all, the Revolution of 1688–1689 is still widely considered "a religious event of the first importance."[5] Bill Speck claims that it was "more clerical than feudal or bourgeois," at least in its initial stages.[6] In the abeyance of Parliament during the latter years of James's reign, Jonathan Scott points out, national leadership effectively devolved upon the Anglican clergy.[7] Similarly, Tim Harris's recent account emphasizes "the crucial role of the Anglican interest, and especially the clerical establishment, in standing up against James's initiatives."[8] Ecclesiastical opposition certainly precipitated the catastrophic crisis that ended the regime of James II, even as many churchmen balked at the constitutional transformations that followed in its wake.[9] Yet there remains widespread disagreement over the social and ideological resources mobilized by the Church of England in its defiance of James II and its collaboration with the regime of his revolutionary successors William and Mary.

Historians have, with a few exceptions, considered the Revolution of 1688–1689 as a crisis in the political theology of the established church and have thus sought for revolutionary Anglicanism somewhere among the church's professed beliefs regarding monarchy and political power more generally. Seldom have historians investigated the church's pastoral practices during the crisis, the myriad ways in which the bonds between clergy and flock were reinforced even as those between church and state frayed.

Revolutionary Anglicanism, it was once widely held, was the leaven of latitudinarianism. An ill-defined strain of theological modernism, variously associated with rationalism, liberalism, and practical ethics, latitudinarianism is frequently ascribed to the putatively moderate clergy that dominated the pulpits of London and Westminster.[10] The term "latitudinarianism" generally signals a broad churchmanship, willing to accommodate some degree of doctrinal and liturgical heterogeneity in pursuit of a common ground of popular Protestantism, anti-Calvinist moral theology, and what was sometimes called "reasonable" Christianity. Latitudinarians are commonly, albeit now controversially, credited with an affinity for natural philosophy and an interest in various forms of reconciliation among the varieties of English Protestantism. During the revolutionary crisis, Thomas Babbington Macaulay claims, "the whole Church seemed to be animated by the spirit and guided by the counsels, of the calumniated latitudinarians."[11] Gerald Cragg credits the latitudinarians with most quickly and most publicly repudiating the Anglican political theology of passive obedience and the divine right of kings.[12] Martin Griffin places the latitudinarians at the vanguard of the revolutionary Church of England, "the most forward and articulate Anglicans" in their support of the Revolution.[13] And Gordon Rupp hails their "manful share in the church struggle under James II."[14] Margaret Jacob, it should be noted, detects among the latitudinarians a profound ambivalence toward the Revolution that gave way to accommodation and support only after the fait accompli of the political and ecclesiastical settlement, and even then not without misgivings. In effect, she claims, latitudinarianism became a revolutionary movement only after the Revolution was complete.[15]

Many scholars, however, have begun to question the utility and coherence of the concept of latitudinarianism as the embodiment of either a distinct religious ideology or an ecclesiastical party within the late-seventeenth-century Church of England. Scholars such as Richard Ashcraft, John Marshall, and John Spurr have ruthlessly deconstructed latitudinarian claims to reason, moderation, and religious liberalism. Spurr even goes so far as to deny the existence of any recognizable latitudinarian party or outlook among the Restoration clergy, considering it mainly a term of Nonconformist opprobrium against those Anglicans most concerned in the repudiation of Calvinist soteriology. The religious rationalism and practical moral theology specifically attributed to latitudinarianism, he suggests, comprised a theological orientation generally espoused among the mainstream of Restoration divines.[16] Gareth Bennett affirms the importance of the London clergy in the Revolution and its aftermath but disclaims their common latitudinarianism, suggesting that most were in fact "moderate Tories," largely bound together by the patronage of the influential Finch family and its high-church scion Daniel Finch, Earl of Nottingham.[17] The latitudinarian faction that Whig historians once confidently placed at the forefront of a revolutionary Anglicanism has been serially dissolved into the mainstream of an intolerant and Erastian Restoration Church of England.

In the light of the chorus of objections to the notion of latitudinarianism, historians have attempted to preserve the social and ideological coherence of the revolutionary London divines by other means. According to Roger Thomas, the city divines at the forefront of the opposition were united by a broader Protestant ecumenism and concomitant antipathy to Roman Catholicism.[18] Tony Claydon brands the opposition churchmen of the metropolis "the Burnetine clergy," linked largely by the court patronage of the Whig cleric Gilbert Burnet, whom William promoted to the see of Salisbury in January 1689, and a common belief in the "mid-Tudor" ideals of "godly magistracy and moral reform."[19] While Claydon believes that the Williamite divines were essentially moderates, who elaborated their justification of the revolution in order "to pursue an ecclesiological compromise between Whig and Tory," Steve Pincus locates them firmly in the Whig camp.[20] Against Spurr, Pincus insists that the men he calls the "low church" clergy were not part of the mainstream of Restoration Anglicanism but comprised a pool of "simmering dissidence within the pre-revolutionary church." These metropolitan low churchmen were not, as Bennett insists, moderate Tories but "had at least as many significant associations with notorious Whigs and advocates of religious toleration," among both Anglican and Nonconformist circles. Bereft of any "distinctive theological outlook," the low-church clergy adopted the broad tenets of revolutionary Whiggery, defending the legitimacy of political resistance, disclaiming coercion in matters of faith, and pressing for a more comprehensive ecclesiastical settlement.[21]

A recent strain of revisionist historiography has attempted to solve the vexed problem of ecclesiastical participation in the Revolution of 1688–1689 by positing an earlier, orthodox insurgency led not by the younger metropolitan divines, but by the reactionary Caroline bishops and their ideological allies among the partisans of the high church. This "Anglican revolution," according to Mark Goldie, effectively absolves the Church of England of the familiar charge of apostasy, that Anglicans hypocritically abandoned their deeply held political theological convictions of passive obedience and divine right monarchy in the face of the aggressively Romanizing James II. Resistance among Anglicans, Goldie insists, occurred entirely "within their existing political catechism," militating not against royal absolutism per se, but rather against a royal absolutism erected on behalf of the confessional rivals of the established church. Goldie thus posits an Anglican revolution, undertaken to restore the intolerant "church absolutism" that prevailed in the first half of the 1680s. The Anglican revolution was designed, according to Gareth Bennett, "to rebuild the Tory system." By October 1688, this revolution had substantially succeeded in pressuring James to abandon his policies on behalf of Roman Catholicism and toleration, thus healing the breach between crown and altar and restoring the Stuart monarchy "to its proper place in the Anglican firmament." The triumphant Church of England then had no need for the invasion of William of Orange the following month or the transformative political revolution that followed the flight of James II. This second, Williamite revolution transgressed the bounds of orthodox political theology and rendered the Anglican platform of church absolutism substantially unsalvageable. The ecclesiastical leadership of the Anglican revolution then retreated into political quietism (and eventually, nonjuring) and left their Tory allies to preserve what was left of a damaged Anglican establishment. Tim Harris also places the traditional supporters of the late Stuart monarchy, "the Tory-Anglicans in England," at the forefront of what he calls "a revolution before the actual Revolution," designed to restore the status quo ante. Harris, it must be noted, suggests that the proponents of Anglican revolution had largely surrendered the revanchist dream of reconstructing a coercive "church absolutism" and had conceded the political necessity of a legislative toleration on behalf of Protestant Dissent as the price of Anglican hegemony. Revolutionary Anglicanism, in this telling, was thus neither Whiggish nor successful, but rather a broadly reactionary movement undermined by the exogenous shock of the Williamite revolution from which orthodox churchmen largely abstained.[22]

The Revolution of 1688–1689, according to a divergent line of revisionism, was neither a latitudinarian coup nor an abortive church reaction. Revolutionary Anglicanism was both reactionary and triumphant. According to Gerald Straka, the Revolution was not a repudiation of traditional Anglican political theology at all; on the contrary, "the Revolution was not a departure, but a restoration of true divine right Protestant monarchy and a return to the national unity of Elizabeth's great days." Anglicans across the theological spectrum justified the Revolution in providential terms, deploying the "divine right of providence" as "a means of continuing in modified form the more personal divine right of Stuart kings." Heavenly superintendence, not popular resistance, had defeated James II and facilitated "a return to the perfect Church-state unity."[23] The influence of Straka's thesis has been enormously amplified by its incorporation into Jonathan Clark's study *English Society 1660–1832*, which claims that the Revolution of 1688–1689 was an instance in which "the Church was defended before the monarchy."[24] In this reading, the Revolution was a successful revolt of church against state, a confirmation of the virtually uninterrupted ascendancy of reactionary high-church Anglicanism.

The problems with such political theological accounts of Anglican participation in the Revolution of 1688–1689 are manifold. First, the demarcations of postrevolutionary ecclesiastical partisanship, terms such as "high church" and "low church," which were not current before the final years of William's reign, have little purchase on the contours of either Restoration churchmanship or theology. The Restoration Church of England was of course by no means theologically or politically monolithic, but its various tendencies and affinities remained fairly fluid and did not correspond to the hardened factions and ecclesiastical parties of its postrevolutionary successor. Historians will continue to ignore at their own peril the powerful and persuasive admonitions of John Spurr and, more recently, William Bulman regarding these anachronisms.[25] Second, party political and party ideological accounts tend to elide the extraordinary degree of collaboration between various circles and networks within the Restoration church, the divisions among which were porous and often had more to do with geography, sociability, and patronage than with party affiliation and ideology. Bulman is correct to point out that the Church of England under James II was characterized by an extraordinary degree of unity, which studies committed to partisan frameworks of analysis remain at great pains to comprehend.[26] Finally, the excessive focus on partisanship and political theology obscures the extent to which a common pastoral agenda and program of religious renewal was shared by a wide swath of churchmen during this period, many of whom would wind up on different sides of the Revolution settlement. The imperatives of Anglican revival were not the province of one ecclesiastical party, nor were they linked to any particular political platform. A political study of the Anglican revival cannot hope to begin with the party political character of its agenda; it can begin only by tracing the vicissitudes of its politicization—or rather, its multiple, often contradictory, politicizations.

Revolutionary Anglicanism cannot be grasped through the lens of political theology. The Revolution of 1688–1689 coincided with a revolution in pastoral practices rooted in the Restoration crisis late in the reign of Charles II. Anglican participation in the Revolution is best understood within the context of this Anglican revival, what one historian has dubbed "a small awakening" afoot in the late Restoration Church of England, particularly in the famously fissiparous capital of London and its environs.[27] The final years of Charles II's reign, John Overton observes, came closest to realizing "the grand idea of a Church truly coextensive with the nation, and adequately supplying all that nation's spiritual wants."[28] Of course, the church of the later Restoration period is largely known for its intransigent royalism, its cherished "theory of religious intolerance," and its growing appetite for the use of coercion in matters of faith.[29] One cannot underestimate the role vicious religious persecution played in propping up Anglican hegemony, but the widespread investment in popular Anglicanism at this time suggests a real cognizance of the limits of coercion.[30] Or perhaps these efforts disclose a lingering mistrust of the House of Stuart, whose serial apostasies may have persuaded some churchmen of the need to provide for the national communion even against the betrayals of its supreme governors. The painstaking work of Anglican renewal in the later seventeenth century thus operated along two potentially divergent orientations: toward court and parish, or toward state and society. The Restoration Church of England was eager to acquire some measure of constitutional security in the supremacy of its royal governor. Yet the church also sought to refurbish its pastoral capacity and devotional life to guarantee some continuity of popular affection irrespective of the vicissitudes of court politics. Even as it hewed closer to the Stuart court, the church seemed oriented toward what John Sommerville describes as "a new foundation in popular opinion, rather than in political might."[31]

James II ascended the headship of an established church undergoing a profound religious revival, one that he perhaps never adequately comprehended. James's domestic program of Catholic aggrandizement unsurprisingly ran afoul of this Anglican revival; and the king came to conceive of the vigorous preaching and pastoral care, organized apologetics, popular sacramentalism, and charitable regard for the Protestant interest abroad that defined this strain of popular Anglican churchmanship as obstructions to his policies. James's numerous pronouncements on behalf of religious toleration were consistently belied by his efforts to disable this dynamic Protestant ministry. He made the terms of Anglican royalism virtually impossible to fulfill and set the bar of loyalty for the Church of England clergy at a virtual abnegation of their pastoral obligation to secure their flocks from Roman Catholic error. James in effect criminalized Anglican pastoral care. In doing so, he imbued the highly establishmentarian revivalist Anglicanism of his brother's reign with an oppositional character that it had not initially possessed. The ascription of disloyalty to the instinctual anti-Catholicism of the Anglican clergy became a fatally self-fulfilling prophecy. James's campaign against the Protestant ministry transformed revivalist Anglicanism into revolutionary Anglicanism.[32] Anglican concern to maintain the integrity of the national communion of the established church cannily acquired a revolutionary force without adopting a revolutionary program. And indeed, the rapid and near total collapse of James's regime at the end of 1688 probably spared the English clergy from the crucible of protracted civil conflict that tested the political theologies of divines in his other kingdoms. The relative ease with which James's successors William and Mary were able to reappropriate Anglican revivalism for the monarchy after the Revolution reveals the enduringly establishmentarian character of the movement.

The Anglican revival of the later seventeenth and early eighteenth centuries was thus the context for rather than a consequence of the Revolution of 1688–1689. Historians have long posited the vibrant, popular Anglicanism of the era—what Dudley Bahlmann famously deemed the "moral revolution"—as the ecclesiastical response to the revolutionary crisis. In fact, this mode of churchmanship might well be considered a precipitant of the Revolution. And this sheds some light on the facility with which William and Mary, with their extensive connections with the London clergy, were able to convincingly claim the mantle of Anglican renewal. Moreover, a prerevolutionary revival permits a much-needed revision of the commonplace conception of the Toleration Act of

May 1689 as an absolute disjuncture between regimes of coercion and persuasion in the maintenance of the Anglican communion.[33] These approaches to the putative problem of religious pluralism coexisted in the later seventeenth century, and indeed the vast majority of techniques that the postrevolutionary church found ready to hand during the era of religious toleration were born in the womb of a persecuting society.

The Anatomy of Revival

Upon his accession in February 1685, James II assumed the headship of an established church in the flush of revival. Over the course of the preceding decade, the church had managed to come to terms with a Stuart monarchy that seemed bent on using its prerogative powers to subvert rather than to uphold Anglican hegemony.[34] The failure of Charles II's final attempt at establishing religious toleration by royal fiat in 1672–1673 occasioned an enduring rapprochement between church and crown. The resultant Anglican royalist fusion of the mid-1670s effectively wedded Stuart commitment to confessional conformity to the Anglican embrace of dynastic legitimism and enabled both the crown and the ecclesiastical establishment to fend off the radical constitutional and anticlerical threat embodied in the rise of the Whig opposition.[35] The Church of England seemed ever more willing to accept a courtly foundation, adopting an increasingly strident political theology characterized by effusive royalism and a reliance on the coercive apparatus of the state for the policing of religious conformity.[36] Yet, the established church did not entrust its national communion solely to state action. It cultivated a wide variety of resources for the reinforcement of communion, deploying the traditional methods of Christian piety, such as preaching, devotional literature, and para-ecclesial organization, within a nascent civil society of popular association and communication.

The decade that followed the Anglican royalist rapprochement of the mid-1670s witnessed a renaissance of Anglican devotional writing that effectively digested the sweeping soteriological reorientation of interregnum Anglicanism, with its staunchly anti-Calvinist emphasis on practical and sacramental piety, into an appealingly popular form. Amidst this "holy living" theology embodied in these tracts was a renewed emphasis on the sacramental life of the church, particularly the Lord's Supper, which coincided with a widespread campaign to restore the Eucharist to the center of Anglican worship. The period witnessed the maturation of a number of the great corporate philanthropies of the established church. And coinciding as it did with Louis XIV's savage pursuit of confessional uniformity in France, the period saw the organization of a peculiarly Anglican response to the imperiled Protestant interest abroad. The Church of England during this period cultivated a genuine institutional regard for the fate of Anglicanism throughout England's burgeoning commercial and territorial empire alongside the first stirrings of a missionary zeal that had long been the province of English Nonconformity.

The city of London stood at the vanguard of the revival unfolding within the late Restoration Church of England.[37] Henry Compton, bishop of London and dean of the Chapel Royal, superintended the learned, popular, and pastorally engaged preaching clergy that staffed the great metropolitan parishes, the city lectureships, and the Chapel Royal at Whitehall.[38] A cavalier of the old school, Bishop Compton compensated for a lack of distinction in either scholarship or piety with the organizational genius befitting one of military mien. Upon his elevation, he immediately took steps to place the customary imperial jurisdiction of the see of London on a sounder footing.[39] The bishop also coordinated the English relief efforts on behalf of the French Huguenot refugees.[40] Compton had been called "the darling of the city and parliament because of his great zeal in the discouragement of papists and popery." Indeed, it was commonly believed that his strident anti-Catholicism had cost him the throne of Canterbury.[41] Less than a week after the nomination of his rival William Sancroft to the primacy at the end of 1677, Bishop Compton summoned the ministers of London to a conference at St. Paul's, where he requested the clergy undertake weekday sermons during Lent, afternoon catechizing, and monthly consultations "about the state of their parish and parishioners."[42] Prominent London clergymen had long assembled informally, but Compton began holding regular conferences among the city divines in the later 1670s and encouraging satellite assemblies among the clergy of the outlying archdeaconries.[43] The fruits of these summits were digested in brief, virtually annual circular letters to the clergy of the diocese, urging vigorous pastoral engagement and a scrupulous maintenance of the canons and rubrics of the church. Even amidst the exultant Anglicanism of the Tory reaction, Compton's missives were wary and defensive, demanding that his clergy consider themselves vigilant watchmen and shepherds. He reflected frequently on the errors of the Roman Catholic Church, devoting his 1680 letter to a refutation of communion in one kind, Latin prayers, and the cult of the saints.[44] Toward that end, Compton called his clergy to a diligent administration of the sacraments and holy offices, ministering to their parishioners in all seasons of life: baptism, catechism, confirmation, and the visitation of the sick. Above all, the sacrament of the Lord's Supper was to serve as the lodestone of Anglican renewal. "The security," Compton reminded his clergy, "not only of every private person, but even of the whole Church, depends on the due observance of this sacrament."[45]

The Anglican revival of the late seventeenth century took great pains to return the sacrament of the Lord's Supper to the center of public worship. The sacrament, it was widely felt, had been unconscionably "denied the blessing of restoration, which all other offices of our worship enjoy."[46] Bishop Compton's first circular letter of April 1679 complained of the "general apostasy" from the sacred institution of the sacrament. He committed his diocese to the "great work" of persuading the people of "the great benefit and necessity of this sacrament." In this they were supported by a vast devotional literature, much of which had been penned by the London clergymen themselves, pressing the necessity of frequent communion.[47] Throughout the 1680s, the city churches demonstrated this renewed emphasis by railing off communion tables and setting them altarwise at the east end of the chancel, as mandated by the Laudian program from the decade before the civil wars. In 1680, Denis Granville, by his own lights "one of the more exact observers of the rubric and sticklers for conformity," set on a foot a sweeping campaign to rectify the omission of weekly communion in the cathedrals and colleges as "the most probable means to revive religion, devotion, conformity and loyalty in the land." The cause found favor with Archbishop William Sancroft, who actively promoted the restoration of weekly communion in cathedrals throughout the province of Canterbury. By late 1685, the cathedrals at Canterbury, York, Oxford, Ely, Worcester, Exeter, Chichester, Gloucester, and Durham were said to be offering weekly celebrations.[48] The diocese of London awaited the reconstruction of St. Paul's Cathedral to reinstate the practice.[49] But meanwhile, Bishop Compton dispatched a circular letter to the clergy of his diocese reiterating the need for a vigorous and "coercive discipline" in the observation of the sacrament.[50] Simon Patrick, dean of Peterborough, restored the regular service to that cathedral around 1684 and preached a series of sermons to his wealthy parishioners in Covent Garden on the necessity of frequent communion.[51] William Beveridge celebrated weekly communions at St. Peter's, Cornhill, and "hath seldom less than fourscore, sometimes six or seven score communicants."[52] At the Savoy, the German émigré Anthony Horneck administered the sacrament to throngs of communicants the first Sunday of every month and at all the great festivals: "So great was the number, that there was need of great help of clergymen to assist in the delivering of the bread and wine."[53] Richard Kidder reported "very great communions and great sums of money given to the poor" in the wealthy east London parish of St. Helen's, Bishopsgate.[54] Edward Fowler of St. Giles's, Cripplegate, reported to Archbishop Sancroft "very comfortable weekly communions" in his parish in 1685.[55] Granville praised the advances "made towards good order and regularity" in the capital, adding that "if they go on as they have done for these two years last past, they may by their good make some amends for the evil example that they have given to the nation" in previous decades.[56]

The campaign to restore the sacrament of holy communion to the center of English worship was not, it must be stressed, a symptom of the arid ritualism with which later Restoration Anglicanism is often charged. The sacrament was widely imbued with profound social instrumentality. Its marginalization in English worship in favor of the more popular sermon, it was feared, seemed to mandate the kind of consumerist religiosity that led to ecclesiological voluntarism.[57] Unlike the sermon, the sacrament of the Lord's Supper was frequently conceived as a guarantor of social integrity. The Book of Common Prayer exhorted communicants to "be in charity with all men." In an increasingly mobile and commercial society, the sacrament was thought to mark off a sphere of sociability qualitatively different from that of everyday life. The communion embodied a form of social intercourse distinct from the sphere of business, with its divergent interests and incessant lawsuits, and from the idle haunts of alehouse and coffeehouse, where one found only "the converse and communion of . . . vain and vicious company." The sacrament was designed to "swallow up all our little piques, and displeasures" that obstructed neighborliness and instill a general benevolence, "a compassionate sense of each other's infirmities, and a tender concern and diligent care for each other's welfare."[58] Indeed, Simon Patrick, perhaps the most popular devotional writer of the later seventeenth century, frequently emphasized the social dimensions of the sacrament in almost Durkheimian terms.[59] "For there are not two cups whereof we drink at his Supper, the one containing the love of Christ, the other the love of our brethren," he wrote, "but we drink both at one draught, and engage to both at one breath."[60]

Most importantly, the sacrament functioned as the cynosure of holy living.[61] Indeed, the complaint that Restoration churchmen "neglected holy living, preferring creedal and ritual formalism to moral reformation," seems not merely unfair, but predicated on a profound misapprehension of the nature of Anglican moral theology.[62] The sacrament was integral to a discourse of moral reformation, confirming the benefits that the communicant received from Christ, which the Durham clergyman Daniel Brevint described as the "maintenance and improvement of life."[63] Moreover, preparation for frequent communion was a painstaking exercise in prayer and self-examination.[64] Amendment of life was thus both the precondition and the outcome of frequent communication. As the great devotional writer John Kettlewell explained, the sacrament "is intended to make a good man better, to carry on repentance in those that have begun it, and to confirm and enlarge every virtue in those who are already possessed of it."[65] In the dutiful preparation for and worthy reception of the sacrament, John Tillotson preached, the Christian was "excited to some good purposes, and put upon some sort of endeavor to amend and reform his life."[66] The campaign for eucharistic renewal in the later seventeenth century was in large measure a clerical and parochial program for the reformation of manners.

Throughout London, Anglican revivalist preaching by metropolitan divines such as the Rhineland émigré Anthony Horneck of the Savoy, William Beveridge of St. Peter's, Cornhill, and William Smythies of St. Giles's, Cripplegate, inspired small groups of young people to assemble weekly for "the mutual assistance and consolation one of another in their Christian warfare."[67] There is a good deal of disagreement over the source of this model of religious association, but John Spurr has convincingly placed these religious societies amidst the Anglican revival in London, underpinned by fervent sacramentalism and a theological orientation toward holy living.[68] A specimen of the rules of one association affirmed that the purpose of the society was "to promote real holiness of heart and life."[69] Evidence suggests that these societies originated in weekend meetings to prepare for the reception of the sacrament of the Lord's Supper, such as Horneck's "preparation sermons" on the Friday preceding communion or the Saturday preparation meetings noted in an unfortunately unidentified provincial town.[70] The sacrament loomed as large in the life of these societies as it did in the devotional writings of the city divines with which they were associated. Membership in a society at St. Martin's-in-the-Fields depended on frequent reception of the sacrament.[71] The rules of the society at St. Giles's, Cripplegate, required members "to partake of the Lord's supper at least once a month if not prevented by a reasonable impediment."[72] A 1681 devotional tract by Arthur Bury, the rector of Exeter College, Oxford, pays tribute to one "holy society" of noble ladies convened for a mixture of sacramental and philanthropic purposes, by "paying our Lord's day, his Supper, and his Poor, their joint rights" through charitable collections and weekly celebration of holy communion.[73] As the decade wore on, such contributions would increasingly be used to endow sermons throughout the city of London "by way of preparation for the Lord's Supper, or to engage a suitable holiness after it," thus reproducing the revivalist energy by which the societies were first founded.[74]

The religious societies were part of a larger wave of para-ecclesial endeavors in the nascent civil society of late Restoration London. As already noted, the metropolitan divines frequently assembled for informal conferences "to consult how they might most efficaciously promote true religion by their ministry."[75] They collaborated in the reconstruction of Sion College and Library, the guild of the city clergy destroyed by the Great Fire, the presidency of which passed among a number of the capital's most eminent preachers.[76] In early 1684, Thomas Tenison solicited the assistance of John Evelyn and Sir Christopher Wren in the founding of a free library on Castle Street in St. Martin's as a suitable resort for the unbeneficed clergy of his parish, the chaplains and tutors who whiled away their free hours in taverns and coffeehouses.[77] Many of the city divines actively contributed to the newly chartered Corporation for Relief of Poor Widows and Clergymen—commonly known as the Sons of the Clergy—a philanthropic entity of interregnum vintage that channeled funds to the families of "loyal and orthodox clergy-men."[78] Thomas Sprat of St. Margaret's, Westminster, gave a rousing sermon at the first anniversary meeting after incorporation, culminating in a broader vision of metropolitan renewal, "a modest, a grave, a religious city," excelling the world in virtue as it already did in size, population, and commerce.[79] Several prominent London clergymen, among them John Tillotson, Edward Stillingfleet, and Edward Fowler, served with eminent Nonconformists as stewards of the Welsh Trust, a philanthropic organization founded to oversee the publication and distribution of "pious treatises in the Welsh language."[80]

In the 1680s, the Church of England, then, was undergoing a national revival that was reducible to neither its rapprochement with the crown nor its willingness to use coercion to maintain the national communion. The church offset its seemingly limitless investment in the Stuart monarchy with a genuine bid for popular affection. Moreover, the church was, as Mark Goldie argues, a "persecuting society," but it was not one that trusted in persecution.[81] The explosion of devotional writings, the campaigns for eucharistic renewal, the cultivation of para-ecclesial organizations such as clerical conferences, charities, and religious societies were clear indications that the church had already discerned the practical limits of religious coercion. Legal action was to be supplemented with vigorous pastoral outreach. And as the extant institutions of the established church proved insufficient to the task of vitally engaging the populace in the national communion, new instruments of popular engagement were developed. Indeed, John Kettlewell was said to remark at the accession of James II that the Church of England was "beginning to flourish more than it had ever since the Reformation," and that it would persist in doing so, "whether supported or not from without, by the civil power."[82]

Court Catholicism and the Opposition to Revival

The metropolis of London and Westminster seemed a less than hospitable environment for the resurgent Roman Catholicism sponsored by the court of James II. From the outset of the reign, the Catholic court was encircled by the vanguard of Anglican revivalism that occupied the great city parishes, the numerous lectureships, and the Chapels Royal at Whitehall and St. James. James's commitment to public and conspicuous Catholicism at court proceeded in the midst of the diocese of the stolidly anti-Catholic "Protestant bishop" Henry Compton, who coordinated and oversaw the activities of the city clergy, superintended the Chapel Royal, and considered himself personally responsible for safeguarding the Protestantism of the king's daughters, Princess Mary and Princess Anne. It is then not entirely surprising that the disabling of the vigorous and dynamic Anglicanism of London soon became one of the central components in James's program of reducing the established church to compliance with his domestic initiatives. His attempts to suppress the Anglicanism of the metropolis and the concomitant alienation of the London clergy transformed Anglican revivalism into a force of opposition. James effectively created a reversionary church in his own capital, the stalwarts of which would most vocally and enthusiastically embrace the regime of his successors.

Upon his accession, James seemed determined to emancipate the English crown from the public Anglicanism with which it was traditionally buttressed. Knowing full well that his brother Charles had been covertly reconciled to the Church of Rome on his deathbed by the Benedictine monk John Huddleston, James could not permit Charles to be interred with the Protestant obsequies of the established church.[83] In an act somehow not befitting the great dissimulator who seldom scrupled at presenting a false face to the public, the late king was "very obscurely buried" on 14 February 1685 in a vault under Henry VII's chapel at Westminster Abbey, "without any manner of pomp."[84] The mean and obscure interment of the late king closed an age of confessional duplicity and ushered in one of dangerous forthrightness. "The face of the whole Court," noted John Evelyn, "exceedingly changed into a more solemn and moral behavior." The next morning, James publicly attended mass in the queen's Catholic chapel at St. James, "to the great grief of his subjects," setting the doors of the oratory wide open to dispel all doubts about the king's religion.[85] In this new spirit of religious candor, James revealed to Archbishop William Sancroft two private papers of the late king repudiating the fissiparous Protestant rule of faith in favor of Roman Catholic infallibility. Sancroft was dumbfounded by the revelation, speechless "almost half a quarter of an hour" before weakly mustering the observation that he "did not think his late Majesty had understood controversy so well" and thought the papers might well be answered. James heartily welcomed the controversy, provided "it be done gentleman-like and solidly," as an opportunity to broadcast to the nation news of his brother's conversion.[86]

By early March, James had erected a Catholic oratory in Whitehall, a placeholder no doubt for the magnificent new Catholic chapel he commissioned Sir Christopher Wren to erect in full public view fronting the street next to Holbein Gate.[87] On Easter Sunday of that year, it was noted, "the rites of the Church of Rome were once more after an interval of 127 years performed at Westminster with regal splendor."[88] The Protestant services at the Chapel Royal were maintained. The chaplains, however, were now instructed (most likely by the courtier bishop Nathaniel Crewe of Durham, who, as clerk of the closet had the specific responsibility of overseeing the private devotions of the king) to bow three times toward the king's empty seat in the closet, rather than offering the single congé, which in the previous reign had been the customary acknowledgment of the absent king. The full liturgical presence and supremacy of the crown was to be affirmed despite the permanent recusancy of its Roman Catholic bearer.[89]

The coronation at Westminster Abbey, presided over by the archbishop of Canterbury and suffused with Anglican ceremonial, proved especially hazardous to the tender conscience of the new king. On 23 April, James and his queen Mary of Modena were crowned in a bowdlerized ceremony designed by Archbishop Sancroft purportedly to abridge the already protracted affair but ostensibly to spare the king from the more aggressively Protestant trappings of the rite. Most conspicuously, the sacrament of the Lord's Supper was omitted, "to the sorrow of the people."[90] The sermon by James's former chaplain, Francis Turner, bishop of Ely, seemed to exacerbate the confessional divide between king and people. His retelling of the accession of Solomon could not avoid mentioning that king's late apostasy into paganism, even as the people of Israel "continued in the worship of God, as they might do without inconsistence whatsoever." Later in the sermon, he extolled the example of Constantius Chlorus, the father of Constantine, who retained only those servants who declined to forsake their Christian faith in pursuit of advancement at court.[91] It was a strange performance in an irregular ceremony beset by bad omens.[92]

Though James proceeded with some measure of circumspection in religious matters during the first year of his reign, Londoners still resented the prominence of Catholicism at court and in the surrounding metropolis.[93] "Some of the ministers here," Thomas Frankland informed his father, "have been called to question for preaching indiscreetly against popery."[94] The bishop of London penned a congratulatory address to the king on behalf of the London clergy, in which he proclaimed the established church "dearer to us than our lives."[95] The address was provocative, but atypical. More loyalist addresses made sport of the bishop's insinuation. The Devon address exulted in the royal declaration on behalf of the church "the words of a King whose word has ever been dearer to him than his life." An address to the king from Merioneth presumed that "the Church of England was dearer to you than to those that made such seditious clamor for its preservation."[96] Not long after his accession, James assured both Compton and Sancroft that he wished their congregations full and pledged to continue the persecution of Protestant Dissenters, but he sternly warned them to curtail preaching against Catholicism.[97] The king's leading minister, the Earl of Sunderland, informed Sancroft that the king "thinks it very unfit that such kind of things should be said in the pulpit, that they are intended seditiously to fill the people with groundless fears and jealousies and are meant against him personally."[98] James personally confronted Thomas Ken, the saintly bishop of Bath and

Wells, over reflections against popery made in his own chapel at Whitehall. The bishop responded by chiding the king for his recusancy: "had you attended your own duty in church, my enemies had missed the opportunity of accusing me falsely."[99] The king complained to Sancroft of the anti-Catholic preaching of Simon Patrick in particular, "a good man," he told the archbishop, but "leaned too much to the two deans (meaning those of St. Paul and Canterbury)," the popular London divines Edward Stillingfleet and John Tillotson. Sancroft retorted that "priests were so busy in troubling our people with questions, that we could do no less than instruct them in the established religion."[100] James clearly bristled at the residual anti-Catholicism of his capital, but his faith in the innate royalism of the Church of England remained as yet unshaken. He had no reason to doubt that the Anglican Tories obtaining substantial majorities in his first Parliament would prove fit instruments of royal policy.

By the second half of 1685, the bishop of London and the clergy of the metropolis had proved truculently opposed to the Catholicism emanating from the royal court. Compton and the leading London divines such as John Tillotson, Edward Stillingfleet, John Sharp, Simon Patrick, Thomas Tenison, and Gregory Hescard, who "have a very good understanding one with another," lobbied Archbishop Sancroft and the other bishops to resist Catholic encroachment in the coming session of Parliament. The London divines found the prelates thoroughly dispirited. Bishop William Lloyd of Peterborough (soon to be translated to Norwich) was desperately afraid of anything that might be construed as a praemunire. Bishop John Fell of Oxford told the London divines that "it was too late, all attempts would be in vain, for popery would come in." It was perhaps not surprising, then, that Compton led the bishops in the House of Lords in protest against the king's employment of Roman Catholics in the army, a manifest violation of the Test Act. In a speech on 19 November 1685, Compton famously compared the Test Act and penal laws to the dikes of Holland: once breached, at any single point inundation would follow. Claiming to speak on behalf of the entire episcopal bench and with "great deference and respect to his Majesty," Compton proclaimed the "whole civil and religious constitution of the realm in danger" and promptly received a standing ovation from the other bishops. "It was a new spectacle in England," wrote Sir John Dalrymple, "to see the bishops opposing the king's will."[101]

When in late autumn of 1685 the Anglican interest in Parliament proved unwilling to comply with the king's domestic objective of Roman Catholic emancipation, James began to rethink his obligations to the established church. He began to cultivate a political bloc composed of the confessional rivals of the Church of England to counterbalance the Tory stalwarts who purported to act in its defense. James also sought to transform Anglicanism itself. His policies and promotions beginning at the end of 1685 were not designed to simply "gag and humiliate the Church of England," as John Miller claims, but to redress the unstable compound of Protestantism and royalism that comprised Restoration Anglican churchmanship decidedly in favor of the latter.[102] James had discerned a surprising potential for opposition in the church's strident anti-Catholicism, its latent nationalism, and its reversionary interests in the Protestant succession of James's daughters Mary and Anne. James sought to neutralize the oppositional potential of Anglicanism in favor of a more fulsome royalism.[103] He therefore took steps to empower a courtly ultra-Erastian Anglicanism over against the mode of dynamic and defiantly Protestant churchmanship that he explicitly associated with his capital.

The king could not but be uneasy amidst the churchmanship of the metropolis, which was a dangerous mixture of popularity and vitriolic anti-Catholicism. "London pulpits ring strong peals against popery," wrote one observer at the beginning of 1686, "and I have lately heard there never were such eminently able men to serve in those cures." When conversing with the king, the Roman Catholic Lord Dover admitted that "the pulpits in London were filled with great and eminent preachers" and expressed an interest in hearing some of the more famous auditors. James replied curtly, "You had better not."[104] James inquired of the Earl of Clarendon, his Lord Lieutenant of Ireland, whether the Protestant ministers in that country had been as indiscreet as those in London, "inveighing very much against popery, even to stir up the people against them," and instructed him that such preaching must not be suffered. In October 1685, the revocation of the Edict of Nantes by Louis XIV cast an especially black pallor over the fortunes of international Protestantism. The French persecutions and the ensuing refugee crisis gave the anti-Catholicism of the London pulpits a fierce new urgency. As the fifth of November approached, the court took steps to contain the national fervency associated with the anniversary of the Gunpowder treason by banning the antipopish processions and bonfires with which it was usually celebrated.[105] Even Francis Turner, bishop of Ely, a former chaplain to James's ducal household and longtime political ally of the king, preached a "violent sermon on the fifth of November" against Roman

Catholicism at Whitehall, earning him James's enduring enmity.[106] The offense was compounded just a few weeks later when the bishop's brother Thomas Turner preached indiscreetly at Whitehall on the "submission of Christians to their persecutors."[107] The capital seemed to infect even the staunchest loyalists with a strain of vituperative anti-Catholicism that bordered on sedition.

The king began to move decisively against London Anglicanism. On 26 December 1685, the popular bishop Henry Compton of London, whose "fame runs high in the vogue of the people," was struck from the Privy Council and removed from his office as dean of the Chapel Royal.[108] The Protestantism of the court was then placed under the supervision of men of more pliant temperament: Nathaniel Crewe, bishop of Durham, was made dean of the Chapel Royal, and Thomas Sprat, bishop of Rochester, was granted Crewe's office of clerk of the closet.[109] The Chapel Royal at Whitehall, once the hub of metropolitan Anglicanism, languished under the courtier Bishop Crewe, who "takes no care to supply it with Protestant preachers." The maintenance of the chapel fell to the sergeant of the vestry, Thomas Haynes, who voluntarily engaged the prominent London clergy to continue the services.[110] In January, James ordered Sancroft to issue a letter to his suffragans instructing them that "no clergymen should preach about anything in controversy between England and Rome."[111] The following month, James ordered the suppression of the popular Sunday afternoon lectures on the catechism; their purpose being to impart and reinforce the doctrine of the established church, they could hardly proceed without some reflection on Roman error. The bishops demurred, pleading the necessity of providing for those who could attend only afternoon lectures and their pastoral obligations as clergy to catechize even regarding points of controversy. As Bishop Compton pointed out, "the behavior of the Romish priests in many places constrain ministers to say more in this particular for the settling of men's minds than otherwise they would do."[112]

James callously delayed the issuance of the royal brief on behalf of the French Protestant refugees in order to excise references to the "cruel persecution in France." The *London Gazette*, the official state organ, remained conspicuously silent on the matter of the French persecutions, and one observer called it "very extraordinary in a Protestant country that we should know nothing of what Protestants suffered." The brief that passed the Great Seal emerged "quite changed, and another turn given to it," reportedly revised at the behest of the French ambassador Paul Barillon d'Amoncourt, but no doubt also with the intention of precluding the wave of anti-Catholic preaching that would likely accompany solicitations from the pulpit.[113] Lord Chancellor George Jeffreys went so far as to revise the archbishop of Canterbury's circular letter accompanying the brief, "to obviate the inconveniences his Majesty apprehends may attend his Service, by any though but seeming reflections."[114] To underscore the delicacy with which James wished his clergy to proceed in the collection, he simultaneously reissued his brother's "directions concerning preachers," a relic of 1662 when English Puritanism still retained a presence in the pulpits of the established church. The new preface recommended the late king's strictures against factious and unquiet spirits, "who make it a great part of their business to beget in the minds of their hearers, an evil opinion of their governors."[115] The injunctions had little immediate effect. Two days after they were issued, Robert Frampton, bishop of Gloucester, preached at Whitehall on "the several afflictions of the Church of Christ from the primitives to this day, applying exceedingly to the present conjuncture." When word of the king's offense at the sermon reached the bishop, he was unmoved, confessing to Archbishop Sancroft "that I spake much to the honor of my dear mother the Church of England is very true and I shall never repent of it." A week later, Thomas Ken, bishop of Bath and Wells, resumed the topic of persecution at the Chapel Royal at Whitehall, exhorting "constancy in the Protestant religion, detestation of the unheard-of cruelties of the French, and stirring up to a liberal contribution."[116] The canon of St. Paul's, Samuel Rayner, perhaps collaborating with Thomas Tenison, soon published an anonymous translation of Jean Claude's *Account of the Persecutions and Oppressions of the Protestants in France*, which sold in the thousands. The work was highly resented at court and ordered burned by the common hangman in May 1686.[117]

Not content with merely neutralizing Protestantism, James sought to enlarge the public profile of the Catholicism that adorned his court.[118] He ordered his Roman Catholic printer Henry Hills to begin publishing the "English sermons preached before their Majesties" at mass, as a public reminder that the devotional heart of the court had migrated to the Catholic chapels.[119] On Whitsunday, the king reportedly touched for scrofula assisted by "his own priests" rather than the clergymen of the established church.[120] James discharged the dean of Windsor, Gregory Hescard, from attending the king's chapel at that palace, "now seized on by mass priests," and rumors began to circulate that the Royal Chapel at Whitehall, where Princess Anne and her household regularly worshipped, would soon be confiscated for the Roman Catholic mass.[121] The Catholicism celebrated at the royal palaces was supplemented by public services often featuring English sermons at the string of Catholic chapels in ambassadorial residences throughout Westminster. Most provocative was the capacious chapel opened at the king's behest on Lime Street within the City by the Englishman James Stamford, the Roman Catholic envoy of the Elector Palatine, "that looks like something else than a place of prayer for his private family." In late March 1686, Lord Mayor Sir Robert Geffrey, accompanied by two sheriffs and a posse of some thirty or forty officers, tried unsuccessfully to halt construction on the Lime Street chapel, for which the king in council rebuked him and ordered construction to continue. "It may reasonably be expected," one observer informed John Ellis, "that in a little time a great many so charactered may follow the example *ad propagandam fidem*." Riots plagued the opening of the Lime Street chapel the following month, placing the City magistrates in the untenable position of protecting unlawful Catholic worship from the fury of Protestant mobs.[122] James also maintained a strange, wheeled wooden chapel in which he could hear mass at the summer encampment of his burgeoning standing army at Hounslow Heath outside of London. Open Catholic worship at the camp worried the Earl of Feversham, the Protestant commander of the king's Life Guards, enough to request that the bishop of London supply Anglican clergymen to minister to the troops and officers. Compton promptly dispatched twelve "of the city clergy to preach there by turns."[123]

London booksellers openly retailed the English sermons of the court and the Catholic chapels throughout the metropolis alongside a steady stream of Roman Catholic propaganda that, with the king's connivance, issued forth from the royal press. Much of this work, such as the Benedictine John Gother's *A Papist Misrepresented and Represented*, aimed to vindicate the doctrine of transubstantiation and therefore directly impugned the eucharistic theology that stood at the heart of Anglican revivalism.[124] John Evelyn complained of "popish pamphlets and pictures sold publicly" throughout the city, with "no books nor answers to them appearing till long after." The London clergy, "chiefly Tillotson, Stillingfleet, Tenison and Patrick," resolved to collaborate upon a series of popular works of Protestant apologetic, modeled on their previous collaborations against English Nonconformity, to counteract the spread of Roman error. Master of the Temple William Sherlock convened a meeting of city divines at his house to craft a "true representation of popery" against Gother's innocuous depiction of the Catholic faith. Churchmen were confident in their ability to counter Roman propaganda. "The arguments lately used in France to reconcile churches and bring in shoals of proselytes," Bishop Turner confidently assured Sir William Trumbull, "have set us in England further off than ever."[125]

James chose this moment to make good on his proposal to Archbishop Sancroft to print his brother's "two papers," in which the late king besmirched "the pretended Reformation here in England" and averred "that none can be that Church, but that which is called the Roman Catholic Church."[126] James clearly sought to overawe the churchmen by interjecting the majesty of both his brother's and his own sovereignty on behalf of Catholic doctrine. But the London clergymen did not relent, and the two papers elicited vigorous, but deferential, Anglican responses from Dean Stillingfleet and Gilbert Burnet, the latter recently exiled to the Continent.[127] Stillingfleet, in particular, prosecuted his refutation of the late king without discourtesy or malice. But John Dryden's defense of the king's papers, insinuating that works of Protestant apologetic were somehow inherently disloyal, exhibited a worrisome trend among Catholic controversialists.[128] It was fast becoming clear that even the most modest rhetoric of Protestant vindication would invite charges of sedition. John Gother's unctuous *Good Advice to the Pulpits* of the following year admonished Protestants that their intemperate refutation of Catholic error was not conducive to the peace of the kingdom. "Men may be taught to be good Christians, without being made bad subjects," he chided, "and the disturbing the government is no necessary preparation for directing people the way to heaven."[129]

The interventions of the king did little to slow the pace of controversy. In spring 1686 John Sharp, dean of Norwich and rector of the large metropolitan parish of St. Giles-in-the-Fields, preached a timely course of sermons on the rule of faith. The sermons were remarkable for their liberal ecumenism, offering an almost shockingly comprehensive notion of a catholic church and dismissing the attempt to put "wits upon the rack oftentimes for the devising and inventing God knows how many marks and tokens whereby to distinguish the true Church from false and pretended churches."[130] Mere months earlier, Sharp's broad-minded ecclesiology likely would have drawn more opprobrium from conservatives in his own communion than from Roman Catholics. However, the enquiries with which Sharp concluded his sermon on 2 May 1686 elicited a hastily drawn paper from one of his auditors "containing an argument for the right that the Church of Rome had to the stile and title of the only visible

Catholic Church." Sharp decided to incorporate a refutation of the paper in his sermon the following Sunday.[131] Despite its reputation, his sermon was a study in moderation. Sharp owned the Roman Catholic Church to be a true church, yet disavowed any possibility of communion with it unless it redressed its manifold errors and usurpations. He did not, however, indulge in any mention of politics or the persecutions on the Continent, tempering his insinuations of heresy against the Roman Catholic Church with frequent affirmations of its soundness in fundamentals. If the term "latitudinarian" retains any ability to adequately convey a style of churchmanship, surely it may be employed to describe these sermons of John Sharp.[132]

Despite the charitableness of Sharp's sermon, word soon spread of its subversive intent. One of Sharp's parishioners at St. Giles, the ultraloyalist licenser of the press Roger L'Estrange, began taking note of "some things that the dean said with his pencil" and reported them to Lord Chancellor Jeffreys at court. Some construed Sharp's concluding remarks concerning apostasy from the Church of England as a reflection on the king. Others believed that the dean was singled out for repudiating the ecclesiological premise of the recently published *Copies of two papers written by the Late King Charles II*. Indeed, it was held by some that the paper refuted in Sharp's sermon of 9 May 1686 was none other than that of the late king. However, the king in his letter to Bishop Compton of 14 June 1686 simply suggested that the dean had preached in violation of the directions concerning preachers issued earlier that year and was therefore to be suspended from further preaching in the diocese of London.[133] Upon receipt of the king's commands, Compton summoned Sharp to Doctors' Commons and simply bid him to abstain from preaching until further word from the king. Compton informed the king of his actions, pleading that he could not execute a summary suspension of a clergyman without judicial proceeding. Sharp penned a petition of profuse apology to the king, but the king and his ministers rather scornfully rejected the dean's entreaties. Lord Chancellor Jeffreys eventually advised Sharp simply "to get out of the way," intimating the court's far graver concern with the open defiance of the bishop of London, "the mark of the envy and hatred of the Romish party at court." Sharp obliged the court with a long retreat in his deanery of Norwich.[134]

The informal methods of exercising the royal supremacy over the established church through the episcopal bench had clearly failed. The primate William Sancroft had proved surprisingly recalcitrant in curbing anti-Catholicism among the Protestant clergy. The bishop of London, convinced that the court aimed "to suspend all the eminent preachers in England," was openly insubordinate. The archbishop of York, John Dolben, had died in April, and the court made no moves toward filling the vacancy. Moreover, the clergy of the established church had managed to tap a surprisingly vast potential for opposition simply within the performance of their ministerial functions. Citing "the extravagancy of some of the clergy," James in early July 1686 delegated his ecclesiastical powers as supreme ordinary of the Church of England to a commission of three ecclesiastics and four lay ministers: the archbishop of Canterbury and the bishops of Durham and Rochester, along with the Lord Treasurer, the Earl of Rochester; the Lord President, the Earl of Sunderland; the Lord Chancellor, George Jeffreys; and the chief justice of the King's Bench, Edward Herbert. The Commission for Ecclesiastical Causes was empowered "to visit, reform, redress, order, correct and amend all such abuses, offences, contempts and enormities" of which the ecclesiastical laws of the realm were cognizant. There was reportedly some comfort among observers in the fact that the commission was composed entirely of "good Church of England men" and that "the defects that were in ecclesiastical authority will now be supplied." But most were not so sanguine. The commission, redolent of the odious Court of High Commission outlawed by Parliament on the eve of the civil wars, was branded "a new court of inquisition." John Evelyn observed that "the main drift was to suppress zealous preachers." Undersecretary of State Owen Wynne admitted "there is no other design in it than to keep our preachers from meddling with polemical points of divinity." One of the loyalist correspondents of the diplomat Richard Bulstrode noted that the new ecclesiastical commission "does indeed somewhat alarm our parsons," offering the mean consolation that "if they keep within those bounds of decorum and respect that becomes them they will not be troubled." Roger Morrice grimly reflected, "The Protestants in France had free liberty, both to preach up the Protestant religion, and to preach and write against popery, till within eight or ten months that they began to torment and murder them."[135]

Six of the seven members of the ecclesiastical commission met on 3 August 1686. Pleading indisposition, the archbishop of Canterbury declined to attend any of the proceedings—a tactic he would use with growing frequency in the coming years to extricate himself from politically unpropitious situations. "The bishop of London," as Gilbert Burnet memorably put it, "was the first to be sacrificed." Cited to appear before the commission the following week, Compton spent the first week in August consulting with the city divines and lawyers, even with "so many evil eyes upon him to observe all his steps, words and deeds." The broad-minded Whig divine Edward Fowler of St. Giles's, Cripplegate, sounded out the handful of clergy remaining in London over the summer on "what was fit to be done if they were summoned before the Ecclesiastical Commissioners." It was suggested that the London divines demur en masse to the jurisdiction of the court, reasoning confidently that it could "never excommunicate the body of the clergy of London." The provincial clergy would "certainly do as they do" in the city, and the enormous trouble of suspending so many ministers "will make the commission impracticable and fruitless." Lawyers with whom Fowler spoke cautioned against owning the jurisdiction of the court, arguing they would indeed all be convicted, "and none will be able to clear themselves by any defense they can make." Fowler informed Compton of his findings, who remained undecided on a legal strategy. Compton then sought the advice of the Whig lawyer Sir John Maynard, a man with a reputation for sagacity, Presbyterianism, and staunch antipopery. Compton informed Maynard that he was prepared to submit to the jurisdiction of the commission, "ready to run all hazards in maintaining the law." Compton appeared before the commission on 9 August, accompanied by ten eminent "doctors of divinity" among the city clergy. The bishop was reportedly "much encouraged, and enabled by the universal concurrence of all the dissenters as well as by all his old friends" among the churchmen. "It was never known of late years," observed Roger Morrice, "that so universal an interest of churchmen, trimmer and dissenters did follow any one cause as now follows his."

At his first appearance before the commissioners, Lord Chancellor Jeffreys asked Compton point blank "why he had not obliged the king's orders that were sent to him for the suspending of Dr. Sharp who had meddled with matters in his sermon that did not concern him and tended to disturb the government?" Compton offered a profuse apology for displeasing the king but seemed to defer on the matter of jurisdiction. He requested that the court's commission be read aloud or a copy provided to him. The chancellor sharply responded that the bishop "could not think they would summon a person of his character before them unless they had authority so to do." He then added caustically that the bishop "might for a penny have seen a copy of their commission at any coffee house," an affront to both the dignity and lineage of the bishop, much "noted and aggravated by the Church and indeed the kingdom beyond." Compton's request for a written copy of the charge against him was also denied. The bishop was again pressed "to give a plain answer to this plain question why he had not obeyed the Kings command for the suspension of Dr. Sharp." Compton requested additional time to secure a copy of the commission and consult with what counsel could be had in a town emptied by the summer heat. The bishop was granted a single week, and then upon a further request, an additional two weeks. When the commission reconvened on 31 August, Compton requested leave to enter a plea as to the jurisdiction of the commissioners, their commission "being contrary to an act of Parliament," but was refused. He further pled that according to canon law he must be tried in the first instance before his metropolitan, for "matters of this nature never came before the Prince but at the second instance and by appeal." This was construed as another plea against the jurisdiction of the commissioners and was rejected. Compton made a final plea against the jurisdiction of the ecclesiastical commission, arguing that the use of the future tense in the letters patent, "to enquire into such offences as shall be committed," prohibited their enquiry into infractions committed before their establishment. This complaint was "looked upon as very trivial," as the commission contained numerous other phrases that encompassed both past and future offenses. Compton finally submitted an answer to the court's question, claiming that though it was not in his power to summarily effect a legal suspension of Sharp, he had indeed advised the dean to cease preaching. And as the dean had abstained from preaching since then, the bishop had effectively complied with the royal command. "If a bare silencing was intended," Compton reportedly argued, "then the king's command was obeyed for that Dr. Sharp had not preached ever since." A week later, the ecclesiastical commission suspended Henry Compton "from the function and execution of his episcopal office," under pain of deprivation from his bishopric. When James was informed of the sentence, he reportedly confessed that he "would have had them to have deprived the bishop."[136]

The established church began to undergo a curious political realignment in the wake of Henry Compton's suspension from his episcopal office. James not only judged Compton and the eminent London clergy as instruments of opposition, he also deemed the stalwarts of the old "Yorkist" party—dynastic legitimists like Archbishop Sancroft and Francis Turner of Ely who had championed the succession of the Duke of York in the final years of his brother's reign—as manifestly unreliable. In their place, he began to cultivate a new ecclesiastical court party composed of courtier prelates and proponents of an ultraroyalist political theology. At the end of 1685, Compton had been displaced at court and council in favor of Bishop Crewe of Durham and Bishop Sprat of Rochester, both of whom served on James's Commission for Ecclesiastical Causes. After Compton's suspension, his episcopal functions in the diocese of London, informally "transacted by the archbishop of Canterbury," were formally conferred upon a more pliant commission consisting of Sprat, Crewe, and Thomas White, a former chaplain to James's ducal household elevated by the king to the see of Peterborough in October of the previous year.[137] In September, Lord Chancellor Jeffreys demanded a list of the names of all "the lecturers of London," presumably to prepare the docket for the ecclesiastical commission.[138] That month, the Stationers' Company began seizing all extant copies of a work called *Episcopalia*, the digest of Compton's circular letters to the clergy of his diocese.[139] The commission dispatched its sergeant to serve the dean of St. Paul's, Edward Stillingfleet, and the three canons residentiary, John Tillotson, Henry Godolphin, and William Holder, with a monitory ordering Compton's suspension posted on the chapter door. The sergeant eventually located Stillingfleet at Lambeth visiting with Archbishop Sancroft and conveyed the commission's orders there. It was a telling sign of the archbishop's alienation from the court that the sergeant's appearance reportedly put Sancroft's family in "great consternation," presuming he had come to summon Sancroft before the commission. The chapter was convened, and over the vocal objections of Tillotson the monitory was posted "without either hand or seal, or any other writing by the Chapter."[140]

Archbishop Sancroft seemed to be following Compton and the eminent London clergy into opposition to the court of James II, a posture for which he was both theologically and temperamentally unsuited. The king denied him any share of managing the diocese of London during the suspension of the bishop. James ignored Sancroft's recommendations for ecclesiastical promotion and instead nominated to the vacant see of Chester the dean of Ripon, Thomas Cartwright, who had won the king's favor with an ultraroyalist sermon on the anniversary of his accession that not only applauded the king's pulpit policy, but proclaimed the Church of England utterly defenseless before the will of the sovereign. To the see of Oxford James nominated the like-minded archdeacon of Canterbury, Samuel Parker, another clergyman of purportedly limitless allegiance to the monarchy. Neither divine allowed a virulent antipathy toward Protestant Dissent to diminish his support for a religious toleration founded exclusively on the royal prerogative. The nominations were widely resented among the bishops, and Sancroft allegedly informed Bishop William Lloyd of St. Asaph that he would delay their consecrations until he was satisfied as to the complaints of his suffragans.[141] In early October, the archbishop waited on the king to explain his absence from the ecclesiastical commission. The king responded with mock sympathy, entirely relieving the prelate of his obligations at court on account of his politically transparent infirmities, "seeing his age and indisposition was such he would likewise excuse him from attending at the Privy Council which meets oftener."[142] Sancroft reluctantly consecrated the two new bishops at Lambeth shortly thereafter on 17 October 1686. Word immediately spread that Bishops Cartwright and Parker would soon be added to the roster of the ecclesiastical commission to fill the vacancy left by the banished archbishop.[143] Though "there was nothing of a holy day at Court," Sancroft's protégé Francis Turner, bishop of Ely, boldly preached again before Princess Anne on the anniversary of the Gunpowder Plot a sermon that no doubt chimed with the strident antipopery of the street processions and city pulpits that season and surely did nothing to return himself or his mentor to royal favor. Sancroft and Turner began to devise a strategy for responding to a seemingly inevitable summons of the archbishop before the king's Commission for Ecclesiastical Causes.[144] The established church was fracturing under the pressure of the court but not, it must be stressed, into camps of high and low churchmen. The strict and hierarchical Caroline bishops and the moderate London divines were both nursing disaffection. At its highest echelons, the established church was divided between a small court party of churchmen willing to collude in Catholic absolutism and a broad-based clerical opposition rooted in the metropolis and steeped in popular antipopery.

The alienation of the London clergy was palpable in what may be considered the final gasp of the Tory reaction. During the summer of 1686, the radical Whig clergyman Samuel Johnson circulated an incendiary broadside titled *A Humble and Hearty Address to all the English Protestants in the present Army* urging English soldiers to desist their service of Roman Catholicism. Already imprisoned in King's Bench for his intrepid 1682 critique of the Anglican doctrine of nonresistance, *Julian the Apostate*, Johnson was seized in May 1686 and incarcerated at Newgate. He was convicted at King's Bench soon after and sentenced on 16 November to pay five hundred marks, stand thrice at the pillory, and be whipped by the common hangman from Newgate to Tyburn. As an added disgrace, Johnson was to be ceremonially degraded from the priesthood before the execution of the sentence in order to spare the established church the ignominy of counting a seditious malefactor among the ranks of its ministry. Johnson was said to have declared at the sentencing, "It is strange I must be whipped for maintaining the laws, and the Protestant religion, when daily are printed books containing treason." From his cassock, Johnson then produced a copy of the Surrey clergyman Edward Sclater's *Reasons for his Conversion to the Catholic Faith*, published that year by the king's printer Henry Hills.[145] Though it was well known that Sclater had received a dispensation from the king to retain his living despite his apostasy from the established church, Johnson demanded the court proceed against him for treason, which it was said "went off with a kind of smile, according to the affections of the people."[146]

The degradation of Samuel Johnson, whose rectory was in Corringham, Essex, fell to the diocesan of London. Some of the bishop of London's friends "thought it a happiness" that his suspension exempted him from those proceedings. Accordingly, Bishops Crewe, Sprat, and White, exercising the episcopal functions of the bishop of London by commission, "did send to about twenty divines of the most conspicuous name and note in London" to assemble at the chapter house of St. Paul's on 20 November. The summons found only twelve of the twenty divines in town, and of those, only seven bothered to attend the ceremony. The remaining five included, significantly, the dean of St. Paul's, Edward Stillingfleet; the dean of Canterbury, John Tillotson; and the dean of Peterborough, Simon Patrick. Two of the absent clergymen informed the bishops that they could not "with a good conscience appear and join therein." A third was reported to have told the bishops that "he would do no more of the Papists' drudgery." Bishop Crewe demanded that the list of divines summoned be read aloud, by which means to expose the refractory clergy, but the assembled clerics protested that "the business should die of itself than be stirred." During the proceedings, Johnson exploited the extraordinary and politically fraught circumstances that prevented his true diocesan from presiding. He demanded to know of the bishops whether they sat by an original commission or as mere surrogates, claiming he would direct his defense only "to the authority they acted by." Johnson insisted he "be degraded by his immediate ordinary . . . and he saw him not there." The bishops responded that they were his immediate ordinary during the suspension of the bishop of London. Johnson replied that he had been informed that the "ordinaryship devolved in such a case upon the archbishop," who was also absent. The bishops disagreed and pressed on with the ceremony. Johnson's cap, girdle, and gown were removed; he parted with the Bible given him "with difficulty," kissing it and tearfully proclaiming that he could not be deprived of its benefits. Johnson told the assembled clergy that "since all he had writ was designed to keep their gowns on their backs," he grieved that "they should be the unhappy instruments to pull off his." After the degradation, Gregory Hescard, dean of Windsor, petitioned Bishop White on behalf of the inferior clergy present that the bishops might "be pleased to mediate with his Majesty for mercy to Johnson." Bishop Crewe was incredulous that any clergyman should have "the confidence to make such a request"; the other two bishops were somewhat more sympathetic. They ultimately decided not to intercede, for as the king had just granted them the favor of allowing the degradation of Johnson—"that the gown might not suffer"—they thought it prudent not to press a subsequent request. On 1 December 1686, Johnson was whipped 317 times on the two-mile march from Newgate to Tyburn. The ordeal of Samuel Johnson was nothing less than a sign of the times. A radical Whig proponent of militant anti-Catholicism and armed resistance to monarchs seemed to garner a good deal more sympathy among the London clergy than the bishops acting in vindication of the orthodox political theology of the Church of England.[147]

Even in suspension, the figure of Henry Compton loomed particularly large in the ecclesiastical opposition. "The bishop does no act of jurisdiction," Burnet wrote, "but really his clergy depend on him more than ever." Through his client William Stanley, the English chaplain to Princess Mary, Compton quietly cultivated his interest with the reversionary court at The Hague. There was talk in the city that Compton might soon be permanently deprived of his bishopric, presumably to make way for a prelate more amenable to the king's designs. Roger Morrice anxiously contemplated a complete decapitation of the London church, envisioning a scenario in which the king's *congé d'élire* to St. Paul's prompted a wave of resignations within the chapter, including most assuredly those of the two deans Stillingfleet and Tillotson. Compton offered a grudging submission to the king within the canonical six months of his suspension, expressly to deny the crown a pretext for deprivation according to civil law, but it went unnoticed. His friends confidently reported that the bishop would not countenance any subsequent summons before the ecclesiastical commission.[148]

At the end of 1686, Compton penned a final meditation on the perils of the established church in a circular letter to the London clergy. His missive skewered the king's pulpit policy and aimed directly at the ultraroyalism of the new court churchmen, affirming that "nothing could be more pernicious to prince or people, than to carry the duty of submission beyond the bounds of just reason or due patience." Somewhat counterintuitively, Compton reasoned that the extreme political theology of the established church posed the real threat to social order. He recommended that his clergy construe the king's prohibition on political preaching as broadly as possible and forbear from preaching the divine right of kings, which could only incite the people to rebellion. Such provocation, Compton reasoned, "would alarm the people with an apprehension that some design were working against their just rights." In other words, the political theology of the established church would not instill obedience in the people, but "dissatisfaction, murmuring, jealousy, and a readiness to rebel," which would in turn serve as a pretext for absolutism. The people must instead look to "the good effect of those remedies we have by passive obedience, Westminster-Hall, Parliament, and what other methods may be." Compton utterly rejected the king's prohibition on controversy, recommending caution and discretion but warning his clergy that "it may fall out, as to be indispensably necessary." There could be no abnegation of their pastoral function. "If the plague be begun in your congregation," he wrote, "you must make haste with your censers. If you see it approaching or hanging over, you must prepare your people, with the best anti-dotes, you can think of." Compton sought to disabuse his clergy of the delusions of Anglican royalism and their vaunted trust in the king's custody of the estab-lished church. Though wrought with a curious (and at times discordant) mixture of Whig and Tory political principles, Compton's letter presented a virtual mirror image of the ultraroyalist Anglicanism gaining ground at court through the likes of Bishops Parker and Cartwright. Compton urged his clergy to abandon the political divinity of the Tory reaction; to vigorously counter Roman error through controversy, preaching, and diligent pastoral care; and indeed to maintain a healthy skepticism of the good intentions of a Roman Catholic king. The bishop's seventh letter to his clergy was nothing short of a manifesto for ecclesiastical opposition.[149]

The Proving Grounds of the Anglican Revival

As James II entered the third year of his reign, the Church of England found its establishment in mortal danger. The king proceeded in early 1687 with his sweeping purge of the Tory Anglicans from all levels of government. He had unmistakably signaled his intention to implement a religious toleration that would include Protestant Nonconformists along with his own Roman Catholic coreligionists in advance of a legislative assault on the penal laws and the Test Acts.[150] The king's court occupied the vanguard of a great wave of Roman Catholic missionary activity in the major cities and throughout the provinces. James had alienated not only the popular metropolitan clergy who fancied themselves the sentries of a besieged Protestantism, but the core of Anglican royalist "Yorkists" who had once embodied the church's unwavering commitment to dynastic legitimism. The king cultivated a party of court churchmen that from either professional or ideological motives advanced royalism as the totality of Anglican churchmanship and gave it a foothold in his Commission for Ecclesiastical Causes. This commission sought not only to enforce the royal strictures against controversial preaching and reform abuses, but more ambitiously to pry from the hands of the established church the great medieval bequest of colleges, hospitals, and charities claimed at the Reformation. The Church of England's legal monopolies over worship, government, and education were all in the process of being dismantled.

This crisis of the established church comprised the proving grounds of the Anglican revival. Having lost the court, the Church of England cultivated an alternative foundation in the affections of the nation. Nowhere more so than in London, the clergymen of the established church, as one divine put it, "took the ready way to popularity" through a program of preaching, pastoral care, theological controversy, and religious charity. As religious persecution abated and Anglican political and institutional monopolies deteriorated, the church relied increasingly on its own powers of exhortation to maintain its national communion.[151] Most importantly, churchmen needed to fortify their flocks against a Roman Catholicism now in political ascendancy. The London divines, acclimated to enormous metropolitan parishes, fickle audiences of all ranks, and a vibrant print culture, possessed a substantial advantage over the foreign-trained Roman Catholic clergy, who were unaccustomed to both preaching and disputation in English as well as to ministering to large congregations. The perceived maladroitness of the Catholic clergy was perhaps exacerbated by the heedless expansion throughout the metropolis of Roman Catholic chapels, which soon outstripped the needs of the miniscule Catholic population and elicited no small amount of derision and resentment among the common people.[152]

In sharp contrast to the sparsely attended Roman Catholic chapels in the city, the thronged services of the London churches became popular rituals of solidarity with the established church, providing forums for public defiance of both the king's pulpit policy and his proselytization efforts. As Compton languished in suspension, the original malefactor in his case, John Sharp, was quietly restored to his ministry in early January 1687. Sharp's return to the pulpit at St. Giles-in-the-Fields brought "an infinite company to the church of all sorts—nobility, gentry and the vulgar." No fewer than a hundred coaches, it was said, turned away upon observing the overflowing of both church and church-yard. Sharp's return to the Chapel Royal at Whitehall in March also attracted "a vast crowd." The newly restored Sharp prudently refrained from controversial preaching on these occasions, but his brethren throughout the metropolis were not so cautious. Edward Pelling, the rector of St. Martin's, Ludgate, warned his audience at Mercers' Chapel on 16 January "against placing any confidence in the promises that papists make to heretics." A few weeks later, Bishop Thomas Ken preached at Whitehall before Princess Anne "and a great crowd of people" on the blasphemies, superstitions, perfidy, and spirit of persecution of the scribes and Pharisees, "so that all the auditory understood his meaning of a parallel between them and the Roman priests." On 23 February, Richard Kidder's sermon at Covent Garden castigated the "blind obedience" of the Roman Catholics and affirmed "the necessity of allowing the judgment of private discretion"—a point vehemently disputed in the *Two papers* of Charles II. Perhaps with the royal designs for her conversion to Catholicism (and that of her uncle, Earl of Rochester) in mind, John Tillotson at Whitehall recommended to Princess Anne the example of Moses, whose steadfast refusal to forsake the religion of his ances-tors for heathen idolatry cost him the throne of Egypt. Against the self-interested apostasy of courtiers, Tillotson urged "a state of afflicted piety before the greatest earthly happiness and prosperity." Indeed, the prohibition of idolatry was such a common cipher for anti-Catholicism that its mere mention raised hackles among the king's supporters. When Robert Frampton, bishop of Gloucester, introduced before his audience at Whitehall a verse from Psalm 115 as his text— "Their idols are silver and gold, the work of men's hands"—an informant who sat among the choristers immediately rose up to inform the court, not even waiting to hear what the Earl of Ailesbury later reassured the king was an "excellent, orthodox, and submissive sermon." The supporters of the king, wrote Richard Kidder, believed "those men ought to be watched who did either speak or insinuate that we were in danger of popery." Homiletics in the capital had by 1687 become sufficiently subversive that such spies were now "posted in all churches." Gilbert Burnet lamented, "Our orthodox clergy are not only inhibited to preach against popery, but are illegally reprimanded, silenced and suspended, for dispatching that duty, which their consciences, offices, oaths and the laws of the kingdom oblige them unto."[153]

The vindication of the Church of England in the pulpit was supplemented by continued efforts in the press and the parishes. The London clergymen strode upon a far greater stage than the court and capital of James II, assailing the major figures of post-Tridentine Catholicism. In 1687, William Sherlock and numerous other London clergymen, including Tenison, Patrick, and Fowler, began publishing the first of what would eventually be fifteen installments of their grand collaborative refutation of the "notes of a true church" that demarcated Cardinal Robert Bellarmine's papal ecclesiology. The young scholar William Wake, a lecturer in the new parish of St. Anne's, Soho (recently carved out of Tenison's sprawling parish of St. Martin's-in-the-Fields), engaged in a running assault on the Gallican Jacques-Bénigne Bossuet, bishop of Meaux, which he believed had "made the king my enemy." In March 1687, Wake informed Trinity College, Oxford, fellow Arthur Charlett of "a design set on foot by some of the most considerable of our clergy" to translate their most formidable works of Anglican apologetic into Latin and French and have them printed in Holland for distribution on the Continent. That year the *London Gazette* began for the first time giving notice of Roman Catholic titles, and the court had ceased to list works of Anglican apologetic in the term catalogues. "We have reason to fear," wrote William Lloyd, bishop of St. Asaph, "that the press may be taken from us." To publicize a struggle that the court seemed intent on suppressing, Wake and his housemate William Clagett, a preacher at Gray's Inn, published a detailed compendium of the recent controversy with the Church of Rome. Just two years into the reign of James II, the churchmen had produced roughly seventy volumes against popery. The number of such works would pass two hundred before the end of the reign, even though, as one newsletter noted, "the press is narrowly watched."[154]

Indeed, all the instruments of Anglican revival were deployed to maintain the communion of the established church. To counter the Catholic missionary presence in the capital, churchmen embarked on a new wave of pastoral and philanthropic activity, "the Protestants," one observer noted, "being resolved not to be outdone in charity by any of a different persuasion." Collections on behalf of the French Protestants continued vigorously apace, particularly in the city of London, the commissioners having paid out some £21,000 by April 1687.[155] In May, the London ministers issued a fresh appeal for the reconstruction of Sion College, receiving subscriptions from city clergymen alongside those of the mercantile interest.[156] The Sons of the Clergy assumed a newfound importance during the reign of James II, as the destitute families of Anglican ministers were often cited by Roman Catholic apologists as an argument for a celibate clergy. Bishop Herbert Croft of Hereford described the philanthropy as "coldly pursued a great while but now is revived and many persons have contributed largely towards it."[157] To compete with the burgeoning Catholic educational establishment—and in particular, its crown jewel, the highly popular nondenominational school opened by Jesuits in the Savoy—Anglicans embarked upon a fresh round of school endowments.[158] In September 1687, Tenison even challenged the Jesuit Andrew Pulton, a teacher at the Savoy, to a religious dispute for the soul of a young apprentice apostatized to the Church of Rome, in which Tenison demanded the Jesuit not "tamper about religion with the Protestant boys who should come to the Savoy-School." The conference, which very closely mirrored the ongoing pamphlet controversies on transubstantiation and the rule of faith, was "managed with much heat, [though] it came to little effect."[159]

The relentless Catholic assault on Anglican sacramental theology did little to diminish the conspicuous piety of the Anglican revival. The patron of the religious societies, Anthony Horneck, in whose parish lay the Jesuit college at the Savoy, was particularly vigilant. The religious societies he inspired persisted throughout the reign of James II, even though "all private meetings were suspected." Though of precarious foundation, the societies participated in the defense of the established church. "Seeing the mass publicly celebrated," one of the London societies set up public prayers every evening at St. Clement Danes, "which never wanted a full and affectionate congregation." Though the king had made his dislike of the city lectures known the previous year, the religious society established a monthly lecture in the same church, "to confirm communicants in the holy purpose and vows which they made at the Lord's table." Other societies survived in a somewhat more liminal state, changing their name from "society" to the more innocuous "club" and assembling in public houses, "under the pretext of spending a shilling or two," rather than privately in residences, which might provoke government suspicion.[160] Under James II, the Church of England began to reap the harvest of Restoration revivalism. Deprived of the countenance of the English state, the church discovered its vast internal resources for the cultivation of popular affection and for the maintenance of its national communion.

The Vindication of the National Church

In a declaration dated 4 April 1687, James II formally abolished by royal prerogative the religious monopoly of the Church of England. The king granted all of his subjects "the free exercise of their religion" and abrogated the confessional bar to both civil and military service of the state. To allay widespread fears that the sweeping transfer of property that accompanied the Protestant Reformation in England might be undone, the declaration twice pledged the king's maintenance of the Church of England "in the quiet and full enjoyment of all their possessions." The king believed this singular favor worthy of public acknowledgment by the church, and the Earl of Sunderland promptly communicated to the court bishops of Durham, Rochester, Peterborough, Oxford, and Chester the royal expectation of some addresses of gratitude. As Tim Harris has illustrated, the court was showered with addresses of thanks from various localities, corporations, commercial interests, and religious denominations throughout the kingdom, though considerably fewer than greeted the king's accession two years earlier.[161]

The subsequent controversy over the addresses, perhaps more than any previous event, exposed the real divisions in the established church between a party of courtier bishops and the clerical opposition based in London and steeped in popular antipopery. The bishops of Durham, Oxford, Chester, and (eventually) Rochester agreed to sign an address, but Thomas White of Peterborough demurred, particularly with respect to the clergy of London, over whom he was now acting diocesan. White informed his brethren that he believed that the metropolitan clergy "were a learned clergy very well settled and resolved." And though the London clergy harbored a greater affection for their present bishop, Henry Compton, "as ever any clergymen had for their bishop," even he would be refused their cooperation in this matter. Bishop Parker scoffed that he had no such opinion of the London clergy, "for their learning or otherwise," but he was certain that they were Erastians and would therefore defer to their king—an oblique reference, no doubt, to the famous 1680 sermons against schism by Tillotson and Stillingfleet and the subsequent controversy that earned them reputations for Hobbism.[162] Parker declared the clergy of London "drunk with the fears of popery, and they must be reduced to their common sense by correction." The bishop of Peterborough proved correct, and prominent members of the London clergy met to coordinate their refusal to sign an address to the king. The court bishops launched a closeting campaign to persuade prominent London clergymen such as the dean of Windsor, Gregory Hescard, and the vicar of St. Mary Aldermanbury, Nicholas Stratford, to support an address, but the bishops were roundly denounced as "*renegados* to the Church of England." Bishop Cartwright lambasted the clergy of London, and "the high opinion they had of themselves," for refusing even a modified address that omitted the indulgence and simply thanked the king for his pledge to maintain the Church of England. Moreover, the London clergy were actively soliciting noncompliance from churchmen in other dioceses. They were joined in this campaign by the Oxford clergy, whose reasons for refusal were "industriously dispersed to hinder addressing" throughout the kingdom. The "Oxford Reasons," as the circulating manuscript was called, comprised a sustained attack on their diocesan Samuel Parker and the court bishops who initiated the address for acting "independently upon their metropolitan and without the previous concurrence of the rest of their order" and breeding "a fatal division among the clergy." James was visibly disgusted with the narrow self-regard evinced even in the handful of clerical addresses that eventually trickled into court. "Can you find nothing to give thanks for," he rebuked the few addressors among the Anglican clergy, "but that one clause that relates to yourselves?"[163]

The controversy surrounding the first Declaration of Indulgence plainly exposed the constraints that pressed against James II's religious policies. First, the Church of England could not be easily governed outside of metropolitical and diocesan channels. Archbishop Sancroft had been banished from the court, and Bishop Compton languished in suspension. The court bishops through whom the king acted were men of limited influence within the church and with the public at large. The court bishops' incompetent and heavy-handed attempts to cajole clerical support for the king's religious policies plainly exacerbated rather than ameliorated the alienation of the church from the court. Second, even deprived of their diocesan the London clergy proved themselves capable of rapid and effective mobilization in opposition to royal policies. Moreover, the London clergy seemed capable of exercising a decisive influence on churchmen throughout the nation—even in loyalist Oxford. Churchmen were now routinely heedless of the royal will, defying the king's pulpit policy and willfully omitting the new prayers for Queen Mary of Modena's celebrated pregnancy.[164]

Third and most important, the king's assault on the Anglican confessional monopoly revived the dormant ideology of Protestant union largely associated with London Anglicanism.[165] The stalwarts of the clerical opposition, Deans Stillingfleet and Tillotson, along with their close friend and ally Bishop Lloyd of St. Asaph had engaged the London Presbyterian John Howe as recently as 1680 regarding a program for comprehending moderate Nonconformists within the established church. Moreover, the city divines most keenly felt the effects of the indulgence not simply because of the proximity of the Catholic court or the marked religious pluralism of the capital, but because the moderate London clergy had made, as John Spurr and Mark Goldie have shown, the farthest inroads with Protestant Nonconformity. It was, the Presbyterian Roger Morrice reasoned, "the congregations of the most religious, and most practical preachers" in the city rather than those of the high episcopal "hierarchists" that had proved most palatable to Dissenters and held the greatest prospects for some future accommodation. The Declaration of Indulgence was not only a fillip for resurgent Catholicism, it threatened to dash the remaining hopes for Protestant reconciliation that moderate Anglicans still cherished. Churchmen watched anxiously as addresses of thanks poured forth from Dissenting congregations throughout the kingdom and grew increasingly convinced that the discredited notion of comprehension appeared the most promising method of maintaining a national Protestant Church of England.[166]

In the wake of James's Declaration of Indulgence, churchmen in the capital and beyond began to sound the long unheard notes of reconciliation with Protestant Nonconformity. In a sermon at St. Mary Aldermanbury near the Guildhall in April, Nicholas Stratford advised the church "to come to a good understanding and coalescencey with the noncomformist dissenters." In a sermon at Whitehall in May, Sancroft's close friend John Lake, bishop of Chichester, expressed his apprehensions of the "danger of popery" and averred that "there was no remedy within human prospect, but by their relaxing and remitting those points of conformity and ceremony that had made the breach between" the church and other Protestants. In a pamphlet circulating in London in the spring of 1687 called *The Ill Effects of Animosities among Protestants in England Detected*, the exiled Gilbert Burnet urged Protestant Nonconformists to enter with churchmen "into a union of counsels and endeavors against popery and tyranny." The Marquis of Halifax's prodigiously popular *Letter to a Dissenter* attempted to reassure a justly skeptical Dissenting interest that the Church of England had repented of its old intolerance. In December, Nicholas Stratford arranged a meeting between the leading Presbyterian William Bates and the veteran advocate of comprehension Bishop William Lloyd in which the two agreed upon "the absolute necessity of [a] good understanding or coalition" between churchmen and Dissenters and a common commitment to maintain the Test Act in a future Parliament. Though Bates would not consent to scheduling Nonconformists' meetings outside of "Church hours," the two men concurred in the need for augmented pastoral engagement within their respective churches "to promote holiness and to confirm persons in the true religion."[167]

The cohesion of the London divines and their tentative spirit of accord with Protestant Nonconformity stood the Church of England in good stead when the king decided to more forcefully exact Anglican complicity in his religious policies. On 27 April 1688, he reissued his Declaration of Indulgence, appending an order in council the following week that the declaration be read from all church pulpits in London on the last two Sundays of May and in all churches and chapels throughout the kingdom on the first two Sundays of June. The Church of England could no longer nurse its grievances with petty disobediences, popular antipopery, and vague overtures toward Protestant Dissenters that had characterized much of the ecclesiastical opposition over the course of the previous two years. The churchmen would comply with the king's directive or be exposed as derelict in their submission, hypocritical in their political theology, and, despite all their professions of concord, inalterably averse to religious toleration.

Historians debate over whom to credit with leading the ecclesiastical opposition at this juncture: the alienated Yorkists, such as Archbishop Sancroft and his protégés Turner of Ely and White of Peterborough, or the popular London divines, with their extensive connections among the Protestant Nonconformists. Although there was almost continual collaboration among them, the initiative, it seems, clearly lay with the London clergy, with leadership conferred upon the bishops as a political and ecclesiological necessity. The ecclesiastical opposition simply could not rest upon an informal body of clergy that lacked any constitutional standing and was, if anything, more alienated from the court than the staunchly Tory diocesans at Lambeth. Within days of the order, London clergymen, including "several considerable divines both of the milder and of the fiercer sort," assembled informally among themselves as well as at the London residence of the bishop of Ely to discuss the reading of the declaration and, more generally, the ever-ascending bar of compliance with the king. On 11 May, a conference of the London clergy at the Temple residence of William Sherlock resolved "that the bishops should be desired to address to the king, but not upon any address of ours to them." In a meeting at Lambeth Palace on the next day, the archbishop of Canterbury and the bishops of London, Ely, and Peterborough (along with Thomas Tenison and the Earl of Clarendon) agreed on the method of petitioning the king. Throughout the crisis, the "Sancroftians" at Lambeth somewhat timorously sought safety in greater numbers and thus solicited reinforcements by inviting to town those bishops they presumed sympathetic to their causes: Peter Mews of Winchester, William Lloyd of Norwich, Robert Frampton of Gloucester, William Lloyd of St. Asaph, Thomas Ken of Bath and Wells, Jonathan Trelawny of Bristol, and John Lake of Chichester. The following day, in search of further reassurance, Bishops Turner and White conferred with some seventeen of the leading London clergymen, including Tillotson, Stillingfleet, Sharp, Patrick, Stratford, Hescard, Sherlock, and Beveridge, all of whom were in support of the refusal to read the declaration, "and so they apprehended most of their brethren to be." Some concern remained, however, among the London divines that their friends among the Protestant Nonconformists would "be much offended at their refusal." To avoid alienating the Dissenters, a brief statement against the reading of the declaration titled "The Comprehensive Sense of the Clergy" was drawn up emphasizing the illegality of the dispensing power upon which the declaration was founded. The clergy denied "any want of due tenderness toward Dissenters," with whom they would willingly come to terms "when the matter comes to be considered in parliament and convocation." Several divines, including Tenison and Patrick, then canvassed the document about the greater body of the London clergy and received the concurrence of somewhere between sixty and eighty of their brethren, whose names were soon conveyed to the bishops at Lambeth. By 16 May, the Earl of Clarendon had been informed "that most of the city clergy had resolved not to read the declaration." One is somewhat hard-pressed to discern the bold leadership and diplomatic skill that Gareth Bennett affords Turner and the other bishops, whose ecclesiological failure of nerve had proponents of *jure divino* episcopacy anxiously awaiting the concurrence of presbyters and schismatics to act decisively. The mobilization that followed the king's order-in-council, though undertaken with the due subordination to the episcopal bench, seemed to confirm the indispensability of the London churchmen to any substantive ecclesiastical opposition. Moreover, the price the city exacted for their support—a commitment to reconciliation with Protestant Nonconformists that would have been virtually unthinkable among the majority of Caroline bishops fewer than three years earlier—was not inconsiderable.[168]

On the afternoon of Friday 18 May, six of the eminent London clergy met with the archbishop of Canterbury and his allied brethren at Lambeth to finalize the petition against the reading of the king's Declaration of Indulgence. A phalanx of London divines conferred with the archbishop and the bishops of London, Ely, Peterborough, and St. Asaph, as well as the recently arrived bishops of Bath and Wells and Bristol, on both the content and the presentation of the petition. It was decided that the bishops then present at Lambeth (though still short of the number summoned) would entreat the king as a body that night, excluding, however, the disfavored metropolitan and the suspended bishop of London. The final petition, written in the archbishop's hand, followed fairly closely on the document circulated by the London divines, emphasizing the settled illegality of the dispensing power and disclaiming any malice toward Protestant Nonconformists. The bishops' petition, however, reaffirmed the "unquestionably loyal" principles and practices of the Church of England, a conceit absent from the earlier document. The bishops' audience with the king late that evening proved what great disparity lay between their respective assessments of loyalty. James was, perhaps not unfairly, incredulous at the positively Whiggish constitutional claims in the petition, furiously sputtering: "The Church of England against my dispensing power! The Church of England! They that always preached it!" The bishops denied that they had ever supported the dispensing power, claiming they had preached "only obedience, and suffering when they could not obey." Here the bishops were on fairly shaky ground: they may have withheld their approval of the dispensing power, but the church had championed prerogative in the past and certainly condemned the coordinate power of Parliament to overrule the king. James was right to sense a rather self-serving lapse in the political theology of the established church. He told the six bishops before dismissing them that he expected to be obeyed.[169]

The events that followed the bishops' petition are exceedingly well known, as is the devastating effect of the petition upon James's religious policies. The petition served as what John Western deems "a national gesture of resistance." There was no small irony in the fact that the bishops took their stand on principles of constitutional government and Protestant solidarity, concerns that had never been foremost among men whose political consciences had been formed during the Restoration crisis and the ensuing Tory reaction. A counterfeit version of the petition—in actuality, a copy of "The Comprehensive Sense of the Clergy"—was in circulation in the city almost immediately after the bishops' audience with the king. According to Archdeacon Adam Ottley, "The business of reading the Declar[ation] has been for some time the chief discourse of the town and it is thought a matter of the greatest moment that has happened since his Majesty's reign." On Sunday 20 May, the declaration was "almost universally forborne throughout all London," unread in all but roughly a half-dozen churches throughout London and Westminster. It fared worse the following week; "in several places where the declaration was read last Sunday," a newsletter reported, "it was omitted yesterday." By the end of the month, another seven bishops had appended their names to the petition, and the London churchmen had begun an active campaign to solicit the refusal of the provincial clergy. The court bishops of Chester, Durham, and St. David's—along with the somewhat conflicted Herbert Croft, bishop of Hereford, and the circumspect Thomas Barlow, bishop of Lincoln—all ordered their clergy to read the declaration but achieved minimal compliance in the provinces. When pressed by the clergy in Hereford not to distribute the Declaration of Indulgence, Bishop Croft plainly blamed the resistance on agitators in the capital, telling his clergy that "the refusal at London preceded only from the rashness of some leading men who would ruin the Church." The bishop of Rochester seemed to comply but half-heartedly, and there was talk that he and Bishop White would be cashiered as commissioners for the diocese of London. Despite the efforts of the king's supporters, Gilbert Burnet reckoned that the declaration was read in only two hundred of the nearly ten thousand parishes in England and Wales.[170]

The court's fateful decision to prosecute the seven bishops for seditious libel catapulted the prelates into national celebrity. They were now confessors not only for the Church of England, but also for the broader Protestant interest, the peerage of the realm, and the ancient constitution. Popular acclaim and the hearty support of the nobility accompanied the bishops at every phase of their prosecution. The king's supporters could not resist highlighting the irony of their newfound popularity. "Time was when there was nothing more abominable, more heinous, or more cried down by the gowned clergy of England than *Vox*

Populi," wrote one loyalist pamphleteer, "now *Vox Populi* is the only *Suprema Lex* that guides them." Summoned before the king on 8 June to answer the information against them, the bishops refused to accuse themselves and declined to give bail "without prejudice to their peerage." James ordered them committed to the Tower, and their transit downriver was watched from the banks with fervent devotion by the London populace. As the bishops descended to the water, the archbishop of Canterbury held out his hand to bless the vast assemblage, saying, "Be dutiful to the King; hold fast to your religion; and God bless you." The watermen on the Thames were heard to be "generally crying 'God bless the Bishops.'" Upon the bishops reaching their place of incarceration, John Evelyn witnessed "infinite crowds on their knees begging their blessing, and praying for them as they passed out of the barge along the Tower wharf." Transported onlookers begged blessings and prayers of the prelates, "as if they were now going to their martyrdom." During the ensuing week, "multitudes of people went to the Tower to the bishops." Among the pilgrims to the bishops that week was a delegation of ten Nonconformist ministers, who later claimed they could "not but adhere to them, as men constant to the Protestant faith." The arraignment of the bishops on 15 June was also "crowded with thousands of people begging their blessing as they passed." The archbishop again urged the onlookers to remain constant in their religion. Numerous bonfires throughout the city of London celebrated the discharge of the bishops upon recognizance that night. One supporter of the king scoffed that it was "incredible what a humor the generality of the people are in about the bishops." He could only reassure himself that "surely people will come to their wits again." Others were less certain. The approaching trial, a correspondent anxiously opined to the government official John Ellis, "is a bad wind that blows nobody good."[171]

If the trial of the bishops at the end of June 1688 was not the culmination of a reactionary "Anglican revolution," neither should it mark the subsumption of the ecclesiastical opposition into a broadly secular national revolution that, as Steve Pincus argues, "deployed the language of liberty rather than that of salvation." The immediate reactions to the trial certainly proceeded in the demotic languages of Protestant nationalism and popular antipopery. The acquittal of the bishops on 29 June was greeted with raucous (and occasionally violent) jubilation throughout the kingdom, described by John Reresby as "a little rebellion in noise, though not in fact," and inaugurated a long season of popular Protestant unrest that stretched through the invasion of William of Orange in late autumn.

Men and women crowded into the churches that night "to return God thanks for so great a blessing with the greatest earnestness and ecstasy of joy lifting up their hands to heaven." The devout young Whig Whitelocke Bulstrode wondered, "If the Apostles had been alive, what could they have done more for their religion, than these bishops did?" In the wake of the trial, Reresby noted, "the parsons now began also to preach more loud and more open against popery than ever." On 8 July, the sermon in the Chapel Royal at Whitehall took as its text Exodus 14:13, "stand still and see the salvation of the Lord, which he will shew to you to day," which was, it was noted, "applied so boldly to the present conjuncture of the Church of England."[172]

In the aftermath of the trial of the bishops, the Church of England did not entrust its deliverance either to the prejudice of the Protestant mob or to the mounting constitutional opposition that in the abeyance of Parliament possessed no institutional footing to speak of. The acquittal of the bishops, Bishop Lloyd of Norwich told Sancroft, "hath mightily revived our drooping spirits." The church thus attempted to shore up its national communion through an intensified program of Anglican revival, which included renewed pastoral efforts in the parishes and an accommodation with Protestant Dissenters to preserve a semblance of conformity. In July 1688, the acquitted bishops and their allies embarked on a new pastoral campaign in their dioceses. "The Bishops that were lately in the Tower," it was reported, "are gone to their respective bishoprics, and have resolved to hold frequent catechizings and confirmations." At Croydon in Surrey, Archbishop Sancroft and Bishop Frampton confirmed several thousands of children. At the end of the month, Sancroft, citing the "great fears of being again made a prey to our merciless enemies of the Church of Rome," began drawing up a program of pastoral renewal in the Church of England. He urged the clergy of the established church "to meditate more of the pastoral care and of the duties incumbent upon you who feed the flock of God . . . that you may not so be satisfied with a bare innocence and blamelessness of life but may study how to shine as lights before your people which will be the best way to gather together your scattered flock and to give authority both to your persons and labors." Sancroft's notes in the summer of 1688 comprise a sweeping program of ecclesiastical reform. He would see weekly communions instituted throughout London, monthly communions in all market towns, and half that number in all other parishes; daily prayers in all major towns; "the use of catechizing indispensably in all churches"; and constant residence of all incumbents in their cures. His list of "things to be endeavored after" included frequent communions, constant catechizing, preparation for confirmation, "amendment of life," visitation of the sick, reformation of manners, vigilant warning "against popery and popish emissaries," "charitable visits to Dissenters," and prayer "for a general union of all Protestant Churches." Significantly, the archbishop recommended that the clergy "meet often and converse much together . . . for mutual assistance in your labors," in precisely the kinds of informal clerical assemblies that Compton and the London clergy had adopted throughout the 1680s. The archbishop digested these in a circular letter issued in late July to the bishops of his province. The letter bristled with antipathy toward Roman Catholicism, instructing the clergy "to take heed of all seducers, and especially of Popish emissaries, who are now in great numbers gone forth amongst them, and more busy and active than ever"; and to preach against "all usurped and foreign jurisdiction" such as that of the pope and the four vicars apostolic recently consecrated to spiritual jurisdiction over the kingdom. No less significantly, the letter radiated a new warmth toward Protestant Nonconformists, instructing the clergy to "have a very tender regard to our brethren the Protestant Dissenters." The indispensable platform of Protestant solidarity required that the clergy take all opportunities of assuring Dissenters "that the bishops of this Church are really and sincerely irreconcilable enemies to the errors, superstitions, idolatries, and tyrannies of the Church of Rome." Sancroft skirted the question of comprehension entirely in his letter, simply exhorting Dissenters "to join with us in daily fervent prayer to the God of Peace, for the universal blessed union of all reformed Churches both at home and abroad against our common enemies."[173]

The resounding call for Anglican renewal and reform at this juncture undermines the competing historiographical frameworks that opt to view Anglican opposition either as a brittle reaction in favor of the unreconstructed confessional state or as part of a broadly secular movement to modernize the English polity. Churchmen gravitated toward Anglican revivalism—diligent pastoral care, frequency of communion, catechizing of children, reformation of manners, and vigilant antipopery—to negotiate the present crisis. Significantly, many churchmen began to perceive comprehension of Protestant Nonconformists as a necessary adjunct to Anglican renewal. Comprehension was embraced as a means of enlarging the communion of the national church and preserving the common prayer. Even as Archbishop Sancroft was formulating his circular letter in July 1688, it was reported that he and the London divines "are said to have had several conferences with the chief of the Dissenting ministers, in order to agree such points of ceremonies as are indifferent between them, and to take their measures for what is to be proposed about religion next Parliament." According to George Every, these informal conversations among the archbishop and the London clergy produced an ambitious agenda for ecclesiastical reform, of which comprehension was only one component. The notes affirmed that "the terms of communion in the established religion be as large as is consistent with the constitution of a national Church." They recommended a review of the liturgy; a more equitable reconfiguration of the size of the dioceses of the church, such "that none be larger than one man can take care of"; the augmentation of poor livings; the construction of new churches in the London suburbs; laws against simony and plurality of church livings; an overhaul of the ecclesiastical courts; and a law "to enjoin the careful catechizing of youth." Sancroft told William Wake that their objective was "to consider how we might not only improve our own constitution but bring over the truly honest & well meaning dissenters to join in communion with us." Wake would later recall, "The design was, in short, this: to improve, and if possible, to enforce our discipline; to review and enlarge our liturgy"; and to forego "some few ceremonies, confessed to be indifferent in their natures, as indifferent in their usage, so as not to be necessarily observed by those who made a scruple of them." Wake further recalled the contemplation of new canons for the reformation of manners; some revision of the collects; "a greater variety of prayers, psalms, and lessons"; and new forms composed for the visitation of prisoners and the sick, for the receiving of proselytes, and for the reconciliation of penitents—in short, Wake said, things "we have been wishing for ever since the Reformation." As Timothy Fawcett has demonstrated, the ensuing liturgical revisions undertaken by Sancroft and London clergymen such as Simon Patrick, Richard Kidder, John Sharp, Edward Stillingfleet, Thomas Tenison, and John Tillotson in the summer and autumn of 1688 were rarely just "low-church" compromises in furtherance of Protestant reconciliation; they were designed for a heightening of devotion and the augmentation of the pastorate. These were the instruments of Anglican revival.[174]

This renewed vigor on the part of the established church soon prompted the Roman Catholics to follow suit. In an attempt to reconfirm his position at the apex of the moral order, James II issued at the end of June a proclamation against the "open and avowed practice of vice, profaneness and debauchery." The leading Catholic clergy embarked upon a fresh round of pastoral engagement. "The

Roman clergy about London," it was reported, "in imitation of the Protestant bishops, begin their circuits very speedily, in order to confirm their youth, and others of their communion." The vicar apostolic Bishop Philip Ellis and the Jesuit Andrew Pulton "confirmed some hundreds of youth (some of them were new converts)" at the Savoy. A pastoral letter from Ellis and the other bishops to the English Catholic laity appeared in defense of this aggressive posture. The legal disabilities of English Catholics permitted only a "private and precarious" devotion, "tending rather towards the preservation of it in your selves, than a propagation of it in others." In light of the king's toleration, the Catholic bishops encouraged the laity, "you are in circumstances of letting it appear abroad, and of edifying your neighbors by professing it publicly, and living up to the rules prescribed by it." The Anglican clergy were outraged at this boldness; they castigated the notion of pastors who "have no flocks," bearing episcopal titles "of remote places," operating by virtue of a long extinguished jurisdiction, directing the recusant laity "not only to continue in their former mistakes, but to use all means for the seducing of others." Sancroft's chaplain, Henry Maurice, decried this intrusion on the Anglican cure of souls as an encroachment on the clergy's pastoral responsibility for "all those who, either of right or actually, appertain to us." The clergy of the established church reckoned all England legally their charge. "It is time for every true shepherd," Maurice proclaimed, "after the example of our Great Pastor when he sees the wolves breaking in upon the flock to be ready to oppose them and to lay down his life for the sheep." Though frequently accompanied by declarations of loyalty to the king, such cries for Anglican renewal subtly traded on an alternative allegiance—one that was perhaps immune to politics: the inviolable obligation of pastor to people.[175]

Conclusion

The ideology of Anglican revival functioned as a mode of antipolitics throughout the reign of James II. This is not to deny that the clergy of the established church, like the English populace at large, espoused a variety of political and constitutional views concerning the limits of the state, the rule of law, and the legitimacy of resistance. It is only to suggest that the centrality of the Church of England to the revolutionary crisis cannot be derived from the ascendancy within the church of some such political ideology. To suggest that a core of Tory bishops behaved like orthodox Tories or that a faction of Whig clergymen in London embraced a Whiggish constitutional program is to say very little indeed and merely awards the Church of England pride of place in the revolutionary crisis as a placeholder for an extant party political system left in abeyance by the suspension of Parliament and the corporate charters.

What was remarkable about ecclesiastical involvement in the revolutionary crisis was the extent to which the Anglican bishops and clergy managed to submerge their opposition to the crown in a program of pastoral engagement. Attempts on the part of the court to proselytize on behalf of Roman Catholicism or to curtail Protestant preaching, lectures, charity, and controversial divinity were met with vigorous clerical engagement in defense of the established church. Yet James had so invested the whole of his kingship in his program of Catholic aggrandizement that the ordinary resistance to the latter expected of the Protestant clergy could not but acquire a broadly oppositional character. Moreover, James's impatience with the anti-Catholicism of the Church of England forced him to adopt a somewhat discordant policy that combined official discountenance of the church with an augmented Erastianism that required routine interference. At no point was James content to simply set the established church adrift in a competitive environment of legalized religious pluralism. Instead, he routinely attempted to disable the church's ability to effectively withstand sectarian competition. The king's ever greater intrusions into the content and conduct of Anglican churchmanship (beyond his encroachments on the legal and constitutional establishment of the church) both undermined his avowal of liberty of conscience and relieved beleaguered churchmen of the burden of mounting a sustained political opposition. In their preaching and writing, their conferences and charities, churchmen could plausibly claim to be simply pursuing their pastoral obligations to their flock. Popular Anglicanism provided a refuge from the problem of Catholic kingship, a contradiction for which the political theology of the established church possessed no practical solution. When a chastened James attempted a reconciliation with his "old friends" of the Church of England in autumn 1688, the bishops requested not only that the king roll back his entire program of Catholic absolutism, but tellingly, that he permit them to present arguments "to persuade your Majesty to return to the communion of the Church of England."[176]

William and Mary, with their extensive ties to London Anglicanism, became the beneficiaries of the Anglican revival. In a letter in late 1688, Gilbert Burnet

urged William to seize upon the instruments of revival to consolidate his position in England. Burnet commended the leading London clergymen to the
prince as men that "deserve more particular regard from your Highness." He
named the architects of the ecclesiastical opposition to James II—John Tillotson,
Simon Patrick, Thomas Tenison, Edward Stillingfleet, John Sharp, William
Sherlock, Gregory Hescard, William Wake, Edward Fowler, and Anthony
Horneck—and explicitly commended their popularity, dexterity in controversy,
conspicuous piety, and moderation, that is, presumably, their inclination toward
accommodation with Protestant Nonconformists. Burnet further urged a restoration of the Chapel Royal at Whitehall and an immediate proclamation in favor
of the reformation of manners, which would "have a very good effect on people's
minds." He was effectively advising William to enlist the "small awakening" in
London on behalf of the Revolution—to restore the revival to its inherently
establishmentarian character for a new Protestant regime. Burnet's 23 December
sermon at St. James before the Prince of Orange, in which the providence of God
was credited with employing the reign of James II toward "the awakening of the
nation," further couched the Revolution in terms of religious renewal. As Tony
Claydon has argued, this sermon would inaugurate a long tradition of presenting
the Revolution as an "opportunity for an Anglican renaissance," the initiation of
a period of ecclesiastical and moral reformation. However, it must be made clear
that this framework was no mere exercise in post facto Williamite propaganda,
rhetorically cobbled together from "mid-Tudor" eschatology to paper over the
constitutional irregularities of the Revolution. The Revolution of 1688–1689 was
welcomed as an unprecedented opportunity for ecclesiastical and moral reformation, precisely because it did in fact present such an opportunity. An emergent
consensus of churchmen believed, in William Wake's words, "that we ought to be
better provided against another time," that Anglican revival was indispensable to
the safety of the Church of England.[177]

The architecture of an Anglican "moral revolution" was thus substantially in
place before the invasion of the Prince of Orange and the ensuing political revolution. Faced with a hostile court and a climate of religious pluralism, conscien-
tious churchmen during the reign of James II began to advance a dynamic and
popular form of Anglicanism cured of its addiction to persecution and the
complacency derived from its establishment. In the crisis of the reign of James II,
the Church of England presented itself as the embodiment of a national moral
and ecclesial community from which the Catholic king had signally recused

himself. And at first blush, William and Mary made every indication of reclaiming this sentiment on behalf of the court. Restored to the Protestant court and reinvested with its properly establishmentarian character, the Anglican revival would soon find itself immersed in the political complexities wrought by the English Revolution.

CHAPTER 2

The Church in an Age of Projects

T he Trinity Chapel on Conduit Street was, in its own peculiar way, a monument to its age. Erected in the fashionable Westminster parish of St. Martin's-in-the-Fields, the chapel stood upon grounds very recently occupied by a strange wheeled tabernacle originally built so that the Roman Catholic king James II could hear mass while encamped with his army at Hounslow Heath. Abandoned by James upon his flight at the end of 1688, the wooden chapel was conveyed the twelve miles to St. Martin's at the direction and expense of the rector Thomas Tenison, where it was intended to serve as a chapel of ease for the outlying parts of his sprawling metropolitan cure. By 1691, with the blessing of the new monarchs William and Mary, Tenison had converted the tabernacle to a building of sturdy brick, though the land not being freehold, he was unsuccessful at establishing an independent parish. A veritable trophy for the Church of England's successful resistance of Roman Catholic absolutism, the new chapel now defied new adversaries. In July 1691, it was dedicated to the Holy Trinity, a mystery of the faith increasingly beset in the postrevolutionary era by an array of anti-Trinitarian heterodoxies. At his inaugural sermon on 19 July 1691, Tenison bid his auditors "to attend to that faith of the Church, now especially that Arianism, Socinianism and atheism began to spread amongst us." That afternoon, the lecturer William Stringfellow preached on Luke 7:5, "For he loveth our nation, and he hath built us a synagogue," in praise of Tenison's numerous "public works for the benefit of mankind, especially to the advantage of religion." Commending the "building and endowing hospitals, libraries, schools" and the procuring of "useful books," Stringfellow's sermon was as much a paean to the future primate as to the broader spirit of institution-building that had accompanied the Anglican revival of recent years.[1] Like Trinity Chapel itself, built from the reclaimed remains of a rolling mass house, Stringfellow's homily celebrated the restless creativity, entrepreneurialism, and experimentation that had come to characterize what Daniel Defoe called the "projecting age."[2]

The Revolution was consummated with a mandate for substantive reform of the established church. During the final months of the reign of James II, churchmen from across the political and theological spectrum were proposing and collaborating on a variety of reform programs, which included comprehension of Protestant Nonconformists, revision of the canons and liturgy, refurbishing of ecclesiastical discipline, expansion of pastoral engagement, and development of the vague program of moral renewal dubbed "the reformation of manners." The Revolution was widely embraced as what Tony Claydon deems an "opportunity for an Anglican renaissance."[3] But, ironically, the events surrounding the invasion of the Prince of Orange, the flight of James II, and the ensuing settlements in church and state effectively shattered the fragile consensus on Anglican reform. In the increasingly polarized environment of the years that immediately followed the Revolution, ecclesiastical reform signally failed to proceed through the formal channels of canonical or statutory redress. On the contrary, much of the reformist agenda advanced, if at all, through less formal, more ad hoc instruments: royal admonishment and circular letters, voluntary societies and chartered corporations, print advocacy and proposals, and the initiative of the laity and lower clergy. Over the course of the final decade of the seventeenth century, the mandate for Anglican reform and renewal seemed to drift away from the court and the episcopal bench, only to be adopted by various projectors and public-spirited individuals operating in civil society. Religion, it seems, was taken up by the culture of enterprise that had seized much of English society at the end of the seventeenth century.[4] The Revolution, rather than inaugurating a period of ecclesiastical reconstruction, seems to have catalyzed an unprecedented wave of organizational innovation and experimentation within (and on the margins of) the established church. In effect, the century's final decade was characterized not by Anglican unity of purpose, but rather by the fragmentation of Anglican reform.

To put it more accurately, a dialectic of Anglican reform characterized the final decade of the seventeenth century. The imperatives of the court and the hierarchy generated projects and proposals among the laity and the lower clergy.

Schemes bubbling up in civil society occasionally found favor with the governors of the church or inspired new initiatives. Dissatisfaction with certain projects as impractical or unorthodox prompted the search for alternatives. It must be remembered that the enduring programs of Anglican renewal that have traditionally dominated the ecclesiastical historiography of this period—the societies for the reformation of manners, the Society for Promoting Christian Knowledge (SPCK), and the Society for the Propagation of the Gospel in Foreign Parts (SPG)—emerged amidst a host of other projects that failed or went unrealized and often proceeded only after other avenues of reform were blocked. Their history belongs as much to the history of ferment as it does to the history of fruition. And that ferment, the restless desire for moral and religious renewal and the wide variety of classes and actors engaged in it, possessed something of a politics of its own—one that is all too often eclipsed by focusing only upon its successes. This chapter offers a historical sketch of the ferment of Anglican renewal in the aftermath of the Revolution of 1688–1689. The eighteenth-century Church of England was shaped by its trials no less than its errors.

The London Ascendancy and the Clamor for Reform

The Revolution was undertaken amidst a spirit of reform in both church and state.[5] Perhaps not surprisingly, proposals for the reform and renewal of the established church loomed increasingly large throughout the crisis. As argued in Chapter 1, James II's incursions against the national communion forced many members of the Church of England to reflect seriously upon the nature and security of its establishment. During the months leading up to and following the invasion of the Prince of Orange in November 1688, calls for some substantive reconstruction and renewal of the church were fairly widespread. Contrary to the prevailing historiographical theory of an "Anglican revolution" designed to reestablish the intolerant confessional polity of the early 1680s, relatively few divines seem to have believed that the ecclesiastical establishment could be secured merely through yet another rapprochement with the Stuart monarchy. Other measures would be necessary to ensure the integrity of the national communion, to facilitate the labors of the clergy amidst the populace, and to heal the breaches in English Protestantism. Even as conservative a figure as Archbishop William Sancroft had by 1688 come to recognize Protestant reconciliation as well as pastoral renewal among the needful things of the Church of

England and had begun to direct his suffragan bishops and clergy to make arrangements "for the better and more perfect establishment" of the church.[6] It is difficult to imagine any outcome of the revolutionary crisis of late 1688 that would have led to a rebuilding of the Anglican temple of the early 1680s.

The ensuing change of state, the displacement of James II by his Protestant daughter and son-in-law, made precious little allowance for ecclesiastical atavism. The churchmanship of London was clearly in the ascendant under the new regime. This was attributable, in part, to the conspicuous refurbishing of court Protestantism under William and Mary. The queen in particular resolved upon her arrival in February 1689 "to do what I could towards making devotion looked on as it ought," receiving the sacrament publicly and instituting singing of prayers and Sunday afternoon sermons.[7] The appointment of Charles Sackville, Earl of Dorset, as Lord Chamberlain and the restoration of his wife's uncle, Bishop Henry Compton of London, to the deanery of the Chapel Royal signaled the displacement of the courtier Bishops Nathaniel Crewe and Thomas Sprat, now tainted as collaborators with the previous regime.[8] Sackville and Compton oversaw "very considerable change made in the king's chaplains," including the appointment of London revivalists like Anthony Horneck, Richard Kidder, and Edward Fowler.[9] Meanwhile, Archbishop Sancroft and the other bishops who refused to acknowledge the new regime had "absolutely declined preaching at court."[10] On 23 February 1689, a body of the London clergy appeared under the direction of Bishop Compton to kiss the hands of the new monarchs, on which occasion both William and Mary expressed "a special kindness for the clergy of London."[11] The London ascendancy was further advanced by the appointment in April 1689 of the dean of Canterbury, John Tillotson, as clerk of the closet, an office that made him a fixture at the court of the new monarchs and gave him "a great capacity of doing good offices for the Church and state."[12] Tillotson chose the popular London preacher William Wake as his assistant.[13] Moreover, Queen Mary named as her own clerk her former chaplain William Stanley, a prebendary of St. Paul's and a client of Bishop Compton.[14] Whitehall once again regularly resounded with homilies extolling the Protestant monarchy and the incomparable beneficence of providence in securing its restoration.[15] On 17 June 1689, such "a great body of the London clergy, the eminentest men, to the number of about 80" took the oaths of allegiance to William and Mary in the Court of Chancery that little other business could be done that day.[16]

There were, however, other factors at work. The withdrawal of Archbishop Sancroft and his allies into political quiescence and, eventually, repudiation of the new regime left the prominent London divines well placed to capitalize on the ecclesiastical settlement.[17] Sancroft's inaction left the high-born and well-connected Compton as de facto primate of all England. And indeed, to avoid the praemunire risked by open defiance of the new monarchs, Sancroft was quite willing to confirm this arrangement by formally empowering Compton to exercise archiepiscopal authority in conjunction with any three other bishops of the province, an instrument indispensable to the reconstruction of the Church of England.[18] The archbishop's acquiescence permitted the king and queen to begin filling the growing number of vacancies on the episcopal bench. By August 1689, death had already claimed five members of the prerevolution episcopate; additional deaths and statutory deprivation for refusing the oaths of allegiance would create another six vacancies by the following April. Unsurprisingly, William and Mary drew heavily upon the London clergy in filling the offices. Of the sixteen men the new monarchs raised to the episcopal bench in the first two years of their reign, eleven (including their first nominee, Gilbert Burnet, a popular preacher at the Rolls Chapel before his exile under James II) held livings in the metropolis during the reigns of their predecessors.[19] By June 1691, the archdeacon of Suffolk, Humphrey Prideaux, observed that "the London ministers get all the preferments," advising his friend John Ellis that Ellis's brother would do better from a curacy in the city than a living in the country.[20] One resentful commentator sardonically wondered of metropolitan clergy, "What is there so pure and inspiring in the air of sea-coal smoke that refines men's wits and makes them wiser than their neighbors in the country?"[21]

To the extent that the Revolution was celebrated in confessional terms, it was depicted as a long-sought opportunity for general reformation, what one divine called "a public reformation in both church and state."[22] The official homiletics of the Revolution had frequent recourse to such tropes, and the major occasions of state and court were often accompanied by reaffirmations of the relationship between the Revolution and the cause of moral and ecclesiastical reform. The Revolution, William Wake told the king and queen at Hampton Court, signaled the coming of "a general reformation, and a true zeal and a perfect charity passing through the world."[23] At the coronation of William and Mary on 11 April 1689, Gilbert Burnet charged the new monarchs with "the encouraging and promoting of a vigorous piety, and sublime virtue, and the maintaining and propagating of true religion."[24] Godly monarchy, however, was no substitute for a zealous clergy, and numerous sermons hailed a renascent church as well. At the consecration of Bishops Edward Stillingfleet, Simon Patrick, and Gilbert Ironside, John Scott, rector of St. Peter-le-Poer, London, preached on Jeremiah 3:15, "And I will give you pastors according to mine heart, who shall feed you with knowledge and understanding." His sermon intimated the fulfillment of God's promise to "raise up in his Church a great many pastors and teachers, eminent for learning and wisdom, piety and virtue," men whose "unwearied activity of their zeal for God and the good of souls" would contribute to the general "reformation of the Christian world." Even the Church of England, "the best and purest Church in the world," hailed Scott, "may still increase in strength, beauty and perfection."[25] Taken in isolation, the homiletics of the Revolution are often cynically dismissed as little more than court-sponsored exercises in Williamite propaganda. Though certainly not without political value for the court of William and Mary, the rhetoric of religious renewal sounded in sermons existed on a broader continuum of programs and proposals for ecclesiastical reform aired publicly and privately throughout the period of political and ecclesiastical crisis and settlement.

Far from imagining that the Revolution would occasion a reversion to the late Stuart confessional polity, clergy and laity from across the political and ecclesiological spectrum were convinced that religious transformation was imminent. Most prominently, there was widespread expectation of some form of reconciliation among English Protestants. The petition of the seven bishops had seemingly acquiesced in it, and the declaration William issued in October 1688 in advance of his invasion had affirmed its place on the national agenda. The Revolution, the royal chaplain Robert Brograve preached before William and Mary, marked "a time designed by heaven for an union with each other."[26] Throughout January 1689, the London divines continued meeting, often in the presence of Daniel Finch, Earl of Nottingham, to work out the terms by which Nonconformists might be comprehended within the established church.[27] On 28 February 1689, the Presbyterian William Bates led about a hundred Nonconformist ministers to address the king and queen, expressing their hope that "the reverend persons who conspire with us" will "consent to the terms of union wherein all Reformed Churches agree."[28] Indeed, many were careful to emphasize the importance of Protestant reconciliation not just to the political settlement, but to any program of religious renewal.[29] Reconciliation, it was hoped, would revivify the common prayer, equip the national church with an infusion of "faithful and laborious ministers," and unify the clergy behind a national reformation of manners.[30]

The issue of comprehension, it must be remembered, was situated amidst a far broader public conversation regarding ecclesiastical renewal. There was, of course, little consensus on either the nature of grievances or the terms of reconciliation, and concerned clergy and laity of all ideological stripes did not hesitate to weigh in—often anonymously. One conservative layman sought to equip the church with greater autonomy and discretion in the election and consecration of bishops, the ordination of clergy, the distribution of preferments, and the administration of the sacraments to unworthy laity.[31] The Whig politician Lord Delamere believed that a law to prevent pluralities and nonresidence among the clergy would more equitably divide the resources of the established church and prevent young ministers from seeking their livings in Nonconformist congregations.[32] Though by no means an advocate of reform, the Buckinghamshire clergyman Abraham Campion hoped that William, "being a pure Protestant Prince come over with designs of a thorough reformation," might at least abolish the clerical dues of first fruits and tenths, which were but "Romish usurpations," illegitimately "transferred upon the king."[33] The eccentric barrister-turned-clergyman Edward Stephens, in mind of his idée fixe of the reformation of manners, urged William immediately to issue a proclamation against vice and hoped that the Convention Parliament would enact "severe penalties" for the punishment thereof.[34] The virtuoso John Evelyn sketched out an ambitious program to expand the social power of the Church of England, recommending reformation of manners, augmentation of poor livings for the clergy of the established church, reform of the poor laws and erection of workhouses, endowment of public libraries furnished with books chosen by the convocation, evangelization of African slaves in the plantations, and establishment of an imperial bishop. He even suggested a registrar of projects, to receive and evaluate all proposals "convertible to the public benefit."[35] As late as April 1689, Evelyn was still discussing the prospect of ecclesiastical reform with both Archbishop Sancroft and Bishop William Lloyd of St. Asaph.[36]

Radical voices demanded even more drastic reforms to the service and structure of the Church of England. The controversial Colchester divine Edmund Hickeringill used the occasion of the Revolution to renew his agitation against unnecessary ceremonies in the liturgy, "to sweep down," as he put it, "the futile and frail Church cobwebs."[37] Another wished to see an end to "all the present constitutions and ecclesiastical corporations in Christendom." In the place of the established church, congregations would elect ordinary men to lead in prayers and praises, while the state would train itinerant ministers in "*Magnum Collegium Christianum*, a large Christian college," to preach the word and administer sacraments on circuits throughout the kingdom.[38] The anonymous author of *The Amicable Reconciliation of the Dissenters to the Church of England* devised a scheme he labeled "congregational episcopacy," by which all tolerated religious assemblies would effectively be comprehended within a pluralistic ecclesiastical establishment, subsisting under the superintendence of state "bishops" of all denominations, commissioned *quam diu se bene gesserint*. An "equally modeled Convocation," in which both church and Dissent were represented, could then be convened to revise the ecclesiastical canons, "reversing the main body of them, having been fitted to the narrow scantling which is unworthy [of] the Church of England."[39]

A host of older reform programs were also brought to bear on the public discussion of the ecclesiastical settlement. In 1689, Francis Bacon's early Jacobean tract *Certain Considerations for the better Establishment of the Church of England* was published with a new preface that testified to the persistence of Bacon's century-old grievances, though "it is now to be hoped that, at this extraordinary juncture, there may be some prospect of redress."[40] The same year saw the republication of Bishop Herbert Croft's controversial 1675 pamphlet *The Naked Truth*, a work of creedal minimalism advocating both Protestant reconciliation and church reform.[41] The somewhat parsimonious comprehension program outlined in the preface to Edward Stillingfleet's notoriously illiberal 1681 work *The Unreasonableness of Separation* was republished as well.[42] The same year, the Whig publisher Richard Baldwin issued a new edition of Edward Chamberlayne's early Restoration tract *England's Wants*, a compendium of proposals for civil and ecclesiastical improvement now directed toward the new monarchs and the Convention Parliament. Like Evelyn, Chamberlayne advocated a battery of social welfare institutions, such as workhouses, hospitals, *montes pietates*, and colleges for virgins, widows, and the elderly. For the Church of England, he recommended the appointment of *censores morum* for the reformation of manners, the erection of a Protestant missionary order, the buying in of tithes impropriated by the laity, and an early morning divine service performed plainly for servants, apprentices, and "the meaner sort of people."[43]

Incidentally, Edward's son John Chamberlayne would oversee the implementation of a number of these proposals in his capacity as secretary to the SPCK, the SPG, and Queen Anne's Bounty.

That Protestant reconciliation and ecclesiastical reform were widely perceived as interrelated is evident from the draft bills that emerged from the Earl of Nottingham's consultations with the bishops and eminent London clergy in early 1689.[44] The toleration bill introduced in the House of Lords on 28 February 1689 was substantially unchanged from an earlier version Nottingham had proposed a decade earlier. However, the companion bill for comprehending Protestant Nonconformists within the established church introduced in the Lords on 11 March 1689 had evolved from its 1680 predecessor. The comprehension bill initially required ministers to approve of the doctrine and worship of the Church of England. It rendered optional the four contested rubrics: the use of the surplice, the sign of the cross at baptism, kneeling at the sacrament, and the provision of godparents. In its initial version, the bill provided a formula for supplementary ordination of those presbyters lacking episcopal ordination, but this was deleted in committee. As an acknowledgment of the significant work that had already been undertaken in previous months by Sancroft and the London clergy, the bill deferred all subsequent amendments to a royal commission consisting of the two archbishops and a number of other bishops and clergy meeting as frequently as necessary "to make such alterations in the liturgy and reformation of the canons and ecclesiastical courts as may conduce to the establishment of the Church in peace and tranquility." This clause was subsequently altered to require the commission to report not only to Parliament, but to the convocation as well—an optimistic amendment, given that the convocation had not transacted any business in more than two decades, but one designed to ensure broader support from the Anglican clergy. And in the likelihood of subsequent revisions to the liturgy and canons, the declaration required of ministers was rewritten to mandate only that one "submit to the present constitution of the Church of England" and conform to the worship and government thereof. Nottingham's amended comprehension bill was sent down to the House of Commons on 8 April. Ten days later, his companion bill for indulgence of Protestant Dissenters outside the national communion was sent down virtually unaltered.[45]

Comprehension, of course, died in the House of Commons. The Commons' far more radical comprehension bill, which accepted ordination in any reformed church as sufficient for orders in the Church of England and allowed scrupulous ministers to provide a curate rather than read the common prayer themselves, was given a single reading on 8 April 1689. After a furious debate, the bill was famously laid aside—it was hoped, "till Doomsday."[46] The Lords' bill received its first and only reading the following day. Neither comprehension bill was ever read again.

The Revolution had effectively alleviated the very pressures of Catholic absolutism that had made Protestant reconciliation seem such an imperative during the reign of James II.[47] But numerous factors, no doubt, contributed to the waning appetite for Protestant reconciliation among members of the Church of England. In the first place, William had already made clear in a speech of 16 March to the House of Commons that he wished to see the Anglican monopoly on office-holding dismantled in favor of "all Protestants that are willing and able to serve." Such a move against the sacramental test not only reinforced Anglican fears of William's undue sympathy for Protestant Nonconformity, but it seriously undermined the rationale for comprehension. After all, comprehension expanded the terms of national communion precisely in order to maintain the preeminence of the established church, a pillar of which was the confessional requirements of office-holding mandated by the Test and Corporation Acts. The king's speech against the test, noted Edward Harley, was poorly received by the "sons of the Church, who resolve to unite in her defense, to keep off any thing that may eclipse her dominion and grandeur."[48] Second, the contemporaneous debates over the oaths of allegiance ended in a signal defeat for the partisans of the Church of England. On 5 April, the Commons accepted the Lords' demand that the oath of allegiance be required of clerical incumbents as well as civil and military office-holders, only managing to append a six-month grace period to the Lords' 1 August 1689 deadline for compliance.[49] The bill placed a number of senior bishops and clergy, among them Archbishop Sancroft and some of the most stalwart opponents of James II's religious policies, in jeopardy of deprivation by the new regime and presaged worrisome new divisions in the body of the church.[50] The prospect of embracing the historic enemies of the established church while turning out saintly confessors for its cherished political theology was just too galling for many loyal churchmen.[51] Third, the ecclesiastical settlement in Scotland cast a long shadow over the comprehension debates in England. On 11 April, just days after the first readings of the two comprehension bills in the Commons, the Scottish Convention laid out the terms of settlement in the Claim of Right, among them the recommendation that episcopacy be abolished as a "great and insupportable grievance and trouble to this nation." The Scottish Convention's charge not only confirmed perennial Anglican apprehensions of militant Presbyterianism, it presented the English church with an omen of its own looming episcopal deprivations.[52] Finally, despite Nottingham's initial conferences with both the London clergy and the bishops, there was widespread grumbling that the church had not been formally consulted in measures that would alter the terms of its communion.[53] On 13 April, a committee of the House of Commons submitted an address to the king requesting that, "according to the ancient practice and usage of this kingdom in time of parliament," he issue writs for the calling of convocation.[54] The king pledged to summon convocation but urged Parliament to proceed with the indulgence for Protestant Nonconformists.[55] A bargain seems to have been struck.[56] The indulgence, widely known as the Toleration Act, received the royal assent on 24 May 1689.[57] The issue of comprehension was dropped in Parliament and reserved for the convocation as "a due respect to the Church."[58]

William delayed issuing the writs for convocation until after the August suspensions of the nonjuring bishops and clergy clarified the extent of disaffection in the ranks of the established church. Even in the face of nonjuring attrition, the king was willing to give the assembly a substantial mandate for ecclesiastical reform. To this end, on 17 September 1689 William commissioned ten bishops and twenty divines to prepare the agenda for this momentous synod, in accordance with the recommendations in the final clause of the Lords' comprehension bill.[59] The commission authorized the nominated divines to recommend necessary alterations to the "particular forms of divine worship"; review the canons of the church, making provisions for the removal of scandalous ministers; and remedy defects in the ecclesiastical courts toward "the reformation of manners either in ministers or people."[60] Unsurprisingly, the divines of the London ascendancy, many of whom had been instrumental in every comprehension scheme over the preceding decade, predominated in the commission. And their sway only increased after the commission convened on 3 October in the Jerusalem Chamber of Westminster Abbey, since conservative, anticomprehension appointees either absented themselves or withdrew early in the proceedings. Of the seven prerevolutionary bishops named to the commission, only Henry Compton of London and William Lloyd of St. Asaph, both early supporters of William and Mary and intimates of the London divines, attended regularly. The remaining members of the prerevolution episcopate either did not attend at all or attended only two meetings before abandoning the commission altogether. The latter were joined by opponents of comprehension among the lower clergy, notably, the Oxford dons William Jane, Regius Professor of Divinity, and Henry Aldrich, dean of Christ Church.[61] This rapid attrition left the commission to the virtually unchecked influence of a largely London-based Williamite core: Gilbert Burnet, bishop of Salisbury; Edward Stillingfleet, dean of St. Paul's (consecrated bishop of Worcester during the sessions); Simon Patrick, dean of Peterborough (consecrated bishop of Chichester during the sessions); John Tillotson, dean of Canterbury; John Sharp, dean of Norwich; the canons of St. Paul's, John Williams and Robert Grove; and the popular London preachers Thomas Tenison, Edward Fowler, and Richard Kidder—all of whom would be elevated to the episcopal bench by William and Mary.[62] Indeed, by the time the commission met, William had already made it clear to Tillotson that he intended him for the primacy, which Tillotson called "a great place, which I dread to think of."[63] Another active participant, the London divine William Beveridge, archdeacon of Colchester, was offered the bishopric of Bath and Wells in 1691 but scrupled at assuming the see of a bishop deprived for nonjuring.[64]

The composition of the new ecclesiastical commission was naturally a point of contention among churchmen. Thomas Tenison described his fellow commissioners as the champions of the Glorious Revolution, writing "these very men with true Christian courage hazarded all that was dear to them in this world, in order to support the Church and the true religion professed by it."[65] But others noted the ideological and geographical bias of the commission, which was dominated by "city divines" and "ministers of the great town," as well as the so-called latitudinarians (a Restoration term rehabilitated as a veritable synonym for Williamites), who had most warmly embraced the new regime. And indeed, charged embittered critics, these divines were richly rewarded by the new court with favors and promotions for their doctrinal and political accommodations. The commissioners, it was complained, were "known to be latitudinarians indeed, and have monopolized Church-preferments."[66] The withdrawn commissioner William Jane derided both the orthodoxy and motives of the remaining commissioners, for they were possessed of "tenderness and moderation enough to part with anything but their Church preferments."[67] An ally of the commissioners, the popular London clergyman William Payne, denounced such charges as scurrilous, dismissing "latitudinarianism" as a bugbear, of which "some timorous old men can hardly speak or hear . . . without trembling."[68] The increasingly isolated London ascendancy that dominated the ecclesiastical commission thus set about the work of ecclesiastical reform amidst an environment characterized by resentment, reaction, and a mounting wariness of change.[69]

In this climate of opinion, the ecclesiastical commission proceeded readily to the less controversial business of liturgical reform.[70] In these areas, the commissioners could safely claim to be simply continuing the work begun at the behest of Archbishop Sancroft in the final months of the previous reign. Indeed, George Every has suggested that the recommendations of the putatively "latitudinarian" ecclesiastical commission probably did not differ markedly from what a commission with more conservative input would have produced.[71] The commission eagerly undertook the work of rendering the service more wholesome. The lessons from the Apocrypha were to be replaced with unobjectionable readings from the undisputed canon of Scripture. The psalms were to be translated anew, and certain psalms (out of course) selected for Sundays.[72] The rubric requiring ministers and deacons to say daily prayers was replaced with one requiring them to exhort their congregations to frequently attend weekday prayers, "especially in the great towns." New collects were written by Simon Patrick (and subsequently revised by Stillingfleet, Burnet, and Tillotson) designed, according to one of the commissioners, "for exciting the devotion of the people."[73] A new rubric mandated that communion be offered monthly in "every great town or parish" and four times a year elsewhere. It further required all ministers "to exhort their people to communicate frequently."[74] Many of these reforms, it should be noted, seem to comport with the revivalist strain in late Restoration Anglicanism. Perhaps unsurprisingly, John Tillotson was hopeful that the commission might undertake "more effectual provisions for the reformation of manners both in ministers and people."[75]

The ecclesiastical commission addressed the points of comprehension with manifestly less resolve.[76] A rubric was proposed to allow a bishop to dispense a scrupulous minister from wearing the surplice while officiating, but it was "not agreed to; but left to further consideration."[77] Similarly, the rubric that allowed parents to forego the sign of the cross in the baptism of their children was proposed and debated, only to be set aside for want of concurrence. The commission was unable to come to any resolution on the reordination of ministers not episcopally ordained, which was debated over four full sessions. This was, of course, a sticking point in any feasible comprehension scheme. Churchmen were largely unwilling to relinquish the necessity of episcopal ordination, while Nonconformists believed any supplementary ordination necessarily impugned the validity of their prior Presbyterian orders.[78] For want of time, the commission failed to take up the "form of subscription" to the articles of the Church of England required of all ministers.[79] When it was pointed out that the commission had thus far done little by way of Protestant reconciliation, Edward Stillingfleet emphasized the priority of Anglican reform. "We sat there to make such alterations as were fit," he told his brethren, "which would be fit to make were there no Dissenters, and which would be for the improvement of the service."[80] After seven weeks of sessions throughout October and November, the members of the ecclesiastical commission ceased their work, uncertain whether they were empowered to continue deliberating during the upcoming convocation.[81]

By the time the convocation was assembling in November, the prospects for any substantive ecclesiastical reform had grown notably dimmer.[82] Elections for convocation, which for the first time saw "great canvassings" on behalf of conservative, anticomprehension clergy, overwhelmingly favored "fierce men" decidedly uninterested in any sort of compromise or reform.[83] "I expect little from this meeting," confessed the London clergyman William Wake, "unless God's providence does wonderfully overrule our passions."[84] Edward Harley was decidedly less optimistic. "We may," he cracked ruefully, "as soon expect a reformation from a convention of infernal spirits as from any of these."[85] William Jane took to print to excoriate the work of the ecclesiastical commission from which he had withdrawn in protest, declaring that it was "not a fit time to make alterations and unsettle the foundations of the Church."[86] Before taking their seats on 6 November, many of the newly elected proctors dined at Sion College with their Tory counterparts in the House of Commons, roundly concurring that "if they abated in anything they betrayed their own cause," resolving instead to "insist stiffly upon all points of conformity."[87] The ecclesiastical commissioner and London divine William Beveridge informed his friend the Scottish episcopal minister Robert Kirk that "many of the convocation, from whom he does not disassociate himself," were for "not yielding a jot."[88] Accordingly, at the second meeting of the convocation on 20 November, Beveridge preached a Latin sermon in which he suggested that the differences between the Church of England and the reformed churches at home and abroad merited only "some disputations in the schools." At this juncture, preached Beveridge, there were no grounds for "any abatements, or any relaxation at all" in the terms of the national communion.[89] The convocation then overwhelmingly chose the foe of comprehension William Jane over the court favorite John Tillotson as prolocutor of the lower house.[90] "A warm party not inclined to alterations carried it against him," noted George Royce, dean of Bristol.[91] The church, it seemed to the London divine William Payne, was fatally divided between "Janites and Tillotsonians."[92] When the convocation reconvened on November 25, Bishop Henry Compton, acting president of the convocation during the suspension of Archbishop Sancroft, reportedly "made a learned speech upon the topic of uniting," reminding the clergy of the pledges of Protestant reconciliation embodied in the seven bishops' petition to James II. These sentiments, however, were drowned out by the mounting intransigence of the clergy, given voice by Jane and Henry Aldrich, dean of Christ Church, Oxford, who "harangued mightily about the beauty of the present settlement of religion." Upon being presented by Compton, Jane applied the cry of *"Nolumus leges Angliae mutari"* to the ecclesiastical constitution—an unmistakable jibe at Bishop Compton, who had borne this motto on his standard when he appeared in arms at Oxford for the Prince of Orange the previous year.[93] The bishop of London soon after adjourned the convocation to await the king's license to transact business.

During the intervening weeks, the advocates of comprehension tried desperately to resurrect the reformist and conciliatory spirit of the previous year.[94] Thomas Tenison argued that churchmen should rejoice that the church "in which they resolve to live and die [shall] have all the strength and beauty added to it which can be given it by commission, convocation and parliament."[95] Another pamphlet, *A Letter from a Minister in the Country to a Member of the Convocation*, which Timothy Fawcett has persuasively attributed to Gilbert Burnet, forcefully reiterated the obligation to reform the established church "by supplying what is wanting, by clearing what is doubtful, by amending what is amiss, and improving what is tolerable and well, so as to make it yet more beneficial and solemn." Like Compton, the author repeatedly invoked the petition of the seven bishops, "the representatives of our Church," as a commitment to Protestant reconciliation. Apparently, the author mused sardonically, the reign of James II was a fit season for comprehension, when churchmen were in no position to affect it, the king was against it, and neither Parliament nor convocation sat to affirm it. Yet now, with clerical engagement, royal favor, and both

Parliament and convocation assembled, he scoffed, the time is suddenly unpropitious. The author lambasted the cant of the new antireformist conservatism obtaining within the established church, whereby clergymen who had previously accepted the wisdom of reform now set their faces against it. "And shall that which was before an infirmity," the author asked, "be adopted into a state of perfection?"[96] For Humphrey Prideaux, archdeacon of Suffolk, the necessity of ecclesiastical reform was self-evident. What, Prideaux wondered, would be the purpose of the present or any other convocation if not amendment and reform?[97] Such attempts to salvage the work of the ecclesiastical commission, to press the urgency of what Prideaux deemed "a moderate and just reformation," flew in the face of widespread clerical sentiment that had come to doubt not only the necessity, but also the very possibility of salubrious reformation.

The convocation reconvened on 4 December to receive from the Earl of Nottingham the king's license to debate matters concerning ecclesiastical reform. The license to the convocation substantially recapitulated the king's charge to the ecclesiastical commission, identifying the same broad areas of reform. To this, the king appended a message to the convocation affirming his "pious zeal to do everything that may tend to the best establishment of the Church of England" and enjoining the assistance of the assembled divines in promoting its welfare.[98] The bishops who constituted the upper house of the convocation then withdrew to prepare a response to the king. Their draft response thanked the king for his commission as further evidence of his zeal "for the Protestant religion in general, and the Church of England in particular." The bishops considered such favors but continuations of the nation's "great deliverance" from "popish tyranny," of which God had made William the instrument.[99] Upon receipt of the bishops' address, the lower house of convocation "fell a whispering and discoursing," evincing "great dissatisfaction" and "uneasiness."[100] The clergy in the lower house lodged numerous objections to the address, disliking in particular the needless mention of the prince's invasion as well as the implication that the calling of convocation was a royal favor rather than a constitutional obligation. Most objectionable, however, was the bishops' seemingly innocuous invocation of the "Protestant religion," which was taken to imply some commitment to Protestant union either at home or abroad. At the ensuing conference, Bishop Burnet defended the inclusion of the term "Protestant religion" as the "common doctrine of the western part of Christendom, in opposition to the errors and corruptions of Rome." The Church of England, Burnet ventured, was but "an equivocal expression," since presumably a successfully Romanized ecclesiastical establishment would have no doubt retained that title. William Jane countered that the term "Protestant religion" was even more equivocal, since it was a term common to "Socinians, Anabaptists, and Quakers," for whose welfare the divines of the established church had no interest in thanking the king. Such complaints among the clergy of the lower house signaled not only a renewed (or unabated) antipathy toward Protestant Nonconformists, but also a mounting anxiety about the integrity of the established church amidst the transnational "Protestant interest" in which the Dutch king had now definitively enlisted England. The final address produced in committee abandoned any gratitude for the summoning of convocation and retained no mention of the Revolution; the king was inelegantly thanked for his zeal on behalf of the "honor, peace, advantage and establishment of the Church of England," which redounded to the benefit of the "Protestant religion in all other Protestant churches." Presented to the king on 12 December, this parsimonious address perhaps conveyed the narrow sentiments of the Anglican clergy more effectively than more effusive earlier drafts.[101]

The protracted struggle over the address to the king exposed both the profound antipathy to Protestant reconciliation on the part of many clergymen and a basic lack of temperamental and procedural accord between the lower and upper houses of convocation. Under the circumstances, then, it is perhaps not surprising that the painstaking work of the ecclesiastical commission was never even taken under consideration during the session. On the contrary, members of the lower house of convocation wished to see the advocates of comprehension censured for their views. On 11 December, the lower house requested that the prolocutor bring to the attention of the bishops in the upper house "several books of very dangerous consequence to the Christian Religion, and the Church of England particularly."[102] The first book named was the Hertfordshire rector Stephen Nye's overtly heterodox *Brief Notes upon the Creed of St. Athanasius*, an attempted refutation of Trinitarian orthodoxy. As I have suggested elsewhere, Nye's anti-Trinitarian works were explicitly (if not entirely fairly) associated with the London ascendancy in general and the ecclesiastical commission in particular.[103] The other books mentioned were the "two letters relating to the present convocation," that is, *A Letter from a Minister in the Country to a Member of the Convocation*, thought to be the work of one of the bishops of the ecclesiastical commission (probably Burnet), and *A Letter to a Friend Relating to the present Convocation at Westminster*, attributed to the Williamite divine Humphrey

Prideaux. These pamphlets were guilty of little beyond a conspicuous lack of charity toward the clerical enemies of comprehension; that they were listed alongside a work of professed Unitarianism goes a long way toward illustrating the extraordinary hostility of the majority of the lower house toward Protestant reconciliation. The clergy of the lower house inquired of the bishops "in what way, and how far . . . the convocation may proceed, in the preventing the publishing the like scandalous books for the future, and inflicting the censure of the Church, according to the canons provided in that behalf, upon the authors of them." Tellingly, Bishop Compton on 13 December, his wariness of the court favorites Tillotson and Burnet perhaps outweighing his active collaboration with the commission, concurred with the clergy regarding the "ill consequence of those books." Upon investigation, however, Compton remained uncertain "how far the convocation might proceed in that affair."[104] The same day, the convocation was adjourned to 24 January 1690 and soon after dissolved with the Convention Parliament without any tangible accomplishments.[105] Several divines soon took to the press to reflect upon the reformist agenda of what Thomas Long called "these two killing *Letters*," the embittered controversy over which spilled into the new year and further divided the church.[106]

The silencing of the convocation at the beginning of 1690 inaugurated what might justly be considered the "lost year" of the postrevolution settlement of the Church of England. During the weeks leading up to the deadline for taking the oaths of allegiance, numerous efforts were made to prevent the looming deprivations.[107] They all fell through. The nonjuring bishops and clergy were duly deprived on 1 February, though William, perhaps unwilling to compound the previous year's failures, made no moves toward either evicting the bishops from their residences or filling the vacant sees.[108] Among the Williamites, there was some hope that "in two or three years time," the nonjuring prelates would be replaced by "the best of the clergy," and there would then be sufficient authority to carry out comprehension and the necessary reformation of the church.[109] In the meanwhile, however, the king's forbearance left a void at the heart of the episcopal bench, including the primacy, which persisted for some fourteen months. Moreover, the interim saw the eruption of a strident and protracted controversy over the doctrine of the Trinity that rapidly assumed unmistakable political overtones, distracting and polarizing an already unsettled church. The Trinitarian controversy consumed the better part of the decade and further postponed the opportunity for substantive ecclesiastical reform.[110] In March 1690, a new convocation was duly elected in conjunction with the calling of William and Mary's second Parliament. However, no commission to transact business was forthcoming, and its assembly that year was a mere formality.[111] At the dawn of the final decade of the seventeenth century, the Church of England began to cast about for new methods and instruments of reform.

The Court, the Bishops, and National Reformation

While the failure of convocation did not signal the end of ecclesiastical reform, it certainly exposed the limits of clerical involvement. The intransigent lower clergy seemed dead set against any innovations in the constitution of the established church, and the depleted episcopate lacked either the coherence or the legitimacy to carry it against them. Amendment could be directed only from the center, and the reform-minded bishops and clergy increasingly relied on the royal supremacy for redress of grievances.

Impeded in both Parliament and convocation, the monarchs applied directly to the episcopate. One week after the dissolution of the Convention Parliament and convocation, on the first anniversary of his reign, William issued royal injunctions to the bishop of London for the better governance of the Church of England. The king's letter, which Compton was to communicate to the bishops of the two provinces (curiously bypassing Archbishop Thomas Lamplugh along with the deprived Sancroft), was an obvious attempt to salvage at least part of the agenda he had put before the ecclesiastical commission and convocation the previous year. William directed the bishops "to apply your selves with all diligence and zeal to the duties of your episcopal function." The bishops were to keep a strict watch over their respective dioceses to ensure that their clergy maintained residence upon their livings, preached plainly and practically "without running into needless controversies," administered the sacraments reverently and often, catechized the youth, and exercised diligent pastoral care over their flocks. Bishops were to take particular care in the examination of candidates for ordination and the disposal of church livings. They were to proceed against those lacking in public duty or personal rectitude "severely and impartially" by ecclesiastical censures. Echoing his previous charge to consider measures "for the reformation of manners either in ministers or people," William added an explicit charge to preach frequently against vice—namely, blasphemy, swearing, perjury, drunkenness, fornication, and profanation of the Sabbath—and to routinely inform parishioners of the panoply of laws prohibiting such enormities. Bishops were to confer regularly with the clergy of the dioceses and inquire into abuses and corruptions "in order to a full and speedy reformation."[112] Though this letter from the king is widely considered the royal authorization of the reformation of manners movement that began in earnest the following year, it is important to point out that nothing in it endorses activism by the laity.[113] Indeed, the substance of William's injunctions differed little from that of Archbishop Sancroft's nineteen months earlier, save for the fact that they emanated from a staunchly Protestant court rather than from a primate in opposition.

The king's orders were communicated down the clerical hierarchy and continued to reverberate throughout the dioceses through episcopal injunctions, visitations charges, and circular letters.[114] Several of the bishops, particularly those with links to the court and the ecclesiastical commission, published recapitulations of the royal injunctions for the benefit of their own dioceses. Gilbert Burnet's injunctions to the archdeacons of the diocese of Salisbury transmitted the king's letter and enjoined his clergy to "pursue all the parts of your ministry with a zeal suitable to the importance of them." Pursuant to the king's call for the reformation of manners, Burnet provided a schedule of vices to be preached against, with all relevant legislation to be duly recited for the congregation. He reiterated the need for sobriety among the ministry, constant catechizing of youth, conferences among the clergy, and careful examination of candidates for ordination.[115] He added the need to rigorously police abuses of the Toleration Act, lest it become an "indulgence to atheism."[116] Simon Patrick's episcopal letter to the clergy of Chester was virtually identical to Burnet's.[117] After Patrick was transferred to the see of Ely in 1691, his successor Nicholas Stratford again reminded the clergy of the need for diligent performance of the offices of baptism, confirmation, and visitation of the sick, along with daily prayers and the frequent administration of the sacrament of the Lord's Supper.[118] Richard Kidder's June 1692 message to the clergy of Bath and Wells enumerated virtually identical methods of pastoral engagement.[119] Edward Stillingfleet's lengthy charge to the clergy of Worcester was a good deal more elaborate, being a veritable meditation on the nature and history of Christian pastoral care. All religions had priests to offer sacrifices, he told his clergy, but only Christianity commissioned "preachers of righteousness, to set good and evil before the people committed to their charge; to inform of their duties, to reprove them for their miscarriages; and that, not in order to their shame, but their reformation."[120] Bishop Compton went even further in his letter to the clergy of London, advocating collaboration with Dissenters in the reformation of manners, "reviving that so much decayed and forgotten virtue among us of Christian charity."[121] All of these charges explicitly cited the king's February 1690 letter as a mandate for pastoral renewal and moral reform.

Surely the most enduring monument to the spirit of pastoral renewal under William and Mary was Gilbert Burnet's 1692 *Discourse of the Pastoral Care*, "the book," the prelate reflected, "that of all my other writings pleases myself best." Commissioned by Queen Mary and John Tillotson shortly after the latter's elevation to the primacy in May 1691, Burnet's *Discourse* seemingly owed a more direct debt to Bishop Stillingfleet's learned and historical *Charge to the Clergy of his Diocese* from the previous year.[122] Burnet began by calling the clergy of the established church to "the completing of our Reformation, especially as to the lives and manners of men." Somewhat audaciously for a work proceeding under such illustrious court patronage, Burnet discerned in the ecclesiastical establishment itself an historical impediment to the work of reform. When the earliest Protestant reformers "felt the warmth of the protection and encouragement that princes and states gave them, they insensibly slackened." They rested content with the legal reformation of doctrine and worship, "but did not study to reform the lives and manners of their people." And indeed, this bifurcation continued to pervade the Anglican ministry, who still believed "that the whole work consists in public functions," preaching the word and administering the sacraments, while the private obligations of pastoral care, "the instructing, the exhorting, the admonishing and reproving, the directing and conducting, the visiting and comforting of the people of the parish, is generally neglected." Burnet's aim was thus to sketch the historical and ecclesiological premises of the Christian pastorate, while providing a practical manual of pastoral conduct. Like his brethren of the Williamite episcopate, Burnet recommended the diligent performance of public functions with "an inward and feeling sense of things that are prayed for in our offices." But any man, Burnet admitted, with sufficient lungs to read prayers and sufficient taste to choose sermons can discharge the legal obligations of the ministry. Burnet thus dwelled on the private labors of pastoral care, "upon which the cognizance of the law cannot fall," and the particular engagements and visitations with the people of the parish, "that so he may know them, and be known of them." Only in this work is the minister's calling truly fulfilled.[123] For an author so indelibly associated with the Protestant monarchy, Burnet's *Pastoral Discourse* often struck a curiously postestablishmentarian tone, underpinned throughout by an inchoate cognizance of the limited instrumentality of state and law in the reformation of the lives of individuals. Upon receipt of the manuscript in April 1692, Tillotson deemed the work "as perfect in its kind as I hope to see anything." The *Discourse of the Pastoral Care*, Tillotson concluded, somewhat wistfully, "will, I hope, do much good at present, and more when you and I are dead and gone."[124]

The court, particularly the queen and the primate, stood at the helm of ecclesiastical reform throughout the early part of the decade.[125] "If I could but hope to do any considerable good to this miserable, distracted and divided Church," Archbishop Tillotson told his friend Robert Nelson in June 1691, "I should esteem it a full recompense for all the trouble which I foresee I must undergo."[126] By the end of that year, it was rumored that Archbishop Tillotson had resumed his earlier efforts on behalf of Protestant reconciliation and was drawing up a comprehension scheme to be introduced in the forthcoming session of Parliament.[127] Shortly thereafter, thirteen of the bishops, eleven of whom were appointed by William and Mary, petitioned the king for a stricter enforcement of the laws against vice, the result of which was the royal *Proclamation against vitious, debauched and profane persons* issued 21 January 1692.[128] At the same time, Tillotson was drafting the heads of a new circular letter to the bishops of his province. The draft enjoined constant residence in their cures for both bishops and clergy, strict care in ordinations, diligent catechizing, visitation of the sick, frequent confirmations, monthly administration of the sacrament and weekday prayers, and dutiful observation of fasts and thanksgivings appointed by the crown. Tillotson also commanded that "his Majesty's letter enjoining preaching against profaneness and vice be carefully observed."[129] On 11 April, Tillotson proposed the heads at a meeting of bishops at Lambeth, which included Archbishop Sharp of York, Bishop Compton of London, Bishop Stillingfleet of Worcester, Bishop Patrick of Ely, Bishop Fowler of Gloucester, Bishop John Moore of Norwich, and Bishop Tenison of Lincoln—all men of late Restoration London, all (save Moore) members of the ecclesiastical commission; the bishops "cheerfully concurred" with the primate's proposals.[130] Given this unanimity, it is unclear why the archbishop's provincial letter was never dispatched. But given the similarity in substance with much of what the bishops had produced in the preceding two years, it is equally unclear why such injunctions were thought necessary. Still, it is difficult to evade the sense that the bishops were somewhat bereft of new ideas for improving the pastoral capacities of the parish clergy.[131] They labored, it seems, simply to find better methods of reaffirming the old ones.

The Devolution of Religious Renewal

By 1692, the postrevolutionary settlement of the Church of England had, for all intents and purposes, achieved its final form. The Revolution had cost the established church its legal monopoly over public worship, as well as the communion of six bishops and some four hundred of their supporters among the lower clergy deprived for nonjuring. The bitter Trinitarian controversy of the 1690s, recognized by many as at least a byproduct of the revolutionary upheavals within the establishment, only served to salt the church's wounds.[132] However, the church had not altered or enlarged in any way the terms of its communion, and although comprehension schemes would continue to be mooted throughout the decade, Protestant reconciliation through statutory means was indefinitely deferred.[133] Moreover, the Anglican dominance of public and political life, underwritten by the sacramental test, remained intact. At court, the monarchs and their allies among the reconstructed episcopate had embraced a modest agenda of ecclesiastical reform based on enhanced pastoral care and the reformation of the manners of both the clergy and the laity. The schedule of national fast days instituted by the court provided opportunities of unprecedented frequency to reaffirm the providential and public obligations of godly reformation.[134]

However, the initiative in moral and ecclesiastical reform was clearly slipping away from the court. The Anglican revivalism of the reign of James II continued unabated through the metropolis of London and Westminster. By 1692, eight parishes in the metropolis offered the sacrament of the Lord's Supper weekly, and another four held the communion service two or three times each month. Some forty-seven churches throughout the city were said to be offering daily prayers. The city churches sponsored approximately twenty-four weekly lectures on various days and an additional twenty-four lectures held monthly.[135] In October 1692, nineteen religious societies were said to be convening regularly throughout the capital, a number that would almost double before the end of the decade.[136] Moreover, zealous members of the clergy and laity were taking it upon themselves to erect new houses of worship to accommodate the teeming population of the metropolis. As mentioned above, Thomas Tenison in 1691 oversaw the founding of Trinity Chapel to better serve the denizens of his enormous Westminster parish of St. Martin's-in-the-Fields. In 1693, Sir George Wheler, the well-traveled clergyman and author of *An Account of Churches and Places of Assembly of the Primitive Christians*, set aside a portion of his lands in the overcrowded East London neighborhood of Spitalfields for the erection of a chapel for the "spiritual relief" of the populace there.[137] Indeed, the Scottish episcopal minister Robert Kirk was so impressed with the religious resources in the capital that he wrote, "if Jacob's ladder to convey people to heaven by a constant instruction of godliness and exercises of devotion be not in London, it is not in the world."[138]

Certainly the most well-known among the initiatives that emerged from this milieu were the societies for the reformation of manners. The first of these, a mere handful of gentlemen, began operating out of the Lincoln's Inn chambers of the barrister William Yates around late spring 1691.[139] This first society sought to advance the reformation of manners largely by encouraging informers to report vice to local magistrates. The society intended to streamline the cumbersome judicial processes by printing blank warrants for a variety of offenses such as swearing, drunkenness, prostitution, and profanation of the Sabbath and providing agents by whom the warrants could be filled out upon receiving information. The informer could then present the completed warrant to a magistrate, swear to its truthfulness, and have the warrant signed and sealed on the spot. The warrant might then be returned to the society's agents for dispatch to the appropriate constable for execution. By August 1691, the society was said to have delivered approximately 140 warrants for moral offenses. "It is a matter of great rejoicing," reported Robert Harley, "that the attempt for reformation of manners succeeds beyond expectation, and the city concurs so far."[140] The society's efforts were publicly countenanced by the queen and received the encouragement of a considerable number of the bishops. The court's blessing allowed this first society to weather an early controversy with the Middlesex justices and the Lords Commissioners of the Great Seal over irregularities in its warrants and its encroachment upon the functions of the magistrates. In the wake of the controversy, Bishop Fowler penned a vindication of the society as answerable to the great hopes for "effectual reformation" sparked by the Revolution of 1688–1689. He challenged the critics of the reformation society "to shew any project better fitted for the attainment of its end, than this throughout is."[141] In March 1692, as a sign of royal approbation, Queen Mary named society members

Sir Richard Bulkeley, Colonel Maynard Colchester, and William Yates to the Middlesex bench.[142] In the next year, two more societies formed in London. By the end of the decade, roughly twenty such organizations were reported to be operating throughout the metropolis.[143]

Though largely secular in terms of personnel and procedures, the societies for the reformation of manners exhibited broad continuities with the Anglican revivalism that informed both the Revolution and the ensuing ecclesiastical settlement.[144] Most obviously, they rather conspicuously laid claim to the providential rhetoric of national reformation that formed the core of Revolution homiletics. "Nothing less than a national reformation will be acceptable in God's sight," wrote one projector, "after England's wonderful mercies and deliverances."[145] It is therefore not surprising that their efforts found favor with Queen Mary and the members of the Williamite episcopate most invested in the propagation of such rhetoric. Williamite bishops frequently preached the biannual reformation sermons at St. Mary-le-Bow, a serviceable venue for periodically reaffirming the providential and revolutionary obligations of moral reform.[146] Second, the reformers often claimed various court efforts at moral and ecclesiastical reform as a mandate for their own.[147] Indeed, their caustic propagandist Edward Stephens did not hesitate to cite the manifest failures of the court as an argument for the societies. The king's February 1690 letter to Bishop Compton was "commendable indeed in itself" but "so defective in respect to what ought to have been done." He elsewhere lamented that the bishops "should be sunk so low in their authority, be become so mean in that esteem and veneration of the people," that they were unable to enact more substantive provisions for the reformation of manners. In Stephens's estimation, the obstructions to reformation through the ecclesiastical hierarchy plainly authorized the mobilization of additional forces among the public.[148] Third, the societies initially sought to situate themselves within the broader ecology of London revivalism. Stephens was careful to describe the members of the first society as "all of them persons of the Church of England, and such as frequent the prayers of the Church and the sacrament."[149] In October 1692, the society dispatched letters to the nineteen religious societies meeting in the city, inviting their members to participate, thus in effect broadening their piety from private devotion to public reformation.[150] This proposed alliance was not merely tactical. Stephens wrote passionately about the need for holy living, frequent communion, reform of the liturgy to "better express the devotion of many pious souls," and the provision of additional churches for the denizens of the capital.[151] And finally, as Craig Rose has demonstrated, the ecumenism of the Anglican societies for the reformation of manners, their early willingness to collaborate with Nonconformists, was widely hailed as an ersatz form of Protestant reconciliation, "a sort of *de facto* union among godly Protestants."[152] Though the failure of comprehension precluded any prospect of ecclesiastical reunion among English Protestants, the cause of moral reform at least offered an avenue for functional collaboration.[153]

Perhaps the reformation societies' most remarkable departure from the prevailing idiom of late Restoration and Revolution-era Anglicanism was their full-throated defense of the principles of voluntary association.[154] Still to some extent imbricated in Restoration-era antipathy toward conventicle, combination, and cabal, the very idea of voluntary association had in the first place to be proved compatible with the public good, lest reformers be charged, as Samuel Wesley put it, with "designing a factious combination instead of a religious union."[155] The legitimacy of association thus became a leitmotif in the literary and homiletic rhetoric of moral reform. The cause of national reformation required a concerted effort among individuals of public spirit. "Single attempts will prove too weak," preached Samuel Bradford to the societies at St. Mary-le-Bow, "whereas the joint and unanimous endeavors of many who will encourage and assist one another, will make iniquity both ashamed and afraid to show itself."[156] The voluntary association possessed tactical advantages unavailable to the private individual or the lone magistrate.

The advocates of national reformation rather cunningly deployed for their own purposes Restoration-era charges against vicious or immoral assemblies. They conjured the specter of a veritable "uncivil society" composed of clubs and societies founded for the enjoyment and furtherance of sin, irreverence, and blasphemy, long the complaint of "the virtuous part of England."[157] Reformers thus argued that the proliferation of such bodies demanded a countervailing movement among the godly, "pious combinations for the overbalancing those of vice."[158] Such models of association, heretofore largely dedicated to sin and schism, might thus be recovered for use by individuals of piety. This rhetoric significantly altered the familiar seventeenth-century tropes of godly magistracy that traditionally accompanied calls for the reformation of manners.[159] Indeed, it seemed to be adumbrating a virtually unprecedented vision of societal autonomy and self-sufficiency.[160] The persistence of social forms deemed injurious to the public good required the propagation of alternative organizations to counteract them. Such rhetoric seemed to imbue society, long the object of national reformations that originated externally in godly rule, the church, or the domestic sphere of family religion, with the capacity for self-improvement.

Given the obligations of entrepreneurialism, competition, and self-promotion that such a vision of social life necessarily entailed, it is perhaps not surprising that advocates of national reformation routinely deployed the language of commercial organization in vindication of their designs. The church itself, preached Samuel Wesley, comprised "a regulated society of men."[161] Like commercial endeavors, national reformation required the pooling of both risk and resources. "This trade," Daniel Chadwick explained, "is not to be driven but by a joint-stock."[162] In commercial forms that permeated urban life, reformers discerned models of efficiency and organization. The establishment of reformation societies was "no other thing than what is constantly done without offense in cases of secular concernment," Samuel Bradford reasoned.[163] Commercial organization provided reformers with a framework for promoting voluntary association that was at once already widely acknowledged as conducive to the public good and substantially free of the negative connotations still attached to clubs and conventicles. Moreover, such language further affirmed the legitimacy of the popular (as opposed to political) initiative that increasingly characterized the work of moral reform. Such entrepreneurialism would long serve as the distinguishing character of English philanthropy.[164]

The growing density of associational life in postrevolutionary England further accelerated the transfer of moral initiative away from the court and the Anglican hierarchy. The ranks of English Nonconformity underwent what can only be described as an organizational revolution in the immediate aftermath of the Revolution, developing institutional apparatuses of enhanced scope and complexity to weather the new climate of religious toleration.[165] In September 1689, a general assembly of representatives from more than one hundred Baptist churches throughout England was convened in London, and a fund of "freewill offerings" was proposed to assist poorer congregations and to train and sponsor missionaries abroad.[166] Baptist associations were meeting regularly in the west (comprising Gloucestershire, Wiltshire, Somerset, Devon, and Cornwall) and the midlands by 1690 and the north by 1691.[167] By June 1690, the Dissenting clergy of Somerset, Gloucestershire, and Wiltshire had established an association of Presbyterian and Congregationalist ministers and even projected the raising of a common fund for charitable purposes.[168] This design was made good in

London the following month, when Presbyterians and Congregationalists established the Common Fund, "by way of benevolence," for the relief of poor ministers, the endowment of new churches, and the training of new ministers, particularly from among the sons of the poorer Nonconformist clergy. The Common Fund was, of course, but a prelude to the even more ambitious (albeit shorter-lived) "Happy Union" of Presbyterians and Congregationalists undertaken in London in March 1691.[169] The "heads of agreement" adopted therein inspired a wave of similarly collaborative endeavors in the provinces, most notably the Exeter Assembly and the Cheshire Classis, both founded in 1691, and the Lancashire Provincial Assembly, founded in 1693. After the collapse of the union, the independent ministers founded their own Congregational Fund in 1695.[170] The Society of Friends had, of course, long been in possession of a comparable national organization in its Meeting for Sufferings. Yet even after toleration delivered the Quakers from the more severe oppressions, the meeting continued to mobilize against the lingering penalties left in place by the Revolution settlement.[171]

Ironically, the English nonjuring clergy soon found themselves in need of similar mechanisms of benevolence. In late 1694, John Kettlewell, deprived vicar of Coleshill, Warwickshire, proposed to the deprived bishop Thomas Ken "the setting up a fund of charity for regular collection and distribution of the same among the poor suffering clergy."[172] At Ken's behest, Kettlewell published his *Model of a Fund of Charity for the Needy, Suffering Clergy* the following January. Like its Nonconformist counterparts, Kettlewell's scheme was designed to consolidate charitable contributions into a single fund, formalize the collection of intelligence on the various hardships of the deprived clergy and their families, and centralize distribution under ecclesiastical superiors—in this case, the surviving bishops who were designated "managers" of the fund. William and Mary's government, however, took umbrage at the public solicitations for what appeared to be a charity brief and summoned Ken before the Privy Council for the illegal usurpation of ecclesiastical jurisdiction. "My lords," Ken replied dryly, "I never heard that begging was part of ecclesiastical jurisdiction."[173]

Such social and para-ecclesial endeavors everywhere shaded into the more nebulous world of projecting that Daniel Defoe famously claimed had come to characterize the age. "Past ages," he remarked, "have never come up to the degree of projecting and inventing, as it refers to matters of *negoce*, and methods of civil polity, which we see this age arrived to." Projects, then, were not simply a matter of commercial development, but of police—that is, in the eighteenth-century sense of the term, social management. Indeed, the lines between commercial enterprise, religious association, and public philanthropy were consistently blurred during this period. Public-spirited individuals routinely traversed these spheres. For instance, the London mercer Thomas Firmin organized relief for foreign Protestants, contributed to the Welsh Trust, was an early member of one of the London societies for the reformation of manners, and promoted a workhouse for linen manufactures in Artillery Lane. In accordance with his anti-Trinitarian religious beliefs, he also proposed religious fraternities modeled on the Anglican religious societies, not "by way of schism or separation from the Church," but only for the especial care of the doctrine of the unity of God.[174] The popular devotional writer William Assheton promoted the reformation of manners in a slew of widely distributed tracts, while actively advancing an insurance scheme for widows to the Sons of the Clergy, the Bank of England, and finally to the Mercers Company of London, which formally adopted his proposal in January 1699.[175] The Glamorganshire industrialist Sir Humphrey Mackworth oversaw the Company of Mine Adventurers, provided basic welfare services such as housing and medical care for his employees, and in 1699 cofounded the SPCK.[176] In December 1700, he scribbled a prayer in his diary: "grant that I may project now for doing of good, as much as I ever did for the world."[177] Around 1700, the freethinker Charles Gildon proposed a national lottery by which to raise enough revenue "to purchase 9 or 10 thousand pounds per annum" in clerical tithes impropriated by the laity.[178] Clearly in the late seventeenth and early eighteenth centuries, commercial and financial forms and religious and moral imperatives freely intertwined.

The vogue for the moral and philanthropic employment of modern commercial and financial forms, it must be pointed out, was tempered by a vague nostalgia for the lost socioreligious institutions of pre-Reformation England.[179] The preface to the celebrated antiquarian Thomas Tanner's work *Notitia Monastica, Or, A Short History of the Religious Houses in England and Wales* offered something of an apology on behalf of the monasteries, "once the glory of our English nation," as institutions at once dedicated to liberality, hospitality, and devotion.[180] The virtuoso clergyman Maurice Wheeler, master of the cathedral school at Gloucester, proposed the foundation of schools at every cathedral and collegiate church throughout the kingdom, "the converting of these ecclesiastical societies into nurseries eminently useful for the education of youth," particularly the sons of the nobility and gentry. A uniform educational system established in the cathedrals, overseen by the bishops, and operated by the canons or prebendaries, Wheeler predicted, would be a greater contribution to the reformation of manners than any "paroxysm of zeal" shown here and there by diligent magistrates.[181] Others went further. The barrister clergyman Edward Stephens, one of the founders of the reformation of manners movement, began administering daily communion to a London religious society in 1692; eventually, he proposed monasteries for Protestants of both sexes.[182] Sir George Wheler, the patron of the Spitalfields chapel and an early member of the SPCK, endorsed the founding of "pious and useful communities," provided they be rendered compatible with the security of both church and state. His tract on family devotion begins with a proposal for the foundation of a Protestant nunnery.[183] In this, Wheler was of course merely echoing the more famous project of the devotional writer and philosopher Mary Astell, whose *Serious Proposal to the Ladies for the Advancement of their True Interest* (first part, 1694; second part, 1697) offered a lengthy and thoughtful justification for such an institution for women of the better sort.[184] It is noteworthy, if not terribly surprising, that the proponents of a suitably reformed monasticism tended generally to align themselves with the cause of high-church Anglicanism; Stephens, Wheler, and Astell all had extensive ties with the nonjurors. However, the fact that the commercially minded and decidedly non-Anglican Daniel Defoe could cite Astell's *Proposal* as something of an inspiration for his "academy for women," in his celebrated *Essay upon Projects* (though dubious of the "bigotry" necessary to "keep up a nunnery"), should illustrate the easy interchange between the conceptual worlds of projects and para-ecclesial organizations.[185]

If such proposals did not explicitly encroach upon the clerical function, many certainly abutted it. Clergymen engaged in the reformation of manners or the exhortation to liberal contributions on a charity brief might find themselves collaborating with projectors and other public-spirited individuals possessed of the conviction that they clearly discerned both the public interest and the optimal methods for its pursuit. Worse, some such individuals believed their engagements perfectly compatible with the realization of individual profit. This was not unpredictably discomfiting to many clergy of the established church. Thus, when the minor poet and playwright Lewis Maidwell proposed his *Scheme for a Publick Academy* to the House of Commons in early 1700, the clergy and the universities were in high dudgeon over what was branded "Mr. Maidwell's nonsensical project." Maidwell proposed the establishment of what he called a *schola illustris* in the City of London modeled after the *académies* in France, where the better sort of youth might be bred up in classical and modern languages, mathematics and natural philosophy, and navigation and "merchant's accounts." The academy would supplement this curriculum with training in "dancing, fencing and riding the great horse," skills necessary for public life and largely absent from a university education.[186] In anticipation of university objections, Maidwell disclaimed the teaching of "logic, or other parts of philosophy," but his critics among the clergy were not mollified. Parliamentary approval of the project, they feared, "might be stretched to authorize him and future governors to set up teachers of university learning, yea, and unsound divinity too." Deeming the project "injurious to the two universities," the clergy used their influence with Tory allies in the Commons to have the plan quashed.[187] The eminent Savilian Professor of Geometry at Oxford John Wallis penned a lengthy set of animadversions on Maidwell's proposal, which vociferously defended the educational establishment of the kingdom and dismissed the scheme (and its continental prototypes) as "so many tricks to draw money from young gentlemen."[188]

Such concerns fed into the general ambivalence of churchmen regarding the array of projects that claimed to advance the national reformation. In the final years of the century, leading churchmen across the political and ideological spectrum voiced significant reservations about the prospects of moral renewal through voluntary associations and reformation societies.[189] Josiah Woodward's *Account of the societies for reformation of manners in London and Westminster, and other parts of the kingdom* appeared in 1699 with the endorsement of five Williamite bishops: Humphreys of Bangor, Stratford of Chester, Fowler of Gloucester, Hall of Bristol, and Kidder of Bath and Wells.[190] Bishop Fowler hyperbolically proclaimed, "our whole bench have never done the 40th part of that service and honor to our Church, that these Church of England laymen have done."[191] Yet some of their brethren were markedly less enthusiastic. When the increasingly conservative Archbishop John Sharp of York encountered a society for the reformation of manners erected in Nottingham in 1698, he confessed to be uncertain "whether these kinds of fraternities and confederations are allowed by the laws of this realm and the constitutions of our church." Sharp was more comfortable with both the religious societies, conducted according "to the rules set down by Mr. Woodward or Doctor Horneck," and the conferences of clergy, "for the promoting [of] religion and reformation in their parishes." But he was decidedly uneasy about the "new methods" of reformation societies, composed of admixtures of clergy and laity, churchmen and Dissenters.[192] The staunch Whig William Nicolson, archdeacon (and subsequently bishop) of Carlisle, was a good deal more strident in his opposition to what he called "the modish societies."[193] Upon discovering reformation societies at Carlisle and Brampton, he furiously lobbied his aged diocesan Bishop Thomas Smith and his metropolitan, Archbishop Sharp, to authorize their suppression. Such organizations, Nicolson declaimed, were "conventicles and unlawful assemblies" that might be licensed under the Toleration Act but were otherwise "without the pale of the established Church."[194] Nicolson particularly distrusted the ecumenical character of these "mongrel combinations," considering them heirs to Richard Baxter's Commonwealth-era Worcestershire Association. "Such linsey-woolsey associations as these," he maintained, "look like the proper manufacture of [Baxter's] Kidderminster, and might be reasonable enough in those days of confusion." However, they had no place under a settled church, "unless it be upon the principle of comprehension."[195] Even Thomas Tenison, archbishop of Canterbury and a staunch advocate of the reformation of manners, fairly resented the initiative of the laity. He recommended to Archbishop Sharp "doing something ourselves," deeming it "most absurd for the college of bishops to be led in such a manner."[196] Sharp, however, saw fairly clearly the way the wind was blowing. He told Archdeacon Nicolson, "it may be doubted whether it be in the bishop's power to stifle or suppress these societies, though he should use his utmost endeavors to do it."[197]

Churchmen committed to moral and religious reform were, then, of two minds concerning the nascent civil society of associations, commercial organizations, and projects. On the one hand, reformers could not but be attracted to the social and organizational technology of civil society. Sociability, entrepreneurialism, promotional press, communication networks, pooled resources, even financial instruments such as lotteries and insurance plans were, for the first time, enlisted in the cause of social and religious improvement.[198] On the other hand, such forms demarcated a sphere that lay outside the traditional ambit of ecclesiastical authority, one that seemed to belong unmistakably to projectors, profit seekers, and Protestant Dissenters. "Projects like parents," one critic noted, "beget their like and multiply wonderfully, projects upon projects, lottery upon lottery, engine upon engine."[199] Organizational innovation harbored the prospect of proliferation beyond the confessional boundaries of the established church, toward either ecumenical alliances with rival denominations or more profane entanglements with commercial or secular enterprises. Moreover, while such organizational forms possessed the extraordinary ability to mobilize individuals and resources in a manner answerable to the reformers' desire to diffuse social responsibility for national reformation, they also threatened to upend the constitutive hierarchies of political and religious life.[200] The cause of national reformation could not, it seemed, be popularized without being substantially democratized. The nonjuror Henry Gandy perceived such efforts as irremediably "tainted with republican, or if you please, Jesuitical principles," fundamentally incompatible with the constitution of the Church of England.[201] The task, then, for Anglican reformers was the development of organizational forms that maintained both confessional integrity and ecclesiological orthodoxy.

The Search for Orthodox Forms

Churchmen during the final years of William III's reign were preoccupied with the search for orthodox modes of social and moral engagement. Indeed, this concern was manifest in both of the major ecclesiastical developments of these years: the campaign to restore convocation and the foundation of the great Anglican societies the SPCK and the SPG. Both movements were predicated on the insufficiency of extant ecclesiastical institutions to meet the challenges of the postrevolutionary religious environment, and both comprised, at least in part, responses to the growing religious and moral autonomy of the "associational world" that lay beyond the Church of England. The Warwickshire clergyman Thomas Bray, whose various ventures and proposals on behalf of the Church of England eventually coalesced into the SPCK, cited the organization of rival denominations as an argument for Anglican engagement. "Whilst the papists, the dissenters, and the very Quakers have such societies for the carrying on their superstitious blasphemous heresies and fooleries," Bray wrote in his proposal, "we have had nothing of this nature yet set up in order to promote the pure and primitive Christianity which we profess."[202] Such complaints stemmed from the church's need for more effective instruments of discipline and religious oversight amidst a civil society already substantially inhabited by increasingly well-organized sectarian rivals.

Nowhere is the canalization of late Restoration Anglican revivalism into the postrevolutionary age of projects more clearly evident than in the early career of Thomas Bray. "I am called a projector (a very mean and contemptible character with such as are accounted men of wisdom)," Bray wrote in 1699, "upon the account of these designs I am continually forming."[203] Bray associated with and was influenced by some of the most famous devotional writers of the late Restoration "holy living" school, such as the nonjuror John Kettlewell and John Rawlet, the author of *The Christian Monitor*.[204] He penned the first volume of his immensely popular *Lectures upon the Church Catechism*, on which his initial reputation was based, in response to the pastoral efforts of the Revolution bishops. Upon relocating to London in 1695, Bray became "conversant with some of those excellent persons concerned in the reformation of manners."[205] Amidst the vogue for institutions of moral reform and social management in this milieu, Bray advanced his scheme for a "penitential hospital for the employing and reforming [of] lewd women," a reformatory to be attached to one of the city churches and placed under the supervision of "some grave matron" and one or two divines who would conduct twice-daily prayers, penances, and "methods of mortification."[206] That Bray referred to the hospital as a "monastery" suggests he was perhaps not unaware of the contemporary proposals for so-called Protestant nunneries afoot, although his idea clearly addressed a far lower social stratum than that of Mary Astell.[207] In 1696, as part of his broader attempt to fortify the Church of England in the plantations, Bishop Compton recruited Bray to serve as his commissary to the colony of Maryland. Even before setting sail for the New World, Bray used his appointment as a perch from which to survey and assess the established church at home and abroad.

Bray's signature project from his term as commissary was the campaign for establishing theological libraries, "to be appropriated and affixed one to each parish in the foreign plantations." These were conceived as a resource "for the poorer among the clergy," who alone might be persuaded to undertake service in America, as well as a magazine of Christian knowledge necessary for the spiritual warfare and sectarian competition such service entailed. Readily endorsed by the two archbishops, and the bishops of London, Lichfield and Coventry, and Norwich, Bray's campaign was an enormous success, raising nearly £2,500 and laying the foundations for more than seventy libraries in North America and the West Indies.[208]

In subsequent iterations, Bray included England and Wales within the scope of the project. He claimed that his solicitations on behalf of imperial Anglicanism were often "met with answers to the effect that we had poor cures and poor parsons enough here in England, and that charity should begin at home," but his domestic designs should not be considered as simply a reappropriation of the imperial project. Indeed, there were significant divergences. Bray initially proposed establishing not parochial libraries, as in the plantations, but lending libraries in the market towns "in every deanery throughout the kingdom," that is, in the ancient districts of the rural deaneries within each archdeaconry. Giving parish clergy access to theological resources would to some extent supplement (if not quite equalize) "the endowments of their vicarages" and go some length toward countering those most prominent causes of popular anticlericalism, ignorance and poverty. Moreover, Bray very clearly proposed his decanal libraries in the context of the Trinitarian and cognate theological controversies of the 1690s, enabling the clergy of the established church "to stand our ground, whilst atheists, deists and Socinians, do so earnestly contend against the faith." Most importantly, Bray conceived the lending libraries not simply as material and financial resources for the provincial clergy, but as functional centers of ecclesiastical life in the provinces. Like many of his generation, he was preoccupied with reviving the function, if not necessarily the medieval office, of the rural dean, the supervisor of religious life and coordinator of pastoral efforts in those parishes geographically distant from the bishop and clergy of the cathedral towns. He imagined that the libraries would serve as a venue for the neighboring clergy "to meet and confer together in," and by their consultations, "to restore more and more by degrees, the ancient use of rural deans." Bray's library scheme, he claimed, was no "mere project." On the contrary, "the ancient discipline of our Church," he contended, "is not so likely to be restored by any other means as by having libraries in our several rural deaneries, for the clergy to meet in, where they may act to such purpose, and according to such powers as shall be allowed them."[209]

Bray's library scheme employed modern methods of fund-raising and promotion to restore the traditional discipline of the Church of England. Indeed, the project aimed at nothing short of the functional reorganization of the diocesan clergy according to the ancient demarcations of the rural deaneries, each of which encompassed roughly ten parishes traditionally subsisting under the supervision of a rural dean appointed by the bishop. Though Bray's unpublished essay on the rural deaneries did not actually propose the revival of the ruri-decanal office, he argued that the disciplinary functions of their chapters could be in some measure restored through deanery libraries. Bray sketched out what he called a "praxis of deanery discipline," by which monthly clerical meetings at the lending libraries, "wholly designed for promoting religion and reformation of manners," could revitalize the collaborative dimensions of pastoral engagement. Parish clergy were annually to subscribe five shillings apiece for the cost of the meetings and additional sums for the maintenance of the library. They were to convene monthly to enquire "by what means and methods we shall best propagate Christian knowledge" and "by what means charity catechetical schools may be raised in our several parishes for the Christian education of children"; to consider the promotion of the "reformation of manners among the profane and dissolute"; and to organize the distribution of devotional works "instructive in faith and practice." In short, Bray imagined his scheme as a blueprint for Anglican renewal, one in which, curiously enough, modern lending libraries raised by subscription and voluntary associations of local clergy might be cobbled into a functional approximation of the medieval disciplinary institutions of the church.[210]

Bray was not alone in seeking new methods of organizing church life in the localities. For instance, the clergy of the archdeaconry of Chester sought "a deputation under the seal" of the Sons of the Clergy "to receive and dispose of such money as they should collect for the relief of poor widows and children of clergymen" within their own district. Like Bray's proposals, this offered a model for empowering the lower clergy to collaborate at levels beneath that of the diocese.[211] Samuel Wesley even suggested that the religious societies of the laity (modeled on the London groups of Anthony Horneck and William Beveridge) might effectively supply the place of the clerical chapters of the decayed rural deaneries.[212] In November 1698, some fifteen clergymen in Bedford resolved to subscribe ten shillings apiece each year and meet monthly "for promoting religion and reformation." They agreed to promote catechizing of youth, diligent visitation of parishioners, endowment of lending libraries, support of poor clergy, and distribution of devotional works to their congregations. The list of recommended volumes included the reformation of manners tracts of William Assheton; the sacramental writings of Beveridge, Tillotson, Patrick, and Ken; and John Rawlet's *The Christian Monitor*. The clergy in neighboring Buckinghamshire formed a similar society at Newport Pagnell the following January.[213]

The question of how to accommodate such forms, both organizationally and financially, within the body of the established church persisted. In 1697, Thomas Bray proposed the founding of a "Protestant congregation, or Society for the Propagation of Christian Knowledge" to oversee the variety of Anglican projects then in the offing at home and abroad. Bray's society was to be incorporated and empowered to meet and consult like the Royal Society and the Sons of the Clergy and to receive "gifts, grants, legacies, &c." in furtherance of its designs. The society was to be composed largely of "the London clergy of chiefest note," with the senior chaplains of both the archbishop of Canterbury and the bishop of London as "standing members." It would also include "some gentlemen of the laity," whose influence over the "generality of the merchants" would serve to enlist the commercial sector in its pious endeavors. For the church at home, the society would serve as a higher form of clerical conference, bringing together "the best of the clergy of the City to consult upon the most material affairs relating to their profession." For the church abroad, it would function as "an honorable counsel to the Lord Bishop of London in his consultations about the affairs of the churches in the foreign plantations," an ersatz cathedral chapter for the bishop of London's imperial diocese.[214] The proposal was warmly received, though incorporation was thought premature.[215] As a preparatory to a chartered organ, Bray endeavored to form a "voluntary society" with a drastically reduced clerical element. Indeed, Bray was the sole clergyman among the five gentlemen who met on 8 March 1699 at the Lincoln's Inn chambers of the Irish lawyer John Hooke and constituted themselves as the Society for Promoting Christian Knowledge.[216] The others came with backgrounds in philanthropy, reformation of manners, and commercial projects.[217]

Less than a month later, Archbishop Thomas Tenison dispatched a letter to John Batteley, archdeacon of Canterbury, in which he clearly articulated the policy of the church with respect to the work of moral and religious renewal.[218] His missive was of sufficient scope and vision to be immediately reissued as a circular letter to all the bishops of his province. The reformation of manners, the primate declared, "belongs more immediately to us, who are the ministers of Christ." Tenison was manifestly conscious of the myriad efforts at moral reform afoot in the capital and elsewhere. His library at Lambeth Palace comprised a veritable clearinghouse for nearly every Anglican project for moral improvement, of whatever practicality or merit, conceived in the second half of the 1690s.[219] In his circular letter, the archbishop somewhat obliquely referred to efforts of the clergy "in the cities of London and Westminster," acknowledging that "the good effects of their diligence have been very evident of late years." But for the clergy of the provinces, Tenison recommended the establishment of clerical conferences in language not terribly dissimilar from that of Thomas Bray.[220] Moreover, were churchwardens and "pious persons among the laity" to be included in their consultations, these conferences would provide an invaluable foundation for "carrying on the reformation of men's lives and manners." He further added the indispensability of catechetical education for children as the surest "foundation for piety and morality."[221] The archbishop of Canterbury had not quite acquiesced to the age of projects, but he certainly seemed to be endorsing the principle of voluntary association among both clergy and laity as a central plank of his program of religious renewal.

As the bishops communicated Archbishop Tenison's letter down through the hierarchy in their respective dioceses, the nascent SPCK resolved to promote the formation of satellite societies throughout the provinces. It would "consider of a certain number of clergyman that may form societies, and give an account once a month to this Society of the state and progress of reformation and of Christian knowledge in their respective counties."[222] In early 1700, the SPCK dispatched a circular letter inviting its correspondents "to engage the clergy to meet frequently together, to consider of the most proper means to carry on these pious designs." This was, the society was careful to point out, no more than what had been "recommended by the archbishop of Canterbury and others the lords bishops in their circular letter in April 1699."[223]

The initial response among churchmen was fairly enthusiastic. Cornelius Yeate, archdeacon of Wiltshire, proclaimed such methods "the great foundation of a general and lasting reformation."[224] In Bedfordshire, where the clergy had begun associating before the archbishop's letter, new societies sprang up in the towns of Shefford, Biggleswade, and Ampthill.[225] William Fenwick of Hallaton in Leicestershire expressed his approval of "the design in every branch and prays that the whole kingdom may unanimously concur" in it. From the Cotswolds, the Reverend Willett of Stretton reported a meeting of eighteen clergymen at Cirencester, where they agreed to promote catechetical instruction and the distribution of devotional literature.[226] In Durham, Archdeacon Robert Booth convened a monthly conference of the clergymen of the deanery of Alnwick, where they agreed "to discourse together and engage themselves mutually and solemnly to prosecute their duties," namely, instruction of youth, frequent administration of the sacrament, distribution of pious books, visiting their parishioners, and promoting family devotion.[227] In north Wales, Bishop Humphrey Humphreys of Bangor issued elaborate instructions to the clergy of Anglesey for their monthly assemblies. Their meetings were to begin with the daily prayers and the reading of Tenison's circular letter; one of the heads of the archbishop's letter was to be considered at every session. The clerical conferences on the island were to maintain a good correspondence with one another, but correspondence with any "foreign society" outside the Church of England was strictly prohibited.[228] By March 1700, the clergy of the deanery Tindeathwy and Menai were meeting monthly. They had resolved to translate William's proclamation against immorality and profaneness into Welsh, to encourage parishioners to bring children and servants for catechetical instructions, and to dispose them to frequently receive the holy sacrament.[229] In Bristol, Arthur Bedford, vicar of the Temple, failed to "promote a society of the clergy" and opted therefore to join the decidedly less orthodox society for the reformation of manners, among whose members numbered many Protestant Nonconformists.[230]

The method of clerical association, however, was by no means universally embraced. Conservatism among the clergy was a widespread obstacle to association. Many, like the clergy on the Isle of Wight, were reportedly "afraid of being accused of novelty, not hearing any precedents of such meetings."[231] In Lincolnshire, "malicious reports against the lawfulness of such assemblies" hindered association.[232] Interestingly, some clergy resented what they took to be the imposition of the model of the Bedfordshire clerical society on the rest of the provincial clergy, complaining that "Bedford and Buckinghamshire clergy had nothing to do to prescribe [to] the rest of their brethren."[233] Clergy around the neighborhood of Malden in Surrey protested that "such meetings are against the law," believing the statutes currently in force "sufficient for the reformation of manners."[234] Moreover, many clergy still harbored an instinctive hostility toward the very principles of voluntary association, reinforced by decades of antipathy toward conventicles. The clergy at Kent, reported one correspondent, charged the SPCK with "reviving of Presbyterian classes encouraging fanaticism."[235] Similarly, the Derbyshire clergy were confident that "friends of the Church would not subscribe to Scottish methods."[236] There remained a pervasive sense that any initiative on the part of the clergy without the leave of their diocesan was simply antipathetic to the constitution of the Church of England.[237]

Beyond the natural conservatism of the Anglican lower clergy was an emergent sense among some churchmen that such methods of voluntary association and collaboration with the laity were deleterious to the independence of the Church of England. At the height of the convocation controversy, the measures recommended by Archbishop Tenison and the SPCK fell well short of the much-desired restoration of synodical authority and discipline. Thus, it is perhaps not surprising that in Kent, clergymen protested the clerical associations as "an usurpation on the rights of the convocation."[238] In Glamorganshire, the campaign was dismissed as little more than "a contrivance to render a convocation useless."[239] In Exeter, Dr. John Osmond agreed to correspond with the SPCK as a "private person" but was dubious of the prospect of anything more formal among the clergy "unless the convocation countenance the matter."[240] Sir George Wheler, an early member of the SPCK, devised a scheme to better reconcile the proliferating clerical conferences with the "primitive" ecclesiology of the Church of England. He proposed the formation of an elaborate hierarchy of ecclesial societies, an "apostolic presbyterion," which "would tend to the restoring of the decayed discipline of the Church, and to the encouragement of virtue [and] holiness."[241] Like Wheler's earlier proposal for a "Protestant monastery," such a scheme goes some lengths to illustrate, on the one hand, the appeal of new forms of religious organization and, on the other, the concern to prevent such forms from transgressing the bounds of ecclesiological orthodoxy.

Conclusion

Archbishop Thomas Tenison's circular letter of April 1699 represented an attempt to contain the forces of national reformation within the existing architecture of the Church of England. Societies of neighboring parish clergy, it was hoped, would serve as the vanguard of the reformation of manners, catechetical instruction, and distribution of pious tracts.[242] Ironically enough, the mobilization of such efforts fell to the nascent SPCK, a para-ecclesial body of laity and clergy with no official standing in the established church whatsoever. Provincial bishops and clergy often did not even know the names of the members of the society with whom they were invited to correspond, and many refused the correspondence on these grounds alone, thinking it "unreasonable to engage with men in the clouds."[243] Yet, the "men in the clouds," the religious reformers, activists, and projectors, it seems, were becoming increasingly indispensable to the

Anglican revival. On the margins of the established church, something like an Anglican voluntary sector seemed to be coalescing. And within a decade, the SPCK, though still but "a society of private gentlemen," would stand at the center of a vast network that connected the Anglican hierarchy and parishes to a host of other societies, projects, and corporations in England, Europe, and the empire.[244]

The insinuation of the SPCK into the constitution of the Church of England effectively instituted the revivalist ferment that characterized the final decade of the seventeenth century. No sooner had the society proposed correspondence with the provincial clergy than it was receiving from them myriad proposals for religious reform touching upon everything from poor relief to church music to the decay of Oriental learning. Indeed, the SPCK explicitly decided to forego incorporation by the crown in order to accommodate precisely this kind of "mission creep." For, "by having no charter," their eighteenth-century secretary Henry Newman would explain, the society could take on a variety of programs to "extend their good offices to all parts of the world."[245] The SPCK effectively imported the entrepreneurialism and innovation of the "age of projects" into the Church of England. The eighteenth century would expose this as a source of both dynamism and instability.

CHAPTER 3

The Antinomies of the Society for Promoting Christian Knowledge, 1699–1720

The Society for Promoting Christian Knowledge (SPCK) was something of a free radical within the body of the eighteenth-century Church of England, bonding with preexistent religious forms and catalyzing new modes of Anglican revivalism. As discussed in Chapter 2, the society emerged from a climate characterized at once by the persistence of Anglican revivalism and the vogue for organizational experimentation and innovation that affected the established church no less than Protestant Nonconformity. While the latter had long been habituated by ecclesiology and political proscription to the virtues of religious voluntarism, the Church of England was, on the whole, less acclimated to it. The established church spent much of the decade rather apprehensively entertaining and engaging in new forms of religious organization answerable to the agenda of national reformation, yet conformable to the ecclesiastical constitution. The SPCK was but one of these forms and plainly benefited from its initial association with causes that had already received the blessing of the hierarchy, namely, Thomas Bray's parochial libraries movement at home and abroad and the clerical societies recommended by Archbishop Tenison. The SPCK was happy enough to claim the mantle of "the reformation of manners," though it took pains quickly to distinguish itself from the controversial societies that bore the name.[1] Indeed, the society seemed to represent not simply the institutionalization of the variety of religious and philanthropic forms that had emerged in the later seventeenth century, but also of the Anglican ferment that had produced them.[2] As such, the SPCK during its first three decades operated at something of a conceptual surplus, proposing and pursuing the designs that opportunity and imagination afforded, though they had formed no part of its original programming. This improvisational quality, along with its peculiar status as an unincorporated entity possessed of the favor but not the official mandate of episcopal superiors, lent the SPCK an extraordinary dynamism in its early years and made it compatible with a wide variety of programs for Anglican renewal. However, such comprehension and flexibility also bred contradictions that over time decisively altered the ideological character of the society.

The SPCK was obviously an instrument of Anglican renewal, but its divergent programming reveals the somewhat limited consensus on what such renewal might have entailed. It was heir to the diversely articulated spirit of revivalism that had informed much of Anglican churchmanship throughout the final two decades of the seventeenth century; but despite its outsized deference to the episcopal hierarchy, the lower clerical initiative and lay collaboration that animated much of its programs were somewhat out of keeping with its Restoration bequest.[3] Indeed, the early SPCK never really sat comfortably within the traditional demarcations of the territorial church or the ecclesiastical constitution. And it is perhaps not surprising that the early society continuously operated amidst the countervailing pull of traditionalism and innovation.

The SPCK routinely presented itself primarily as a resource for the parish clergy, an aid to fulfilling the pastoral obligations outlined by the bishops in numerous letters throughout the 1690s: the reformation of manners, catechetical instruction, and positive engagement with those outside the communion of the established church.[4] To these ends, it recommended fairly newfangled instruments such as clerical associations, charity schools, theological lending libraries, and the distribution of works of practical piety and popular apologetics. Naturally, this beneficent and supplemental role predominated in the early society's promotional literature, which betrayed a persistent anxiety to assure skeptics of its legitimacy. But the society was never content simply to reaffirm the Anglicanism of the parish. It made early and enduring commitments to engaging those souls that tended to fall outside the remit of the territorial Church of

England. Even leaving aside the American concerns of Thomas Bray's commissarial office, the SPCK consistently sought to address mobile and nonparochial sectors of the population such as sailors, soldiers, merchants, and prisoners. Perhaps even more ambitiously, it also soon became the vanguard of ecumenical engagement throughout the British Isles and continental Europe. During the reign of Queen Anne, leading members spoke openly of the society's engagement on behalf of the so-called Protestant interest—a loaded term generally favored by Whigs and low churchmen during this period, for whom it covered the range of positions presumed necessary for preserving the Revolution settlement and the Protestant constitution, including a geopolitical commitment to the Grand Alliance against Bourbon France; fidelity to the Protestant succession of the House of Hanover; and a posture of reconciliation with the Protestant churches at home and abroad.[5] Such policies, it must be remembered, were by no means universally embraced across the political and ecclesiastical spectrum in early-eighteenth-century England. Thus, it is well enough to say, as Craig Rose does, that the SPCK was founded "to reassert the spiritual and political primacy of the Church of England in the nation."[6] But there was, it must be emphasized, precious little consensus over what such primacy entailed or which policies best conduced to its maintenance. The society very plainly inherited the very contradictions—Anglican or Protestant, narrowly confessional or broadly ecumenical, traditionalist or modernizing, dynastic legitimism or the Protestant succession—that had haunted the Anglican revival since the reign of James II.

Perhaps this explains why it has proved so notoriously difficult for historians to assess the ideological commitments of the SPCK during its earliest decades. Indeed, the polarization of historical opinion on the politics of the society is nothing short of remarkable. The SPCK has been alternately associated with both high- and low-church Anglicanism, Whiggery and Toryism. W. K. Lowther Clarke, for instance, asserts that "the tone of SPCK Churchmanship had from the first been set by [the deprived bishop of Bath and Wells Thomas] Ken and [Robert] Nelson, the Nonjurors."[7] T. C. Curtis and William Speck considered the SPCK the province of "high churchmen and Tories, even Jacobites."[8] Tina Isaacs associated the society with "High Church Tories."[9] Andrew Porter deemed the early SPCK "a small group of high church Anglican reformers."[10] Similarly, Donald Gray, in a biographical sketch of Thomas Manningham, bishop of Chichester, cites membership in the SPCK as "further evidence of his high-church sympathies."[11] Other historians discern a rather different ideological complexion. The broader postrevolutionary reformation movement, of which the SPCK was but one component, has long been associated with Whiggery and "Revolution politics."[12] Garnet Portus tended to view the manifold societies operating under the rubric of national reformation as "on the side of the Whig party in their outlook."[13] Similarly, Gareth Bennett deems almost the entire wave of religious voluntarism during this period as something of a low-church alternative to the strident clericalism of the high-church movement.[14] John Gascoigne believed the SPCK to be "closely associated with the latitudinarians."[15] In considering the ideological commitments of the SPCK, historians have tended to resemble the blind men and the elephant of the old fable, extrapolating the contours of the whole from any recognizable aspect or figure. Reproduced through citations and passing references in the wider historiography of the period, such misconceptions accrue into outright distortions.

A handful of historians, however, have added some welcome nuance to the scholarship on the early SPCK. Mary Gladwys Jones recognized that the early membership of the society embodied "different schools of thought within the Church, the latitudinarian, non-juring and High Church parties." But she unhelpfully subsumes these differences in a common "puritanism," defined neither doctrinally nor ecclesiologically, but simply as "the expression of an austere and devout religious temper."[16] Eamon Duffy has gone further, arguing that the SPCK was "the continuation of a long-term preoccupation with the conversion of the nation," historically rooted in a tradition of godliness common to both Anglicanism and Dissent. Only the "political environment," Duffy somewhat vaguely suggests, dictated an agenda of Anglican hegemony rather than one of Protestant reconciliation.[17] David Hayton explains the ideological diversity of the SPCK in political terms, underscoring the preponderance of "country interest" politicians among its ranks, whose vigorous sense of civic virtue naturally aligned with the imperatives of moral reform.[18] Daniel Brunner and Jeremy Gregory have also offered useful assessments of the ideological pluralism of the early society.[19]

The work of Craig Rose, however, has most directly assailed the myth of ideological homogeneity in the early SPCK. According to Rose, the SPCK was devoted to the maintenance of Anglican hegemony in England, a cause that appealed to a "wide spectrum of opinion within the Church of England." Studying the remarkable variety of political and ideological commitments of the early members of the society, Rose discerns what he calls "the bipartisan nature of the SPCK," exemplified in its enduring (and, in his estimation, mostly successful) commitment "to remain aloof from the political strife of the Augustan age."[20]

Rose is to be heartily commended for thoughtfully addressing the antinomies of the SPCK. The society was by no means ideologically monolithic in either its origins or its ideals. However, Rose is entirely too sanguine concerning the enduringly "non-partisan stance of the SPCK in an intensely partisan era."[21] Over the course of the first two decades of the eighteenth century, the SPCK, an organization founded by Whigs and Tories, high and low churchmen, evolved into a bastion of "church Whiggery," possessed of a firm commitment to the Hanoverian succession.[22] Rose systematically ignores or misinterprets the numerous moments of ideological and ecclesiological conflict that occurred in the society during this period.[23] And in doing so, he overlooks the SPCK's unmistakable drift toward Whiggery. Many of the Tory and high-church members Rose cites as evidence of the nonpartisan nature of the early society had by the final years of the reign of Queen Anne significantly reduced their involvement or withdrawn altogether.[24] Rose is correct to disclaim any ab ovo commitment on the part of the SPCK to a particular political or ecclesiastical party, but his insistence on successfully sustained nonpartisanship during the first two decades of the eighteenth century cannot account for the eventuality of just such a commitment.

Over the course of the early eighteenth century, the SPCK, an organization founded and initially joined by a politically and ideologically heterogeneous assortment of churchmen, became increasingly identified with church Whiggery, Hanoverianism, and the so-called Protestant interest. As such, this preeminent engine of Anglican renewal seemed to possess diminishing appeal to many of those who identified with the "church party" of Tory Anglicans. This realignment must be considered in light of two factors. First, the growing antipathy of Tory and high-church Anglicans to reformed Protestantism during the reign of Queen Anne rendered the ecumenical engagements of the SPCK increasingly unpalatable. Second, the burgeoning sacerdotalism of high-church Anglicanism in this period diminished the appeal of a voluntary association seemingly animated by the combined efforts of an activist laity and a court episcopate. These factors may serve to account for the subtle but unmistakable high-church disenchantment with the SPCK during the first two decades of the eighteenth century. More broadly, they help illuminate the polarization of the Anglican revival into opposing programs of religious renewal. This chapter and the following two will address this process.

An Atlas of English Benevolence

During an era of intensifying political and religious polarization, the ideological diversity at the heart of the early SPCK was remarkable indeed. Among the society's five founders were two Tories: the Glamorganshire gentleman and industrialist Sir Humphrey Mackworth, who represented Cardiganshire and Totnes in the parliaments of Queen Anne, and the peer Francis North, Lord Guilford, who served on the Privy Council and the Board of Trade during the Tory ascendancy of Anne's last years.[25] Another founder, the west countryman Maynard Colchester, served from 1701 to 1708 as a Whig MP for Gloucestershire of a markedly "country persuasion."[26] The Irish-born judge and barrister John Hooke, whose Lincoln's Inn residence hosted the society's earliest meetings, had served as a justice in north Wales and deputy justice of Chester. He denied political affiliation but owed his November 1700 promotion to sergeant-at-law to the patronage of the Tories Lord Guilford and Sir Nathan Wright.[27] Hooke did, however, find himself on the opposite side of the debate over the occasional conformity bills from high-church society members Humphrey Mackworth and Philip Stubbs, who wrote vociferously in support of the measures.[28] The lone clergymen among the founders, Thomas Bray, was both an ardent Hanoverian and a close associate of deprived clergymen such as John Kettlewell and Digby Bull. He owed his Warwickshire rectory of Over Whitacre to the pious but disaffected nobleman William, Lord Digby, a patron of the nonjurors. In 1706, he was presented to the London living of St. Botolph's, Aldgate, by the Lincoln's Inn barrister Samuel Brewster, an early SPCK member of Jacobite sympathies.[29]

The first wave of new members was equally diverse. The talented linguist and courtier John Chamberlayne, a self-described "unchangeable Whig," was elected to the society in its second month and served as its first secretary.[30] The Pembrokeshire Whig MP Sir John Philipps of Picton Castle was no doubt well known to the founders before his election on account of his tireless legislative efforts against blasphemy and profaneness.[31] The society was joined by several Lincoln's Inn barristers: John Comyns, who would serve as Tory MP for Maldon for much of the first quarter of the century; and two others of notable high-church piety and nonjuring sympathies, the aforementioned Samuel Brewster and William Melmoth, who scrupled at the oaths to William and Mary and idealized the deprived John Kettlewell in his 1711 devotional classic *The Great Importance of a Religious Life Consider'd*.[32] Sir Edmund Turnor, Tory MP for Orford, was elected to the society in May 1699.[33] The first additional clerics proposed were two London low churchmen, the devotional writer and propagandist for the reformation of manners movement Josiah Woodward, minister of Poplar, and Henry Shute, a former chaplain in William's army and lecturer at Whitechapel.[34] In June 1699, the nonjuring gentleman Robert Nelson, a man his contemporaries described as "addicted to piety," was elected to the society.[35] Nelson's incredible affinities and connections were redolent of the markedly less fractious prerevolutionary Church of England. The pupil of the eminent moral theologian George Bull, bishop of St. David's, and the disciple and executor of Kettlewell, Nelson nevertheless remained close with the stalwarts of London Anglicanism, Archbishop John Tillotson and the physician-clergyman John Mapletoft, the long-serving vicar of St. Lawrence Jewry.[36] He was intimate with nonjuring and Jacobite communities in London and Shottesbrooke, though his long service in the great Anglican societies and the Royal Society ensured his close affiliation with the leading lights of church Whiggery and English natural philosophy. Like his friend Thomas Bray, his somewhat contradictory churchmanship embodied the antinomies of the Anglican revival.[37]

Despite the prominent involvement of numerous Tory MPs and gentlemen, clerical subscription to the early SPCK tended to come predominantly from the ranks of Williamite clergy and low churchmen. The bishops invited to join were prelates of the London ascendancy: Edward Fowler, bishop of Gloucester; John Williams, bishop of Chichester; Nicholas Stratford, bishop of Chester; Richard Kidder, bishop of Bath and Wells; and Gilbert Burnet, bishop of Salisbury. On the whole, the Caroline bishops (with the notable exceptions of Bishops Compton and Lloyd) were somewhat less amenable to the society's designs. Jonathan Trelawny of Exeter was reportedly "utterly averse thereto," and the clergy of Durham "could not obtain one farthing" from their diocesan Nathaniel Crewe for society programs.[38] By way of contrast, Simon Patrick, bishop of Ely, was informed of the society's work in May 1700 and reportedly "thanked God for it" and promised "to give it all the countenance he could."[39] Clerical correspondents to the society were naturally drawn from across the political and ideological spectrum. However, among the subscribing clerical members residing in London, low churchmen predominated.[40] Indeed, early clerical members such as White Kennett, curate of St. Botolph's, Aldgate; Richard Willis, dean of Lincoln; William Hayley, dean of Chichester; John Evans, rector of Llanaelhaiarn, Carnarvonshire; Thomas Frank, archdeacon of Bedford; and the bishop of Worcester's son and namesake William Lloyd, rector of Fladbury, were all prominent members of the low-church opposition in the lower house of convocation during the reign of Queen Anne.[41] Their involvement in the society, it must be noted, did not discourage the enlistment of Tory churchmen such as Thomas Manningham, rector of St. Andrew's, Holborn, or Sir George Wheler, the disciple of the leading nonjuror George Hickes and a man reputedly sympathetic to his mentor's cause.[42]

The institutional penetration of the early society was as impressive as its remarkable political and ideological diversity. Its membership embodied a vast network of social and philanthropic organizations throughout the kingdom. Indeed, the SPCK comprised a virtual map of the social and institutional life of postrevolutionary England. Given its base in London and its appeal to the clergy, significant overlap with the governors and fellows of Sion College, the guild of London clergymen, is perhaps not surprising. Society members John Mapletoft, White Kennett, Philip Stubbs, Thomas Lynford, and Lilly Butler all served as governors of Sion College in the first two decades of the eighteenth century. The college subscription lists reveal even more extensive engagement by SPCK members.[43] The same was true of the Sons of the Clergy, the charity for the families of Anglican ministers, which had served as something of a model for the society in its early years.[44] Active SPCK members Sir John Philipps, Josiah Woodward, Arthur Bedford, Thomas Manningham, and Frederick Slare, among others, served as governors of the corporation.[45] The society monitored local charitable endeavors for the relief of clergymen's families and was consulted during attempts to incorporate local branches of the Sons of the Clergy in Cheshire in 1700.[46] Kennett harbored hopes that extant corporate Anglican philanthropies might be repurposed to address the glaring problem of clerical poverty—for instance, that the Sons of the Clergy might obtain a new charter, "with powers enlarged for the taking and disposing of all charitable gifts and legacies, that should be assigned for the help and benefit of the poorer vicars and curates." He even suggested that the newly formed Society for the Propagation of the Gospel in Foreign Parts (SPG) had hopes of "looking at home as soon as those more urgent occasions were served abroad."[47] Accordingly, when in 1704 Queen Anne indicated her desire to apply the entirety of her revenue from the first fruits and tenths to supplement the livings of the poorer clergy, she established a corporation fashioned after the other chartered entities of social provision of that era.[48] Like its sibling organizations, the corporation of the governors of Queen Anne's Bounty was empowered not merely to apply state revenues to redress clerical poverty, but also to solicit and distribute charitable contributions from the public.[49] Moreover, the appointment of John Chamberlayne, successively secretary to the SPCK and the SPG, as secretary to Queen Anne's Bounty cemented the latter's connections with the Anglican philanthropic establishment, as did the appointment as treasurer of stalwart SPCK member Edward Tenison, a cousin of the archbishop of Canterbury, who had recommended him for the post.[50] Queen Anne's Bounty was frequently cited alongside the other institutions of the Anglican revival; it was, as William Dawes put it in a 1709 sermon, "all of a piece with those other good works which we have of late happily been carrying on here at home."[51]

The SPCK was similarly well integrated into the medical establishment in London and Westminster, numbering among its activist core numerous prominent physicians such the German-born Frederick Slare, an eminent member of the Royal College of Physicians; Gideon Harvey, physician to the Tower of London; and John Locke's friend John Mapletoft, who left his Gresham College professorship of physic to seek ordination in the Church of England, eventually succeeding Benjamin Whichcote as vicar of St. Lawrence Jewry.[52] Society clergy reinforced these connections through various hospital chaplaincies. Philip Stubbs served as the first chaplain of the newly founded Greenwich Hospital for disabled seamen.[53] Josiah Woodward ministered to the decayed and disabled merchants in the East India Company hospital in Poplar.[54] Another core member, the London clergyman Richard Mayo, described as "the most constant attender of all their meetings," long served as chaplain to St. Thomas Hospital in Southwark.[55]

Born of the ferment of the final decade of the seventeenth century, the SPCK took pains to align with the various new forms of religious association. Most commonly noted was its connection to the reformation of manners movement in London and elsewhere.[56] Early on, Thomas Bray was "conversant with some of those excellent persons concerned in the reformation of manners."[57] Another one of the society's founders, Maynard Colchester, had been instrumental in founding the first reformation society in the capital. His colleague in that endeavor, the Irish baronet Sir Richard Bulkeley, was among the earliest recruits of the society, for which he became lay correspondent in Dublin in June 1700.[58] The first bishop proposed to the SPCK, Edward Fowler of Gloucester, had penned a well-known defense of the reformation societies in 1692.[59] The society's early correspondents for Bristol included Arthur Bedford, vicar of Temple parish, the merchant Sir John Duddlestone, and the Whig MP Robert Yate, all of whom had been leading figures in the Bristol society for the reformation of manners.[60] The SPCK numbered among its ranks the reforming Whig magistrates Whitelocke Bulstrode, the Middlesex justice whose zealous charges from the bench bristled with antipathy to profaneness and vice,[61] and John Disney, the Lincolnshire justice whose several compendia of laws against immorality were produced with significant assistance from society members.[62] In May 1700, the society resolved to maintain "a good correspondence" with both the societies for the reformation of manners and the religious societies.[63]

The SPCK tried to take a more active role in the management of the religious societies. On 25 January 1700, the society was informed "that there are several religious societies that want and desire advice," an extraordinary request to an organization that still claimed only a handful of lower clergymen among its residing members.[64] The next month, the Bedfordshire correspondent Thomas Frank proposed that the corresponding clergy endeavor to "undertake the management of such religious societies that do meet in their parishes" as a means to reset the societies on a strictly parochial footing and to subject them more closely to the parish church. By this method, he reasoned, "the clergy may prevent strangers meddling with their charge."[65] And, it went without saying, such parochial societies might more easily be kept free of the interdenominational contamination common to the reformation societies. The SPCK committee established that year to inspect the proceedings of the religious societies further recommended that all members of the latter assist "in giving information of any notorious immorality."[66] In its early years, the society vigorously promoted and defended the religious societies in the teeth of opposition from critics. Society clergy "inspected the several orders of the religious societies, in order to answer the objections raised against them" and circulated promotional literature such as Samuel Wesley's "Letter Concerning Religious Societies" and Josiah Woodward's *Account of the Rise and Progress of the Religious Societies in the City of London*.[67] By 1705, it was reported that the religious societies in

London had contributed roughly £100 of the SPCK's operating budget of approximately £800.[68]

The SPCK was even more intimately involved with the entities founded to carry out the various branches of Thomas Bray's program of Anglican renewal. It concerned itself with the oversight of Bray's scheme for the promotion of parochial libraries, until a separate organization, the Trustees for Erecting Parochial Libraries and Promoting Other Charitable Designs, was founded in 1705. Overlap with the SPCK was extensive, and the Massachusetts-born layman Henry Newman served as secretary to both organizations after 1708.[69] Predictably, the two societies were often taken as a single entity.[70] The SPCK also closely monitored and encouraged the founding of catechetical schools for poor children throughout the capital and the kingdom. As numerous historians have noted, the SPCK itself did not establish charity schools; its role in the movement was largely advisory and promotional. But it zealously kept tabs on independent efforts throughout the country; distributed organizational, promotional, and instructional materials; and maintained a close working relationship with the Society of Trustees for Charity Schools in London, a body drawn from the various school trustees throughout the metropolis.[71] The SPCK's closest and most well-known sibling was, of course, the incorporated SPG.[72] The interpenetration of the SPG and SPCK in terms of personnel, methods, and ideals is so well established as to not require further elaboration here.

The SPCK was thus an atlas of English benevolence. From its earliest years, its meetings and prodigious correspondence connected representatives of a wide spectrum of social and religious initiatives—first in England, and then eventually throughout Britain, continental Europe, and the world. On 18 April 1700, society members began debating whether to seek incorporation under the terms of the recently passed Act for the Encouragement of Charitable Gifts and Dispositions. Looking to the chartered Sons of the Clergy, SPCK members argued that incorporation would confer social and political legitimacy and legal standing in court; would permit the society corporately to acquire and hold lands and monies in mortmain; and would grant the society an institutional permanence above the mutable piety of the public-spirited. With the incorporation of the sibling SPG under the Great Seal in June 1701, the plan for an incorporated SPCK was "wholly laid aside by the society."[73] Obviously, the effect of incorporation is purely a matter for speculation, but it is unlikely that a society whose remit was fixed by royal charter would have been nearly as open to the variegated concerns and connections of its members and correspondents in the capital, the provinces, and abroad. It is, at the very least, worth noting that neither of its incorporated siblings, the Sons of the Clergy or the SPG, evinced anything like the "mission creep" that characterized the SPCK during the first half of the eighteenth century. The society resolved early on to "always decline the intermeddling with all matters which are foreign to their religious designs," but there was wide latitude within the rubric of "religious designs."[74] The SPCK was, as the antiquarian Humphrey Wanley described it upon being nominated as its first clerk in 1700, simply "a religious society": "The members are lords temporal and spiritual, knights, eminent clergymen and gentlemen. These by their joint contributions in money and their counsels make it their business to stop the current of debauchery and profaneness and promote the salvation of men's souls and that by several prudent methods; some whereof are the printing good books, and founding charity schools, &c."[75] From its inception, the SPCK was defined more by its lofty ideals than by any fixity in its methods or personnel. Such an orientation could not but leave the society peculiarly exposed to the vicissitudes of ecclesiastical and civil politics.

The Reinforcement of Parish Anglicanism

The SPCK harbored aspirations of both conservatism and innovation. In the first instance, it conceived of itself as a resource for the parish clergy of the established church. The society's domestic agenda was at this level deeply conservative, largely designed to reinforce the boundaries of the parish and strengthen the hand of the clergy against the traditional enemies of the Church of England—rival denominations and the irreligious. After all, the society informed its correspondents in early 1700, "the faithful discharge of all parts of the ministerial care is the ordinary means that God has enjoined for the preserving and propagating of Christianity, and regulating the lives of those people who profess it." To supplement the clergy's primary pastoral obligations, the society recommended the formation of clerical conferences among local clergymen, the erection of schools for poor children, and the distribution of pious tracts among parishioners.[76] There was some hope that society programming in the parishes or lobbying in the metropolis might help to curb the toleration.[77] But the society's methods, even at their most aggressive, were decidedly noncoercive. While its pastoral and parochial ideals were redolent of the revivalist Anglicanism of the late Restoration, its means were indisputably postrevolutionary.

Indeed, the SPCK did more than merely recall the devotional ardor of the Anglican revival; it quite literally reproduced many of its most popular expressions. Late Restoration Anglicanism was extraordinarily well represented among the devotional tracts distributed by the society during its first two decades. Specifically, SPCK literature broadly renewed the seventeenth-century call to holy living that had become the hallmark of Restoration anti-Calvinism. For instance, John Rawlet's immensely popular *The Christian Monitor* (1686), "a persuasive to an holy and religious life," was undoubtedly among the most recommended in the society's tracts.[78] Rawlet's grave admonition, "be not so weak as to think you may be saved by a good belief alone," chimed with the practical anti-Calvinist moralism of his friends Richard Baxter, John Tillotson, and Thomas Bray.[79] Such literature seemed to tap a vein of anti-Calvinist "holy living" theology that informed both the fervent sacramentalism and the latitudinarian moralism that comprised Restoration divinity. With the whole of English Protestant devotional literature available for republication and distribution, the SPCK unreservedly gravitated toward the writings of the early 1680s.[80] To adapt a phrase from Heiko Oberman, the society sought to reap the harvest of Restoration theology. As a result, its book selections signally failed to align with the divisions of postrevolutionary ecclesiastical partisanship.

The SPCK had to overcome the sharp divisions created by the Revolution of 1688–1689. Society literary offerings in the early eighteenth century included late Restoration devotional works by the likes of Tillotson, Patrick, Beveridge, Thomas Comber, Kettlewell, Rawlet, and William Allen, men who now represented vastly different strains of churchmanship in an increasingly factious church. Such works were evocative not of a lost godliness associated with Puritanism, as Eamon Duffy suggests, but rather of the post-Puritan "devotional revolution" occurring within late Restoration Anglicanism, the last great and more or less concerted effort to incorporate the populace of England fully into the life and offices of the established church.[81] Collectively, they bespoke a unity of purpose that the Revolution seemed to have fractured.

The parish clergy clamored for a renewal of such efforts. "Correction for practical atheism is the general cry," the Dorsetshire minster Thomas Curgenven informed the society in 1700, "the Church wanting no champions for doctrine and instruction."[82] Restoration classics of sacramental piety, such as Beveridge's

Sermon Concerning the Excellency and Usefulness of the Common Prayer (1682) and Tillotson's *Persuasive to a Frequent Communion* (1683), possessed the additional value of channeling the reformation of manners directly into the public offices of the Church of England.[83] In 1701, an elated Hugh Todd in Penrith reported thousands of books "chiefly related to the H[oly] Sacrament" distributed throughout the diocese of Carlisle; "almost every one of them has brought a communicant to Church more than usual," and with them, a "visible reformation of manners everywhere."[84]

The charity schools promoted by the SPCK were also intended to reinforce the bonds of national communion. By the beginning of the third decade of the eighteenth century, the SPCK reported the founding of more than thirteen hundred schools, educating roughly twenty-three thousand students in reading, writing, arithmetic, and catechetical lessons.[85] Craig Rose has convincingly overturned the prevailing historiographical interpretation of the charity schools as essentially secular institutions of social discipline. On the contrary, they were instruments of Anglican confessionalization designed primarily to secure the lower orders of society in the communion of the established church.[86] The chief design of the charity schools, according to the rules circulated by the SPCK in its annual *Accounts*, was "the education of poor children in the knowledge and practice of the Christian religion, as professed and taught in the Church of England." As such, the society insisted that schoolmasters be not only members of the Church of England, but frequenters of the holy communion, serving with the approval of the parish minister and the license of the bishop. The children were to be instructed in the church catechism and brought to services twice every Sunday and holiday. Schoolmasters were to notify the parish minister as soon as a sufficient number of students were ready to be catechized in the church.[87] White Kennett's popular instructional manual *The Christian Scholar* even hoped that such schools would lessen "the irreverence and disrespect shown to the ministers of God," to which anticlericalism he attributed a good deal of the corruption and debauchery of the age. Anything that served to reinforce the bonds of obligation between parishioner and priest, he wrote, "will help to reclaim this city, and in time reform this nation."[88] The service to the security of the Church of England was a common theme of both the instructional and promotional literature of the charity schools. The charity schools, William Wake, bishop of Lincoln, told the assembled trustees, promote unity in the church communion "by bringing up our children from the beginning in the same doctrine and worship; and love of our established Church."[89] Throughout the promotional literature for the schools, the utilitarian aims of education, discipline, and training were commonly subsumed into the broader objectives of Anglican acculturation.[90]

The SPCK also worked to fortify parish Anglicanism against sectarian rivals. Generally speaking, the society formulated no policy with respect to moderate Nonconformists. Early correspondents in the provinces initiated local "endeavors to reconcile the dissenters," but these were hardly countenanced by the society.[91] Although occasionally requested, pamphlets against Nonconformity or schism did not comprise any substantial part of society literature.[92] The society's third secretary, Henry Newman, an American of Puritan stock, simply recommended "outshining the Dissenters in acts of piety and virtue" as "the most effectual means for weakening their interest."[93]

The society's vehement opposition to Quakerism, however, belied its generally nonconfrontational stance with respect to Protestant Nonconformity. The first item on the agenda of the SPCK's first meeting was a consideration of the work of the combustible Scottish Quaker apostate and provocateur George Keith "towards the instruction and conversion of Quakers."[94] Two days later, the nascent society resolved to procure some official recognition for Keith's anti-Quaker mission and to distribute his tracts "up and down the kingdom."[95] In May 1699, the society agreed to sponsor Keith's missionary efforts against Quakers throughout England. That month, Keith set out with 250 pamphlets to harass Quakers into conformity at the society's expense.[96] He would continue to evangelize throughout England over the next two years. The correspondents generally cheered his mission, hailing his visits and then complaining vociferously that the work came to no good end "because the clergy do not pursue the victory in his absence."[97] Though correspondents wished that Archbishop Tenison would formulate a coherent program against the Society of Friends, the SPCK had little to offer beyond the distribution of literature. Keith's broadside *A Serious Call to Quakers* was in great demand among the corresponding members.[98] In early 1702, the society conferred with another anti-Quaker activist, Francis Bugg. Bugg was granted £26 10s in credit for the purchase and distribution of books, and the society agreed to purchase one hundred copies of his tract *The pilgrim's progress, from Quakerism to Christianity*.[99] Works by Keith and Bugg, alongside the anti-Quaker tract *The snake in the grass* by the Irish nonjuror Charles Leslie, soon became mainstays in the canon of the early SPCK. In 1702, Keith was dispatched to New England to continue his work of reclaiming Quakers under the authority of the newly formed SPG.[100]

The society's efforts against domestic Catholicism were similarly diffuse. Colin Haydon's estimation of the society as "an official spearhead in the drive against Catholicism in England" seems considerably overstated.[101] The SPCK acted as little more than a monitor of Catholic activity in England. Initiative lay with the local correspondents, and the society typically responded to reports of Catholic proselytizing or conversions with shipments of anti-Catholic literature.[102] Anti-Catholicism loomed large in the charity school literature, which hailed each school as a "fortress and frontier garrison against popery," but such gestures were more likely imbricated in the rhetoric of Anglican revival than targeted at actual communities.[103] The society's active anti-Catholic programming tended to ebb and flow with national anxieties stoked by dynastic or geopolitical crises.[104] Though the religious indulgence did not apply to Roman Catholics, SPCK efforts against popery in England did not differ markedly from those against Quakerism. The society could only supplement the endeavors of local clergy with pious works and hearty encouragement.

The early SPCK thus assumed an overtly conservative posture, even as it operated amidst a world of legalized (and de facto) religious pluralism. Its initial programming was not, like seventeenth-century Puritanism or eighteenth-century Methodism, corrosive of parish religion. On the contrary, the society's most well-publicized endeavors such as book distribution and charity schools served to reinforce the parochial communion of the Church of England. Despite its substantially lay character and its anomalous status within the ecclesiastical constitution, the SPCK disclaimed any interest in innovation or encroachment upon the clerical cure of souls. Initiative in much of its programming was ideally to remain with the minister and the local authorities, with the society consigned to a supplemental and promotional role. But the SPCK found it exceedingly difficult to confine its interests to parish Anglicanism. After all, it had been founded in accord with the capacious imperial vision of Thomas Bray, which was almost immediately augmented by the influx of members from the maritime, military, and mercantile sectors. The SPCK retained the imprint of their concerns long after the SPG was chartered as a separate entity with responsibility for "plantations, colonies and factories" abroad.[105] Indeed, the SPCK appealed to many who saw it not as reinforcement of the territorial church, but precisely as a vehicle for overcoming the limits of Anglican territoriality. In the SPCK, many Anglicans discerned a means of adapting the established church to a dynamic and increasingly global English society.

Beyond the Parish

The SPCK took an early and abiding interest in populations that fell outside the traditional demarcations of parish life.[106] Outreach to displaced sectors such as seamen, soldiers, merchants, captives, and prisoners required a good deal more creativity than the revivifying of parochial communion, which naturally operated within an extant structure of religious practice and ecclesiastical authority. Nonparochial populations, however, lived and worked in the interstices of the territorial Church of England, the jurisdictional divisions of which offered little by way of accommodation for mobile sectors. The SPCK (and later the SPG) endeavored to engage the acephelous English chaplainry that ministered to such populations. In doing so, the society found itself operating in the liminal ecclesiastical space between the hierarchies of the insular church and the array of deracinating military, naval, commercial, and penal institutions in which growing numbers of Englishmen subsisted. Alongside its commitment to the reinforcement of traditional parochial religion, the SPCK was forced to engage in the work of ecclesiastical modernization.

Almost immediately after its founding, the SPCK secured connections with the maritime sector.[107] Thomas Bray believed that his parochial libraries would be of particular use in English seaports, where missionaries and chaplains often tarried on account of weather or war. Such libraries, Bray proposed, would serve as little outposts of the established church to the maritime and merchant communities.[108] In 1701, Bray proposed the establishment of lending libraries for the entire fleet, presumably consisting of pious books for the use of both seamen and chaplains.[109] Soon after its founding, the SPCK began to attract other clergymen affiliated with maritime communities. In December 1700, the society named the naval chaplain Patrick Gordon, author of the popular geography textbook *Geography anatomiz'd*, "correspondent for the Navy." Gordon immediately submitted his "Proposals for Christian Instruction of Seamen" for the consideration of the society, though they were deemed to be impractical.[110] Soon after, Thomas Shewell, naval chaplain and rector of the Thameside parish of Gravesend, became a correspondent, pledging "to disperse the books and papers of the Society amongst the seamen." From aboard the *Barfleur* at Spithead, a ninety-gun ship of the line in the Channel fleet commanded by Sir Cloudesley Shovell, Shewell urged the SPCK to lobby for the appointment of a chaplain general for the entire fleet.[111] The Admiralty obliged by empowering the clergyman William Hodges "to inspect and oversee the lives and behaviors of the rest of the chaplains of the ships." In August 1701, the society initiated correspondence with Hodges aboard the *Triumph* at St. Helens on the Isle of Wight, who pledged the distribution of society literature throughout Sir George Rooke's Channel fleet.[112] Both Philip Stubbs, author of *The Religious Seamen* and chaplain to the seaman's hospital at Greenwich, and Josiah Woodward, the East India Company minister, joined the society in late 1701.[113] In early 1702, George Stanhope, vicar of the dockside parish of St. Nicholas, Deptford, and author of *The Sea-Man's Obligations to Gratitude and a Good Life*, also became a correspondent.[114] Days after the elevation of Queen Anne's husband Prince George of Denmark to the largely honorific position of Lord High Admiral of England, the SPCK delegated members to approach the prince for the allocation of funds "toward the furnishing of her Majesty's seamen and soldiers on board the Fleet with good books."[115] Interestingly, the Admiralty board felt that such an application would have been more properly made by the archbishop of Canterbury or the bishop of London—further evidence of the anomalous status of the society in the corridors of civil and ecclesiastical power.[116]

The substantial maritime contingent among both the residing and corresponding members of the early SPCK ensured a persistent concern for the spiritual lives of English seamen—particularly after England resumed hostilities with France at the outbreak of the War of the Spanish Succession in early 1702. Society engagement with English seamen was largely confined to the distribution of pious books, but this task it performed with energy and diligence.[117] Society member Josiah Woodward's small tracts against vice were immensely popular for this purpose. In 1701, Patrick Gordon requested seven thousand or eight thousand copies of Woodward's *A Kind Caution to Prophane Swearers* "in order to be distributed through the whole Fleet."[118] In June 1701, the society dispatched a thousand copies of Woodward's *A Disswasive from the Sin of Drunkenness* to Sir George Rooke and a thousand copies of the *Caution to Swearers* to John Benbow, who commanded the Downs Squadron.[119] In December 1701, the society sent a shipment of some four hundred books to residing member James Vernon for distribution to men of the *Mary Galley*, a thirty-two-gun fifth rate upon which his younger brother Edward, the future hero of the Battle of Porto Bello, was serving as volunteer-per-order.[120] In October 1702, the society resolved to distribute pious tracts "amongst the sick and wounded in the hospitals in and about London."[121] The following year, it began targeting naval and shipping communities in Bristol, Portsmouth, Woolwich, Gravesend, Plymouth, and elsewhere.[122]

The literary centerpiece of SPCK outreach to the maritime sector was undoubtedly Josiah Woodward's *The Seaman's Monitor: or, advice to sea-faring men*. Named after John Rawlet's classic of Anglican piety, the *Seaman's Monitor* was to be the most enduring example of that emerging subgenre of eighteenth-century English religious writing: devotional literature for mariners.[123] "As the good success of sea affairs is one of the principle concerns of this our island," so the chief concern of all patriots and churchmen must be the souls of English seamen, who were "under God, the chief strength and defense of our nation, and the means of its wealth and commerce."[124] *The Seaman's Monitor* was a complete manual of shipboard conduct, conversation, and worship and therefore a favorite instrument of Anglican engagement with the fleet throughout the eighteenth century. The SPCK continuously distributed it during the War of the Spanish Succession, even overseeing a translation into Dutch.[125] In the summer of 1723, George I ordered *The Seaman's Monitor* reprinted, and the SPCK distributed some ten thousand copies throughout the fleet.[126] The tract was republished in 1767 and then again during both the American and French revolutionary wars.[127]

The recommencement of hostilities with France induced the SPCK to take English soldiers within its ken. Robert Hales, the society's unofficial emissary to the Protestant churches on the Continent, applauded its efforts on behalf of mariners but implored the society to "not forget the land army."[128] In the summer of 1701, the SPCK invited Woodward to draw up another tract to facilitate its efforts among the land forces.[129] He completed *The Soldier's Monitor, being Serious Advice to Soldiers* in October, and the society ordered five thousand copies printed.[130] As with the Royal Navy, the society had no official channel of contact with the army. The members inquired after a "chaplain-general of the English army" but turned up nothing. The society proceeded again through informal channels, submitting the *Soldier's Monitor* to the general officers of the armed forces for approval.[131] A list of all English garrisons was drawn up, and the former army chaplain Henry Shute was asked to devise a scheme for distributing pious books among them.[132] A small number of the book were placed in the hands of the commander-in-chief John Churchill, Earl of Marlborough, and his brigadier-general John, Lord Cutts, in the Netherlands. Thousands more were lodged with William Thorold, an Anglican chaplain in Rotterdam, for distribution throughout the English forces on the Continent.[133] In April 1702, several thousand books were dispatched to Sir Richard Bulkeley in Dublin, "to disperse amongst her Majesty's soldiers in Ireland."[134] The SPCK continued to claim an interest in the spiritual lives of English soldiers throughout the early eighteenth century.[135] In the aftermath of the Jacobite rising of 1715, the SPCK thought it wise to "to present a packet of little practical books to the King's Guards in Hyde Park," a total of some five thousand horse and foot guards.[136] In 1722, George I ordered ten thousand copies of *The Soldier's Monitor* dispersed among the troops in England.[137]

The SPCK also took an interest in prison reform decades before future members James Edward Oglethorpe and John Perceval championed the cause in Parliament in the late 1720s. At first glance, this interest would not seem to comport with the concern for mobile populations that animated the society's outreach to soldiers and sailors. But the English jails also housed populations removed from parish life, beset with moral peril, and irregularly served by a disorganized chaplainry. In January 1700, Bishop Compton tasked the nascent society with considering "some means for the better instructing and regulating the manners of the poor prisoners" incarcerated in London and Westminster.[138] Henry Shute, lecturer at Whitechapel (and perhaps familiar with the conditions of the debtors' prison in that neighborhood), produced a lengthy set of proposals "toward the reformation of Newgate and the other prisons in and about London." He recommended a litany of new regulations for the prisons in the metropolis and their supervision by a committee composed of aldermen, common councilors, and (interestingly enough) "some members of the society for reformation." To remedy the neglect of religion, Shute advocated a sufficient salary for the ordinary (chaplain), visitation by neighboring ministers, books of devotion for the prisoners, daily prayer and monthly sacraments, and "that all prisons (for debt especially) be considered as parochial cures."[139] Shute's proposals were laid before the Lord Mayor and sheriffs, where they presumably languished. In early 1702, however, Thomas Bray and Philip Stubbs began visiting prisons throughout the city and, "being affected by the sight of so many miserable objects of pity," distributed charity and devotional books.[140] Paul Lorraine, the new ordinary of Newgate, was invited to become a correspondent of the society.[141]

Resorting to its cherished method of intervention, the SPCK resolved in early 1702 to distribute packets of devotional books "to each county gaol in England." In addition to the usual complement of Rawlet's *Christian Monitor* and various tracts by Josiah Woodward, the society included John Kettlewell's *Office for Prisoners* and *Prayers for Prisoners under Sentence of Death*.[142] The packet of books, it was hoped, would render prisoners "better fitted to living soberly and piously for the future in this world; or in case of condemnation at the approaching assizes religiously to depart out of it."[143] During the following months, society correspondents reported dispersing the books throughout jails in Exeter, Reading, York, Derby, Bedford, and New Sarum.[144]

Society members continued to press "the necessity of reforming prisons" but were often content with the provision of Anglican ministry and offices.[145] Reports trickled into the society of overcrowded prisons in Bristol and London, "altogether unprovided with the means of divine service."[146] In late 1710, the society initiated a campaign for better provision of church services in the Marshalsea Prison in Southwark, even taking up a subscription for the salary of the chaplain. Society members John Chamberlayne and the Tory MP Edward Jennings lobbied Sir John Bennett, judge of the Marshalsea, "to give leave some upper room of the Marshalsea Prison may be fitted up for divine service." Bennett consented, and the society was willing to pay the expense of outfitting the room with a desk and pews.[147] In 1715, one Mr. Davies, chaplain of the Marshalsea, reported to the society on the barbarous conditions inside the prison, suggesting that more than two hundred debtors "have been starved to death in that prison in the space of years past." He asked that society members, "who are well wishers to humanity," press members of Parliament to "find some expedient to prevent the little barbarities for the future." As the MPs Samuel Bracebridge and Thomas Cave were then preparing a bill for the relief of poor debtors in King's Bench and other prisons, society members looked forward to a public enquiry "extended to all the prisons in the kingdom," which Henry Newman confessed would "disclose such a scene of cruelties . . . not to be equaled in Turkey nor in Barbary itself."[148] Society concern for the deplorable condition of English jails and prisons in large measure prompted its embrace of the parochial workhouse movement during the third decade of the eighteenth century.[149]

The society's interest in the spiritual lives of English captives abroad was something of a natural development from its regard for both mariners and prisoners. Captain George Delaval's negotiations with the sultan of Morocco for the redemption of English slaves in Morocco were well publicized in the press.[150] In the spring of 1700, the court issued a charity brief "toward the redemption of English captives" in the Moroccan capital in Meknes.[151] In October of that year, Josiah Woodward moved that the SPCK offer something for the "English captives in the island of Ceylon," whose plight presumably came to his attention through his connection with the East India Company. The society dispatched fifty copies of Woodward's own *Letter of Advice and Comfort to the English Captives Who Suffer in Slavery in Foreign Parts.*[152] It never formally adopted the cause of English captives abroad, but their spiritual welfare remained a residual concern throughout the early eighteenth century. The Scottish correspondent James Kirkwood repeatedly directed the society's attention to the redemption (or at least consolation) of English and Scottish captives.[153] And leading member John Chamberlayne lobbied the Junto Whig secretary of state, Charles Spencer, third Earl of Sunderland, on behalf of "the slaves in Algiers."[154]

The improvisational quality of SPCK engagement with nonparochial populations at home and abroad illustrates the unprecedented adaptability of the organization. The society was able to respond, albeit often with little more than correspondence and shipments of books, to various sectors as their need became manifest. What ensued was something of a virtuous circle: the society attracted representatives of groups ill-served by the established church, who in turn directed members, resources, and even public attention toward those groups, enlarging the society's mandate for outreach. And yet in engaging mobile or displaced groups, the SPCK not only pressed up against its own limitations as "a society of private gentlemen," but pressed up against the limitations of a territorial church establishment bereft of both religious orders and an international episcopate.[155] Moreover, as the SPCK became an instrument of ecclesiastical expansion, it increasingly found itself engaged in ecumenical interaction with the churches of the so-called Protestant interest. And there the society's mandate was tenuous indeed.

The Protestant Interest Abroad

The SPCK inherited not only the Anglican revivalist fervor that had accompanied the Revolution of 1688–1689, but also the intractable domestic and international confessional tensions that had permeated the crisis and its aftermath. In this sense, the SPCK was a true child of the Revolution and heir to its religious duplexity. For the Revolution embodied, on the one hand, the particular deliverance of the established church from Catholic absolutism and unlimited toleration by royal fiat and, on the other, England's restoration as the bulwark of the so-called Protestant interest, when it resumed the Elizabethan alliance with the United Provinces and assumed headship of the international coalition against Catholic France.

These dual identities animated the spirit of Protestant reconciliation that both preceded and followed the invasion of William of Orange and the overthrow of the Stuart monarchy. And yet, their incompatibility was exposed in the failure of comprehension and the collapse of the addled convocation of 1689, in which conservative Anglican churchmen could hardly bring themselves to acknowledge the alliance of the Church of England and the Protestant churches beyond England. These tensions were only exacerbated by the death of Queen Mary in 1694 and Anne's son William, Duke of Gloucester, in 1700, by which hopes for a native English (and, of course, firmly Anglican) dynasty were effectively extinguished. The preservation of the Revolution settlement thereafter required a Protestant succession in the Lutheran House of Hanover and a political union with Scotland, which ensured the identity of the crowns, yet left the new nation of Great Britain with both an episcopal and a presbyterian church establishment on either side of the Tweed. The geopolitical vicissitudes and ruinous expenses of the protracted War of the Spanish Succession during the reign of Queen Anne further embittered many English churchmen toward the very notion of a common "Protestant interest" among the allies. From one perspective, the Revolution had salvaged the Church of England from popish domination and reawakened the English to the mortal threat of French Catholic hegemony in Europe. But from another, it had inaugurated religious pluralism, Anglican schism, the prospect of an alien dynasty, dual ecclesiastical establishments, and seemingly unlimited engagement on behalf of Dutch and German enemies of episcopacy. By the first decade of the eighteenth century, the Revolution's benefit to the Church of England was very much in question.

The initial openness of the SPCK with respect to ideology, designs, and membership very quickly exposed the organization to these contradictions. On the one hand, many of the early correspondents in the provinces welcomed the society as an engine of Anglican confessional entrenchment at home—a resource for the parochial clergy in its struggles against irreligion, popery, and dissent. Indeed, it would not have been unfair to perceive the society as a means for helping the established church navigate the unprecedented religious and political environment—characterized by religious pluralism, burgeoning freedom of association, and a virtually unregulated press—wrought by the Revolution. On the other hand, elements in the activist core of residing members in London and correspondents in Europe came to conceive of the society as a vanguard of Protestant internationalism on the world stage. From this vantage, the SPCK was not the antidote to the Revolution, but rather its continuation by other means. It was thought to be the embodiment of the revivified Protestantism of 1688. As William of Orange was held to be "the great restorer of the liberties of Europe," wrote a correspondent on behalf of the Protestant clergy in the Swiss city of Neuchâtel, "so they consider the Society as the restorer of piety and good manners."[156] These identities existed in tension. The SPCK commitment to Anglican confessional aggrandizement at home was not readily compatible with the conciliatory and collaborative Protestant internationalism that this broader reformation movement entailed.

From its inception, the SPCK was welcomed as a vanguard of Protestant internationalism, the religious analogue to England's augmented military posture in Europe during the wars against Louis XIV. The introduction to Josiah Woodward's third edition of the *Account of the Rise and Progress of the Religious Societies* (1701) suggested for the first time an international context to the new wave of religious voluntarism in England. The new edition, significantly the first since Woodward joined the SPCK, included testimonials of the international response to religious and reformation societies in England, including the warm approval of the Huguenot Protestant internationalist Pierre Jurieu and the famed Saxon Pietist August Hermann Francke of Halle, who had been named a foreign correspondent of the SPCK just eight weeks after the society was founded.[157]

Thus, it is not entirely surprising that many chose to view the nascent SPCK not as an instrument of Anglican confessional militancy, but rather as further evidence of English collaboration in finishing, as the Swiss theologian and correspondent Jean-Frédéric Ostervald put it, "the great work of the Reformation," long hindered by Protestant disunion.[158] M. De Beringhen, a lay correspondent and member of a society of Huguenot refugees at The Hague "for carrying on the like designs," imagined the SPCK as potentially the first in a network of like-minded societies throughout Europe, charged with monitoring and maintaining the Protestant interest. On behalf of the residing members, John Chamberlayne responded favorably to the proposal of "forming committees like ours in London in all the Protestant states throughout Europe."[159] Ostervald perceived the Protestant ecumenism of the society as its greatest glory.[160] From Saxony, Francke welcomed a correspondence with the society, anticipating that "many benefits by its means will accrue to the whole Christian church; especially a stricter union among Protestants."[161] Even an ailing John Locke, a well-wisher to the fledgling society, was "very glad to see such a spirit raised for the support and enlargement of religion." And he too lit upon the ecumenical imperative: "Protestants, I think, are as much concerned now as ever, to be vigorous in their joint endeavors, for the maintenance of the Reformation."[162] Interestingly, another English observer demanded that the cause of Protestant internationalism and antipopery be the SPCK's primary purpose, going so far as to propose an alternative organization whose sole function would be "to maintain the Reformed religion against the growth of popery." As the anonymous projector ruefully observed, "if we don't seriously apply our selves to this, all our other societies will at last be useless."[163]

Within its first year, the SPCK established correspondence with both reformed and Lutheran groups in the Netherlands and Germany. However, during its first decade, the society was largely preoccupied with the Protestant churches of the Swiss cantons, which were not only of enormous strategic importance on the eve of the recommencement of hostilities in Europe, but also undergoing something of liberal insurgency against the Calvinist orthodoxy of the Formula Consensus.[164] Both geopolitical and theological conditions in the Swiss cantons oriented their clerical leaders toward England and made them particularly receptive to a formal correspondence with the representatives of the established church. The indefatigable traveler Robert Hales of Bekesbourne, Kent, appears to have initiated contact with the SPCK while abroad in Switzerland in late 1700.[165] He was soon after adopted as the society's primary emissary to the continental Protestants.[166] The society's correspondence with Hales and his numerous Swiss contacts revealed an anxious and hidebound reformed church establishment in the cantons, "surrounded with papists" and "very jealous of all innovations." The Swiss, Hales reported, had no need for an equivalent society as charitable expenditure was carefully monitored by the magistrate, education was relatively well provided for, and an "excellent discipline [was] observed amongst them." Moreover, self-organization smacked of separatism, and as Ostervald reported of Bern, "everybody there that appears for reformation is branded with the name of pietist."[167]

The Swiss clergy, however, were starved for English works of devotion and divinity—particularly those of the "holy living" style of piety favored by the society. The German translation of Woodward's *Account of the Rise and Progress of the Religious Societies* published in Berlin was already well known among the Swiss clergy when Hales arrived, and translations of the works of Anthony Horneck and Gilbert Burnet were already afoot in St. Gall. Hales commissioned translations of several society staples, including Woodward's *Caution to Swearers* and *A Pastoral Letter from a Minister to His Parishioners* into both German and French for refugee Huguenots and the embattled Protestants of Orange and the Vaudois. The society correspondent, John Jacob Scherer, minister of St. Gall, undertook translations of Rawlet's *The Christian Monitor* and Theophilus Dorrington's *Familiar Guide to the Right and Profitable Receiving of the Lord's Supper* and claimed he was "willing to translate into German or Latin any good book that comes from England." In May 1701, Hales undertook the translation of John Kettlewell's *Measures of Christian Obedience* and noted the circulation of German translations of some thirty of Archbishop Tillotson's sermons.[168]

Of course, the literary exchange with the Swiss churches was not solely one way. In 1703, SPCK clerk Humphrey Wanley and member George Stanhope translated Ostervald's great catechism *The Grounds and Principles of the Christian Religion*, which soon became a fixture in SPCK and SPG packets.[169] Even more ambitious was Ostervald's revision of the liturgy of Neuchâtel, which borrowed liberally from the Book of Common Prayer.[170] The liturgy caused something of a sensation in England, even before it was translated by John Chamberlayne and published with an epistolary preface by the Prussian chaplain and Protestant internationalist Daniel Ernst Jablonski in 1712.[171] Churchmen from across the political and ideological spectrum perceived the liturgy as a blueprint for Protestant reconciliation along broadly Anglican lines—at least in terms of worship, if not episcopal polity. Even the Irish nonjuror and Jacobite Charles Leslie thus deemed the Neuchâtel liturgy "a great instrument of bringing many of the Calvinists into a nearer conformity with the Church of England."[172]

For the Swiss churches, however, the *correspondence fraternelle* with the Church of England was first and foremost intended to secure English countenance and protection for continental Protestantism during the War of the Spanish Succession. The Swiss generally held, Robert Hales informed the SPCK, "that the Protestant interest does depend upon the welfare of England."[173] The Swiss churches clearly saw in the SPCK's correspondence and literature not only a fillip to their own domestic movement for Protestant revivalism and reformation, but also the prospect of some more formal political commitment from the English state. Thus, the Swiss correspondents routinely pressed society members at home to procure from the church or government some formal accreditation for Hales's mission.[174]

The SPCK envisioned an even more comprehensive role for Hales, as "a gentleman with a public character to intend the interest of this nation and of our holy religion," as John Chamberlayne advised Secretary of State Robert Harley in 1704.[175] A memorandum drawn up by the society recommended that Hales be "appointed commissioner to investigate the position of Protestants in various states," a kind of errant commissioner for monitoring and maintaining the rights of Protestants in accordance with the treaties of Westphalia, Ryswick, and Altranstädt. The document envisioned Hales as something of a liaison between the Protestant courts of Great Britain, the Netherlands, Prussia, Hanover, and Hesse-Cassel and the various Protestant communities throughout Europe—the very nexus of states, churches, and peoples that comprised the Protestant interest.[176] Such a scheme, it must be noted, was implicitly predicated on the maintenance of a continental alliance to which Tory and high-church Englishmen were increasingly opposed. Regard for the Protestant interest abroad naturally impelled the SPCK toward an embrace of Whig internationalism—"as if our good works and our arms were to spread their glory together through all Europe," as White Kennett put it.[177]

The commission for Hales was not forthcoming, but the SPCK had effectively secured a reputation as the defender of Protestant minorities throughout Europe.[178] The early society dispatched works of piety and consolation to refugee communities in Britain, Europe, and America.[179] And by 1705, society members had begun a collection "for the relief of the Protestant ministers and gentlemen, slaves in the French king's galleys."[180] But here again, the cause of reformed Protestants abroad reportedly garnered precious little sympathy among high-church clergymen in this period.[181] In 1709, Queen Anne naturally drew upon the members of the SPCK and its sibling corporation, the SPG, to staff her commission for the relief of the mostly Lutheran emigrants driven from the Rhine Palatinate by the impositions of French forces and their Roman Catholic Elector William of Newburg. The case of the so-called poor Palatines, as White Kennett wrote, "did not lay before the body of the Society, yet several of the members in their respective situations were very instrumental in the first relief of them."[182]

The relief of the poor Palatines sharply divided public opinion along party lines.[183] Whigs and low churchmen tended to favor the relief and resettlement of the refugees, an expression of England's broader diplomatic and confessional commitment to the Protestant interest in Europe. For Tories, however, the Lutheran refugees, exempt by the terms of the Whig Naturalization Act of 1709 from having to conform to the established church, embodied the burgeoning spiritual and material costs of their continuing involvement in the continental war and the anti-French alliance. As if the persistence of Protestant Nonconformity at home were not troubling enough, Englishmen were now being asked to import new and impoverished Dissenters into the kingdom.[184] Unsurprisingly, SPCK involvement in the commission was almost entirely limited to the society's Whiggish and Hanoverian ranks. Commissioners and society members Sir John Philipps, Dr. Frederick Slare, Henry Shute, Robert Hales, John Chamberlayne, John Hooke, Thomas Bray, and Wilhelm Heinrich Ludolf, secretary to the prince of Denmark, operated largely under the auspices of the Earl of Sunderland, the Junto Whig secretary of state.[185] The two London clergymen appointed to execute the queen's charity brief for the refugees were White Kennett and Lilly Butler, both SPCK and SPG members and outspoken low churchmen.[186] Chamberlayne used the opportunity of their collaboration to recommend to Sunderland the work "of the several religious societies erected in this nation," including the SPCK, taking great pains to underscore their loyalty to "revolution principles" and the Whig interest. Chamberlayne explained that "the large majority of the gentlemen who compose all the societies mentioned . . . are staunch Whigs, and will always be so as long as the Whigs are the supporters of our religious and civil rights."[187] This was a noticeably different profile than that contained in the society's professions of nonpartisanship and inclusivity.

The engagement of SPCK members on behalf of the poor Palatines marked not only the culmination of a decade of concern for the welfare of Protestant refugees, but also the maturation of the society's relationship with the expatriate community surrounding Prince George of Denmark's Lutheran Royal Chapel at St. James.[188] John Chamberlayne was a "gentleman waiter" in the household of Prince George. The prince's first chaplain, the Danish Lutheran J. W. Mecken, began attending SPCK meetings in late 1699. Mecken constituted the society's first link to the Scandinavian world, shipping parcels of SPCK material to Denmark, Sweden, and Holstein in 1702.[189] Prince George's one-time secretary Wilhelm Heinrich Ludolf was elected a corresponding member in December 1700. Ludolf became one of the society's strongest links to the Halle pastor August Hermann Francke, whose reformist Pietism chimed with Ludolf's own radically ecumenical vision of a "universal Church."[190] It was the well-connected Ludolf who first secured for Francke's disciple Anton Wilhelm Boehm a position as court preacher in the Lutheran Royal Chapel of Prince George, and from there, entrée into the circle of Anglican clergy and gentlemen surrounding the SPCK, affiliations Boehm retained for the rest of his life. One of the most stalwart members of the SPCK in its second decade, Boehm became the society's primary ambassador to the Lutheran world—"the life and soul of our correspondence in religious affairs with Germany and Denmark," as Secretary Henry Newman eulogized in 1722.[191] Boehm also developed a productive relationship with the society publisher Joseph Downing, through whom he became the primary conduit of Lutheran Pietist works into the English-speaking world.[192]

Perhaps Boehm's greatest achievement was facilitating SPCK sponsorship of the Lutheran mission to southern India. In 1704, Prince George's nephew, King Frederick IV of Denmark, undertook the sponsorship of a Lutheran mission to the Danish colony of Tranquebar on the Coromandel Coast of India. The king's agents managed to procure two Germans to undertake the mission, Bartholomäus Ziegenbalg and Heinrich Plutschau, former students of the Pietist Francke. Ziegenbalg and Plutschau's mission, which formally began with their arrival at Tranquebar in 1706, was virtually unknown in England until Boehm began actively publicizing the work. In 1709, Boehm and Joseph Downing brought forth a collection of the missionaries' letters in English under the title *Propagation of the Gospel in the East*, dedicated to the Church of England's formal instrument of missionary expansion, the SPG, and its president, Archbishop Tenison. Boehm's introduction was a manifesto of Protestant revival, hailing the Tranquebar mission as evidence of "some little sparks perhaps of spiritual life" glowing among the "frozen over" churches of the Protestant world.[193]

Boehm's collection, "which has occasioned large contributions towards propagating the gospel in the East Indies," was something of a sensation in England and its empire. As Henry Newman related, the SPG, "considered that their charter confined them to Her Majesties plantation in [the] W[est] Indies declined concerning themselves in it," but the SPCK, "being under no restraints but the laws of the land and common discretion," warmly embraced the mission.[194]

In September 1710, the SPCK made a formal commitment to assisting the Danish mission in Tranquebar. Within a few months, the society had opened a subscription toward the mission and charged a separate "Malabar committee" with overseeing fund-raising and correspondence.[195] "The Lord be praised for this unexpected support come from England!" hailed Ziegenbalg from Madras.[196] In the spirit of the late Robert Boyle and in keeping with the character of its domestic and continental distribution of books, the society undertook the publication of the New Testament in Portuguese, to be used by the missionaries.[197] Within a year, the society had collected £434 4s 9d on behalf of the Protestant mission; the sum had doubled to £870 by the end of 1711, nominally raised for the printing of the Portuguese New Testament but largely "expended in necessaries sent to India or remitted to the missionaries."[198] Josiah Woodward used his connections with the East India Company to procure at least nominal support from the company, which agreed to ship supplies to the missionaries free of charge.[199] The society sponsored Jonas Fincke, the schoolmaster at a German school in London, to serve in Tranquebar as a printer for the mission. Along with Fincke, the society sent a printing press, sets of fonts, one hundred reams of paper, and £100 in silver. In February 1712, the society shipped by the East India Company fleet £366 15d in pieces of eight, three hundred Portuguese translations of the New Testament, and two other crates of books, designed as the foundation for two lending libraries at Fort St. George and Bengal.[200]

Sponsorship of the Danish mission to Tranquebar laid bare the antinomies of the SPCK. The collaboration could really be understood only in a spirit of broad-based Protestant ecumenism, utterly free from the Anglican confessional aggrandizement that marked much of the society's domestic agenda. Indeed, for many, this was the great benefit of the mission. "Such endeavors are laudable," wrote Boehm, "as have a tendency to bring" the divided churches "to a Christian moderation."[201] Ziegenbalg prayed that English support presaged a grand Protestant alliance in the field of missionary endeavors.[202] Even Henry Newman hoped that English commitment would serve "to animate foreigners to assist in promoting so excellent a work."[203]

However, the SPCK possessed no real mandate for Protestant reconciliation, and the irregularity of an Anglican voluntary society sponsoring Lutheran conversions in the East Indies did not go long unregistered. Ironically, it was Archbishop Tenison who first queried the propriety of this arrangement. In December 1713, the society's Malabar Committee convened to investigate complaints of doctrinal and ecclesiological incompatibilities between the mission and its English sponsors. The ensuing controversy delivered a blow to the improvisational ecumenism that the society had been quietly pursuing since its inception. And indeed, as Henry Newman informed John Chamberlayne, "The major part seemed to wish the matter had never come in question before them." The committee acknowledged that "it was no secret to them that the missionaries are Lutherans, or at least pass for such." The denomination of the missionaries had not been deliberately concealed, but rather downplayed in hopes of maintaining the appeal of the Danish mission among English donors. Clearly, a dominant element in the SPCK conceived such cavils as trifling before the grand providential imperative of enlarging the kingdom of Christ. It was the policy of the society that better "the heathen should be Lutheran Christians than no Christians."[204] Archbishop Tenison disagreed, going so far as to inform the society "that he would advise the clergy strongly against taking in the least bit further or in assisting in any way such a mission which aimed at planting sectarian Lutheranism."[205] The controversy did not curtail SPCK support for the Danish mission, but it did expose an unrelievable tension between the society's confessional and ecumenical objectives.[206]

Ecumenical engagements closer to home were no less problematic for the society. It had long considered the Scottish Highlands, at least indirectly, as part of its domestic mission field.[207] Early SPCK members Samuel Brewster of Lincoln's Inn and Vigerus Edwards of the Inner Temple put forward a proposal to erect libraries in the Highlands, which the society recommended to corresponding members as a "design with the same nature as their own."[208] In 1704, the General Assembly of the Church of Scotland adopted the parochial libraries scheme as its own, "a project set on foot by some piously inclined in this and the neighboring nation of England," and directed its thanks to "the Society in England for Propagating Christian Knowledge."[209] Informal links between the SPCK in London and various reformist ministers in Scotland persisted throughout the decade. After the Union of 1707, society members sought to establish more formal ties with several individual Scottish Presbyterians, a move that apparently caused some controversy which required consultation with the bishops.[210] In November 1708, the society formally invited the clergymen William Carstares of Edinburgh, Robert Baillie of Inverness, and John Stirling of Glasgow to become corresponding members, all of whom accepted.[211] Society members were delighted with the correspondence, John Philipps writing, "nothing is so likely to establish the Union and improve it to the best ends as a communion of good works."[212] And indeed, SPCK members consulted their northern correspondents on several of their more ecumenical projects, such as the relief of the poor Palatines and the Tranquebar mission.[213] The society, Henry Newman wrote to Robert Baillie in January 1709, "have been extremely pleased with your readiness to promote the interests of religion in north Britain."[214]

The Scottish correspondents soon after entreated Queen Anne for letters patent incorporating them as a distinct society, which she conferred on 18 August 1709.[215] The agenda of the Presbyterian Society in Scotland for Propagating Christian Knowledge (SSPCK), which comprised the erecting of charity schools and distribution of pious materials, closely mirrored that of its Anglican counterpart. From England, John Chamberlayne immediately seized "the opportunity of laying the foundation of a friendly intercourse betwixt the two Societies, whereby they may be helpful to each other in the common cause of promoting the interests of the Christian Reformed Church."[216] The correspondence naturally appealed to those members who had since the SPCK's inception cherished the vision of an international network of like-minded voluntary associations comprising the vanguard of the Protestant interest. But such a vision was by no means universally embraced in London. The Union, with its confirmation of the Presbyterian establishment in Scotland and its neglect of any indulgence for the proscribed Scottish episcopal clergy, was already widely resented by English Tories and high churchmen.[217] A correspondence between the SPCK and its Scottish counterpart could only, it seemed, reproduce precisely the ecclesiastical contradictions instituted by the Union. For the Anglican society to ally itself with an organization that aimed at promoting the interests of a church which was constitutionally antipathetic to episcopacy was more than inappropriate, it was grossly self-defeating. Society member Benjamin Wood, curate of Wherwell, Hampshire, vehemently opposed the correspondence. Professing ample respect for the Kirk, Wood nonetheless predicted scandal for the London society, whose members already purportedly "leaned too much towards the dissenters." How would the SPCK respond to its critics "when we are observed to court a correspondence and invite assistance from persons that are supposed enemies to our ecclesiastical establishment and encouragers of those among us that are so." Anxious for the society's reputation, Wood feared that "some will be apt to conclude the sweet council we [the two societies] take together is like to have sour consequence."[218] Ultimately, the SPCK declined the correspondence on proprietary rather than ideological grounds. As a voluntary association, Newman informed Carstares, the SPCK "have never yet gone further than a private correspondence" with affiliates in England and abroad. The formal recognition of "an incorporated body" like the SSPCK appeared to be "inconsistent with the privacy which they have hitherto aimed at."[219] When once again confronted with the contradictions between its confessional and ecumenical impulses, the SPCK took refuge in its unincorporated status, afraid to be caught brokering the accommodation with Scotland that its mother church was as yet unwilling to make.

The SPCK commitment to the Protestant interest abroad seemed at times to divert the society from its original purpose as an instrument of Anglican confessionalization. Moreover, despite the continuing affiliation of Tories and nonjurors, the embrace of the Protestant interest often seemed to push the society to commit to overtly Whiggish ideals such as the Grand Alliance, the Hanoverian succession, and the imperatives of Protestant reconciliation—ideals that had diminishing purchase on Tory Anglicans during the reign of Queen Anne. Frictions over these contradictory orientations appeared occasionally at meetings or in exchanges among members, but there were no open ruptures by which the society might be firmly enlisted in one camp or another. It quietly struggled to maintain its immunity from the devastating effects of the "rage of party" that polarized English politics and society during this period. But even as the SPCK imagined itself to be standing still amidst the political and religious torrent of Anne's last years, it was impelled almost imperceptibly toward the Whigs and the low church.

The SPCK and the Hanoverian Succession

The final years of the reign of Queen Anne sorely taxed the vaunted inclusivity of the SPCK. Prominent members (if not always the society itself) had acted on behalf of a series of causes that increasingly troubled the Tory Anglican conscience: the Union, the relief of the poor Palatines, the war against Catholic France, and the Hanoverian succession. The society's commitment to the Protestant interest abroad placed it out of step both with a Tory politics that repudiated the Grand Alliance and with an illiberal and flagrantly antiecumenical Anglican high churchmanship that denied the validity of the nonepiscopal churches in Britain and on the Continent.[220] Both positions, it was not unfair to conclude, tended toward Jacobitism and threatened the Hanoverian succession to which many society members were deeply committed. Tory antipathy to the Union, the House of Hanover, and the Protestant interest, it was said, derived "from certain bigoted notions of Church-communion."[221] The complex of political, ecclesiological, and dynastic commitments that came to define Tory Anglicanism at the end of Anne's reign were very difficult indeed to reconcile with the agenda of the SPCK.

By the final years of the reign of Queen Anne, the SPCK had begun to take on a noticeably altered political and ecclesiastical character. Just a decade beyond its commendably bipartisan origins, the activist core of the society was composed largely if not exclusively of men of broadly Whiggish and low-church allegiances. Indeed, the presence of the founders had diminished dramatically by this period. The SPCK met with a quorum 259 times in the five years before Anne's death (28 July 1709–29 July 1714). John Hooke attended four of these meetings before his death in 1712; Lord Guilford attended three; Thomas Bray, two; and Humphrey Mackworth, a single meeting. Although Maynard Colchester continued to subscribe to the organization until his death in 1715, he attended no meetings during this period. In terms of sheer presence, the society was clearly dominated by a more Whiggish element: the treasurer Henry Shute attended 228 of the 259 meetings in this same period; John Chamberlayne, 192; Richard Mayo, 168; the Shropshire gentleman John Tayleur of Roddington, 177; the Inner Temple lawyer Vigerus Edwards, who received government appointments under Sir Robert Walpole, 135; the Whig MP Sir John Philipps of Picton Castle, 111; and the Whig magistrate Daniel Dolins, 82. And, of course, the presence of the New England–born Henry Newman, whose influence over the society extended far beyond his lengthy service as secretary, was presumably near constant. Numerous high churchmen, it must be noted, remained dedicated in their service to the society, but there were notably fewer with comparable attendance records during this time: the reconciled nonjuror Robert Nelson was present at 168 meetings; the Tory banker and philanthropist Henry Hoare, 77; and the devotional writer William Melmoth, 72. Robert Nelson's death in January 1715 further diminished the already waning high-church presence in the society.[222] Of course, attendance is by no means an absolute indicator of engagement, but it is arguably a far better one than mere membership, which Craig Rose and others have drawn upon to paint an enduringly bipartisan profile of the SPCK during this period.

Moreover, the composition of the society and its activities at this time soon began to tell upon its reputation. Even as the local charity schools that the SPCK promoted (but neither managed nor controlled) were acquiring a reputation for Jacobitism and an uncompromising strain of high-church divinity, the society in London was increasingly branded an instrument of low churchmanship.[223] The SPCK, reported a correspondent in the high-church bastion of Oxford, was "not so much objected against, as suspected in his neighborhood."[224] The society complained of opposition from what Henry Newman called "the violent opposers of Whiggish charity."[225] Even when the society "have industriously avoided the unchristian disposition that has been so fashionable of late years," complained Newman on a separate occasion, "yet they could not escape being called the Presbyterian Club."[226]

The SPCK was increasingly torn between the political inclusivity that had long been the hallmark of its organization and the commitment to the Protestant interest and the Hanoverian succession that loomed ever larger in its operations. It struggled to accommodate these stresses, resolving first to exclude "turbulent people" from attending meetings and "to prevent all debates that tend to destroy the Christian charity by which the Society subsists."[227] The same year, the society adopted a standing order "that they do not meddle with controversial books." Yet, it soon found itself straitjacketed by its own pretensions to political neutrality. As the mounting fear of Jacobitism among the correspondents increased requests for anti-Catholic materials, the society claimed that its new rule prohibited the consideration of such requests, "or any books relating to popery." A debate ensued on 12 February 1713, and the order was promptly reversed. The society complied with the requests of correspondents, dispatching hundreds of copies of anti-Catholic works by Archbishop Tillotson and Bishop Bull.[228]

As the society wrestled with its pretensions of nonpartisanship, a secret committee was formed by its more vehemently anti-Jacobite members— including Newman, Hales, Bray, Dolins, Mayo, Shute, and the Huguenot Claude de la Mothe—"to watch the advances to popery, and to meet weekly to communicate to one another such intelligence as came to their knowledge, and to consider of the best means to countermine the devices of the enemies to the Protestant succession." Their task, reflected Thomas Bray, was "to awaken the nation both against popery and the Pretender." The group met at de la Mothe's house until his death in October 1713 and continued to meet weekly in the city thereafter, where Newman reported they "go on as well as one can expect in these times wherein so much caution is necessary."[229] In 1713, the society began to make formal overtures toward the House of Hanover. In April 1713, the University of Helmstadt–educated scholar Johann Holling was named a correspondent for Hanover.[230] In August, Henry Newman wrote to Princess Sophia, asserting that the work of the SPCK in England "has laid such a foundation for securing the Protestant religion and of consequence the succession of your illustrious family to the throne of these kingdoms as will I hope for ever frustrate all attempts to introduce popery or overthrow the settlement on which the future happiness of this nation so much depends."[231] By this time, Robert Hales had settled in Hanover and began acting as the society's emissary to the electoral household.[232] "As to political affairs," Newman anxiously wrote to Hales, "we are very unsettled and can hardly ever be otherwise till the H[ouse] of Hanover come hither to give us a prospect of a race of princes never to be extinct."[233]

Leading society members rapturously greeted the accession of the Elector George of Hanover to the throne of Great Britain in August 1714. Newman was positively awestruck at the miracle of the Protestant succession. Just weeks before, he noted, the rage of party blew "with such vehemence that some even dared to give odious insinuations of the most august family of Hanover," while others "dared publicly to avow the interest of the Pretender." The bishops in the country "expected in a few months to have the crown of martyrdom." But now, "a profound tranquility we thought not possible" overspread the land. The Protestant succession was "not less miraculous, nor less seasonable than our late happy Revolution was."[234] Thomas Bray commended Hales for promoting the work of the SPCK and the SPG to the electoral family, even proposing that the new king's daughter-in-law Princess Caroline "would vouchsafe to become the royal patroness of them."[235] There was even some talk of the SPCK offering a formal address to her husband, the future king George II, but it was decided that such a compliment "from a voluntary society to a prince of the blood shall be thought a presumption." If the prince "is pleased to countenance their designs," wrote Newman, "he will have as many opportunities of doing it as effectually as if he stood in the relation of a member."[236]

The SPCK soon took steps to formalize its commitment to the new dynasty. The members of the society's anti-Jacobite cell conferred to determine "how far their aims were accomplished by the happy accession of King George to the throne." They resolved to consider "wherein they can yet be serviceable to the Protestant interest at home or abroad."[237] In the summer of 1716, the society began to discuss the requirement of prayers for the royal family at their weekly meetings. One member balked at the imposition, complaining that such prayers "carried in them something like a Test insinuating as if there were some members that could not pray for the King." Other members claimed that the requirement flew in the face of the society's cherished inclusivity and was unbecoming to "a Society that had hitherto acted in concert for promoting the interests of religion separate from any political considerations." But these reservations emanated from a dwindling minority. When the committee formally submitted the prayers on 19 July 1716, they were unanimously adopted.[238] In November 1716, the society resolved to "break off all correspondence" with members who could not take the oaths to George I.[239] The death of Robert Nelson the previous year at least spared the society the discomfort of expelling one of its most pious and long-serving members. In tandem with these efforts, Archbishop William Wake launched an effort to monitor "disaffection to King George and his government" and purge Jacobitism from the charity schools. As far as the SPCK was concerned, the cause of the Church of England and the cause of Hanover were one and the same. Once again, the Anglican revival recommitted itself to the Protestant monarchy.

Conclusion

The early SPCK may perhaps best be understood as the Church of England—bishops, clergy, and laity—rethinking aloud its obligations to the state and society wrought by the Revolution of 1688–1689. The late-Restoration agenda of confessional entrenchment, which served the church so well during the crisis of the reign of James II, was renewed in the society's program of supplementing parish pastoral care, promoting charity schools, and countering Nonconformist or Catholic encroachment. But even as the SPCK sought to reinforce the religious demarcations of a traditional society, it found itself called to trace the contours of a modernizing one. The society originated, at least in part, in Thomas Bray's vision of an imperial church; imperial expansion along with the unprecedented military and naval mobilizations of the wars against Bourbon France reaffirmed the need for a less insular, more dynamic Anglicanism. England's (and later, Britain's) enhanced military and commercial presence on the Continent, not to mention its restored place at the vanguard of the Protestant interest, engendered an ecumenical recommitment to the Reformation and the shared destiny of its churches. The more the society understood its own ideals as ultimately inseparable from those of the Revolution, the more ardent its devotion to the Protestant succession became. The broad base that characterized the society at its founding narrowed considerably. Jacobites and nonjurors were cut off. There was, of course, nothing to bar Hanoverian Tories and high churchmen from continuing to participate, and indeed, many did. Yet, their diminished presence in the society's activist core suggests that they were perhaps drawn to alternative modes of Anglican renewal, most prominently, the contemporaneous efforts in the convocation of the province of Canterbury.

At the dawn of the Hanoverian age, the SPCK threw a long shadow over the eighteenth century. It stood at the very origins of the so-called age of benevolence. And indeed, few developments in the social ministry of eighteenth-century Anglicanism at home and abroad could not be traced, directly or indirectly, back to the SPCK and "the constellation of noble designs" (in White Kennett's memorable phrase) in which it resided.[240] However, the political significance of the society must not be overlooked. Above all, during its first two decades the SPCK served as a dress rehearsal for the church-Whig alliance that came to define the structures of Georgian churchmanship in the first half of the eighteenth century.[241] One only need consider the astounding number of SPCK members elevated to the episcopal bench during the first decade of the Whig ascendancy: William Wake, archbishop of Canterbury (1715); Richard Willis, bishop of Gloucester (1715) and Salisbury (1722); Edmund Gibson, bishop of Lincoln (1716) and London (1723); Edward Chandler, bishop of Lichfield and Coventry (1717); White Kennett, bishop of Peterborough (1718); Hugh Boulter, bishop of Bristol (1719); Joseph Wilcocks, bishop of Gloucester (1722); Thomas Green, bishop of Norwich (1721) and Ely (1723); Edward Waddington, bishop of Chichester (1724); Samuel Peploe, bishop of Chester (1726); and Francis Hare, bishop of St. Asaph (1727). All of these men appeared on the rosters of the society's corresponding or residing members before their elevation to the bench, and many continued their involvement with the organization along with various other instruments of Anglican renewal afterwards. In these relationships, one can glean something of the multidimensionality of the eighteenth-century Anglican establishment. After 1714, the Church of England was bound not only to the Hanoverian monarchy, and the burgeoning Whig state, but also to the flourishing culture of Anglican voluntarism subsisting within civil society. Upon this infrastructure, the age of benevolence proceeded.

CHAPTER 4

Sacerdotalism and Civil Society

The 6 December 1705 meeting of the House of Lords had been set aside for the peers spiritual and temporal to debate the high-church and Tory charge that the Church of England was in danger. Amidst the arguments for and against, Gilbert Burnet, bishop of Salisbury, rose to speak. Against the resolution, he testified to an established church in the full flush of revival. Burnet hailed the renaissance of pastoral care, particularly in London, "constant prayers, frequent communion, diligent catechizing, faithful visiting of the sick, especially," he could not resist pointing out, "by those low church clergy they called low church men." Beyond the pastoral revival in the parishes, there was the explosion of Anglican voluntarism. He noted that "the society for reformation of manners set up in London and other parts had contributed considerably to the suppression of vice." Burnet pointed to the newly established Anglican societies, the Society for Promoting Christian Knowledge (SPCK) and the Society for the Propagation of the Gospel in Foreign Parts (SPG), which "had done a great deal in instructing men in religion, by giving away great numbers of books in practical divinity, by erecting libraries in country parishes, by sending over very able divines to the plantations abroad . . . and setting up schools to breed up the children in Christian religion." He pointed out that these programs were funded entirely by "voluntary contributions," further evidence of an engaged and devout English public; although, he rather waspishly observed, "in truth very little from those who appear so very for the church."[1] The Anglican revival, the evidence of which was apparent throughout England and its empire, precluded the endangerment of the church. The claim would soon become commonplace in Whig and low-church vindications of the security of the post-revolutionary establishment.

To understand the character of early-eighteenth-century Anglicanism, it is necessary to comprehend the ways in which the reigns of Anne and George I generated such wildly contradictory assessments of the fortunes of the established church. The church was either undergoing a revival, the first signs of an incipient age of benevolence and Christian enlightenment; or it was in mortal peril, threatened from without by irreligion and dissent and from within by the "false brethren" who would betray it to its enemies. Both appraisals, of course, apprehended something of the nature of early-eighteenth-century Anglicanism. The Anglican revival, characterized by pastoral renewal, organizational experimentation, and unprecedented institutional innovation, unfolded against a background of mounting consternation for the endangerment of the established church. And given that these developments were by no means isolated from one another, one might presume them to be reciprocally negating—and yet they were not. The revival did little to ameliorate anxiety over the church in danger; the warnings of danger did not signal the failures of the revival. That proponents of the revival were unable to mollify the prophets of Anglican doom suggests, on the one hand, the possibility of some political or ideological defect in the character of the revival, or, on the other, the incongruous standards by which critics evaluated it. Either possibility indicates ecclesiastical polarization so profound that it had rendered the Church of England, on some level, incomprehensible to itself. The parties of high and low church were not simply speaking past one another; they were speaking what increasingly seemed to be mutually unintelligible languages of churchmanship.

Therefore, it is necessary to appreciate something of the postrevolutionary development of Anglican high churchmanship, both juring and nonjuring, to understand first, its reservations regarding the Anglican revival that proceeded under the leadership of the Williamite bishops and the Anglican societies; and then, its sponsorship of an alternative program of Anglican renewal predicated on the refurbished disciplinary apparatus of the established church. Why and in what ways was the Church of England believed to be in such grave danger in the postrevolutionary era? How was this danger effectively to be averted? These are difficult questions to answer. The rhetoric of "the church in danger," like all effective political languages, was a capacious and potentially contradictory discourse, suitable for a wide variety of applications. And indeed, the vulnerabilities of the established church were assessed differently not only between the juring and nonjuring communions, but sometimes within each. Moreover, like all political languages, that of "the church in danger" was often deployed with breathtaking cynicism as little more than a fillip to Tory political fortunes, a point rarely lost on critics. And so, such an analysis must proceed by way of a hermeneutics of charity, attempting to glean from disparate sources, some of them nakedly instrumental in intention, a coherent sense of ecclesiastical crisis.

The premise of Anglican high-church discontent in the postrevolutionary period, this chapter argues, was the pervasive sense of *the loss of the ecclesial*.[2] The church's danger was, for high churchmen, existential. They feared, above all, the disappearance of the Church of England as a "distinct society," that is, a form of human sociality reducible to neither the political state nor the multiplicity of associations subsisting in civil society. Anglican high churchmanship in this period was persistently informed by the dual apprehension of both state and society, the social logics of which—coercion on the one hand, and voluntarism and transaction on the other—were both considered utterly alien to the constitution of the church. This double-sidedness pervaded Anglican high church-manship at this time. The fear of the state that Anglican high churchmen gleaned from the invasive regimes of James II and William III had done nothing to allay their traditional abhorrence for the sect. And so, the postrevolutionary high-church movement set its face against both state and society, renouncing alike the Erastianism of Thomas Hobbes and the voluntarism of John Locke. In this, the Anglican high-church movement arguably gazed more penetratingly than its contemporaries into the very heart of religious modernity, which, apportioning the world between sovereignty and sect, reserved no other grounds for the church as a distinct society.[3] Anglican high churchmen felt themselves threatened not only by an intrusive state and a religiously pluralistic society, but also by an attenuated conceptual field incapable of recognizing anything else. Vindicating a sovereignty not rooted in violence, and an association not derived from mere interest, high churchmen seemed to be speaking a dying, if not quite dead, language.

The postrevolutionary Anglican high-church movement was thus consumed by fear of encroachment; it believed the integrity and independence of the Church of England to be under relentless assault. The sacral life that it alone embodied was everywhere transgressed: interference in its polity and discipline by the state, impropriation of its resources by the grasping laity, performance of its offices by rival denominations, and usurpation of its functions by voluntary associations. The Anglican high-church movement was, at some level, a revolt against sacrilege, the manifold contaminations of the sacred by the profane (or worse, pretenders to the sacred, which amounted to the same thing), the sources of which seemed to be ubiquitous.

Given the Anglican high-church movement's dual apprehensions of an aggrandizing Erastian state and the legalized proliferation of rival sects, it became necessary for it to articulate an ecclesiology premised on both the sovereignty and independence of the Church of England—a sovereignty, however, dissimilar from that of the state, and an independence dissimilar from that of the sect. Postrevolutionary Anglican high churchmanship was thus characterized by an increasingly robust sacerdotalism, which stressed the indispensability of the priesthood and the priestly, sacramental function to Christianity. Sacerdotalism usefully cut both ways for high churchmen. This discourse invoked the inviolability of the episcopally ordained priesthood as an order of men "set apart," against both the intrusions of the political state and the pretensions of the nonepiscopal sect or the solitary enthusiast. For Anglican high churchmen, the priesthood, and the sacramental mysteries of which it alone was the sole custodian, formed the very sinews of communion. Through the sacramental ministrations of the episcopally ordained priest, the individual Christian participated at once in the historical church founded in Christ's commission to the apostles and in the eschatological community that comprised the body of Christ. The logic of the church's claim to embody a distinct, visible society was, in the final analysis, soteriological.

Though this strain of sacerdotalism was first embraced by the nonjurors, its basic imperatives soon came to permeate the whole of Anglican high churchmanship. The early decades of the eighteenth century are often seen as a high-water mark of post-Reformation English anticlericalism.[4] However, it is seldom recognized that such assaults on ecclesiastical authority expressly proceeded in the face of these ever more strident assertions of priestly power. The sacerdotalism of the Anglican high-church movement thus formed a vital part not only of the background of early Enlightenment investigations of religion, but of the whole of English politics during this period. Indeed, the exaltation of the priesthood attaining greater prominence in Anglican high-church ecclesiology was the vanguard of a broader social vision, one predicated on the radical autonomy of sacred things: the polity, clergy, offices, resources, and holy occasions of the church were all to be considered "set apart" from the common intercourse of English state and society. Religion was not to be construed merely as correct belief or right action, but as faithful participation in this distinct sphere of the sacred, the demarcations of which were, like checkpoints and border crossings, kept by the sentries of the church. From this vantage, the ubiquitous cry of "the church in danger" may be understood as more than a mere political slogan, but rather as a genuine alarm, a warning signal against transgression and invasion. And indeed, from this perspective, the Anglican revival, with its lay character, its giddy improvisations and casual ecumenism, its affirmation of the religious instrumentality of both state and society, may well have appeared as the work of so many spies and false brethren.

The Social and Ecclesiastical Thought of the Nonjurors

The character and content of what may be called counterrevolutionary Anglicanism was dramatically altered first by the deprivation of the nonjuring bishops and clergy in February 1690 and further by the consecration of new bishops to the vacated sees fourteen months later. Before the deprivations, counterrevolutionary churchmen were content to base their opposition to William and Mary on the shopworn political theology of Restoration Anglicanism, with all of its extravagant royalism and concomitant political quiescence. Indeed, their substantial contribution to the so-called allegiance controversy over the legitimacy of the new regime—much of it by way of refuting the quondam nonjuror William Sherlock's revolutionary turn in *The Case of allegiance due to sovereign powers stated and resolved*—largely involved the reaffirmation of the cherished doctrines of passive obedience and nonresistance to divine right monarchy.[5] These writings, on the whole, rarely strayed very far beyond the boundaries of prerevolutionary Toryism, even as the lay stalwarts of the Tory party were making their peace with the new establishment.[6] The deprivations of 1690, however, and much more so the intrusions of the Williamite bishops the following year, transformed the whole tenor of counter-revolutionary Anglicanism. The exaltation of the monarchy that had long formed the heart of Tory political thought gave way to an unmistakable circum-scription, if not outright negation of the civil power over sacred things.[7] The repudiation of revolution yielded pride of place to the declamation against schism.

The Revolution of 1688–1689 provoked a crisis in the traditional political theology of the Church of England. The deprivations and new consecrations, however, prompted a crisis of ecclesiology.[8] Defenders of the Revolution queried its opponents not on their opposition to the new regime, but on whether such opposition constituted legitimate grounds for withdrawal from the communion of the established church.[9] The Williamite classical scholar Humphrey Hody's ill-fated translation and publication of a selection from the Baroccian manuscripts in the Bodleian Library was intended to prove that historically, the intrusion of new bishops in the place of deprived ones was no grounds for schism, unless the new bishops were deemed heretical.[10] The nonjurors were not pressed on their Jacobitism, but rather on their schism—or rather, the schism to which they consigned the whole of the revolutionary church establishment. Obviously, their objections to the so-called immoral prayers to William and Mary inserted into the liturgy of the Revolution church blurred these lines considerably, but very few nonjurors considered these, in and of themselves, sufficient grounds for withdrawal from the public worship.[11] The initial question of the nonjurors' continuing loyalty to the exiled Stuart dynasty was rather quickly subsumed into a markedly different controversy over their continuing adherence to the deprived bishops.[12]

This shift had an unmistakable effect on the tenor of the nonjuring movement. The nonjurors committed the being of their church not to the supremacy of the exiled crown, but to the communion of the deprived bishops. As such, the identity of the nonjuring church was never really that of a reversionary establishment, maintaining its Erastianism in abeyance until the king could once again come into his own. The nonjuring church comprised, on the whole, a movement for ecclesiastical autonomy. The nonjurors were, as their leader George Hickes, the deprived dean of Worcester and a bishop in the nonjuring communion, described them, "confessors for the independent rights of the Church."[13] Indeed, the nonjurors routinely tempered their loyalty to James II with a fulsome commitment to the spiritual monarchy of the lawful episcopate, and by extension, the independence of the church.[14] These allegiances were, of course, by no means mutually exclusive, but nor were they identical; and the nonjuring Church of England, strictly speaking, dated the schism not to the deposition of 1689, but to the deprivations of the following year.[15] Consequently, the nonjuring movement's intellectual and polemical preoccupations during its first decades were with the critique of Erastianism, or state interference with the church, rather than with dynastic legitimism. Obviously, one should not overstate this point: the bishops and clergy were, after all, deprived for refusing to transfer their allegiance from James II to William and Mary; but it bears emphasizing that the nonjuring movement, by and large, embraced a distinct ecclesiological platform that was neither reducible to Jacobitism nor necessarily shared by all the partisans of the House of Stuart.[16] Indeed, many nonjurors routinely assailed the predations of James and William as more or less identical intrusions into the autonomous life of the church. The potential for divorcing their consummate regard for the independence of the church from the cause of political Jacobitism afforded the nonjurors an influence with their conforming brethren that their counterrevolutionary dynastic politics might have otherwise precluded.

The catastrophe of the Revolution, and the ensuing deprivations and new consecrations, demanded clarity from the profound ambiguities of Restoration Anglican ecclesiology. For now, lamented the Irish nonjuror Charles Leslie, "there were bishops and anti-bishops, and opposite altars set up," a true church arrayed against a nation in schism.[17] The nonjurors could no longer claim the luxury of an overdetermined church, rooted at once in the political establishment, jure divino episcopacy, and the historical nation.[18] Faced with what they considered an unlawful regality, a rival establishment, and the widespread alienation of national affections, the nonjurors made a singular investment in the apostolic institution of episcopacy. To this end, they seized upon a strain of Restoration Anglican ecclesiology derived in large part from the third-century bishop Cyprian of Carthage and propagated in the later seventeenth century by the likes of Bishops John Fell and John Pearson and the historian (and future nonjuror) Henry Dodwell.[19] Under the influence of Cyprian and his modern editors and expositors, the nonjurors exalted episcopacy to the level of a spiritual monarchy, the presence of which was indispensable not just to the good order, but to the very being of a church.[20] For the nonjurors, the diocesan bishop embodied the principle of ecclesiastical unity and was thus the very guarantor of sacramental efficacy. The regular succession of bishops from the apostolic age to the present was the only reliable preservative of divine authority and hence the only indisputable channel of sacramental grace.[21] As Dodwell asserted, "on the reasonings of St. Cyprian," in his *Vindication of the deprived bishops*, for the Christian "all hopes of pardon of sin, of the Holy Ghost, of eternal life, on performance of duty, were confined to the visible communion of the Church," which "could not appear but by their visible communion with the bishop, and head of the Church, and the principle of its unity."[22] Dodwell explicitly rejected Nonconformist and low-church ecclesiologies that identified the church with the depositum of true faith and orthodox doctrine, which he considered the mark of the sect. Faith alone was of no avail beyond the visible communion of the bishop, and thus the revolutionary church could not plead the orthodoxy of the Williamite bishops as grounds for continued communion.[23] In nonjuring thought, the bishops served as guarantors of a radically exteriorized religiosity, legitimated through unbroken apostolic succession and reaffirmed in the cultus of sacramental worship.[24]

The church, for nonjurors, was precisely as Cyprian had described it: *plebs Sacerdoti adunata et Pastori suo grex adherens*, a people united to their bishop, and a flock adhering to their pastor. The church was, then, a polity not unlike the state, albeit one constituted not by coercion, but by, as the nonjuring clergyman John Kettlewell wrote, "a spiritual subjection and dependence of people to their bishops."[25] The church was a polity bound by a spiritual power, which as nonjuring bishop Jeremy Collier pointed out, "is neither any gift of the people, or held by commission from kings and princes: it springs from a greater original, and derives no lower than heaven itself."[26] The church was what George Hickes called "a priestly polity" and a "spiritual corporation."[27] Dodwell even more colorfully referred to it as "a polity of angelic men."[28] The restlessness with which nonjurors seemed to run through the available linguistic resources of sociological description was rather remarkable, as if no extant model of temporal social or political organization quite grasped the being of the church.[29]

Most crucially, the church embodied a form of authority fundamentally different from that of the state. The nonjurors were proponents of what Mark Goldie has described as the doctrine of the two societies, the Christian political theory that apportioned the lives of individuals between the two "coterminous, yet distinct spheres" of church and state.[30] The nonjurors believed Christians to be properly subjected to two different monarchies, the temporal rule of the crown and the spiritual rule of the bishop. These regimes would ideally subsist in harmony with one another, but they could not be fused.[31] "The sacred and the civil," explained Charles Leslie, "were like two parallel lines, which could never meet, or interfere; for these two authorities lie in two distinct channels."[32] For nonjurors, the spiritual power derived from Christ through his apostles and exercised by the bishops remained wholly external to the coercive power embodied in political states.[33] The nonjurors therefore had fiercely to resist

Constantinian notions, which suggested that the conversion of the Roman Empire had somehow altered the being of the church, that is, had incorporated it into the structures of the civil state and subjected its spiritual authority to that of the imperium. Allowing the spiritual power of the monarchy, wrote Collier, would "put a period to the apostolical succession and dissolve the Church into the state."[34] This put nonjurors at odds not only with the more extravagant notions of the royal supremacy established over the Church of England by Henry VIII at the Reformation, but also with the implications of some of their more robust pronouncements on behalf of the divine right of kings. The right by which monarchs might indefeasibly claim to govern, though divine in origin, was not actually spiritual in operation and therefore afforded them no authority to interfere with the ministrations of the church. This was a curious divine writ, to say the least, which did not in fact run in the realm of the sacred. In any case, these qualifications of civil power quickly told on the tenor of the controversy over the deprivations. Nonjurors protested not simply against the actions of an illegitimate Revolution state, but against the intrusions of the state *tout court*. The powers claimed by James II, William III, or for that matter the Grand Turk were all alike and equally external to the spiritual constitution of the church.[35]

The deprivation of the bishops by the Revolution state, then, struck at the very axis of ecclesiastical communion, the independent and irrefragable relations that bound pastor to flock. The temporal power was thus arrogating the right to suspend and reconstitute the operations of spiritual power, which amounted to a wholesale nullification of that power by which the church subsisted. This monstrous encroachment, Henry Dodwell warned the newly consecrated primate John Tillotson, will "make it impossible for the Catholic church to subsist as a distinct and independent society on the state, which will fundamentally overthrow the very being of a Church as a society."[36] The question for nonjurors was not one of policy, but of polity; the deprivations were an existential threat to the life of the church as the nonjurors conceived it.[37] As the Suffolk nonjuror Nathaniel Bisbie reasoned with an eye toward the destruction of episcopacy in Scotland, "if the state hath such a power to deprive a bishop of his Church, as they have put John [Tillotson] upon William [Sancroft], may they not put William upon John again, and at length Jack Presbyter upon both?"[38] The nonjurors struggled to underscore the radical dissimilitude of church and state; the deprivations were no more valid than "if the states of England should make laws and enact penalties for the states of Holland," wrote Bisbie.[39] Charles Leslie went even further, branding the deprivations "a confounding of heaven and earth."[40]

The pressing need to defend the church as a spiritual society independent of the state imbued the nonjuring movement with an expansive sense of the sacred, and a heightened sensitivity toward all forms of encroachment. For the nonjurors, religion took on a conspicuous externality quite out of step with the radical interiority enshrined at the heart of the Protestant tradition. "Religion," wrote John Kettlewell, "ought not to stand on scattered individuals, but to be born up by communions, or pastors and people or by regular societies."[41] Religion denoted a kind of sociality: membership in a distinct society, which for the nonjurors comprised adherence to the lawful governors of that society and participation in the offices that those governors alone were commissioned to perform. Christians, wrote Henry Dodwell, possessed an "unavoidable duty to continue in its [the church's] external visible communion, and in subjection to its visible head." Only in this adherence, "they will continue their right to the invisible communion of the spirit."[42]

The insistence upon the irreducibly corporate nature of religion informed the nonjurors' particular antipathy toward what they branded enthusiasm. Nonjurors like Charles Leslie refurbished the mid-seventeenth-century critique of religious inspiration into a general critique of religious individualism.[43] Leslie's monumental work of anti-Quakerism *The snake in the grass* assailed the Society of Friends for substituting for the divine and historical authority of the church an "extraordinary commission of immediate divine revelation."[44] The Quakers abjured nearly all the externalities of religion, even the visible sacraments instituted by Christ himself, and instead "turned all into a mere allegory performed within every man's breast."[45] Improbably enough, Leslie was just as unsparing in his denunciation of the enthusiasm of deists and freethinkers, who also clamored after an individualized religion utterly bereft of external and visible ordinances. The deists were joined with the Quakers, warned Leslie, all of whom conspired to "throw off the succession of our priesthood . . . together with the sacraments and public festivals."[46] In the estimation of the nonjurors, religion was in danger of being atomized to mere belief—John Locke's famous "inward persuasion of the mind," ungrounded in historical authority, unmoored from external communion, and ultimately untouched by sacramental mysteries.[47] The church, observed Leslie, groaned beneath "a neglect of the outward signs and seals, pledges and means of grace, whereby God guarded and fenced the soul and spiritual part of his religion."[48]

For the nonjurors, the priesthood served to dispense these outward signs and seals that demarcated the visible communion of the church and ratified its ultimate soteriological function. Deriving its sacerdotal authority from the apostolic episcopate to whom the power of the Spirit was historically committed, the priesthood functioned as a sanctified and separate order of "men set apart" as the stewards of divine mysteries.[49] And as such, the priesthood was, in effect, the instrument by which the visible society of the church was governed, for it alone regulated access to the spiritual benefits of the society. Citing Melchizedek, the mysterious priest-king of Genesis 14:18, and Christ, "the eternal archetypal Melchizedek," George Hickes described the priesthood as possessed of both priestly and kingly powers and the power to administer the sacramental mysteries instituted by Christ, and in doing so, "to administrate his sacerdotal kingdom." Endowing the priesthood with what Hickes called "rectoral, or ruling authority" was the logical corollary to the nonjurors' conception of the church as an independent "political house or society," a bounded order of sociability possessed of its own constitutive integrity.[50] In such a vision, the priesthood could only be conceived as part of the apparatus of spiritual government.

The sacerdotal kingdom was administered sacramentally.[51] The sacraments both legitimated the spiritual rule of the priesthood, whose performances, because divinely and historically authorized, could alone find merit with God; and constituted the spiritual subjection of the laity, whose faithful participation in the offices ensured their continuing membership in the spiritual society of the church. Anglican sacerdotalism was thus underpinned by a robust sacramentalism. "The spiritual power," wrote Henry Dodwell, "is grounded in the power of rewarding and punishing spiritually, by admitting to, or excluding from the spiritual benefits of the society."[52] The episcopally ordained priesthood, those bearing an authentic commission "to officiate betwixt God and man," governed by regulating access to the instruments of salvation left by Christ in the sole custody of his church.[53] The Anglican sacraments of baptism and the Eucharist together comprised the means of incorporating individuals into the visible society of the church, and thereby communicating its soteriological benefits.[54] As the church was an outward, visible society, it required some "outward and visible form of admitting men into it." The sacrament of baptism constituted "our admission, initiation, or birth into the society of the Church." Without some physical demarcation of membership, warned Leslie, the church could not claim to be a distinct society, "for it could not then be distinguished from the rest of mankind."[55] Nonjurors accordingly laid great stress on the Anglican rite of confirmation, in which baptismal vows were renewed at the age of discretion. Though denied sacramental status in the Church of England, the episcopal prerogative of confirmation underscored the spiritual subjugation that membership in the visible society entailed.[56]

In his infamous *Epistolary Discourse, proving, from the Scriptures and the First Fathers, that the Soul is a Principle Naturally Mortal*, Henry Dodwell pressed the sacramental imperatives of nonjuring ecclesiology well past the bounds of orthodoxy.[57] He asserted that the human soul is naturally mortal. A person qualified for immortality, he argued, only "on account of the spiritualizing of his soul by the union of the spirit with it," which occurred only in the canonically performed sacrament of baptism—or rather, began in the priestly sacrament of water baptism and was completed only in the exclusively episcopal "spiritual baptism" of confirmation. In accordance with his rigorously Cyprianic ecclesiology, Dodwell argued that individuals derive their immortality from Christ not immediately, but "from some one principal person who was designed by God as the principal of their unity, upon whom they would depend if they would entitle themselves to the same spirit." In other words, salvific immortality was sustained only in communion with the bishop. Those who broke communion or otherwise sinned were denied the immortalizing spirit; they were instead immortalized immediately by God in the "second death" of damnation.[58] Dodwell was roundly condemned as a heretic. Even those who made it past his provocative title, acknowledging that natural mortality did not amount to the actual mortality of the soul advanced by some freethinkers, still rejected the radical sacerdotalism of the thesis.[59] Others found his sacramental theology utterly self-serving, a contumacious heresy to which he had been driven by "the desperate cause of the new schism."[60] Many saw little but rank Jacobitism ornamented by meretricious patristics. In the end, as John Tutchin's *Observator* put it, Dodwell "teaches that there's no salvation in the Communion of the present Church of England, as establish'd on the Revolution-foot."[61] Dodwell's thesis was by no means accepted, even among the majority of nonjurors, but his lapses from orthodoxy are telling.[62] In his account of the sacrament of baptism, Dodwell furnished his ecclesiology with a metaphysical as well as a soteriological foundation.

The sacrament of the Lord's Supper provided the basic grounds of Anglican communion.[63] Again developing a strain of seventeenth-century Anglican churchmanship, nonjurors (and many sympathizers among the conforming clergy) roundly emphasized the sacrificial nature of the Eucharist.[64] They rejected the merely commemorative ceremony that the contemporary prayer book seemed to favor, mourning the loss of the rich sacrificial language that had been present in the communion services of the 1549 prayer book and Archbishop Laud's Scottish prayer book of 1637.[65] The nonjurors considered the sacrament not just commemorative, but what the ablest expositor John Johnson of Cranbrook (himself a juring clergyman, though a theological ally of George Hickes) called "representative," in an extraordinarily literal sense, meaning that which again makes present. In re-presenting Christ's propitiatory and expiatory sacrifice on the cross, the consecrated elements were themselves propitiatory and expiatory. And as such, they were representative not merely for the people, but also in the sight of God, ever procuring from him the effects of Christ's death, "as if we had his very body and blood present to the father." The sacrament, it must be stressed, neither repeated the sacrifice on the cross nor supplemented the merits derived from it. It merely applied the general pardon bought by the cross to the individual communicant.[66] The sacrificial interpretation of the Eucharist had unmistakably sacerdotal implications. The minister was more priest than pastor, actually transacting with God, rather than merely bringing his flock to remembrance of the event of the crucifixion. These sacerdotal implications were not lost on critics, who believed the sacrificial interpretation of the Lord's Supper "an opinion revived of late for advancing the honor of the clergy."[67]

The charge was not wholly unwarranted. The nonjurors championed an intercessory priesthood possessed of a virtually judicial power of absolution. Eschewing the church's traditional notion of a merely declaratory form of absolution, promulgating Christ's general promise of pardon for the sincerely repentant, the nonjurors affirmed the necessity of sacerdotal absolution for the remission of sins.[68] Remission of sins, they claimed, was mediate rather than immediate; and the priestly absolution was not merely declarative, but active and peremptory. In his "Hypothesis concerning Sacerdotal Remission of Sins," Henry Dodwell set out to prove that "no truly penitent person can expect remission of sins . . . by virtue of the penitence itself, without the divine bounty and indulgence accepting it." Such acceptance, he argued, could not be expected outside the "ordinary means" of remission instituted by Christ and the sacraments, particularly that of the Eucharist. As the priest alone possessed "dominion" over the sacraments, his "consent and approbation" were deemed necessary toward securing the pardon of the penitent. Of course, Dodwell did not doubt that God was free to dispense his "extraordinary uncovenanted mercies" at will; he merely warned sinners against trusting in such prodigies. Christ instituted the sacramental offices expressly for "the preservation of the priest's authority."[69] This position gained ground among nonjurors (and like-minded juring churchmen) throughout the early eighteenth century and was promulgated to spectacular effect by the likes of Thomas Brett and Roger Laurence at the end of the reign of Queen Anne—to the mounting horror of Whig clergymen.[70] The leading low churchman White Kennett castigated those who would make "the power of forgiving sins as great in the priest as it was in Christ Jesus himself."[71]

The nation witnessed with particular dismay the realization of such sacerdotalist principles in April 1696. Three nonjuring clergymen, Jeremy Collier, Shadrach Cook, and William Snatt, ministered at the execution of two Jacobite conspirators, Sir John Friend and Sir William Parkyns, condemned for their involvement in a plot to foment an insurrection in the midlands and the north in advance of a French invasion and the assassination of King William.[72] Just before the sentence was carried out, the three clergymen jointly laid their hands upon the condemned men, publicly and solemnly declaring them absolved of their sins. The scandal was manifold. First, the public ministration of nonjurors was distasteful enough, a sacerdotalist defiance of the Revolution state that had deprived them of their public offices but could not curtail their spiritual authority. Second, the ceremony was apparently performed without any public confession; the absolution of unrepentant traitors might seemingly imply some measure of approval for their plot on the part of the attendant clergymen. And indeed, the last testaments of Friend and Parkyns that surfaced soon after their deaths revealed the conspirators to be not merely impenitent, but positively contumacious in their crimes.[73] Finally, and perhaps most egregiously, the sins of the two conspirators were remitted in a rite altogether unknown to the Church of England.[74]

One week later, the two archbishops and twelve bishops issued a formal denunciation of the ceremony as a "manifest transgression of the Church orders" and a "profane abuse of the power Christ hath left with his ministers." The bishops bristled in particular at the collective performance of the rite; for, though Collier had not attended upon Friend, nor Cook and Snatt upon Parkyns, the three divines absolved the two conspirators cooperatively. Thus, each clergyman had a share in absolving a man of whose confession and repentance he had no direct knowledge. The bishops inferred that the divines thereby deemed individual repentance either unnecessary or unwarranted.[75]

The ensuing controversy turned upon both politics and ecclesiology. Jeremy Collier immediately took to print to vindicate his involvement in the absolution. He had judged Parkyns's repentance sincere, and as circumstances had prevented him from offering private absolution, he absolved him publicly at the earliest opportunity. Collier pleaded for the orthodoxy of the rite, which in the absence of any particular office for condemned criminals simply grafted the primitive practice of imposition of hands to the "Visitation of the Sick" as it stood in the Anglican liturgy.[76] Moreover, he claimed it was vital that the absolution be performed according to some set form, rather than "left to the liberty of extempore effusions, which rather become a Calvinistical elder, than a presbyter of the Church of England."[77] Most defiantly, Collier pleaded the general independence of spiritual power, lamenting the state of postrevolutionary England, where "the functions of the priesthood and the assistances of religion and the reading of public liturgy are grown a crime."[78] The Church of England, he claimed, was not required to justify its absolution of sinners before the government and the public.[79] Collier denounced the divinity of his critics, which "comes from Selden, or Erastus, or else from Hobbes' *Leviathan.*" Indeed, without the power "to bind and loosen," the Church of England was not a church at all, but a mere "court-invention, and a politique design."[80] Enacting the entire drift of nonjuring thought in miniature, Collier contended not for the legitimacy of the Jacobite cause, but for the independence of the church from the state. The state, however, was not to be scorned. Cook and Snatt were both arrested and convicted of absolving traitors at King's Bench on 2 July 1696, though they were released with only a censure. Collier, however, fled prosecution, and though he reemerged in public without penalties the following year, he nominally remained an outlaw throughout his life.

If, as is often claimed, there was little that was wholly unprecedented in the thought of the early nonjurors, their political alienation—in principle, from the Revolution establishment, and in practice, from the Roman Catholic court at St. Germain—afforded them the luxury of clarifying the Anglican tradition.[81] The result of these clarifications was a vigorous articulation of ecclesiastical independence, founded on the principles of Cyprianic episcopacy and enacted through the sacerdotal ministrations of the priesthood. The tenor, if not always the letter, of nonjuring ideals pervaded early-eighteenth-century Anglican high churchmanship. And if the nonjurors were not readily able to attract the mass of conforming clergy to their cause, they at least managed to revive in their brethren a due skepticism of state power and a healthy sense of the autonomy of the sacred.[82] Indeed, the sacerdotalism of the nonjurors—along with its opposite, the strident anticlericalism of the freethinkers—effectively defined the polarity of early-eighteenth-century Anglican churchmanship. Their influence on the rhetoric of the "church in danger" during the reign of Queen Anne was unmistakable.

The Church in Danger

The disaffection of juring high churchmen did not impel them to embrace nonjuring principles during the reign of William and Mary.[83] Indeed, the import of such principles would have ill-served the conformist clergy who, having grudgingly accepted the legitimacy of the revolutionary monarchy and episcopate, had no immediate desire to see either invested with unaccountable sovereignty over state and church.[84] On the contrary, Anglican high churchmen during the reign of William frequently expressed their discontent in the political language of "country ideology," the traditional English commitment to responsible government and the defense of traditional rights and privileges against executive aggrandizement.[85] High churchmen found in the robust constitutionalism of country ideology a means to secure what they referred to as the "rights of the clergy" against the courtly designs of crown and bishops alike. During the latter part of William's reign, Anglican high churchmen trained their fire not on the civil state per se, but on the royal supremacy and the supine Williamite bishops, the "Church-Empsons and Dudleys," who colluded in its augmentation.[86] On a platform of "ancient constitution," Magna Carta, and the coronation oaths, conformist high churchmen set out to defend the traditional liberties of the established church from what they deemed "the boundless authority of sovereigns in Church-matters."[87]

This country or constitutionalist mode of the postrevolutionary Anglican high-church movement informed the great ecclesiastical controversies of the final years of William's reign. Many of these turned explicitly on the question of limits to the royal supremacy over the established church. The agitation to restore the dormant ecclesiastical assembly of convocation was conducted almost entirely in these terms.[88] The manifesto of this campaign, Francis Atterbury's *Letter to a Convocation-Man*, asserted in almost Whiggish language that "a convocation is as much a part of the constitution as a parliament itself." Atterbury did not, in fact, make his case on the nonjuring principles of the independence of the church from the state.[89] On the contrary, he pressed to insulate the lesser organs of the constitution from royal interference, of which the nearly ten-year suspension of convocation was a most troubling example.[90] The Somerset clergyman Samuel Hill went so far as to compare the suspension of convocation to the quo warranto proceedings against the city charters under Charles II and James II.[91] This high-church antipathy toward royal aggrandizement soon informed other controversies as well.[92] The proceedings of Archbishop Tenison and his Williamite allies against Thomas Watson, bishop of St. David's, for simony and peculation throughout the later 1690s exacerbated high-church fears of an overmighty court, which soon found expression in the unlikely voice of the Scottish radical Robert Ferguson, a stalwart of country principles.[93] Perhaps caught up in the broader drift of Toryism from court to country, Anglican high churchmen during the final years of William's reign contented themselves with constitutionalist retrenchment. They nursed their disaffection with petty aspersions of the king and the Revolution, lamenting the "horror" of "the affairs of the Church under his administration."[94] But on the whole, Anglican high churchmen during the reign of William conceived of their alienation in political rather than ecclesiological terms.

Ironically, the accession of Queen Anne in March 1702 inaugurated a new era of intellectual contiguity (if not quite collusion) between nonjurors and the juring high churchmen.[95] One might have presumed otherwise, that Anne's dynastic legitimacy and devout Anglicanism would have gone some lengths to fully reconcile churchmen to the Revolution establishment, salving the troubled consciences that might have induced them to hearken unto nonjuring recriminations. But the opposite turned out to be the case. Having pinned their disaffection on William and his bishops, Anglican high churchmen could not but be disappointed with the broad continuities in ecclesiastical policy under Anne. Far from reconciling them to the Revolution, the reign of Anne disabused many high churchmen of their instinctual, Tory Erastianism, rendering them manifestly more receptive to nonjuring conceptions of ecclesiastical independence. A pronounced sense of clerical grievance and an outsized regard for the externalities of devotion soon came to permeate the whole of Anglican high churchmanship. The ideological affinity between jurors and nonjurors was such that the intemperate likes of Charles Leslie could, even while papering over the crucial dynastic question, effectively become a leading spokesman on behalf of Tory causes.[96] This concord was only reinforced when in 1705, Henry Dodwell and several prominent nonjurors signaled their intention to rejoin the communion of the established church after the death of the last of the deprived bishops still claiming their sees—an event that occurred just five years later.[97]

The debate over occasional conformity, the annual taking of communion in the Church of England by Dissenters in order to qualify for civil employment under the Test and Corporation acts, was the most striking point of intellectual alignment during the reign of Queen Anne. The prevention of occasional conformity had become something of a Tory obsession during the first decade of the eighteenth century.[98] The advocates of a bill to penalize qualified office-holders who attended Nonconformists' meetings during their tenures reasoned that such an act would serve as a foundation for the new queen's reign, just as the Toleration Act had inaugurated that of her predecessor, an act in favor of the church to answer the prior act in favor of Dissenters.[99] Inspired perhaps by a sermon from the Oxford firebrand Henry Sacheverell the previous summer, William Bromley, the Tory MP from Oxford, introduced a bill to prevent occasional conformity during the first session of Anne's first Parliament. Easily carried by the substantial Tory majority in the House of Commons, the bill was delivered up to the Lords in December.[100] There, it was laden with amendments that diluted its force and rendered it unacceptable to its initial proponents; it died in conference between the houses. In late 1703, the Tory propagandist Charles Davenant's *Essays upon peace at home, and war abroad* appeared with a lengthy assault on the occasional conformity bill conducted in largely politique terms. Bearing the approval of Lord Treasurer Sidney Godolphin and a dedication to Queen Anne, Davenant's paean to "moderation" seemed to signal the court's growing distaste for revising the terms of the ecclesiastical settlement.[101] After an all-night debate, Bromley introduced a second occasional conformity bill on 26 November 1703. Two weeks later, the bill was carried in the Commons by eighty-three votes and delivered up to the Lords with great pomp by some two hundred members. The Lords narrowly rejected it by twelve votes; significantly, fourteen Williamite bishops voted with the majority.[102] The remainder of the parliamentary session culminated with the dismissal or resignation of several prominent

Tory Anglicans from the ministry. In closing the session, the queen lamented the lack of "moderation and unity" among the members. Unchastened, the Tory Anglicans resolved the following autumn to "tack" the occasional conformity bill to a revenue bill necessary for maintaining the war effort against France. The bill was crushed in the House of Commons, 251 to 134, with numerous prominent Tories voting with the majority.[103]

The controversy over occasional conformity was, as Geoffrey Holmes judged, "the most bitterly contested of all the battlegrounds of the political parties" in the early part of Anne's reign.[104] Opponents of the measure were quick to impute flagrantly counterrevolutionary motives to its supporters, surmising at every turn the collusion of Jacobites and nonjurors. In the House of Lords, the Whig Lord Charles Mohun warned "that if they passed this bill they had as good tack the pretended Prince of Wales to it." Bishop Burnet pointed directly to the encouragements of Charles Leslie, "furiousest Jacobite in England."[105] Leslie himself was quick to dismiss what had become a fairly standard charge in the rhetorical arsenal of early-eighteenth-century Whiggery: "Everything they don't like brings in the P[rince] of Wales!"[106] And yet, the allegation was not, in this case, wholly unfair.

Nonjurors were disconcertingly prominent in the debates over occasional conformity; their activism on behalf of the cause remains more than a little perplexing. On the one hand, they generally did not worship in the parish churches; they deemed their conforming brethren of the established church to be in schism for their adherence to the bishops intruded by the Revolution state. They seemed to be actively campaigning in defense of a church in schism and a state in rebellion against its lawful sovereign. On the other hand, the nonjurors remained intensely hostile to Nonconformity and perhaps discerned in the occasional conformity bills a means of curtailing Dissenter influence on policy. And even the nonjurors were perhaps not wholly free from political cynicism, recognizing the benefits that would surely redound to the Tory party from any diminution of Whig political clout. It would not have been unfair for them to perceive in the Tory party wholly better prospects of healing the schism, and perhaps even restoring the main branch of the Stuart line. However, the nonjurors may have had a genuine ideological investment in the repudiation of occasional conformity.

At stake in the occasional conformity controversy was the externality of communion, the notion of a church as a singular and visible society. Christ, wrote Henry Dodwell, "owns no body of men for his but his Church, nor any Church for his but that which is in covenant with him by baptism and our eucharistical sacrifice." Communion, then, consisted of firm adherence to spiritual governors and faithful participation in the offices that those governors alone were authorized to perform. The sacraments, particularly that of the Lord's Supper, were the "bonds of external union, so that they who united in the sacraments were united in the orthodox communion."[107] The sacramental test was not merely a task to be performed, an annual participation in an Anglican rite, but an indicator of permanent communion, of membership in the society of the church. The practice of occasional conformity was objectionable not merely because it gave Nonconformists access to political power. The occasional conformist was a rebuke to the very soteriology and sacramental theology that underpinned nonjuring ecclesiology; for if one "can communicate without communion," one could then partake of the body of Christ without being incorporated into that body.[108] The nonjurors could by no means allow this without damage to their social ecclesiology. The occasional conformist's "communicating with the Church upon some occasion," wrote William Higden, "no more makes him a member of our Church than a visit at my neighbor's house makes me an inhabitant, or my lodging once or twice at an inn makes it my home."[109]

The nonjurors thus sought not merely to curtail the practice of occasional conformity, but to demonstrate the impossibility of its very principle. Occasional conformity—or occasional communion, as they sometimes more emphatically called it—was a contradiction in terms, an oxymoron, "like rebellious loyalty, orthodox heresy, the north south wind." The terms could not be meaningfully reconciled for, as Thomas Wagstaffe put it, " 'communion' denotes Church-membership, and an intimate and mutual union between the parts; but 'occasional' denotes straggling and wandering and no union at all."[110] To nonjurors, occasional conformity was premised upon a flawed construction of religion that considered the sociality of communion somehow ancillary to salvific faith. This was, of course, to dissociate the saving truth of Christianity from the church in which such truth was rendered operative.[111] Nonjurors could by no means allow communion, membership in the spiritual society of the church, to be divested of its soteriological function. The occasional conformists and their enablers, charged Dodwell, are "ruining all lasting and obliging principles of unity and firm communion; and leave all at liberty, whether they will or will not maintain any one communion."[112]

The opponents of the bills chose to mount their defense of occasional conformity in the queen's own watchword of "moderation."[113] Moderation was associated with a truly catholic spirit, an unwillingness to permit putatively indifferent matters such as liturgy and church government to divide the body of the faithful. The occasional conformist, then, was no hypocrite, one who annually forsook his own congregation to qualify for office. On the contrary, the occasional conformist, wrote James Owen, was "one of a catholic spirit and confines not his communion to any one sect or party of Christians, but has an universal and comprehensive charity towards all that belong to the mystical body."[114] Such a man, wrote the Irish lawyer and SPCK founder John Hooke, "believes the holy catholic Church, takes himself to be a member of that Church, and consequently believes it his duty to refuse communion with no party of Christians."[115] Such a view made nonsense of the very concept of schism, implying that the divergence and multiplication of churches in England and abroad had done nothing to rupture the body of Christ. Claims for moderation seemed to press well beyond the logic of toleration, a merely political indulgence for those fundamentally in error; moderation not only presumed religious pluralism, but something like denominational interchangeability.[116] Moving between churches did nothing to hinder one's access to the means of salvation.[117] Such a position either rendered all Protestant churches equally orthodox or made ecclesiastical communion wholly exterior to soteriology.

Obviously, the nonjurors and many Anglican high churchmen could not abide either of these implications. They saw in occasional conformity, and the cry of moderation with which it was defended, the true face of religious modernity. Moderation, sneered one opponent of occasional conformity, was "a virtue of more modern complexion . . . calculated for the present state of things, a sociable and useful virtue"[118]—for moderation entailed plurality and equality of communions in the church of Christ, and the concord and politeness such equality required, a "lukewarmness" befitting Laodicea.[119] Worse, moderation seemed to imply that the choice among multiple communions was a matter of personal preference—and not even a binding one.[120] "To separate from a Church with which we can communicate without sin is schism," wrote Thomas Wagstaffe. "And if this be not the case, there can be no such thing as schism in the world, nor no such thing as a Church. 'Tis only a voluntary society which men may enter into and recede from at pleasure."[121] The nonjurors' hatred of voluntarism was the corollary to their contempt for Erastianism; whereas the latter threatened to subsume the society of the church into the coercive machinery of the state, the former relinquished the church to the associational and commercial logic of civil society. The church would be but one society among the variety of voluntary associations and contracts into which individuals' interest habitually led them. And such "independent societies," wrote Samuel Grascome, "make the Catholic Church a rope of sand."[122] The church would be no more than a sect or a club bereft of any obligation to adherence, "to which there goes no more than to be of this opinion; and they might change from one to another ten times a day, or, as a man may change his lawyer or physician without any hazard or penalty."[123] The proponents of occasional conformity, wrote Robert Nelson, "speak of churches, 'tho of different communions, as gentlemen do of seats in the country, and choose one before another for ease and convenience sake."[124] This fear that communion would be infected with a kind of commercial logic, the consumer mentality of a "mercantile conscience," permeated high-church tracts against occasional conformity.[125] The church, they reckoned, was no less imperiled by the penetration of the market than by the encroachment of the state.

The repudiation of Queen Anne's recommended policy of moderation soon became a centerpiece of Tory Anglican polemic. At pains to articulate the danger to the Church of England under an Anglican queen, a Tory Parliament, and a well-established episcopal church, Tories resorted to a kind of "paranoid style" in which moderation was a cover for collusion between the avowed enemies of the Church of England and the manifold traitors and false brethren within its own communion.[126] In June 1705, the Tory propagandist James Drake's incendiary *Memorial of the Church of England* used the failure of the occasional conformity bills and the exodus of the Tory Anglicans from the ministry to proclaim the church in danger. Drake accused the ministry of the Duke of Marlborough and Sidney Godolphin, their Whig allies, and the Williamite bishops of betraying the Church of England, preaching "indifference to the interests of the Church under the specious, deceitful name of moderation." Moderation, "the trade of hocus-pocusing and playing fast and loose with religion," struck at the very being of the church. Its proponents taught, above all, "that there ought to be no distinction amongst Protestants." Drake surmised an alliance of courtiers, Whigs, atheists, Scottish Presbyterians, and English fanatics against the Church of England. The ideological incompatibility of this imagined crew was of no account, "since through the ruin of the Church lies the common road to all their ends, even the devil's hand is welcome to pull it down." To save the endangered Church of

England, Drake looked to a purer breed of Anglican leaders than the current ecclesiastical governors. He called upon the handful of prerevolutionary bishops "who do not owe their promotion to [the Whig Junto ministers] Sunderland and Somers," the high-church stalwarts in the lower house of convocation, and the lower clergy "who want only to be headed and countenanced" to exert themselves in defense of the church. Simmering with resentment, Drake let slip a thinly veiled threat: "The principles of the Church of England will dispose men to bear a great deal; but he's a madman that tries how much."[127]

Given the inflammatory tone of this *Memorial*, it is not surprising that authorities were initially uncertain whether to attribute the piece to Tories within the establishment or to nonjurors and Jacobites outside of it.[128] Indeed, many critics lit precisely upon the diminishing daylight between the nominally distinct camps.[129] The whole tenor of high-church opposition was now set by "Leslie and his brood," and few critics could overlook the irony of those "who at the same time that they pretend to write for the Church and state, acknowledge neither, defaming one with the name of schism, and the other with that of rebellion."[130] The freethinker John Toland took the occasion to indict the entire sacerdotalist drift of Anglican high churchmanship; "intoxicated with the grandeur and splendor of the ancient patriarchs and councils," he wrote, the juring and nonjuring clergy alike seem "more concerned to preserve the hierarchy than the Protestant religion."[131] By August 1705, *The Memorial of the Church of England* had been presented to the grand jury of London and Middlesex as a "scandalous and traitorous libel" and ordered burned.[132] The suppression of the *Memorial*, however, did little to quell the pervasive sense among Tories and high churchmen that the church was indeed in very grave danger.

Perhaps congenitally incapable of doubting their own loyalty and orthodoxy, Tories and high churchmen grew increasingly careless with the antiestablishmentarian—even counterrevolutionary—tenor of their rhetoric. Whigs and supporters of the ministry were more than happy to advance their political rivals all the rope they needed to hang themselves. On 30 November 1705, the Junto Whig Lord Halifax cunningly requested that the House of Lords set aside a day to enquire into the supposed dangers of the church, which now loomed so large in Tory Anglican polemic. Barreling headlong into the trap, the Earl of Rochester, one of the leading aristocratic patrons of the high-church movement, rapidly seconded the motion. Thus, on 6 December, the Tories in the house foolishly lined up to impugn the security of the Church of England with a litany of grievances, all in the presence of her sacred majesty Queen Anne, then present in the chamber, unbeknownst to the peers.[133]

The Tory performance in the debates was a debacle. Disorganized and disrespectful, the Tories proceeded to deploy unfiltered the polemic of their most scabrous propagandists. Indeed, their case exposed a profound absence of any substantive Tory consensus on the perils facing the ecclesiastical establishment, merely a restless paranoia ranging after a surfeit of real and imagined enemies. Unsurprisingly, numerous Tory peers placed the failures of the bills against occasional conformity atop the list of dangers. To the grievance of occasional conformity, both Rochester and Nottingham added the menace of the established Kirk in Scotland and the absence of toleration for Episcopalians there. Rochester further complained of the absence of the Hanoverian heir to the throne, who might settle among them "in order to be fully acquainted with us and our constitution and thereby enabled to prevent any evil designs upon the Church and state." Sympathetic bishops followed suit with grievances of their own. Bishop Compton railed against profaneness and irreligion, a standard complaint, but hardly one with overt party associations. He further complained of the licentiousness of the press, citing a crop of radical Whig writers in both press and pulpit, including Edmund Hickeringill, John Toland, and Benjamin Hoadly. Archbishop Sharp cited the increase of Dissenters and the proliferation of unlicensed Dissenting academies, urging that judges be consulted about some means toward their suppression.[134]

The Whigs, particularly the bishops, not only parried Tory attacks with ease, they did so in a manner that made the Tory peers appear alternately extremist and mercenary. The Tory peers were tied to their party's most intemperate elements, particularly the insolent lower clergy and the nonjurors. Lord Halifax scoffed at the urgency with which Tories requested the presence of the Hanoverian heir, reminding them that at the time of the Act of Settlement, highchurch clergy had denounced Princess Sophia as an "unbaptized Lutheran." Lord Wharton sincerely hoped that Archbishop Sharp's intended suppression of the Dissenting academies would naturally include the nonjurors' schools, particularly the one in which the archbishop's sons had been educated. Similarly, Bishop Burnet complained of the growing influence of the nonjurors over the conforming clergy. Bishop Patrick decried the rabid high churchmanship in the universities, "in danger of this love of politics, which thrusts out arts and sciences." Patrick further complained about the lower clergy's pretensions to independence, "the undutifulness of the clergy to their bishops, and the difficulty they had to govern them regularly." In this, even Compton was forced to concur, reporting the calumny clergymen heap upon their bishops, "as if they were in a plot to destroy the Church." Bishop Lloyd similarly marveled at the insolence of the lower clergy, remarking, "I have been called fanatic in my own diocese and my brethren are called Low Church, i.e. betrayer of the church."[135]

Moreover, the Whigs decried the shameless opportunism of the Tories. To this end, they could not resist dredging up the reign of James II, when a genuine existential threat to the established church elicited from Tories not protest, but complicity and collaboration. Halifax ridiculed those lords still in the house, Rochester most prominent among them, who had sat on James's ecclesiastical commission yet now complained of the church in danger. Wharton even joked that he had prepared for the debate by consulting *The Memorial of the Church of England* to better inform himself of the dangers the church faced. He found there nothing more troubling than the fact that Buckingham, Rochester, and Nottingham were out of office.[136]

The Whigs, by way of contrast, celebrated a Church of England that was not only secure, but undergoing an unprecedented religious revival composed of new voluntary associations and corporations, a renewal of pastoral care, and new ecumenical initiatives. Tory and high-church discontent allowed the Whigs effectively to claim the Anglican revival and all its works as their own, undertaken on a platform of the "Revolution principles" of which they were the sole custodians. The low church blithely claimed the high ground. In the end, the motion was a spectacular failure, mustering only thirty votes to the sixty-one against it. Moreover, its supporters had been forced to own their disloyalty, publicly aspersing the soundness of Queen Anne's governance of her own beloved church. The resolution that passed was a resounding vindication of the Revolution settlement, which affirmed that the "Church of England by law established and rescued from the extremest danger by King William III of glorious memory is now by God's blessing under her Majesty's reign in a most safe and flourishing condition." All those who would insinuate otherwise were branded enemies to the queen, the church, and the kingdom.[137] As a coda, the queen soon after issued a proclamation condemning *The Memorial of the Church of England* and those "who falsely, seditiously and maliciously suggest the Church of England as by law established to be in danger at this time."[138] The high-church movement was now at its apogee from the court of Queen Anne.[139] The Whigs had managed to drive a wedge between the clericalism and the royalism at the heart of Tory ideology.

The Rights of the Christian Church

The Anglican high-church cry of the "church in danger" rapidly acquired the quality of a self-fulfilling prophecy. Even as the nonjurors and their conformist allies indicted an ever expanding circle of conspirators in a campaign against the church, their opponents clearly recognized that extravagant sacerdotalism would only breed radical anticlericalism. "The more we exalted the powers of the Church and clergy," warned the Whig clergyman John Hoadly (elder brother to the future bishop of Bangor), "others would the more sink and trample them."[140] And thus, the great age of early English enlightenment anticlericalism was at one and the same time an era of virtually unprecedented clerical self-assertion. The fatal dialectic of ever higher followed by ever lower articulations of religious authority came to define the field of political and ecclesiological controversy during the first two decades of the eighteenth century. Accordingly, ecclesiastical politics was warped by the intellectual pressures generated by this polarity.[141] Thus, within just months of the defeat of the "church in danger" resolution, an erstwhile Roman Catholic and former pupil of George Hickes published what would remain the most thoroughgoing assault on clerical authority to appear before the start of the Bangorian controversy during the reign of George I.

Matthew Tindal's extraordinary 1706 work *The Rights of the Christian Church asserted, against the Romish and all other priests who claim an independent power over it* was almost a photographic negative of nonjuring ecclesiology.[142] As the nonjurors and high-church sympathizers contended mightily for a corporate vision of the church, reducible to neither the coercive state nor the individual conscience, Tindal directly apportioned religion between these two authorities. He admitted the social dimensions of religion, which gave the state a positive interest in upholding those aspects of religion conducive to civic life, while preserving for the individual the radical soteriological freedom that he considered the core of Protestantism.[143] Exorcised from this framework, then, was the very notion of an autonomous spiritual power, at once independent of the state and binding on the individual conscience.

In effect, Tindal replaced the nonjurors' cherished doctrine of the two societies, the parallel sovereignties of church and state over the souls and bodies of men, respectively, with a radical bifurcation of the nature of religion itself. To the extent that religion inculcated morality, it fell under the cognizance of the sovereign state.[144] To the extent that religion was epistemological, and involved the apprehension of saving truths, it was reserved for the inviolable conscience of the believer. He simply denied the existence of any tertiary religious arena—social, but not political; spiritual, but not individual—in which ecclesiastical authority might obtain. Scholars disagree on the precise recipe by which Tindal managed to integrate robust Erastian claims for state authority over religion with an argument for religious toleration redolent of John Locke, but there is widespread agreement that such an amalgamation left no room for priestly authority.[145]

Adopting Locke's contractual account of the origins of political society, Tindal maintained that humans departed the state of nature only "for defense of themselves and properties," and not for the formation of ecclesiastical society.[146] As a result, the state could claim jurisdiction only over those aspects of religion "necessary for the support of human societies." This highly circumscribed Erastianism enshrined the state with largely negative religious obligations: the prevention of blasphemy, perjury, irreligion, and profanity. The positive religious obligations of the state did not extend beyond the bare bones of natural religion: the existence of God, his providential concern for the affairs of humanity, and the duty of honoring him. The state's obligation to prevent sin and irreligion was but a subsidiary function of its constitutive obligation to protect life and property. Humans had contracted no further than this, and therefore, with respect to the saving content of any religion, they remained within the state of nature. By limiting recognition only to those powers contracted at the foundation of the state and those powers enduringly reserved by the individual, Tindal left no redoubt wherein an autonomously spiritual authority might reside.[147]

Tindal thus advanced a model of religion that quite deliberately allowed no special province for the priesthood. Anglican high-church sacerdotalism was boxed out, on the one hand, by a qualified Erastianism, in which the state was concerned with religion only so far as it contributed to public virtue; and on the other, by a Lockean voluntarism predicated upon the possession by individuals of a "natural right of judging for themselves in matters of religion."[148] In this scheme, the ministrations of the clergy were extraneous to both the peace of the commonwealth and the worship of God. Thus, Tindal set about exposing the fallacies of sacerdotalism. He did not, like the freethinkers with whom he is often associated, simply catalogue the imagined historical malignancies of the priesthood. On the contrary, he sought to deconstruct the logic by which an intercessory priesthood was interjected into the economy of salvation. The spiritual monarchy championed by the nonjurors and high churchmen subsisted by the power of the keys commended to the clergy, that is, the power of admitting or excluding to the regular means of salvation. But this construction yielded the exceedingly strange phenomenon of a visible and outward society that somehow lacked the power to act visibly and outwardly upon its members. As ecclesiastical punishments like excommunication were neither visible nor external, the church claimed only a spiritual power, which "binds the inward man." But Tindal could not substantiate what such a nebulous power might consist of, for coercion could be exercised only temporally (over the body) or eternally (over the soul). The former belonged to the state, while the latter belonged to God alone. The claim of the clergy to bind and loosen in the next world was, for Tindal, "the most horrid blasphemy." Otherwise, the priests themselves would be worthy of divine worship, "since the power of damning and saving is in them, and God himself is no more than their executioner." And indeed, Tindal added reassuringly, any clergyman, if pressed, must surely admit that "God will not reward a good, or punish an ill man, more or less for their decrees."[149]

The priest, then, does not actually claim a judicial power of salvation and damnation, but only the power of admitting or excluding from communion with the church on the pretense that beyond its pale "there's no visible means of salvation." But this power of excommunication derived not from any apostolic commission, but, Tindal asserted, echoing Locke, from the very principles of human association, "the practice of all private societies, companies and clubs, who daily exclude those members who act not conformably to the rules they have agreed on." He proceeded to demonstrate that the Christian power of excommunication adhered in the flock rather than in the priest, traditionally requiring the consent of the whole congregation. Historically, excommunication amounted to little more than "avoiding the conversation of an ill man." In the hands of the grasping and ambitious clergy, Tindal accused, the principle became tantamount to damnation. Indeed, those who should have the greatest investment in reclaiming this lapsed soul were facilitating its banishment from the kingdom of God. Excommunication became the rod of priests, not in furtherance of their sacred function, but only "to advance their interest and power." The deterrent force of excommunication could redound to the benefit of the priesthood only if the penalty was a matter of soteriological efficacy rather than merely social convention. Priests, therefore, "made it their business to persuade the people that receiving the Lord's Supper was necessary to salvation, and that only they had a right to give it."[150]

The function of the clergy, then, was essentially ministerial, not sacerdotal. If the congregation chose an officer to minister in the performance of holy rites, it did so "for order['s] sake only, and not on account of any peculiar spiritual power which those who are set apart for the doing of them have from heaven." Tindal did not doubt the foundational work of Christ and the apostles, merely the notion that their commission descended through a particular lineage. Moreover, what had the parish priest to do with the apostles? The latter possessed the power to work miracles, but the modern ministry, he asked, "what mission can these gentlemen pretend to?" They were at best functionaries, "commentators, note-makers or sermon-makers on those doctrines which the ambassadors of God once delivered to the saints." Their commission to perform the offices of religion derived not from Christ, but from the agreement of the congregation in which they were to be performed. "All ecclesiastical power," Tindal boldly asserted, "has no other foundation than the consent of the society."[151]

Matthew Tindal's *Rights of the Christian Church* advanced something a good deal more radical than a vision of Christianity shorn of its priesthood. The work offered a compellingly modern sociology, in which the concept of spiritual power—power not originating in the individual or the sovereign state (the latter being, in any case, on Lockean principles, only an amalgamation of individual powers)—was utterly extirpated. Although not above dabbling in the petty anti-clericalism that characterized the works of contemporaries like Sir Robert Howard or Charles Blount, Tindal's work was not an exposé on the historical iniquities of the priestly caste, but an account of power in human societies so immanent that it virtually precluded the very idea of religious authority. That this was used not in defense of a civil religion, but rather on behalf of the "Church of England as by law established" was perhaps even more troubling to proponents of ecclesiastical independence, for it left the polity of the church intact but subordinate to the state and deprived of its sources of historical and spiritual legitimacy. In doing this, Tindal's work confirmed the whole thrust of nonjuring critiques of the Revolution establishment. Indeed, in its oscillation between Erastianism and voluntarism, Tindal's ecclesiology clearly struck critics as something of a grotesque of the established church.[152]

At the heart of Tindal's book, juring and nonjuring critics alike quite rightly discerned the specter of laicization, an emptying out of spiritual authority into the state and the individual. And unsurprisingly, both wings of Anglican high churchmanship lined up to vindicate the spiritual authority of the priesthood.[153] The responses are significant not so much for their novelty or ingenuity, but rather as further evidence of the penetration of sacerdotalism into the main-stream of Anglican thought.[154] The linguist and scholar William Wotton assailed Tindal in a sermon at Newport Pagnel, Buckinghamshire, titled *The rights of the clergy in a Christian Church asserted.*[155] The royal chaplain, Peter Nourse, preached his *Vindication of the Christian Priesthood* before Bishop Trelawny in August 1708, asserting, "we ought to magnify our office, for 'tis plain we are not (as some would have it) mere creatures or precarious officers of the state, but true ministers of Jesus Christ."[156] In 1707, Hickes brought forth his previously written treatise *On the Christian Priesthood* to counter Tindal's sociology of religion; all nations, he pointed out, have "agreed in the notion of the priesthood, and the difference between the sacred and the civil power."[157] No less significant was the extent to which the conforming clergy in mobilizing against Tindal came to recognize and embrace the double-sidedness of the nonjuring critique. The church was endangered at once from the heavy hand of the sovereign state, which would render Christianity as nothing more than a "political religion," but also from the moderation and latitude of a pluralistic civil society. Critics perceived quite clearly that Tindal's system, and perhaps the Revolution establishment upon which it was based, was designed "to take away the rights of the Church and establish the rights of No-Church at all," that is, the rights of state and sect that were but mere pretenders to spiritual authority.[158] For a growing number of clergy, Tindal's *Rights of the Christian Church* had the force of clarifying the profundity of the crisis facing the Church of England.

The Lay Baptism Controversy

The sacerdotalism of Anglican high churchmanship reached a crescendo in the so-called lay baptism controversy of 1708–1715. In many ways, this campaign against the validity of sacraments administered by nonepiscopally ordained ministers, much more so than the notorious (but theologically unremarkable) sermons of Henry Sacheverell, signaled the extremity of Anglican high churchmanship during the final years of the reign of Queen Anne. Sacheverell's Toryism was stolid and naïve, a reaffirmation of Caroline political theology in which the fact of the Revolution was to be shouted away by volume and vituperation. His incredible celebrity, enhanced by his impeachment in 1710 and the ensuing electoral fallout, has come to embody the specter of Anglican high-church revanchism in the later years of Queen Anne's reign.[159] But Sacheverell's throne and altar conservatism was by no means representative of the most reactionary elements of the high-church program in these years. The critics of lay baptism, such as Thomas Brett and Roger Laurence, were pressing the sacerdotalism beyond the bounds of Tory establishmentarianism. Indeed, the account of sacerdotal authority at the heart of their writings seemed at times to transgress the very boundaries of the Reformation. As Gareth Bennett once put it, these men "represented a clerical dream-world."[160] Such figures were not typical of the mainstream of Anglican high churchmanship, but the profound unwillingness of conformist bishops and clergy to condemn their ideas suggests the growing appeal and at least tacit acceptability of such doctrines within the Church of England. Apprehensions of the danger to the church had grown so acute that virtually all vindications of priestly authority were welcomed in its defense.

The complaint against baptism by those not in holy orders had been a standard grievance of churchmen throughout the later seventeenth century.[161] However, the increasingly sacerdotalist cast of Anglican high-church thought prompted some to broaden the definition of laity at the heart of the complaint to include all those lacking episcopal ordination. In March 1708, Roger Laurence, a Nonconformist layman, to resolve his gnawing doubts about the validity of nonepiscopal sacraments, sought rebaptism from John Betts, a reader at Christ Church, London. Because of the irregularity of the performance, neither the vicar of Christ Church nor the bishop of London was informed of the rite. Soon after, Laurence published an anonymous defense of the service titled *The Invalidity of Lay Baptism*.[162] Citing the nonjuror George Hickes, among other authorities, Laurence advanced an extreme sacerdotalism in which he denied soteriological efficacy to sacraments administered by those lacking episcopal ordination. Cribbing a metaphor from the contemporary debates over the act for naturalization of foreign Protestants, Laurence likened baptism to the conferral of holy citizenship. As naturalization, and the conferring of all the benefits it entails, was the known prerogative of the magistrate, so baptism in the church was the prerogative of the spiritual governors. Christians would be as foolish to think themselves secure in the rights conferred by nonepiscopal baptism as foreigners who had received their citizenship from an ordinary subject. Such was lay baptism, a bogus naturalization in the kingdom of heaven conferred by one with no authority to grant it. The implication of Laurence's thesis was clear: sacraments performed outside of the episcopal church were not valid. He claimed an initial ambivalence with respect to the Protestant churches abroad, but his warning to English Nonconformists, "living under that episcopal government which they refuse to acknowledge and submit to," was unmistakable: "I fear their case is very dangerous."[163]

During the following years, Laurence's critique of lay baptism gained vocal adherents among a conforming clergy desperate for some confirmation of the viability of their spiritual power.[164] Bishop Burnet openly decried the uncharitableness of this "conceit lately got in among us that denies all who are not baptized among us to be Christians, shuts them out of Christ's covenant, and thinks them no better than heathens." He linked these positions with the "monstrous errors" of Henry Dodwell's widely ridiculed *Epistolary Discourse*.[165] The learned Thomas Brett, rector of Betteshanger, Kent, published a letter defending Laurence's position, congratulating the layman for defending "the spiritual rights of the clergy, which I fear some of our own orders are too ready to oppose."[166]

The controversy was rapidly expanding to include the broader question of priestly power, and the intercessory role of priests in the procurement of grace. Roger Laurence further developed his soteriology in a 1711 work titled *Sacerdotal Powers*, arguing, as Henry Dodwell had done, for the necessity of priestly absolution to pardon sin. Thomas Brett followed suit, preaching a sermon titled *On Remission of Sins* at the Chapel Royal on 5 November 1711 and then again in London churches the following two weeks. Brett's sermon equipped the episcopally ordained clergy with a virtually judicial power of absolution. Brett, like Dodwell, denied that penitence merited divine pardon; it merely qualified one for the peremptory act of priestly absolution.[167] Auditors reported back to Archbishop Tenison "that he [Brett] urged the necessity of the absolution of the priest much further than is consistent with the doctrine of the Church of England."[168] White Kennett denounced Brett as "a fashionable defender of some notions of Dr. Hickes and the Jacobite party."[169]

The leading low churchmen were predictably scandalized by the new strain of sacerdotalism gaining ground among their brethren. On 22 February 1712,

Robert Cannon, archdeacon of Norfolk, moved to put the lower house of convocation in mind of the "false and dangerous doctrine" in Brett's sermon *On Remission of Sins*, which he did not find consonant with either Scripture or the doctrine of the Church of England.[170] Tellingly, the high churchmen in the majority rallied to defend Brett. The dean of Carlisle, George Smalridge, admitted that he might not be able to defend every passage in Brett's sermon but moved that if the lower house were to concern itself with censuring books, "they should rather fall upon those that had depressed the authority of the Church too low than upon such as had raised it too high," such as Matthew Tindal's *The Rights of the Christian Church*.[171] Another member objected "against meddling with a clergyman when there were so many lay writers who were much more obnoxious to our censure and condemnation of them." The low churchmen were unmoved by the latter argument, saying that "in any reformation of doctrine or discipline we should begin with ourselves, and call any of our own brethren to account much sooner than strangers." Unwilling to have to defend Brett's extremist doctrines, the prolocutor Francis Atterbury managed to have the question set aside.[172]

Balked among the lower clergy in convocation, the low-church bishops moved to address the question of lay baptism directly. On 22 April 1712, the bishops then in London assembled at Lambeth Palace for the customary Easter Tuesday dinner with the archbishop. At dinner, the conversation was dominated by "the great offense given by the sermon of Dr. Brett asserting the invalidity of lay baptism and extending it to the foreign Churches as well as to our dissenters at home." All the prelates present, including the increasingly conservative archbishop of York, John Sharp, agreed that "some public notice ought to be taken to prevent the farther scandal that would otherwise be given abroad and at home by such uncharitable and dividing doctrines." Tenison worried openly of the reports that numbers of Nonconformists were seeking rebaptism in the city churches, insisting that "such a call to be rebaptized was never the sense or practice of the Church of England." Tenison resolved to revoke the discretionary power allowed ministers to baptize adults seeking communion with the Church of England and to stipulate that all adult baptism required the consent of the diocesan.[173] That week, the archbishops and bishops agreed to issue a short declaration against the new doctrine of the invalidity of lay baptism, which Tenison thought "short and plain and (I hope) inoffensive."[174] The statement simply affirmed that it was the judgment of the catholic church of Christ, and the Church of England in particular, "that such persons as have been already baptized in or with water in the name of the Father, Son and Holy Ghost ought not to be baptized again."[175] But the consensus began to fracture. William Dawes, bishop of Chester, "expressed his dislike of that way of proceeding."[176] On 28 April, Archbishop Sharp confessed to Tenison that he could not endorse the declaration, "For I am afraid this would be too great an encouragement to the Dissenters to go on in their way of irregular, uncanonical baptisms." Several other bishops, Sharp added, concurred with him.[177] It is worth remembering that sixteen years earlier, Archbishop Tenison was able to solicit significant support from the Tory bishops for his intervention against the nonjurors' absolution of Sir William Parkyns and Sir John Friend. By the end of the reign of Queen Anne, even moderate high churchmen were unwilling to check the increasingly reactionary sacerdotalism gaining ground among the lower clergy.

The archbishop fared no better in convocation. On 14 May, Tenison and the bishops sent down their declaration against the doctrine of the invalidity of lay baptism.[178] The Gloucester proctor Henry Brydges railed bitterly against the declaration, claiming that the vital business of the queen was being left undone so the bishops could "countenance schism and give the Dissenters a cordial for the loss of their occasional conformity." Brydges concluded with a motion that the declaration from the archbishop and the bishops be ignored. White Kennett reported that the speech was so mean-spirited that even reliable high churchmen like George Smalridge "shook their heads and seemed very much troubled and ashamed for him."[179] Nevertheless, faced with the possibility of "giving some advantage to schismatical baptism," the majority in the lower house carried the motion that the paper be laid aside. A declaration against Brett and his allies among the nonjurors and within the church could not at that time be considered "because of the inconveniences manifestly attending such a declaration especially at a time when the authority of the Christian priesthood was openly struck at by some and the advantage of an episcopal mission so much undervalued by others."[180] The lay baptism controversy sputtered on in the ensuing years. Tenison and his allies continually threatened to press the issue of their proclamation in convocation, while Oxford University astoundingly conferred a master's degree on Roger Laurence seemingly in approbation of his sacramental theology.[181]

The lay baptism controversy typically has been read as a theological cipher for the politics of the Protestant succession. There was no question that

Jacobitism lingered not far below the surface of the debate. After all, denying the validity of sacraments performed outside of episcopal communion tacitly granted the Roman Catholic James Francis Edward Stuart a clearer title to heavenly grace than his rival the Lutheran Elector George of Hanover. Moreover, the abjuration of the Pretender required by parliamentary statute after the Hanoverian succession did finally prompt both Brett and Laurence to abandon the established church for the communion of the nonjurors, in which both were eventually ordained bishops.[182] However, it is important to remember that both men had made their initial case for the necessity of episcopal communion within the Revolution establishment; no part of their case against lay baptism impugned the legitimacy of the Revolution Church of England. Their sacerdotalism was not, at least at first, freighted with the burden of the nonjuring schism. And this must have accounted, in no small part, for its broader appeal to the mass of conforming clergy. The high-church clergy of the Church of England grasped after any account of spiritual authority that was at once elevated above the sect and emancipated from the state. Even those bishops and churchmen who had serious reservations about the orthodoxy of Brett and Laurence did not wish to see the promulgation of a censure, which they feared would further derogate the power of the priest in the eyes of the nation.

In the heat of the controversy, low churchmen of all ranks began a campaign against the sacerdotal pretensions they saw gaining ground throughout the established church. These men singled out the "independency of the Church upon the state," the notion of a "proper sacrifice in the sacrament of the Lord's Supper," "the necessity of sacerdotal absolution for the remission of sins," and the invalidity of lay baptism as doctrines born of what John Turner deemed a misguided "zeal to support the sinking power of the priesthood."[183] Spurred on by nonjuring ripostes, the low-church campaign against sacerdotalism plowed inexorably forward toward the bishop of Bangor Benjamin Hoadly's explosive 1716 tract *A Preservative against the principles and practices of the nonjurors both in church and state*, the work that set the stage for the consuming ecclesiological controversy that bears his title.[184]

In what was surely a sign of the times, Bishop Gilbert Burnet issued a new edition of his most cherished work, *A Discourse of the Pastoral Care*, in the final years of his life. To this veritable manifesto of Anglican revivalism, born of the profound religious hope of the Glorious Revolution, the bishop appended a new preface in which he systematically assailed "the raising [of] the power and authority of sacred functions beyond what is founded on clear warrants in Scripture," and along with it, the notions of ecclesiastical independence, the sacrificial Eucharist, sacerdotal absolution, and the "unchurching" of the nonepiscopal Protestants at home and abroad. He considered the rejection of these doctrines to be essential to the identity of the low churchmen, among whom he ranked himself, and all those who "rejoiced in the Revolution and continue faithful and true to the settlement then made, and to the subsequent settlements."[185] Such priestly pretensions had no place in Burnet's pastoral ideal.

Conclusion

The most enduring work produced in the nonjuring and high-church milieu of the reign of Queen Anne was neither a political sermon nor a piece of controversial divinity. At the height of the occasional conformity controversy, the nonjuror and philanthropist Robert Nelson published his astonishingly rich *Companion for the festivals and fasts of the Church of England*. This enormous compendium of holy days and occasions was intended not only as a practical aid to observance, but a quiet vindication of the ecclesiology of Anglican high churchmanship. "Except we will acknowledge some power in the Church, to determine the modes and circumstances of public worship and to oblige us in indifferent matters," Nelson wrote, "it is impossible there should be any settled frame of things in any Christian society in the world." Nelson's *Companion* went beyond the vindication of the spiritual authority of the priesthood to affirm the whole being of ecclesial life that subsisted beneath that authority. Ecclesiastical communion was more than just subjection to spiritual governors; it was an enduring sociality lived in both space and time.[186] And naturally, evidence of encroachment was met with ever more strident affirmations of inviolability. The sacerdotalism of the nonjurors unfolded into a broader cult of exteriority within the Church of England, a more than aesthetic concern for the external demarcations and orders of ecclesial life that would be the nonjuring schism's primary legacy to eighteenth-century Anglicanism.[187] The conception of the church as a visible, distinct society naturally engendered a concern for the material emblems of communion—the hierarchy, liturgy, sacraments, and offices—the outward terms and trappings of membership in a spiritual corporation. By the end of the century, Nelson's *Companion* had run to nearly thirty editions.[188]

The danger to the church, then, was the dissociation of religion from communion. The Anglican high-church movement and the nonjurors conceived of religion as belonging rather than believing, membership in a society enacted through adherence to its governors, observance of its canons, and constant and faithful participation in its offices. They relentlessly assailed the increasingly pervasive sense in eighteenth-century England that religion consisted primarily of correct belief or moral behavior. For once communion became more or less ancillary to salvation, the church would fall prey to the prudential and politique management of the state, the rivalry of denominations of equal validity, or utter dispensability in the eyes of enthusiast and rationalist alike. And so the Anglican high-church movement was prompted to weave its soteriology ever more finely into the fabric of its ecclesiology, to the point where those outside the communion of the church were considered, as Henry Dodwell assured his readers, "actually under the power of the Devil."[189] They responded to the widespread cry of irreligion and profaneness during this time by reaffirming the inviolable bonds of ecclesiastical communion. The nonjuring squire Francis Cherry scribbled a telling quote from Francis Bacon in his commonplace book: "Heresies and schisms are greater scandals to the Church than corruption of manners."[190]

From this vantage, one can perhaps begin to comprehend the ambivalence of high churchmen toward the Anglican revival as it was then unfolding. They were broadly supportive of programs, such as the charity schools, designed to entrench English men and women firmly in the communion of the Church of England. However, they often looked askance at the mere reformation of manners, which considered judicial suppression of vice an end in itself. Moreover, their inestimable regard for the powers of the clergy and their constitutional traditionalism could only have been alienated by newfangled, lay-dominated organizations such as the SPCK. Certainly, they would have wanted no part of the SPCK's numerous ecumenical engagements at home and abroad, all of which seemed to confer legitimacy on nonepiscopal denominations whose irregularity high churchmen were at great pains to stress.

One must not overstate the case. As we have seen, nonjurors and high churchmen, at least initially, participated in entities like the SPCK with energy and enthusiasm. However, it was abundantly clear to contemporaries that the leading Anglican high churchmen of the reign of Queen Anne expended their energies elsewhere. Rather than embrace the financial and organizational instruments of civil society to promote the cause of religion, Anglican high churchmen turned toward the traditional institutional resources of the established church. As we shall see, they gravitated toward an alternative religious revival, one predicated on augmenting the spiritual power and presence of the Church of England over national life.

CHAPTER 5

The Moral Counterrevolution

At its inception at the turn of the eighteenth century, some Anglican clergymen denounced the Society for Promoting Christian Knowledge (SPCK) as an encroachment upon the rights and function of the long dormant convocations of the Church of England. One must remember that the society was founded during one of the more contentious controversies to trouble the peace of the church in the postrevolutionary era, the wide-ranging debate over the constitutional and ecclesiological status of the church synods known as the convocation controversy. Since the mid-1690s, one of the central planks of Anglican high churchmanship had been the restoration of the provincial assemblies of the established church, which had been, apart from the brief and fruitless revival of late 1689, in abeyance since 1664. Yet it is not immediately obvious why a small London voluntary association composed of members of both the laity and the clergy, as well as its campaign to organize provincial clergy into clerical societies, would be perceived as "an usurpation on the rights of the convocation," or worse, "a contrivance to render a convocation useless."[1] But, in fact, such complaints were not uncommon. Influential voices in the Anglican high-church movement discerned in the postrevolutionary wave of Anglican voluntarism and lay activism an invasion of the rights and functions of the clergy. Only through the lens of an increasingly contested Anglican revival does this embryonic conflict come into focus. The same impulse toward religious renewal that impelled the organizational experimentation of the reign of William and Mary informed the agitation to restore convocation as an instrument of ecclesiastical discipline and reform. That proponents of the latter campaign could look askance at participants in the former suggests the emergence of a rival strain of Anglican revivalism, one that placed a greater emphasis on augmenting the social power of the clergy and refurbishing the traditional institutions of ecclesiastical discipline. This movement may be conceived as a "moral counterrevolution."

Given the growing prominence of sacerdotalist regard for the unique powers and privileges of the priesthood in early-eighteenth-century Anglican high churchmanship, it is perhaps not surprising that some clergymen looked with misgiving at the collaboration between court bishops and voluntary associations that characterized the program of religious renewal during the reign of William and Mary. The fiery Henry Sacheverell threw down the gauntlet in his savagely partisan 1702 tract *The Character of a Low-Churchman*, in which he complained that

> instead of the ancient, primitive discipline of the Church, which has for so many ages secured its religion from vice and immorality, schism and heresy we have substituted in its place a society for the reformation of manners, wherein every tradesmen and mechanic is to take upon him the gift of the Spirit, and to expound the difficult passages of Scripture, and every justice of the peace is allowed to settle its canons and infallibly decide what is orthodox and heretical. And now to what end or purpose must all these alterations be made, and this mongrel institution be brought into the Church? But only to insinuate an insufficiency in its discipline, to overturn its ancient, genuine constitution, to betray its powers into the hands of lay eldership and fanaticism, and to leave it dependent and precarious on the will and humor of the senseless and giddy multitude?[2]

Like his nonjuring contemporaries, Sacheverell feared the dissolution of the church into state and civil society, the transfer of its prerogatives into the hands of an activist laity and a zealous magistracy. Like-minded high churchmen, then, sought to staunch the leakage of sacred authority out of the established church by undertaking the reconstruction of ecclesiastical discipline.

This "moral counterrevolution" comprised a rearguard defense against the laicization of religious life putatively embodied in Anglican voluntarism.[3] The term is intended to invoke two well-known historiographical constructs pertaining to this period: Dudley Bahlmann's characterization of the reformation of manners movement and allied associations as part of "the moral revolution of 1688," and Gareth Bennett's suggestion that the high-church agenda of the convocations of the reign of Queen Anne represented "an Anglican attempt at counter-revolution."[4] Both authors were too quick to map these competing Anglican revivals onto the geography of postrevolutionary party politics, effectively assigning Whiggish and Jacobite orientations to voluntarist and sacerdotalist campaigns, respectively.[5] The assignment of political affiliation, or more crudely, revolutionary and counterrevolutionary orientations, to these campaigns gets one only so far. After all, as we have seen, Anglican voluntarism in the postrevolutionary period, for all its avowal of "Revolution principles," was largely impelled by the failures of the Revolution state to undertake the work of ecclesiastical renewal. Moreover, high-church efforts, despite their prerevolutionary nostalgia and sentimental Jacobitism, could hardly look to the highly Erastian Restoration church, which had bartered away its ecclesiastical assemblies, to model a movement rooted in convocation and founded upon notions of ecclesiastical independence and the rights of the lower clergy. The term "moral counterrevolution," I hope, captures some sense of the Anglican high-church opposition not to the Revolution per se, but rather to the spirit of ecclesiastical "projecting" and improvisation that the limitations of the Revolution settlement had seemingly made necessary. The moral counter-revolution intended to rescue, as it were, the work of ecclesiastical renewal and reformation from civil society and reground it firmly in the disciplinary institutions of the established church.

One cannot but be struck by the extent to which the high-church agenda of the convocations of Queen Anne mirrored that of the SPCK and allied organizations. Whereas the SPCK sought to organize informal neighborhood clerical societies, the convocation advocated the restoration of the rural deaneries. Whereas the SPCK distributed works of piety and devotion, the convocation sought to police and censure works of heterodoxy. Whereas the SPCK promoted charity schools, the convocation sought to curtail the proliferating academies of sectarian rivals. Whereas the SPCK championed the societies for the reformation of manners, the convocation sought to rehabilitate the ecclesiastical courts. Whereas the SPCK identified with what it perceived as a burgeoning revival in the established church, the convocation reported on a dire state of religion in postrevolutionary England. Given the parallels in their agendas, it becomes increasingly clear why contemporaries might have accused the variety of religious societies and corporations of promoting an ersatz discipline compared with the genuine article advocated in convocation.

Obviously, the lines were not always so starkly drawn. As we have seen, numerous high churchmen remained engaged with organizations such as the SPCK in this period, and indeed, as late as March 1711, a committee on charity in the lower house of convocation was still recommending the establishment of charity schools and parochial libraries, two projects long associated with the SPCK.[6] Nevertheless, real divisions were apparent. The leading high churchmen in the lower house of convocation, particularly those associated with Christ Church, Oxford—Henry Aldrich, Francis Atterbury, George Hooper, and George Smalridge—had largely eschewed participation in the Anglican societies. And, as we have already seen (Chapter 3), those SPCK members who sat in the lower house of convocation at this time were much more likely to side with the low-church opposition to Atterbury and his allies. Perhaps unsurprisingly, the "Representation of the State of Religion" produced by high churchmen in convocation in early 1711 went out of its way to disparage voluntary efforts as broadly insufficient for the task of religious renewal.[7]

Positing a competition between distinct strains of Anglican revivalism in the first two decades of the eighteenth century, of course, necessitates the identification of a winner. In this, there can be little controversy. The civic Anglicanism sponsored by the SPCK and allied organizations was enshrined in the missions, hospitals, and workhouses of the mid-eighteenth-century age of benevolence in Britain and its empire. Meanwhile, the moral counterrevolution was, by any standard, a colossal failure. The restored convocation of the early eighteenth century achieved next to nothing before succumbing to royal suspension in 1717 at the outset of a long season of Whig ascendancy over the established church. The Anglican high-church movement during this period did not fail because it was politically counterrevolutionary; quite the contrary, the movement seemed to grow increasingly politically counterrevolutionary as its failures mounted. Political and institutional obstruction to high-church social and religious objectives stoked antagonism toward a Revolution settlement that was increasingly identified as a bar to religious renewal and propelled the dangerous clerical fantasy that ecclesiastical autonomy would fare better by a Catholic restoration than the Protestant succession. In truth, the failure of the moral counterrevolution stemmed more from the institutional deficiencies of the established church itself, the Erastianism and episcopal domination of which had been routinely reaffirmed to high-church acclaim over the course of the preceding half-century. There was precious little a movement rooted in the lower clergy could accomplish in an established church reconstructed after the political and religious crises of the mid-seventeenth century to militate against threats to royal and episcopal superintendence. Nevertheless, Anglican high churchmen during the reign of Queen Anne adumbrated a program of religious renewal rooted in traditional institutions that comprised a genuine alternative to the kinds of civic and associational projects promoted by the likes of the SPCK. The coming of the eighteenth-century age of benevolence cannot be fully understood without accounting for this program's foreclosure.

The Return of Convocation

"If ever there was need of convocation, since Christianity was established in this kingdom," wrote Francis Atterbury in his powerful *Letter to a Convocation-Man*, published at the end of 1696, "there is need of one now."[8] With these words, Atterbury committed the nascent postrevolutionary high-church movement to the cause of convocation—first, to the restoration of the ecclesiastical assemblies, and then, having achieved that, to their functionality in the realms of ecclesiastical discipline and reform. For the next twenty years, the fate of Anglican high churchmanship would be intertwined with that of convocation. The genius of Atterbury's *Letter* was its ability to channel widespread, albeit inchoate, clerical discontent with the Revolution settlement and the unchecked theological excesses of the Trinitarian controversy into a movement to restore the provincial assemblies of the established church.[9] Evincing an almost unparalleled fluency in the evolving languages of postrevolutionary Toryism, the *Letter* fused the constitutionalist tropes of "country ideology" with the nascent paranoia of "the church in danger."[10] When it served his purposes to assail the prerogative of the monarch to suspend the convocation, Atterbury cheerfully traded on the touchstones of Whiggery—the Magna Carta, the coronation oaths, and "many of the popular pamphlets in the two last reigns"—to affirm the limits of the royal supremacy.[11] The sovereign was no freer to dispense with convocation than he or she was to dispense with Parliament. Atterbury rested much of his case for the constitutional necessity of convocation on the so-called *praemunientes* clause traditionally appended to the writs that summoned the bishops to Parliament. The clause directed the bishops "to attend upon the king in parliament" with their deans, archdeacons, and proctors from their cathedrals and diocesan clergy, thus implying a parliamentary foundation for the lower house of convocation. The *praemunientes* clause furnished Atterbury with what he conceived as an "argument of invincible strength to establish the necessity of convocations meeting as often as parliaments."[12] Moreover, the *praemunientes* clause, implying a direct summons from king to bishops to lower clergy, had the added benefit of dramatically curtailing the role of the archbishops in convening their provincial assemblies and thus, perhaps, limiting their direct authority over the bodies.

Perhaps most remarkably, Atterbury's *Letter* spoke directly to the grievances and resentments of the clerical subaltern. On their behalf, Atterbury complained of "the neglect with which they are used, and the methods that are taking of making them useless," presumably by Archbishop Tenison and his Williamite allies, who dominated the episcopal bench. While their diocesans governed the church from court and their seats in the House of Lords, the lower clergy "are in no other capacity of serving the Church and kingdom." The restoration of convocation, particularly on the basis of the *praemunientes* clause, finally afforded the lower clergy their rightful powers and place within the English constitution— particularly in this moment of constitutional redress, "when the rights of all other bodies are so tenderly preserved."[13]

Although some were incredulous at Atterbury's cynical blend of country ideology, "Revolution principles," and clerical resentment, the *Letter to a Convocation-Man* permanently altered the character of postrevolutionary ecclesiastical politics.[14] It not only succeeded in placing the restoration of convocation high on the broader Tory political agenda, it effectively goaded the Williamite bishops and clergy into affirmations of the royal supremacy so immoderate as to further impair their reputations as defenders of the rights of the church.[15] The Williamites' plea "for the boundless authority of sovereigns in Church-matters" exposed them as little more than shills for the court. Atterbury went so far as to compare the Williamite defenders of the royal supremacy to the episcopal creatures of James II, Bishops Samuel Parker and Thomas Cartwright, who colluded with the monarch in "new schemes of Church government twelve years ago."[16] In the wake of the *Letter*, a staunch clerical opposition to the court Whigs and their episcopal allies emerged, coalescing around the demand of restoring convocation to its proper constitutional status. And indeed, the Tories, hoping to capitalize on the waning powers of the Whig Junto, quickly discerned the political benefits of this clerical agitation. Thus, when William, turning again toward the Tories in December 1700, offered Laurence Hyde, Earl of Rochester, the lord lieutenancy of Ireland, Rochester demanded the recall of convocation as his primary condition for service. The king pledged to allow the convocation to meet and transact business alongside the new Parliament convening at the beginning of the new year.[17]

Convocation, convened twice during the final two years of the reign of William and then more or less concurrently with Parliament during the reign of his sister-in-law and successor Anne, would thus become a permanent feature of the landscape of civil and ecclesiastical politics during the first two decades of the eighteenth century—setting off that era from the long sweep of English church history between the Restoration and the mid-nineteenth-century age of reform, during which the assemblies remained, for all intents and purposes, in abeyance.[18] Indeed, it would not be unfair to consider the restoration of convocation the most significant achievement of the postrevolutionary Anglican high-church movement. And yet, convocation was by no means an ideal platform for the revolt of the lower clergy. True, the bicameral structure of the convocation of the province of Canterbury gave the disaffected clergy in the lower house a virtually unprecedented public forum from which to take cognizance of the welfare of the established church. From there, the clergy could secure a modicum of independence not only from the Williamite bishops, whom they now vehemently opposed, but also from the handful of prerevolutionary Tory bishops such as Thomas Sprat and Jonathan Trelawny, whose trimming and complacency they could no longer abide. And yet, convocation was an institution ill-suited to the polarized political environment into which it was conscripted. The body's jurisdiction and range of debate were hemmed in by the royal licenses with which it was convened.[19] The lower house, consisting of 145 clergymen—deans, archdeacons, and the elected proctors of the diocesan clergy—had an uncertain degree of procedural autonomy from the upper house, in which sat the 21 bishops of the province of Canterbury under the presidency of the archbishop. Moreover, the precedents governing the role of an opposition in the lower house or disagreement between the two houses were obscure—the historical record being spotty and frequently subject to time-consuming disputation.[20] The various protestations and obstructions employed by the majority in the lower house in hopes of some leverage on its superiors were by and large ineffective, further entrenching the gridlock with which the Williamite bishops (who had been rather indifferent or opposed to the assembly from the outset) were not wholly displeased. Upon the initial assembly of the restored body in January 1701,

Atterbury already suspected that "a settled resolution is taken of rendering convocations insignificant and useless."[21]

Securing the recall of convocation was one matter, but refurbishing the body as an effective instrument of ecclesiastical renewal was quite another. Convocation was simply not institutionally accustomed to either divisive party rancor or an extraordinary degree of disharmony between the houses; such factors significantly impaired the basic functionality of the assembly. And indeed, the early convocations of the eighteenth century were largely consumed with interminable procedural squabbles, mostly occasioned by the determination of members of the lower house to secure some measure of operational autonomy from the bishops. In this, the convocations of William's reign set the pattern for those of his successor.

The exasperating convocation of February to June 1701 was dominated by the lower house's efforts to affirm and exercise the powers to adjourn itself and to meet synodically during the intervals when the bishops of the upper house were not assembled. These powers, asserted the dean of Christ Church Henry Aldrich and the dean of Canterbury George Hooper, were "necessary to secure all other rights and liberties of the inferior clergy; nay, and of the utmost consequences to the preservation of the Church itself."[22] The substantial high-church majority in the lower house chafed at the authority claimed by Archbishop Tenison as president of the convocation to determine unilaterally the times and duration of assembly. "Such a power," wrote the deans, "might be so abused as to defeat all the ends of our meeting."[23] This was perhaps not an unreasonable conjecture. The first convocation of the eighteenth century assembled at Westminster Abbey on 10 February 1701, where George Hooper was chosen prolocutor of the lower house. But already, Whig clergymen were bragging "with great confidence, that the convocation will be allowed to do nothing after they have presented the prolocutor."[24] Hooper was duly admitted by the bishops on 21 February, after which the archbishop sent down his instrument of prorogation to the lower house. Reassembled on 25 February, the lower house immediately set about business, establishing a committee to inspect the convocation precedents and draw up a report regarding the powers of the archiepiscopal presidency over adjournments and prorogations.[25] During the session, word again came down from the upper house notifying the lower house of the archbishop's prorogation. The prolocutor set aside the archbishop's schedule and continued to transact business until the lower house acknowledged its adjournment. From this point, the lower house began complying ever more loosely with the archbishop's prorogations, delaying the reading of the instrument until the business of the session was completed and even assembling as a house in the morning on synodical days before the arrival of the bishops. When pressed by the archbishop on the irregularity of these proceedings, the majority in the lower house, with "a very few only dissenting," affirmed on 6 March two propositions: first, "that the lower house of convocation is not broken up by a bare signification that the upper is adjourned," and second, "that the lower house may meet and sit and act, if it see cause, in a time intermediate between the sessions of the upper."[26]

By the end of March, the lower house had begun openly to defy the archiepiscopal schedules of prorogation. On 27 March, Hooper returned from the upper house with a schedule of prorogation in his hands. Rather than it being executed, however, a vote was put whether to continue to transact business, which was carried overwhelmingly in the affirmative, prompting a small exodus of opposition clergymen from sessions they now considered illegal.[27] Four days later, the committee on adjournments adopted a report that affirmed the power of the lower house to adjourn itself. Despite the pleas of William Beveridge "in defense of the power of the metropolitans over their provincial synods," the house accepted the committee report by a huge majority.[28] On 8 April, the whole of the lower house was called before the bishops and berated for the irregularity of its proceedings. Archbishop Tenison then prorogued the convocation for an entire month "in such a manner," related Hooper and Aldrich, "as to let us know it might be done at pleasure." The majority of the lower clergy promptly returned to Henry VII's Chapel, where the question was put whether "they looked upon themselves as adjourned or not." They unanimously declared that they did not and adjourned themselves to the following morning.[29] Though the bishops had departed for the lengthy Easter recess, the lower clergy continued to assemble and transact business throughout April in what some critics lambasted as a "Rump convocation."[30] Upon convocation reconvening according to the archbishop's schedule, Tenison pronounced the work of the intermediate sessions "void and null and of dangerous consequence," effectively foreclosing the possibility that some reconciliation between the houses might redeem an otherwise intractable assembly. White Kennett pined for "the good old subordination of presbyters to bishops." Edmund Gibson lamented that the convocation had become "a scandal to the Church," confessing, "the best thing we can hope for now is a speedy prorogation."[31] Gibson got his wish on 25 June, when the convocation was dissolved along with William's penultimate Parliament. The controversies spilled over into the public sphere that summer, with churchmen high and low producing competing accounts of the preceding session.[32]

Even amidst these obstructions, the high churchmen in the lower house of convocation were able to lay the foundations for their agenda of ecclesiastical renewal. Upon their own initiative, the lower clergy established committees for overseeing the vital areas of church reform. In March 1701, the lower house established a committee "for inspecting books written against the truths of the Christian religion."[33] Shortly thereafter, the house established another committee to consider "the methods of curbing the open immoralities of the age" and yet another for the suppression of the Dissenting academies.[34] On 15 March, a committee was appointed "for considering the methods of propagating the Christian religion in foreign parts."[35] (This was, it must be noted, just two days before the SPCK debated the possibility of seeking a royal charter for its missionary endeavors.) The extent to which these foundations paralleled contemporaneous efforts in civil society should be obvious. Clearly, efforts were afoot to re-embed these functions within the express purview of the clergy.[36] White Kennett believed the objective was to establish convocation as a "standing committee for religion," to which would ultimately fall an even wider range of religious functions: recommending fasts and thanksgivings; addressing occasional conformity; advancing the clergy onto commissions for assessing taxation, "to prevent the oppression and distinguishing burden of parsons and vicars"; recalculating the movable feasts in the liturgy; and stopping "the licentiousness of the press."[37] And indeed, in December 1701, one self-described gentleman "of the old Cavaliers' principles" called upon the lower house to set aside the fruitless squabbling "concerning prorogations, adjournments, continuations, *in hunc locums*, schedules, intimations, commissaries, *Praemunientes* clause, and I know not what stuff more." He urged the clergy to bury their personal piques and animosities in St. Margaret's churchyard and set about the vital work of ecclesiastical reform concerning "religion, reformation of manners, propagating the gospel in the American plantations, censuring heretical books, the good of the universities, grievances, &c."[38] Progress on these objectives, however, was quite limited in the latter convocations of William's reign, save for the censuring of heterodoxy—and even that hardly advanced beyond the lower house.

The censuring of heterodox books had loomed extraordinarily large in the Anglican high-church rationale for restoring convocation. The brief, addled convocation of 1689–1690 had moved to condemn the anti-Trinitarian writings of the Hertfordshire clergyman Stephen Nye, as well as the two procomprehension *Letters* penned in defense of the proceedings of the prayer book commission. Thwarted in convocation by episcopal trepidation and royal dissolution, Anglican high churchmen during the ensuing decade clamored for some method of effectively resolving the protracted dispute over the doctrine of the Trinity and cognate theological controversies. Consequently, advocates for the return of convocation routinely cited the unchecked proliferation of heterodoxy as evidence of the profound lapse of discipline.[39] Citing the "various opinions and heresies of late published and vindicated," Francis Atterbury pleaded, "a convocation seems necessary, not only for the sake of the faith and doctrine of the English Church, but even to preserve the belief of any revelation."[40] Thus, even without royal license to pursue heretics, the lower house of the restored convocation naturally assumed that it possessed a mandate to vindicate orthodoxy.

In March 1701, the lower house quickly established a committee for inspecting heterodox books, naming as chairman William Jane, former prolocutor and veteran of the Trinitarian controversy.[41] The committee thereafter immediately took up consideration of John Toland's notorious *Christianity not Mysterious*, a work already five years old but long a mainstay of Anglican high-church obloquy.[42] After two weeks of examination, the committee concluded, *nemine contradicente*, that Toland's work "was writ with a design to subvert the fundamental articles of the Christian faith."[43] The committee's report recommended that "some speedy course ought to be taken for the suppressing of this and all other books of the like mischievous nature and tendency."[44] The lower house appended to the report an index of heretical propositions contained in Toland's work and submitted both to the bishops on 20 March, inquiring "what effectual course may be taken to suppress this, and all such pernicious books already written."[45]

The bishops in the upper house balked at the report. They harbored no sympathy for Toland but resented the initiative of the lower clergy, who had made findings of error unprompted and now merely sought the concurrence of the bishops.[46] The upper house took no action for two weeks, until pressed by a deputation from the lower house. The bishops then simply resumed the position taken in the convocation of 1689–1690, informing the lower house that, having consulted with lawyers, "they find not how they can censure any such books judicially, without the king's license which they have not yet received." Any move to do so, they found, put them all at risk of praemunire.[47] The lower house responded with a whole declamation against the bishops' operative theory of convocation, denying not only that the proceedings against Toland's book comprised "any occasion to consult with lawyers," but that the convocation even required the king's license in such matters. Moreover, it could not refrain from adding, had Archbishop Tenison been truly zealous for the cause of the church, "they might very well hope his Grace might easily have obtained from his Majesty whatever might have been found needful to suppress such books."[48] The leadership in the lower house was quite happy to score political points, where disciplinary measures were not forthcoming. And indeed, the nonjuror Charles Leslie publicized the fecklessness of the bishops as further evidence of the lassitude of the postrevolutionary Church of England.[49] Responding to high-church critics, Edmund Gibson somewhat lamely fell to invoking the twice-told tale of the Williamites' "undaunted opposition to popery" under James II.[50] Hooper and Aldrich scornfully retorted that the church now possessed "so many enemies round about us, what honor is it to the bishops to have opposed that single one?"[51]

The lower house responded to the bishops' rebuff with an act of extraordinary provocation. Returning from the Easter recess in spring 1701, it took up Bishop Gilbert Burnet's recent study of Anglican doctrine *An Exposition of the thirty-nine articles of the Church of England.* "Yesterday," bragged the Westminster prebendary Peter Birch, "it was my fortune to attack a great man, the Bishop of Salisbury . . . This makes some noises here and marks out a servant [of the Church] who is not afraid." On 16 May, the lower house resolved upon three articles: first, that Burnet's treatise expounded the articles contrary to the sense of their framers; second, that it expounded them contrary to the plain meaning of the words; and third, that it gave an historical account of the articles "as tended to the turning all the clergy of the Church of England out of their livings." A committee under William Jane was tasked with substantiating the charges.[52] On 6 June, the lower house delivered to the bishops a general complaint against Burnet's work, but its terms were vigorously rejected. A committee of the bishops determined that "the lower house of convocation has no manner of power judicially to censure any book" and that it was in the wrong for entering upon examination of the work of a bishop of the Church of England without leave of the upper house. The bishops further complained that the absence of specifics in the complaint of the lower house rendered their representation "defamatory and scandalous."[53] A detailed index of Burnet's doctrinal lapses in the *Exposition* was prepared, but the prorogation of the convocation that month prevented any further consideration by the upper house. As Martin Greig has made clear, the *Exposition*, with its generous allowance for diversity of opinion in doctrinal matters, was largely assailed as a "platform laid for comprehension" with Dissenters at home and Protestants abroad.[54] It is, of course, completely unclear why the lower house believed its indictment of a sitting bishop, particularly one with a scholarly reputation as immense as that of Gilbert Burnet, would somehow fare better than its thwarted assault of the rogue Irish deist John Toland. Burnet's sin, latitude and a surfeit of ecumenical charity, hardly rose to the level of heterodoxy; and listing the *Exposition*, a work that claimed the imprimatur of the episcopal hierarchy, alongside *Christianity not Mysterious* simply strained credulity. The lower house's disciplinary aspirations were frequently undermined by its unhinged resentment of William and his episcopal bench, and in this case, the house simply succumbed to the temptation of a foolish political stunt. This would by no means be the last time the lower house took to reflecting upon the Revolution settlement and its custodians, particularly when it found its higher ambitions for religious renewal obstructed.

In the immediate aftermath of the convocation of 1701, ecclesiastical partisans began positioning themselves for fresh confrontation in the convocation to be convened with the new Parliament at the end of the year. Atterbury was at great pains to insist that the new convocation be assembled on the basis of the *praemunientes* clause, "the very ground-work and basis of all the interest which the lower clergy of this Church have in the state."[55] The campaign to promote the execution of this clause was seen as vital toward circumscribing the presidential authority of Archbishop Tenison and securing the independence of the lower house of convocation. Moreover, political realities intruded: as war loomed on the Continent, the Earl of Rochester was slipping out of the king's favor. High churchmen desperately needed a constitutional mechanism more sound than the changing fortunes of Tory ministries in order to ensure the continued sitting of the convocation.[56]

In the summer of 1701, the ecclesiastical parties fell to open electioneering. Francis Atterbury steeled his clerical brethren against episcopal intimidation in the choice of proctors, which "must certainly go a great way towards procuring such a lower house as will sacrifice its rights and liberties to the upper."[57] There was evidence that the campaign was bearing fruit. "The poor country parsons, that know nothing of this matter," reported one observer of the Gloucester elections, "were instructed to vote for such as would assert their rights against the usurpations of the bishops."[58] Nor was the low-church opposition above out-of-doors politicking either. In December 1701, the diocese of Worcester elected as proctors the sons of two stalwart Williamite bishops, William Lloyd, son of the present bishop of that diocese, and James Stillingfleet, son of his predecessor, the late theologian and controversialist Edward Stillingfleet. William Hallifax, rector of Old Swinford, penned an "application" to the new proctors, purporting to be the sense of the clergy of that diocese. He urged the proctors first, to "pay all due and canonical obedience to the most reverend, the metropolitan as the sole president of the whole body of the convocation"; second, to endeavor the election of a prolocutor who shared their reverence for archiepiscopal authority; third, to "never consent to any intermediate adjournments, or private meeting of the lower house"; and finally, to lay aside all animosity and prejudice in consideration of those matters licensed by the supreme head of the church, the king.[59] The instructions were decried as an imposition upon the lower house's freedom of deliberation, and Hallifax was personally denounced as one who aimed to enlarge toleration, legalize occasional conformity, and abolish the annual thirtieth of January memorial for the royal martyr Charles I.[60] The zealous and embittered politicking that accompanied the electoral campaigns of the summer and autumn of 1701 virtually guaranteed that the brief convocation of winter 1701–1702 would stall over the same issues as its predecessor.

The convocation that opened on 30 December 1701 and coincided with the final three months of William's life was heir to the disputes that beset the previous assembly. Robert Woodward, dean of Salisbury, was elected prolocutor over the somewhat more moderate (or at least less confrontational) William Beveridge, archdeacon of Colchester.[61] Woodward had just been confirmed in his chair on 13 January when the schedule of prorogation was handed down from the archbishop of Canterbury. Woodward received the paper and informed his brethren that it was but "a paper by which their Lordships had adjourned themselves."[62] The debate over separate adjournments renewed immediately.[63] Beveridge intervened, saying, "Mr. Prolocutor, I beseech you, I adjure you in the name of Jesus Christ not to open our first meeting in such contempt and disobedience to the archbishop and bishops of the Church and in giving such offence and scandal to our enemies."[64] But the heightened rhetoric of the preceding season had rendered such moderation unfashionable. The following week, the majority proceeded to what White Kennett deemed "the most express acts of contempt and defiance," arrogating to themselves the right to commission and hear a thirtieth of January sermon, to appoint committees to meet at intermediate sessions, and to adjourn the lower house without regard to the schedule.[65] On 28 January, Edwin Sandys, archdeacon of Wells, proposed the revival of the committee to inspect books written against the Christian religion. William Hayley, dean of Chichester, and Charles Trimnell, archdeacon of Norfolk, suggested the house defer until after the settlement of the procedural disputes. When they were overruled, Trimnell demanded an inquiry into "the custom of inspecting such books." Atterbury rebuffed him, boldly asserting that "there could be no doubt but we have a power to declare books to be pernicious."[66] The minority low-church opposition settled on a strategy of obstruction, questioning the provenance of every apparent procedural innovation and ultimately on 9 February 1702 lodging with the bishops a formal protestation against the conduct of the majority.[67]

The lower house of convocation nearly came to blows on 12 February when the prolocutor, Robert Woodward, fell ill and deputed Henry Aldrich, dean of Christ Church, to serve as his replacement in the chair. Privately, the low churchmen White Kennett and John Mandeville agreed to accept the deputy on behalf of the minority, provided that the approval and confirmation of the archbishop was secured. Both parties concurred, but Kennett and Mandeville were prevented from informing the archbishop by the Winchester proctor William Needham, who insisted that such an application to the bishops would "raise some difference rather than preventing it." The application was thus delayed until after prayers, at which time Atterbury endeavored to obstruct any message from being sent, insisting upon the right of the lower house "to take a sub-prolocutor, and that the bishops ought not at all to intermeddle with it." With no clear prolocutor in the chair and suddenly uncertain whether they were in fact sitting synodically, members of the lower house fell to riotous debate. In order to compose the differences, William Beveridge and John Wickart, dean of Winchester, opted to convey to the bishops the "instruments of substitution," the paper formally deputizing Aldrich. Archbishop Tenison admitted the members, heard the instruments read, and ordered them to withdraw. In their absence, the majority in the lower house "had in a tumultuous manner resolved that Dr. Aldrich should keep the chair" and dispatched William Jane, George Hooper, and William Finch to inform the bishops of its resolution—though the three men were not admitted to the Jerusalem Chamber. The bishops finally summoned the entire body of the clergy to the upper house, where Tenison deemed the controversy "an incident of great moment" and prorogued the convocation for two days for further deliberation. As the clergy withdrew, Atterbury indefatigably cried out, "Away to the lower house! To the lower house!" The Lincoln proctor John Mandeville turned on him and asked whether "he was not ashamed to always be promoting contention and division." Atterbury indignantly replied that he "was not ashamed to be for the rights of the clergy."[68]

The point was rendered moot by Woodward's death the following day. In respect to the memory of the deceased prolocutor and the Ash Wednesday solemnities, Tenison adjourned the convocation to 19 February. Reconvening on that date, the archbishop informed the entire assembly that "no synodical business is yet, by royal authority, laid before the convocation," and whatever business they might have was obstructed by the "unsettled" formularies and "debates about methods of proceeding." Both war and the Easter season approached, and Tenison felt that the energies of his clergy might better be expended among their flocks. The interminable controversies that had marred these sessions threatened to damage irreparably the credit of the clergy with the wider public, who had lately been made privy to the troubles of the assembly through pamphlets and public intelligences. Tenison would allow further deliberation on the nominee to replace Robert Woodward, after which the convocation was prorogued for the season.[69] Unsurprisingly, several members of the lower house insisted upon further assemblies.[70] Their efforts, however, were soon arrested by the death of King William III on 8 March 1702.[71]

The two convocations of the last years of William's reign were, for all intents and purposes, bereft of tangible accomplishments. Yet even amidst the deadlock, it is possible to discern the first stirrings of a moral counterrevolution. The actions of the lower house, Francis Atterbury told the clergy of his archdeaconry in Totnes, were "absolutely requisite towards retrieving the honor and advantage of an English synod, and *making it useful to all the great purposes of religion for which it is designed*."[72] Clearly, the clergy of the lower house harbored ambitious designs for ecclesiastical renewal that included the reformation of manners, censuring of heterodox books, promotion of Anglican education, and propagation of the gospel—objectives that had for the most part lately fallen to activists in the voluntary sector. And significantly, though the movement was not conceived as an attempt to reverse the Revolution settlement, it very quickly acquired counterrevolutionary overtones. Most notably, Anglican high-church designs in the lower house of convocation and elsewhere increasingly proceeded upon the platform of "the rights of the clergy," against state and sect alike—a slogan that resonated unmistakably with the sacerdotalism of the nonjurors. Unsurprisingly, conciliatory nonjurors like Thomas Ken, the deprived bishop of Bath and Wells, observed how the lower house of convocation "do now very worthily assert the rights of the clergy" and thought it might be a fit instrument for ending the schism.[73] The lower house's relentlessly petty aspersions of William and the Revolution settlement could only endear it further to the nonjuring wing of the Anglican high church.[74] In this light, the lower house's continuing disrespect for the bishops took on manifestly counterrevolutionary shadings. Surely, one observer surmised, "Laud, Sheldon or Sancroft" would never have met with such hostility from the inferior clergy.[75] Significantly, just as the Anglican revivalism of the burgeoning voluntary sector was coming broadly to identify itself with "Revolution principles," the Anglican high-church renewal centered upon the lower house of convocation was marked by a growing alienation from the Revolution and its works.

An Alternative Anglican Revival

The convocations of Queen Anne hardly fared better than those of her predecessor. At least initially, Anne's vaunted regard for the established church did not extend terribly far beyond her late brother-in-law's concession of assembling the convocation during Parliament. The queen may have been a traditionalist in ecclesiastical matters, but she was by no means a sacerdotalist and thus harbored little sympathy for the pretensions of the recalcitrant lower clergy. Like her predecessor, she withheld from the convocation a license to transact business synodically, a virtual guarantee that its meetings would be preoccupied with exasperating procedural and constitutional questions rather than with substantive matters of ecclesiastical reform. This proved to be a somewhat foolish tactic, as the clergy in the lower house were often more reckless and subversive in vindicating the so-called rights of the clergy than in addressing questions of religious renewal, about which there was a far broader consensus. On numerous occasions, Queen Anne complained about the lower house's encroachments upon the royal supremacy over the Church of England, most famously pledging in February 1706 "to preserve the constitution of the Church of England as by law established" and "to maintain our supremacy and the due subordination of presbyters to bishops as fundamental parts thereof."[76] By 1708, Anne and her ministers had, through continuous prorogations, effectively returned convocation to the state of constitutional abeyance in which it spent the better part of William's reign.[77] Only the Tory ascendancy after 1710 restored the assembly to (admittedly limited) functionality and even induced Anne to license the body to transact business concerning a wide range of ecclesiastical questions for the first time in her reign.[78] This decision, it may be argued, exposed the radical incompatibility of the convocation with the postrevolutionary establishment in both church and state and effectively set the assembly on the path toward its own destruction just seven years later.[79]

The lower house of Anne's first convocation took the opportunity of the new reign to reissue its call for Anglican renewal. In December 1703, the lower clergy again put the bishops in mind of "the daring licentiousness of the press," by which heterodoxy and atheism proliferated, "to the great dishonor of God, the apparent hazard of many souls and the exceeding scandal of Church and nation." The lower house begged the bishops for some synodical intervention "and a stop put to so growing an evil."[80] After the Christmas recess, the lower house delivered an even more ambitious agenda.[81] In a representation conveyed to the bishops in February 1704, the clergy of the lower house compiled a list of ecclesiastical grievances in dire need of redress. Reflecting the provenance of the representation, many of the complaints addressed the erosion of clerical authority in the localities, alongside other deficiencies in parochial life and worship. The clergy complained of clandestine marriages and private baptisms administered outside of the parish church; irreverent and disorderly behavior during divine service; the negligence of churchwardens in making due provision for administration of the sacrament of the Lord's Supper; and the failure to discipline ministers, "who read not the Common Prayer distinctly, reverently and entirely." The clergy also protested persistent lay encroachment upon tithes, which necessitated costly and vexatious lawsuits with parishioners. Special indignation was reserved for the manifold failures of ecclesiastical discipline in the localities: the "defective presentments of churchwardens," excessive fees in ecclesiastical courts, abuses in the commutation of penance, and the enervation of ecclesiastical censure. Such lapses manifestly impaired the reformation of manners. They also complained of Dissenting academies proliferating throughout towns and provinces beyond episcopal supervision and promoting principles "as tend to perpetuate the schism we now labor under and to subvert the established constitution."[82] Francis Atterbury described the agenda as "giving life to the discipline of the Church in every respect."[83] And though the themes outlined—reformation of manners, policing of heterodoxy and Dissent, the refurbishing of parochial worship—were fairly commonplace concerns across the spectrum of early-eighteenth-century Anglicanism, they were articulated here with a particular emphasis on vindicating the rights and authority of the clergy of the established church. In April 1704, Archbishop Tenison promised to see all complaints rectified, although he strongly implied that diocesan visitations were perhaps the more suitable forum for redress.[84]

The high-church clergy that dominated the lower house of convocation were wary of alternative avenues of religious renewal. As societies for the reformation of manners proliferated throughout the kingdom and clergymen even clamored for inclusion on the commissions of the peace, churchmen in the lower house of convocation looked to the revival of ecclesiastical discipline.[85] "An ecclesiastical synod is *a society for reformation*," they proclaimed in 1703, "established by apostolical authority, by the constant usage of the catholic Church and by the laws and customs of this nation." Only the convocation, they insisted, could effectually undertake the "public reformation of manners," without risking the danger to church and state posed by "unauthorized societies."[86] The restoration of convocation, it seemed, had only sharpened high-church antipathy toward reformation societies and other social projects, all of which threatened the derogation of clerical authority.[87] "Throw down these societies of reformation," thundered Isaac Sharpe's high-church mouthpiece "Orthodoxus" in his 1704 dialogue *Plain-dealing*, "and restore to the Church her right and just privileges."[88] The vicar of St. Andrew's, Plymouth, John Gilbert was somewhat more charitable, commending the zeal of the reformers but insisting upon "a more effectual remedy, that is to say, the restoring of the Church discipline." After all, Gilbert reasoned, the formation of reformation societies and other instruments of religious renewal implied some defect in ecclesiastical discipline and "seems to carry with it a reproach to the society of the Church."[89] Faced with lay competition from both voluntary and civic institutions, the lower house of convocation set out to refurbish the traditional institutions of ecclesiastical discipline.

The restoration of the rural deaneries had loomed particularly large in post-revolutionary visions of ecclesiastical reform. The rural dean, or archpriest, was an incumbent delegated to oversee the operations of a district of usually ten parishes within a diocese. The office possessed a particular responsibility for moral regulation. "The proper office of a rural dean (however constituted)," wrote Edmund Gibson in his *Codex juris ecclesiastici Anglicani* of 1713, "was the inspection of the lives and manners of the clergy and people within their district."[90] Enthusiasm for the revival of the office, it must be stressed, was by no means confined to the Anglican high-church movement. Stalwart Williamites such as Bishops Burnet and Gardiner also urged the restoration of the dean-eries.[91] And as discussed in Chapter 2, Thomas Bray advocated the restoration of the rural deaneries while envisioning his parochial libraries and clerical societies as veritable replacements for the decayed office. In 1701, the future nonjuror Thomas Brett lamented the disappearance of the office throughout England, "to the great prejudice of the Church, which by this means loses a very useful, not to say necessary officer, to preserve and maintain its discipline."[92]

The challenge of Anglican voluntarism, and the reformation of manners movement in particular, lent new urgency to the restoration of the rural dean-eries. James Metford, rector of Basingham in Lincolnshire, urged the deploy-ment of rural deans in the work of moral reformation as "the best spies upon creeping heresies and schism." He argued for the ultimate futility of moral refor-mation by singular incumbents, as well as by lay and clerical associations. "In truth," he wrote, "nothing less than a strong united stream of all Church power and countenance will be able to carry away these heaps of corruption, the nuisances of parochial religion."[93] The leading high churchman Francis Atterbury used his 1708 address to the clergy of Totnes to appeal for the restora-tion of the office. He reflected equivocally on the societies for the reformation of manners: "Far be it from me to condemn the zeal of those persons who with good intentions entered on that desirable work, however unqualified they may be for it." But Atterbury suspected anticlerical designs behind the work of the societies, "to take the inspection of manners out of their hands to whom it most properly belongs," namely, the priesthood. Indeed, Atterbury gave voice to a pervasive anxiety on the part of high churchmen that the new wave of Anglican

voluntarism "gives us no very comfortable prospect of procuring any enlargement of the powers we already possess in matters appertaining to religion and
virtue, or of retrieving any of those we have lost."[94] For high churchmen, the
rural deaneries were particularly appealing as a means of resisting the transfer of
pastoral and disciplinary functions to the voluntary sector.

When the ascendant high-church movement finally in January 1711
procured a royal license for the convocation to transact business, the assembly
was specifically tasked with the refurbishing of the rural deaneries.[95] On 10
March, a committee of both houses, presided over by three Tory bishops,
Trelawny of Winchester, Sprat of Rochester, and Ofspring Blackall of Exeter, met
to consider proposals for reconstructing the office. The committee recommended that a canon be drawn up to delineate the powers of a rural dean. A
minister in Trelawny's diocese wrote the bishop specifically urging that the
admonitory function of the rural deans be preserved and enhanced. The rural
dean, armed with the power to issue solemn and public censures upon the
refractory, would, he believed, "do more towards reforming a single man's
morals, than the minister's whole year's preaching to them."[96] This component of
the office was explicitly preserved in the committee's first report. The rural deans
would oversee the moral and social lives of the parishioners of their assigned
districts:

> As particularly to enquire into the manners of the clergy and people; to visit
> and examine the state of parochial churches and chapels, with the chancels of
> the same; together with the ornaments and utensils thereunto belonging; as
> also the manses of rectors and vicars; and all other ecclesiastical endow-
> ments, and likewise to enquire into the condition of schools, hospitals and
> the several gifts and legacies bequeathed to pious and charitable uses. And
> after such due inquiries to acquaint the bishop or other ordinary with any
> notorious crimes, scandals, errors or defects in eccles[iastical] matters or
> persons within the district of the said deanery. That so if upon private admo-
> nition there does not follow a due reformation, then legal process may issue
> thereupon.[97]

The rural dean was reconceived as not only a supervisor of local manners and
mores, but also the overseer of the physical plant of the parishes. Even more
remarkably, the dean was imagined as something of a clerical ambassador to the
burgeoning philanthropic community, a visitor of schools, hospitals, and other
endowments. Clearly, the office was redesigned as a means of asserting clerical

superintendence over the entire machinery of social and pastoral engagement, both civic and voluntary.

The revival of ecclesiastical discipline also required the repair of deficiencies in the ecclesiastical courts.[98] The overhauling of ecclesiastical jurisdiction had actually lingered on the ecclesiastical agenda at least since William charged his first convocation with improving the church courts for "the reformation of manners either in ministers or people" (see Chapter 2).[99] And indeed, the lower house of Anne's first convocation complained extensively to the bishops regarding lapses and abuses in the ecclesiastical courts, in particular, that "the sentence of excommunication hath been rendered less awful and effectual than it ought to be."[100] The lower clergy observed that the custom of regularly denouncing persons excommunicate in the parish church and cathedral of the diocese had fallen by the wayside. Moreover, commutation of penance—the paying of fines to evade prosecution—had degenerated into institutionalized bribery.[101] This practice tended to discourage the parish officers from presenting offenders in the first place, particularly the affluent, for they would not hazard their own fortunes in arresting one whose crime would likely go unregistered and unreformed. Furthermore, the fee itself would often go to "private disposal" instead of the public and charitable uses stipulated by the canons.

Again, the royal license procured in 1711 authorized the consideration of what high churchmen deemed a vital component of reviving ecclesiastical discipline. The queen specifically tasked the convocation with addressing "the abuses in excommunication and in the commutation of penance," and a committee of both houses began considering a program for reform on 5 February 1711.[102] The committee resolved to petition Parliament to equip the ecclesiastical courts with a writ *de contumaci capiendo*, which would permit the courts to issue arrest warrants for a range of offenses that did not merit the highest spiritual sanction of excommunication, the force of which had long dulled through overuse and negligent enforcement. The committee further recommended that all commutation of penance proceed at the discretion of the bishop, rather than the court officers, and that a register be kept of all commutations and the uses to which the monies were applied. In February 1712, the committee further recommended that an act of Parliament be procured to ensure that one-third of the fine paid for commutation of penance be appropriated to the founding and maintenance of the local charity school.[103] Interestingly, the low-church minority in the lower house demurred at the committee's resolutions, complaining about the prospect of investing the ecclesiastical courts with the authority to order imprisonments not only for excommunication, but for any contempt of court, "a two edged sword to be given to the eccles[iastical] judge." They further complained "against the viciousness of offering to get commutat[ion] money established by Parliament," as if something untoward was implied in regulating the disposal of collections. Most likely, these gripes did not reflect substantive objections to the reform of the church courts as much as the low-church opposition tactic of lading all resolutions with endless procedural complaints.[104]

Such proposals reveal an Anglican high-church movement patently unwilling to abandon the traditional ecclesiastical functions of moral oversight and sanction to either state or civil society. And indeed, the movement is to be credited with recognizing the acuity of the threat.[105] But the ambitions of the lower house of convocation in the early eighteenth century suggest a movement exercised as much by the voluntarism associated with the incipient age of benevolence as by the anticlericalism associated with the English Enlightenment. The Anglican high-church movement no doubt recognized the danger posed by irreligion and secularism, but more shrewdly, it seemed to recognize the more subtle danger posed by the alternative combatants of irreligion and secularism—an activist laity, voluntary associations and projectors, and even the magistracy. Anglican high churchmen (like the nonjurors for whom they were growing increasingly sympathetic) discerned in eighteenth-century English society both the disappearance of the sacred and its purported multiplication as a variety of social actors attempted to perform functions once reserved for the church. In attempting to reground some of these functions in ecclesiastical institutions, the lower house of convocation aimed not only to revive the spiritual and moral life of the established church, but to do so in a way that ultimately vindicated the rights and prerogatives of the clergy.

The Policing of Heterodoxy

A perennial concern of the lower house of convocation during its postrevolutionary revival was, of course, the policing of heterodoxy. Voluntary associations distributed popular refutations of Roman Catholic and Quaker doctrines. At the (virtually) annual lectures endowed by the natural philosopher Robert Boyle, Anglican divines held forth on the cogency of revelation and the incoherence of deism and atheism. Even the two universities were on occasion sufficiently provoked to declaim against particularly egregious doctrinal lapses.[106] But from the inception of the postrevolutionary campaign to restore convocation, Anglican high-church partisans were determined to see the ecclesiastical assembly enshrined with authoritative powers to intervene against heterodoxy. Despite the general uninterest of the bishops, who remained broadly unconvinced of the constitutionality of such proceedings, the lower house remained peculiarly tenacious in its attempt to establish synodical censure as part of the regular machinery of ecclesiastical discipline. During Anne's first convocation, the lower house practically begged the bishops to tend to the safety of the established church, "to have all due regard to the soundness of its doctrine, and to labor some effectual provision against its being corrupted and depraved."[107] Episcopal inaction concerning heretical books prompted the lower house to renew its plea a year later, to little avail.[108]

Stymied by questions of procedure, as well as episcopal reluctance, the lower clergy of the high-church interest engaged in public recriminations. In a published letter to a friend in Berkshire, Francis Atterbury affirmed his commitment to liberty, both civil and ecclesiastical. "But liberty is indulged too far," he wrote in 1706, "when it degenerates into such boundless license, as shall undermine the foundations of religion and government." He proceeded to reproduce large passages from the day's most infamous works of freethinking: Charles Blount, John Toland, Sir Robert Howard, and Matthew Tindal were all given their due.[109] In another sign of confluence between the juring and nonjuring wings of the Anglican high-church movement, George Hickes commended Atterbury's work the following year.[110] In a particularly intemperate Ash Wednesday sermon in 1707, the Irish clergyman Francis Higgins invoked the church of Sardis from the book of Revelation as a warning to the Church of England, "its very angels, watchmen, or bishops . . . sunk into such a lifelessness, stupidity and lethargy, as to need a voice from heaven to rouse them." Higgins did not equivocate in locating the source of modern godlessness in that "most unaccountable liberty not only in conversation but in books publicly printed and sold about our streets."[111] The nonjuror Charles Leslie published a postscript to Higgins's sermon, depicting an exchange between the preacher and Archbishop Tenison. Higgins was made to accuse the archbishop of negligence, comparing his feeble investigations of heresy with the energy expended "to have an account of the discourses of men such as I am."[112] The inferior clergy, harboring no doubts regarding their competence and jurisdiction to prosecute heresy, rounded upon enemies within the church for their manifest inaction.

Persisting throughout much of the reign of Queen Anne, the paralysis was tested by the publication of Anthony Collins's brief tract *Priestcraft in Perfection* in early 1710. The freethinker assailed the authority of the Church of England, disputing the legitimacy of the first clause of the church's twentieth article, by which it claimed power "to decree rites and ceremonies, and authority in controversies of faith." Collins asserted that the clause had been passed by neither Elizabeth's convocations of 1562 and 1571 nor Parliament and in fact appeared in no copies of the articles before the age of Archbishop William Laud. The clause, Collins charged, was a blatant forgery, a sacerdotalism inimical to the spirit of Protestant liberty, now perpetuated only by "the proceedings of the high church priests of this day."[113] Interestingly, juring and nonjuring churchmen began actively collaborating in their response; Francis Atterbury was in regular contact with the nonjurors George Harbin and Hilkiah Bedford regarding Collins's book.[114] "All helps from all hands will be welcome," Atterbury wrote to Harbin, "and shall be thankfully acknowledged."[115] The response issued under Bedford's name vindicated the authority of the Church of England, arguing that "that power is so essential to the Church that (as I have shown) it could not be a Church without it." Bedford tarred Collins as a disciple of Matthew Tindal, "not so much an enemy to popery, as to priesthood."[116]

The assault on ecclesiastical power clearly struck a nerve with the convocation. When it returned from a nearly two-year hiatus amidst the Tory ascendancy of 1710–1711, the lower house was again determined to make use of its purported disciplinary powers. At the outset of the new convocation, the bishops drafted a letter to the queen in which they pledged to "ever be watchful against the growth of atheism and immorality, of heresy and schism and superstition." After a decade of inactivity on this front, the majority in the lower house found the commitment laughable on its face. The inferior clergy once again reminded the bishops of their duty, "to lay seriously at heart the dangers with which the Christian religion is encompassed from . . . the Tolands and the Collins's of this age."[117] The lower house, it seems, was most aggressive (and the bishops most wary) in confronting errors that tended to derogate priestly authority.

In this light, then, it is perhaps not entirely surprising that it was the brazen Arianism of the Newtonian natural philosopher William Whiston that ultimately broke the deadlock between the houses.[118] Whiston's lapses, for which he was dismissed from the Lucasian chair of mathematics at Cambridge in October 1710, were historical and Christological, rather than overtly anticlerical in the sense of Toland or Collins.[119] Moreover, the audacious dedication of his grand exposition of anti-Trinitarian divinity *Historical Preface to primitive Christianity reviv'd*, to the convocation of Canterbury, piled provocations atop one another. In a rare display of consensus, the lower house of convocation concurred in proceedings against Whiston's *Historical Preface*. On 9 March 1711, William Binckes lodged the initial complaint, requesting the customary (and customarily fruitless) address to the bishops, "what course may be taken with that book and the author of it." Surprisingly, the motion was seconded by the opposition stalwart White Kennett, dean of Peterborough, who launched into a lengthy speech on the matter. "It is now high time," Kennett said, "to complain of so great a scandal to the Christian religion."[120] Moreover, as Whiston had boldly dedicated the work to the convocation itself, inaction by its members, Kennett reasoned, might be taken for sanction. Finally, unlike Toland and Collins, Whiston was a priest in the Church of England and therefore the particular responsibility of the synod.[121] On 12 March, in a committee of both houses in the Jerusalem Chamber, the new prolocutor Francis Atterbury casually mentioned the possibility of proceeding against Whiston's book. The bishops remained dubious, but Atterbury "seemed to be well assured that the power of punishing heresy was in the convocat[ion] as a proper court." Two days later, the former prolocutor George Hooper, subsequently elevated to the see of Bath and Wells, vehemently denounced Whiston in the upper house. On 16 March, the inferior clergy formally submitted to the bishops an address against the *Historical Preface*, and a committee was formed to consider the work.

There was still no consensus about precisely how and by what right convocation might proceed against an author. The convocation entertained three options—not including the more scholarly procedure of an examination of both the author and his writings. The whole synod might act as a court of judicature, "proceeding to censure and excommunication immediately"—the position no doubt favored by Atterbury and his allies in the lower house. In an alternate method of proceeding, the archbishop might preside alone over a court of audience and rule *assidentibus et consentientibus Episcopis*, with no input from the lower clergy. Finally, the convocation might simply vote a synodical censure upon Whiston's writings and then refer him for punishment to the court of his diocesan.[122] Archbishop Tenison discussed the three alternatives in his letter to the whole convocation, 11 April 1711, in which he suggested, "the two last seem to be most plain and clear in point of legality," but the first was doubtless "the most solemn."[123]

Legislation of both the Reformation and Restoration era had left convocation in a precarious position with respect to heresy. Erastian to the core, Tenison deemed the safest course was "to make an address to the queen and beg advice and instructions how to proceed legally in this affair of Mr. Whiston." Significantly, Tenison's resolution met some resistance among his suffragan bishops, several of them—Compton of London, Sprat of Rochester, Hooper of Bath and Wells, and Bull of St. David's—voting against consulting the queen. Dining with White Kennett and Edmund Gibson at Lambeth on 18 April, Tenison brooded that "some of the bishops had been too forward to assume a power of judicature." Still, the motion had been carried against them, and on 17 April, Bishops John Moore and John Hough were dispatched to inquire of Queen Anne, "How far the convocation, as the law now stands, may proceed in examining, censuring and condemning such tenets as are declared to be heresy by the laws of this realm; together with the authors and maintainers of them." The queen referred the question to twelve judges and her attorney and solicitor general.[124]

The queen's counselors were of two minds on the legality of proceeding against Whiston. Eight of her majesty's judges, along with the attorney general, Sir Edward Northey, and the solicitor general, Robert Raymond, argued that convocation might proceed "to examine, censure and condemn" heretical tenets "and the authors and maintainers thereof" as long as a right of appeal to the queen was preserved in accordance with her ecclesiastical supremacy. A minority of four judges dissented from the decision, affirming that the proper jurisdiction in matters of heresy lay in the ecclesiastical courts of the episcopate.[125] On 8 May 1711, Anne commended the findings to Archbishop Tenison and bid him convey their sense to the two houses. "We cannot doubt," she wrote to the Metropolitan, "but the convocation may now be satisfied they may employ the power which belongs to them, in repressing the impious attempts, lately made to subvert the foundation of the Christian faith."[126]

The convocation did not proceed judicially against William Whiston. On 11 May, Tenison ordered Bishops Trimnell and Bull to confer with four delegates from the lower house "in order to examine the doctrine contained in the said book and compare the same with the doctrine of the Church of England." The lower house sent two members from each party: Tenison's lieutenants Edmund Gibson and White Kennett, along with the high churchmen George Smalridge and Jonathan Edwards, principal of Jesus College, Oxford. Observers couldn't help but notice that the bishops seemed to have "taken the opinion of the four judges before that of the eight judges." Atterbury abstained from participating in what he perceived as a capitulation, that is, "proceeding against the doctrine without proceeding at the same time against the person." Indeed, the overwhelming majority of the lower clergy shared Atterbury's sentiments; they "seemed to apprehend it as a design of avoiding all process against the man and declaring only against his tenets."[127]

Ultimately, the convocation merely produced a report of twelve heretical propositions in Whiston's book, and a thirteenth—his claims of authenticity for the spurious *Apostolical Constitutions*—as "impious and such as tended to disturb the canon of Scripture." Even Whiston himself was perplexed at the anticlimax.[128] On 12 June, Tenison decided to submit the citation of Whiston to the queen by his commissary "for her approbation." The lower house thought this method indecorous. White Kennett recorded in his journal that even Queen Anne felt "it ought to have been presented to her in a more solemn manner." Kennett clearly shared Whiston's own sense of anticlimax; he reported the conclusion of the affair to his friend Samuel Blackwell: "the censure of him was delivered for royal approbation, the paper was dropped, and no intimation of desiring another copy, or any farther proceeding."[129]

Besides the head of William Whiston, Archbishop Tenison had denied the lower house the long-sought powers of synodical censure. The extraordinarily rare congruence of royal connivance, bipartisan consensus, and legal standing was insufficient to elicit from the primate anything more than a bare examination of suspect doctrine. The reluctance of Tenison and his allies to act more vigorously against Whiston remains a matter of conjecture, but it is not unlikely that they dreaded the inevitable politicization of ecclesiastical censures. Anglican high churchmanship was clearly in the ascendant during the latter half of the reign of Queen Anne, and it had arguably grown even more dangerous since the violence and political fallout surrounding the Whig prosecution of the Tory churchman Henry Sacheverell the previous year.[130] High churchmen had long used aspersions of heterodoxy as a political cudgel against Williamite divines, and Tenison was unwilling to hand his enemies a dagger with which to cut his own throat. Indeed, the subsequent controversy surrounding the anti-Trinitarian writings of the celebrated London theologian Samuel Clarke was settled even more quietly by the bishops the following year, with virtually no input from a seething lower house.[131] Francis Atterbury fumed while the convocation "sit still and do nothing to oppose this torrent of irreligion, though that be their proper business, and the peculiar reason for which their assemblies are now kept up."[132]

The year after his citation by the convocation, William Whiston published a proposal "for erecting societies for promoting primitive Christianity." He observed the remarkable improvements in religion and public morality accomplished "by fixed and formed societies, voluntarily entered into and heartily promoted by many worthy persons." Whiston pledged his cause of primitive truth and Arian Christianity to "try the same useful method of regular societies."[133] That an accused heretic could emerge from synodical proceedings to publicly promote his heresy through voluntary associations speaks volumes about the altered religious ecology of early-eighteenth-century England. The holy synods of the established church were everywhere traduced by civil society.

The Present State of Religion

The moral counterrevolution, like much of the postrevolutionary Anglican high-church movement, was animated by the pervasive sense that the established church was in crisis. In the flush of the Tory ascendancy, Queen Anne was willing to afford the clergy an opportunity to provide some testimonial of the church's danger. She charged the convocation assembling in November 1710 with producing an account of "the present state of religion particularly with respect to atheism, infidelity, heresy and profaneness."[134] Like the "church in danger" debates five years earlier, the assignment exposed the continuing absence of any consensus on the state of religion in postrevolutionary England. As a result, the two houses of the convocation produced two fundamentally incompatible reports, which divided in large measure over the meaning and methods of the Anglican revival and its debts to the Revolution of 1688–1689.

The prolocutor Francis Atterbury engaged the task with great relish. His joint committee of both houses produced an exhaustive catalogue of national sins. Atterbury's "Representation of the State of Religion" comprised something of a counterhistory of irreligion in England.[135] Against the prevailing rhetoric of national reformation in which the Restoration court of the Stuarts figured as the wellspring of all vice, Atterbury located the original source of the current infidelity in the mid-seventeenth-century crisis of the English polity, "that long, unnatural rebellion, which loosened all the bands of discipline and order," the English civil wars. In Atterbury's narrative, the Restoration era functioned as a kind of salve—irreligion being "checked and kept under for a time" by the dread of popery and the firm hand of the state upon the press and public opinion. "As soon as these fears were removed, and those restraints were taken off, it broke out with the greatest freedom and violence."[136] The Glorious Revolution, while delivering the nation from popery and vindicating the rights of Englishmen, effectively dissolved the political and ideological infrastructure by which rank atheism and infidelity had been long kept at bay. Atterbury offered a cursory nod to the contemporary activism of the Anglican voluntary sector—"societies have been formed, and funds of charity raised"—but damned them with faint praise before damning them outright. "It must be confessed," he wrote, "that all the endeavors which may hitherto have been used, by public or private persons, to stop the growth of this evil, have proved ineffectual."[137] The Revolution was depicted as a blow to those serviceable means by which the Restoration church and state had kept irreligion in check; voluntarism had proved a poor substitute.

Atterbury's jeremiad rebuked virtually the whole of Augustan culture. He assailed religious toleration, the freedom of the press, the excesses of the scientific revolution, and the intellectual climate of freethinking.[138] The culture that had emerged amidst these new and dangerous indulgences was manifestly hostile to the established church, and Atterbury repeatedly complained of the pervasive anticlericalism of the age. In a line that might have come from any nonjuror, he grieved to see the cherished ecclesiology of Anglican high churchmen besieged by enemies who "have endeavored utterly to root out of men's minds all notion of a Church as a society instituted by Christ . . . to blend and confound this spiritual society with the temporal." And like the nonjurors, Atterbury discerned an antidote in the independence of the church, particularly the liberty of convocations, by which "some way may be found to restore the discipline of the Church, now too much relaxed and decayed, to its pristine life and vigor." Atterbury's aggrieved and incendiary "Representation" contained a manifesto for the entire moral counterrevolution: only an independent convocation armed with the power of ecclesiastical censure and entrusted to rebuild the infrastructure of ecclesiastical discipline could provide a bulwark against the tide of irreligion loosed by two revolutions.[139]

The polemical thrust of Atterbury's "Representation" did not go unnoticed in the ecclesiastical assembly. On 21 March 1711, opposition members in the lower house grumbled that the report was "a very artful piece sparing the reigns of K. Ch[arles] II and K. James II, loading the Revolut[ion] and reign of K. Will[iam] and invidiously charging the late ministry," that is, the Whigs and their allies. The "Representation" was received with equal suspicion in the upper house, where, White Kennett reported, "it was generally disliked as being too long and too much in the declamatory way."[140] Whig bishops puzzled at the seemingly irrelevant reflections upon the conduct of the War of the Spanish Succession and the religion and manners of the Dutch—rhetorical mainstays of the Tory party during the reign of Anne but utterly tangential to the task at hand.[141] The bishops rejected the draft nine votes to seven, and by the same margin affirmed to draw up their own report on the state of religion.

The "Representation" drawn up by the bishops reproduced significant portions of Atterbury's draft but softened the language considerably. For instance, the civil wars of the previous century still received their share of obloquy, but the commendation of the Restoration was dropped, along with aspersions regarding the effect of the Revolution of 1688–1689. The bishops abandoned the complaint against anticlericalism and encroachments upon the rights of the clergy, which had so characterized the earlier draft. More importantly, their depiction of the state of religion was not nearly as bleak as that offered by Atterbury's committee. Instead, the bishops depicted a monarch and her subjects collectively and heartily engaged in the national struggle against infidelity. In this vein, they lauded the work of the Anglican voluntary sector, mentioning the publication and distribution of devotional works, pointing to the missionary and educational efforts of the religious societies, and singling out the Boyle Lectures "in defense of the Christian religion against all the adversaries of it." They further observed that as a result of the religious activists, "divine service and sacraments have of late been oftener celebrated and better frequented than formerly." As befitting the current governors of the Church of England, the outlook of the bishops on the current state of religion was cautiously but unmistakably optimistic.[142]

The two competing representations on the state of religion constituted yet another impasse in the proceedings of the convocation. By May 1711, the documents had not been reconciled.[143] The differences between them were not merely stylistic, they were broadly ideological. In June, White Kennett offered an impassioned defense of the bishops' "Representation" on the floor of the lower house. At stake was the legacy of the Revolution itself.[144] The bishops' "Representation," unlike that of Atterbury and his allies, "does by no means detract or seem to detract from the honor of the Revolution nor from the glory of her Majesty's reign." Kennett castigated the fiction "that no sins or scandals under which we now suffer did grow up in former reigns and none of those mischiefs happened to the Church or to religion in all that interval between the happy Restoration and the late Revolution." Moreover, the "Representation" of the bishops prominently acknowledged "her Majesty's care of the Prot[estant] Succession, which had been forgotten" in Atterbury's account. Finally, the bishops had paid due tribute to the work of the religious activists in the Anglican voluntary sector, whose endeavors the lower house "had forgot or had passed over with slight implications only. They are the many good things that help to balance if not atone for the evil" of irreligion. For Kennett, as for a growing number of church Whigs, the prospering causes of Revolution, revival, and the Protestant succession were all of a part.[145]

The two representations were never reconciled, nor was either version ever presented to the queen as stipulated in her royal license. Shortly after the session of convocation ended with that of Parliament on 12 June 1711, both versions were surreptitiously published.[146] The controversy spilled out into a polarized public sphere still addled by the trial of Sacheverell and the religious riots of the previous year. In the *Examiner* of 21 June 1711, Jonathan Swift laid culpability upon the doorsteps of the episcopate.[147] Further obstruction by the bishops in the face of the "deluge of profaneness" explicitly catalogued by the lower house bordered upon contumacy.[148] Matthew Tindal, inveterate enemy of ecclesiastical power, excoriated the "Representation" of the lower clergy as a work of cunning priestcraft. "After having in the most pathetic terms made the lamentable description of the iniquity of the times," he wrote of the lower house, "they declared that in this sad state, they saw no way to prevent the growth of infidelity, heresy, profaneness, &c. but by enlarging the power of the clergy."[149] Daniel Defoe agreed, vigorously defending the liberty of the press and denouncing the revival of ecclesiastical discipline proposed by the lower clergy as "some kind of Protestant Inquisition."[150] The lower house of convocation, Tindal explained, "cry for more power for the Church," insisting the latter would never be safe from danger until "holy discipline prevails." Like other Whigs and low churchmen, he countered that religious revival could proceed only on the foundations of the

Revolution. "God be thanked," he concluded, "that the Revolution and reformation of manners began together, and that the latter has been carried on to so great a height by men of revolution principles."[151]

The "Representation" produced by Atterbury and his allies encapsulated the politics of the moral counterrevolution. Anglican high churchmen did not set out to undo the Revolution settlement, nor were their initial visions of ecclesiastical renewal necessarily redolent of the courtly and highly Erastian churchmanship that prevailed during the Restoration. On the contrary, their program of ecclesiastical renewal acquired a counterrevolutionary valence only in the face of royal ambivalence, episcopal obstruction, Erastian interference, and competition from the burgeoning voluntary sector. When finally invited to account for the embattled state of religion in England, Anglican high churchmen ultimately lit upon the Revolution and its aftereffects. And to the extent that the Revolution comprised the true source of the church's endangerment, Anglican high churchmen could not but feel the whole of the postrevolutionary establishment in church, state, and society arrayed against them. They finally found themselves at odds not only with the constitution in church and state, but with the emerging national identity of England as a Protestant kingdom redeemed by Revolution and national reformation. In disputing the latter, they impugned the former. And thus, while the bishops and other men of "revolution principles" celebrated a nation in the throes of Anglican revival, the high churchmen could only advance what White Kennett denounced as "a bedroll of the sins and follies of the nation."[152]

Conclusion

Anglican high churchmen during the reign of Queen Anne undertook a movement to augment the social power of the priesthood, refurbish the traditional institutions of ecclesiastical discipline, and vindicate the rights of the clergy. This campaign, catalyzed by encroachments upon clerical functions and prerogatives, quite obviously paralleled efforts afoot elsewhere in the church and civil society. Frequently, it drew ideological sustenance from the sacerdotalist ecclesiology of the nonjurors, with its cogent and sophisticated regard for the peculiar domain of clerical authority. And yet, the results of this campaign were meager. Convocation did indeed assemble fairly regularly throughout the first two decades of the eighteenth century until its suspension and virtual abolition in

1717, but it remained bogged down in procedural morass throughout the period. The ecclesiastical censure of the assembly, such as it was, remained of little account. Its proposals and reports toward ecclesiastical reconstruction languished, for the most part, in the upper house and disappeared with each dissolution. Rather than serving as an instrument with which to curb the public sphere, the convocation spurred further pamphlet skirmishes and produced more fodder for theological and political controversy out of doors. By 1711, White Kennett confessed, "We have done nothing in convocation to any purpose but that of making more noise."[153] When controversy over Benjamin Hoadly's sermon on the kingdom of God embroiled the established church early in the reign of George I, convocation proved to be its victim rather than its arbiter.

Why did the moral counterrevolution fail? Obviously, the obduracy of the revolutionary episcopate proved an insurmountable obstacle to ecclesiastical reform. Moreover, there was an institutional barrier. The Anglican high-church movement had invested virtually everything in convocation, a cumbersome body more suitable for deliberation than legislation. It is telling that the only two even temporarily successful achievements of the moral counterrevolution, the fund for building fifty new churches throughout London and Westminster, and the Schism Act, which purported to reestablish the Anglican monopoly on education, were enacted in Parliament.[154] Moreover, the genuine independence of the two houses of convocation remained insufficiently defined throughout the era. The sibling convocation of the province of York was unicameral. This fact alone (not to mention the mere existence of another ecclesiastical assembly within the kingdom) undercut high-church claims on behalf of the lower house of a spiritual power equivalent to the temporal power of the House of Commons. The lower house seemed to have no institutional recourse in the face of inertia in the upper house; hence its constant applications and representations to the bishops, supplemented by its frequent appeals to the Commons, the queen, or public opinion. Convocation was an archaic and conservative institution, and the lower house was clearly the subordinate element within it. This was hardly the most advantageous platform from which to actuate a reconstruction of the moral and social order of the kingdom.

The second barrier was constitutional. The Anglican high-church interpretation of the *praemunientes* clause of the parliamentary writ notwithstanding, the English constitution did not really take cognizance of the lower clergy as a distinct corporate entity. Thus, the rallying cry of the "rights of the clergy" possessed no meaningful constitutional resonance—even if it did serve the Tory political ends of crying up the endangered church. Ironically, the aggressive episcopalism of the Church of England reconstructed at the Restoration to militate against the ecclesiological leveling of Presbyterianism or independency had probably rendered the notion of the "rights of the clergy" even less plausible. This irony was not lost on William Sherlock, who clearly delighted in tarring the actions of the lower house with the logic of "puritans . . . and the Scotch Presbyterians" bent on "changing episcopal government for a presbyterian parity."[155] The Church of England offered precious little ecclesiological purchase for the claims of the inferior clergy against their own diocesans.[156] Thus, tensions between the two houses more often than not led to institutional paralysis.

But the antipathy was, of course, not so much personal as ideological. As we have seen, the Anglican high-church interest in the lower house came to conceive of the program of ecclesiastical renewal in direct opposition to the Revolution establishment. The high-church movement's indispensable devotion to monarchy and episcopacy became increasingly difficult to square with the obstruction of the bishops and the unshakable commitment of Queen Anne to the royal supremacy "and the due subordination of presbyters to bishops."[157] The lower clergy responded by acting out. One of their communiqués to the upper house brazenly qualified the bishops with "the greater part of whom are of K. W—'s [King William's] creating," as if to insinuate some fundamental illegitimacy.[158] Anglican high churchmanship lurched into incoherence. As one commentator noted, "Many of the sons of the Church have risen up against their fathers the bishops through a misconceived apprehension that themselves were vindicating the cause of the Church against bishops that were endeavoring to subvert it."[159] By April 1712, White Kennett was compiling a paper "reciting many passages out of late sermons and discourses directly impugning her Majesty's supremacy."[160] The Anglican high-church movement eventually found itself alienated not just from the Revolution settlement, but from the ecclesiastical constitution itself. On their own, the lower clergy lacked either the constitutional or ecclesiological standing to spearhead church reform.

The failure of the early-eighteenth-century moral counterrevolution, its terminal alienation from the Revolution settlement and the national identity, opened the way for an eighteenth-century age of benevolence rather than one of sacerdotalist discipline. Obviously, this was only one factor in the making of the age of benevolence, but one that has been curiously overlooked. The reactionary attempt to reground in institutions of ecclesiastical discipline many of the social and moral functions lately taken up by actors in civil society was phenomenally unsuccessful. Perhaps, then, the thriving civil society, with its culture of voluntarism, that came to characterize British social life in the eighteenth and nineteenth centuries was not so much, as Whig historians might have us believe, the byproduct of a weak state.[161] Perhaps it was the byproduct of a weak church.

CHAPTER 6

The Blue Water Policy of the Church of England

The members of the great Anglican societies of the early eighteenth century were particularly fond of a verse favored by the Hebrew prophets: "The earth shall be full of the knowledge of the Lord, as the waters cover the sea" (Isa 11:9, Hab 2:14).[1] In the mouths of clergymen whose church had thus far seemed virtually rooted to the soil of its island territory, it was more than a little romantic to accord the process of ecclesiastical expansion an almost diluvian relentlessness. And yet the verse might have captured something of the peculiar fluidity of Anglican development amidst England's burgeoning commercial and territorial empire. When the Anglican revivalists of the late seventeenth and early eighteenth centuries contemplated ecclesiastical expansion, they envisioned a church fit for an "empire of the seas": an informal, imperial pastorate oriented not just to the boundaries of the territorial empire, but toward the widening sweep of global British commercial and geopolitical interests.[2] Their objective was not simply to incorporate English territories under the jurisdiction of the established church, but rather to accommodate into the Anglican communion the moving parts of empire: the merchants, soldiers, sailors, strangers, and slaves that bound fort, factory, and plantation to metropole. By orienting Anglican ecclesiastical expansion toward England's "blue water" empire, churchmen of the turn of the eighteenth century were able to fashion a novel imperial ecclesiology—one that had no need of either the papal mandates that lent theological ballast to Latin empires or the millenarian eschatology that informed the imperial evangelism of radical Protestants.[3] The proponents of Anglican revivalism looked toward neither flag nor miter, but rather toward the ledger—as befitting the clergy of a commercial empire. "The limits of our Savior's kingdom," proclaimed Patrick Gordon, naval chaplain and missionary for the Society for the Promotion of Christian Knowledge (SPCK), would be extended "as far as English sails have done for traffic."[4]

With respect to ecclesiastical expansion, the church adopted what might be a called a "blue water policy," that is, a primary orientation toward England's maritime and commercial empire.[5] This formulation has, I believe, two major advantages over the notion of an "imperial Anglicanism" favored by other historians.[6] First, the notion of an ecclesiastical blue water policy does not artificially segregate Anglican activism on behalf of the colonial church from other modes of ecclesiastical expansion. Many of the personnel and organizations that mobilized on behalf of the "king's church in America" were involved in establishing an Anglican presence in the forts and factories of continental Europe and Asia— sites of British commercial and strategic interest, but by no means outposts of British sovereignty. Second, this formulation neither assumes nor requires that ecclesiastical expansion proceeded with the concurrence of the state. Historians who depict Anglican expansion as "the ecclesiastical arm of eighteenth century imperialism" tend to imply that church and state were engaged in a common project of imperial consolidation.[7] Yet, there is no reason to assume that ecclesiastical expansion was somehow free of the institutional pluralism, improvisation, and ideological contestation that characterized any of the other dimensions of imperialism in this period.[8] One might even go so far as to say that the fundamental limits of establishment capacity and concern for ecclesiastical expansion helped create the space for the public promotion, organization, and experimentation that characterized Anglican efforts abroad in the early eighteenth century. It would be fundamentally misleading to treat the panoply of Anglican expansionist projects—from the Society for the Propagation of the Gospel in Foreign Parts (SPG) to the Rotterdam church to the Codrington plantation to George Berkeley's Bermuda College—as expressions of a monolithic imperial policy. On the contrary, these were all manifestations of an established church struggling with the fact of its own insularity. Rather than conceiving of these endeavors as part of a broader metropolitan campaign to impose the Church of England upon territories under the English crown, they might be better understood as efforts at the *de-territorialization* of Anglicanism, a process of rendering the established church less dependent on the political, diocesan, and parochial structures that had proved difficult if not impossible to reproduce abroad.

The Anglican revival of the late seventeenth and early eighteenth centuries was, in truth, only moderately successful in establishing the Church of England abroad. Nevertheless, its effect on the moral consciousness of Britons in the eighteenth-century age of benevolence was profound. The organization and promotion of Anglican expansionist projects during the first half of the eighteenth century had the effect of dramatically expanding the "sympathetic imagination" of metropolitan English men and women.[9] Such efforts allowed an established (and downright telluric) church plotted in the insular dioceses of England and Wales to begin reckoning the far-flung populations affected by English global commercial and strategic interests within its moral purview.[10] This increasingly capacious pastoral concern, and the promotional and organizational structures in which it was embodied, must be comprehended within the genealogy of modern British humanitarianism. Anglicanism, rather than the abstract universalism of the later Enlightenment, provided the initial framework in which the suffering and deprivation of vulnerable populations could be contemplated at a distance. Without minimizing the later contributions of enlightenment and evangelical awakening, it must be recognized that modern English humanitarianism was, in the first instance, a problem of ecclesiology.[11]

The Late Restoration Revival and the Church of England Abroad

The later Restoration period witnessed, as part of the broader revival of Anglicanism, the emergence of a newfound regard for the fate of the church abroad.[12] Restoration statesmen and churchmen were slow in summoning anything resembling the energy with which Archbishop William Laud addressed the issue of ecclesiastical expansion in the years before the civil wars.[13] In 1672, for instance, there was an abortive effort to install one of Charles II's cronies in exile, Alexander Murray, as the first bishop of Virginia, although the scheme foundered when the soundness of both the proposed American episcopal endowment and the candidate's character were questioned.[14] Such efforts notwithstanding, the cure of imperial souls still rested with the bishops of London, whose diocesan authority over the empire and the English abroad was largely customary, albeit underpinned by several periodic grants of ecclesiastical jurisdiction by the crown.[15]

The elevation of the militantly anti-Catholic solider-turned-cleric Henry Compton to that see in December 1675 (and to the Privy Council the following month), however, inaugurated a new period of conscientiousness regarding the imperial church.[16] Compton immediately took steps to place the imperial jurisdiction of the see of London on a sounder footing. In January 1676, he applied to the Lords of Trade and Plantations "that enquiries be made concerning the authority of the bishop of London over foreign plantations." When the search turned up only a 1633 order placing the ecclesiastical affairs of the Merchant Adventurers trading company under the jurisdiction of the bishop of London, Compton lobbied for a more formal mandate. He was granted diocesan authority over the English garrison at Tangier in North Africa, long known as a hotbed of popery among the ranks of the English military.[17] A series of orders conferred upon the bishop of London the oversight of the entire international chaplaincy, mandating that no minister or schoolteacher be installed in any colonial or foreign cure without certification by the bishop of London of the candidate's orthodoxy. Compton successfully pressed the committee to insert a clause into the instructions to colonial governors "that God be duly served, and holy days and the sacrament administered according to the rules of the Church of England."[18] Of course, it must be remembered, that this patchwork and usually ad hoc authority was by no means beyond challenge. When Compton's successor John Robinson pressed for the establishment of ecclesiastical courts on the island of Barbados in 1717, the planters of that island disputed the bishop's authority as merely customary and without legal standing. The ensuing investigation by the Board of Trade found that diocesan jurisdiction over Barbados or any of the colonies had never been formally attached to the see of London.[19]

This nascent concern for the church abroad was not confined to the upper echelons of church and state. The broader public was gradually becoming invested in the work of ecclesiastical expansion during this period. In June 1681, the orientalist Humphrey Prideaux reported "a design de propaganda in fide" among the scholars at Oxford, undertaken at the behest of Bishop Compton and the East India Company.[20] Barnabas Oley, vicar of Great Gransden in Huntingdonshire at his death in 1684, endowed a farm and tenement in his parish for charitable purposes, among them "propagating the Christian faith" by the king with the advice of the bishops and according to the doctrine of the Church of England. Upon Oley's death the following year, Sir Leoline Jenkins, the sober Tory statesman, endowed two fellowships at Jesus College, Oxford, for clergy to "go out to sea in any of his Majesty's fleets . . . and in case there be no use of their service at sea, then to be called by the Lord Bishop of London to go out into any of his Majesty's foreign plantations."[21] At the same time, Jenkins's friend Edmund Bohun penned a tract advocating the evangelization of African slaves in the English colonies, which, however, failed to secure a license for publication.[22] Bohun's voice would have joined that of the Anglican clergyman Morgan Godwyn, who produced in the final years of the Restoration a series of hugely influential works exposing the moral consequences of Anglican lassitude abroad.

Morgan Godwyn was no rabble-rouser. His royalist Anglican credentials were frankly impeccable. Both his great-grandfather Thomas Godwin and his grandfather Francis Godwin had been bishops in the church. His father Morgan served as archdeacon of Shropshire and a prebendary in his father's diocese of Hereford before his ejection during the civil wars, after which he kept a school in Newland in Gloucestershire. The younger Morgan was educated at Brasenose College, Oxford, before transferring to Christ Church, where he received his bachelor's degree in March 1665.[23] His clerical pedigree and prospects made his departure for Virginia the following year all the more unusual. Godwyn spent roughly four years in Virginia, ministering in the parishes of Marston and Stafford, before departing for Barbados. He returned to London around 1679–1680, where he was made rector of Woldham, Kent, and in 1681 vicar of Bulkington, Warwickshire. Drawing on his ministries abroad, Godwyn began to publish and preach on the deficiencies of the Church of England in the plantations. One can surmise that he became comfortably ensconced in the climate of the Tory reaction of the early 1680s. He dedicated his major work, *The Negro's & Indians advocate*, to the fiercely royalist primate William Sancroft. He corresponded with the Anglican historian and future nonjuror Henry Dodwell.[24] He dedicated his final publication, the sermon *Trade preferred before religion*, to James II upon his accession to the throne in 1685.[25]

The importance of Godwyn's writings are somewhat broader than their idée fixe of evangelizing African slaves in the American plantations.[26] His larger purpose was to invest the very notion of empire with a sense of moral custody. In the dedication of his first work to Archbishop Sancroft, Godwyn claimed that his purpose was "to implore relief for those myriads of hungry and distressed souls abroad; most of them within the English dominion, though without their care."[27] The sin of empire lay in the inescapable fact that commercial and territorial expansion had failed to engender any concomitant enlargement of moral responsibility. The failure of English settlers to oversee the conversion of African slaves and the neighboring natives was not merely a sin of omission; it underpinned a broader, anti-Christian imperialism, in which the "needless and troublesome charge about religion, cannot enter into such, who for the most part know no other God but money, nor religion but profit." In other words, Godwyn was not merely reminding the English colonists of their Christian duty to propagate the gospel. He was indicating the measure of moral and spiritual obligation implicit in English dominion abroad.[28] Godwyn's was not an evangelical call to make disciples of all nations but a somewhat more modestly paternalistic call to apply the tenets of "family religion" to all the souls that dwelt in the English dominions. "Our negroes and Indians, slaves and tributaries," he preached throughout London and Westminster in 1685, "all of them [are] the subjects of this kingdom (and should be also of our care)."[29]

Godwyn was not simply upbraiding his auditors in the capital for avarice. He was challenging the strict territorial logic at the heart of the Protestant Church of England. Its communion was not to be conceived as the accumulation of territories under the control of the English crown, but rather as the aggregate of souls with which the nation was engaged. He anticipated the retort of his auditors, "What have they to do with those abroad?" But he did not recognize the distinction between the domestic and imperial concerns of the Church of England; commerce in the broadest sense justified communion. The souls abroad "justly claim a share in our spirituals, whilst we enjoy so much of their temporals." The ecclesiological distinction between metropole and periphery was invalid. Godwyn distinguished only between an empire circumscribed by English interests and the greater world. He invoked the old adage regarding the proper sphere of charity in order to dramatically broaden the regions of English concern: "Our charity in this case ought most properly to begin at home; I mean amongst the subjects and tributaries of our plantations; and not rather (as some I have heard have projected) in such remoter places where we are less related."[30] Godwyn's imperial vision might (with apologies to Benedict Anderson) be conceived as "imagined communion": an empire consecrated through the offices of the Church of England would effectively transmute Britons and colonials, African slaves and American natives into a single people.[31] "So powerful are the bonds of religion to unite the minds of men," he wrote, "though of most different and even contrary interests . . . making men to forget their own people, and their father's house and joining them in affection to the most distant strangers."[32] The humanitarian musings of the conservative Anglican cleric were void of enlightenment ideals; they proceeded exclusively from ecclesiological considerations.

Although Godwyn's fate after the Revolution remains unknown, his influence upon the advocates of ecclesiastical expansion was enormous. His ideas remained current among the nonjuring community at the manor of the Jacobite squire Francis Cherry at Shottesbrooke, Berkshire.[33] Godwyn's associate Henry Dodwell was a fixture of the Shottesbrooke scene.[34] Despite their alienation from the Revolution establishment, Dodwell and his nonjuring associates were known to lobby Archbishop Thomas Tenison and others on "doing God service in the plantations."[35] Cherry's nonjuring chaplain Francis Brokesby explicitly publicized Godwyn's ideas in his 1708 tract *Some Proposals Towards Promoting the Propagation of the Gospel in Our American Plantations.* The eccentric nonjuring physician Francis Lee, an associate of Robert Nelson and Dodwell, was also known to lobby the ministry of Robert Harley with numerous philanthropic projects for "the improvement of our American colonies."[36] Nelson, perhaps the most important habitué of Shottesbrooke, was of course an early and enduringly active member of several of the great Anglican philanthropic organizations of the early eighteenth century and was the strongest link between the nonjurors and the Anglican voluntary sector. Ironically, Cherry had appointed White Kennett, a former Anglican royalist well on his way to becoming a zealous church Whig, to the rectory at Shottesbrooke. Kennett, like Nelson, was also heavily engaged in the Anglican societies, and he too became intimately familiar with the ideas of Morgan Godwyn. As a member of the SPG in 1706, Kennett on numerous occasions pressed for the republication of Godwyn's works.[37] Godwyn's influence on the society was prominently featured throughout Kennett's manuscript collection of materials for a history of Anglican missionary efforts, compiled during the reign of Queen Anne.[38]

As with late Restoration Anglican revivalism at home, such gestures on behalf of the church abroad were not without oppositional potential. Neither Charles II nor James II was particularly sympathetic to the expansionist Anglicanism pressed by Compton and his allies. After all, the Anglican royalist alliance that underwrote the political security of the government at home was substantially unnecessary abroad, where both monarchs were free to court Roman Catholicism and Protestant Nonconformity.[39] Moreover, the imperatives of late Stuart imperial policy made religious pluralism a demographic necessity.

Late-seventeenth-century colonial foundations in the mid-Atlantic and the Carolinas simply could not afford the kinds of confessional restrictions that might prove a bar to attracting settlers.[40] In the absence of the religiously inspired "great migrations," which peopled the early-seventeenth-century colonies of New England and the Chesapeake, late Stuart foundations generally relied on tolerationist policies to attract and maintain the levels of population necessary for viability.[41] Royal indulgence abroad thus further undermined the late Stuart monarchs' professed regard for the security of the established church. Englishmen were not without hope that the restoration of the Protestant monarchy in 1689 might provide fresh opportunity for reviving the fortunes of the church abroad.

Anglican Ecclesiastical Expansion and Civil Society

The Revolution of 1688–1689 did, in fact, reinvigorate the Church of England abroad. In the aftermath of the crisis, the Church of England was established by law in the colonies of Maryland, New York, and South Carolina. Prominent and richly endowed episcopal congregations founded in the major port cities of Boston, Philadelphia, and New York became centers of Anglican culture even amidst the religious pluralism and alien establishments of the northern and mid-Atlantic colonies. At the end of 1689, Bishop Compton appointed as commissary to the colony of Virginia the Scottish episcopal priest James Blair, who was equipped with visitational and disciplinary power over the church there. In 1693, Blair founded the College of William and Mary as the first Anglican seminary in the New World. Compton's second appointment, Thomas Bray, commissary to Maryland, planted parochial libraries in the colonies and founded the Anglican SPCK and SPG.[42]

Amidst the flush of revivalist energy that followed the Glorious Revolution, Anglican expansion became not merely an establishment program, but a wider societal concern. A growing chorus of voices within the burgeoning postrevolutionary public sphere renewed Morgan Godwyn's lament for an empire that had outstripped the communion of its mother church.[43] Moreover, cognizance of the institutional limitations of the established church (and perhaps the distractions of a burgeoning English military-fiscal state preoccupied with the secular concerns of war and empire) impelled Anglicans to rethink the organizational footing of ecclesiastical expansion. Bray, for instance, envisioned the participation of a robust voluntary sector, those people, "who have put the ministers of God in a capacity of so instructing the people, by making a provision for the acquisition, maintenance and propagation of Christian knowledge. Such are those who have been the founders of churches, schools, colleges, and libraries . . . such charities, which directly tending to the everlasting happiness of the souls of men."[44] As Anglicanism lacked the missionary orders and international episcopate possessed by its Roman Catholic rival, Richard Willis, dean of Lincoln, could only "hope the charity of our people will now help to supply the defect and take away this reproach from our Church and nation."[45] The Anglican missionary Patrick Gordon imagined a national outpouring for the propagation of the gospel abroad: the five-hundredth part of the annual income of every freeholder, the two-hundredth part from every merchant, and one-hundredth from every clergyman, "priest and people unanimously combine[d] together in carrying on this most Christian design."[46] The movement for Anglican ecclesiastical expansion was very much a creature of civil society, fueled by lay activism and charitable contributions, countenanced but hardly directed by the ministers of the British state. Indeed, the publicity and solicitations of this movement became another important (though hitherto largely unrecognized) conduit by which the fact of the empire was interjected into eighteenth-century metropolitan life.[47]

Though established by royal charter in 1701, the SPG was cognizant during its first decades of its dependence upon civil society—particularly the mercantile sector in the metropole.[48] At one of the very first meetings of the society, it was ordered that all residing members in London "be desired to apply to the eminent merchants of the city especially such of them as do trade to the plantations for their benefactions towards the promoting the designs of this society."[49] At the first anniversary sermon of the society, presented yearly at the London parish of St. Mary-le-Bow, Richard Willis addressed his plea for the advance of the gospel within the empire "in a particular manner . . . to the consideration of this great city, and especially to those who are grown rich by the trade of the plantations."[50] In 1711, Queen Anne appointed Trinity Sunday for the reading of a charity brief on behalf of the SPG from all the pulpits of London, Westminster, and the liberties. The brief yielded some £2,900 in charitable contributions.[51] Mindful of this success, the queen issued a second charity brief for the society in London and Westminster three years later in May 1714.[52]

Nor was public enthusiasm by any means limited to monetary donations. On a visit to London in May 1707, the saintly Thomas Wilson, bishop of Sodor and Man, attended a meeting of the SPG and formally offered the Isle of Man as a suitable locale for the erection of a college to train American missionaries. The bishop assured the society that the Manx were a frugal, sober, and seafaring people, ideally bred "for the service of the Church in America."[53] A tiny seminary was indeed erected under Wilson's direction, though it was largely eclipsed by the prospects of a missionary college to be established on Barbados.[54] The latter was the bequest of Colonel Christopher Codrington, whose will in 1710 left three sugar plantations on that island, stocked with "three hundred negroes," from which to furnish a seminary with "a convenient number of professors and scholars to be maintained there, all of them under the vows of poverty, chastity and obedience, who shall be obliged to study and practice physic and chirurgery as well as divinity, that . . . they may indear themselves to the people and have the better opportunities of doing good to men's souls whilst they are taking care of their bodies."[55] The sermon delivered at Codrington's funeral hailed the gift as a noble example to be imitated by the English merchant community, "consecrating some part of their great estates, to conversion and instruction of those infidels, to whose labor under providence they owe their wealth and affluence."[56]

Ensconced at the heart of the metropole and needful of the beneficence of the commercial and maritime sectors, the SPG advanced a vision of empire in which trade might be enlisted in the service of the gospel. Its quarrel was not with trade per se, but with its ultimacy—"trade preferred before religion," as Godwyn's sermon had put it. In his 1712 anniversary sermon before the SPG, White Kennett, dean of Peterborough, listed among impediments to advancing the kingdom of Christ trade driven by "secular interest and gain, rather than the seeking the glory of God and the good of souls."[57] Trade and religion were rarely depicted as alternative engagements with the wider world. Indeed, as George Stanhope, dean of Canterbury, observed in 1714, the former could serve as a channel for the latter: "the mutual intercourse, set on foot between countries remote from each other, for the sake of traffic and temporal convenience, has all along been one great instrument of imparting useful knowledge, where it was wanted. This was the case of learning and philosophy, among the ancients. This is the case of arts and sciences in every age: This in part has been and will, we trust, be more and more, the case of our most holy faith."[58] Other advocates of ecclesiastical expansion discerned in British global trade more than merely a means of propagating the gospel abroad. Commercial engagement engendered the obligation of spiritual engagement. Clergy frequently inverted St. Paul's disavowal of remuneration for preaching the gospel at 1 Corinthians 9:11: "If you have reaped so much of their carnal things, or by their means," asked William Stanley, dean of St. Asaph, in 1708, "is it not fit that they should reap your spiritual things, or by your help and means?"[59] Such remarks did not, in fact, imply a purely evangelical call to go forth and make disciples of all nations. Nor, it should be noted, did they suggest that the spiritual jurisdiction of the Church of England abroad should simply shadow the territorial sovereignty of the crown. On the contrary, the church was accommodating its pastoral responsibilities to those souls comprehended within the global sweep of British commercial interests. "Where are the fruits of your religion," asked John Williams, bishop of Chichester, in 1706, "when you have under your care those vast dominions which is called the *English Empire*; and from whence you draw so much of your emoluments to enrich and pleasure your selves at home?"[60] The principle conviction of the early-eighteenth-century advocates of Anglican expansion was that communion followed interest: material profits incurred spiritual debts.[61] As long as these debts went unpaid, English trade could be arraigned for irreligion. "Our commerce therefore does not commence truly Christian," George Stanhope lamented, "till it proceeds upon a principle of charity. Of charity to all, but especially to the spiritual wants of them, to whom we apply for the increase of our temporal comforts."[62]

Anglican expansion thus required that the church overcome its own terrestrial ecclesiology.[63] In order to do this, the movement fixed particularly upon trade as the precondition of Anglican concern. Anglican concern with the peoples of the world, Robert Nelson explained, presumed "a settled correspondence and commerce with them, as to the things of the earth."[64] This commercial orientation goes some length in explaining the institutional innovation and experimentation that characterized the movement. The Anglican voluntary sector dispatched missionaries; founded chapels; distributed devotional materials; and established parochial libraries, charity schools, overseas seminaries, and philanthropic colonies—projects geared not toward imposing confessional homogeneity on the dynamic and pluralistic empire, but rather toward establishing an informal, imperial pastorate to minister to a mobile and increasingly far-flung Anglican communion. This was the blue water policy of the Church of England.

Anglican Expansion in Europe

Even as the Anglican societies began devoting resources to augmenting the Church of England in the American colonies, activists remained committed to the establishment of an Anglican presence throughout the commercial and strategic outposts of the English maritime empire. This was not limited to sites that fell under crown jurisdiction. Locales claiming substantial English (or British) presence or strategic significance attracted the attention of activists no less than the formal dominions of empire. Indeed, the Anglican societies and their members directed a substantial part of their attention not to building the king's church in the New World, but to accommodating the English commercial and military presence throughout Eurasia and Africa.

For instance, the foundation of an Anglican church at Rotterdam for merchants and sailors became something of a cause célèbre early in the reign of Queen Anne.[65] Unsurprisingly, the main proponents of the project were drawn overwhelmingly from the personnel of the SPCK and the SPG, though the matter was never a formal concern of either organization.[66] The Anglican church at Rotterdam was to be "the first public national Church out of her Majesty's royal dominions."[67] Its advocates touted "the benefit which their posterity, strangers and seafaring men may find in the public enjoyment of their religion in a foreign country in communion with their native Church."[68]

Anglican activists readily, albeit informally, adopted this project as their own. The Rotterdam church's pastor, William Thorold, was chosen as a corresponding member of the SPCK in 1701.[69] The leading SPCK and SPG activist Robert Nelson was a tireless advocate on the fledgling church's behalf. In March 1703, Nelson wrote his friend Samuel Pepys, a man with long ties to the navy, to inform him of this "pious work," noting the unusual level of enthusiasm for the Rotterdam church in the military establishment.[70] In the age of the great wars against Louis XIV such enthusiasm is perhaps not surprising: soldiers and sailors often found themselves beyond the ambit of the established church. The trustees for the Rotterdam church cited contributions to the church from fourteen regiments and subscriptions from another five commanders.[71] Indeed, the captain-general of the armies, John Churchill, Duke of Marlborough, took a particular interest in the establishment of the church, and the trustees took pains to give him credit, writing in February 1704 that "the great concourse of seafaring men enjoy the exercise of their religion by his Grace's establishment of a Church of

England here" in Rotterdam.[72] The Rotterdam church was roundly considered the beginnings of a larger Anglican profile on the Continent, one befitting a nation that in the wake of the Glorious Revolution aggressively resumed its identity as "the great bulwark of the Reformation."

The same expansionist sentiment in the Church of England soon fixed upon the free port of Leghorn on the Ligurian Sea in Tuscany. The increasing prominence of the British merchant community at that port, along with the growing British naval commitment in the Mediterranean, naturally drew the attention of the Anglican societies in London. Thus, in 1705, along with his commission as British envoy to Florence and Genoa, Dr. Henry Newton, a learned civilian, took with him to Italy the informal proposal of his patron Archbishop Tenison, ex officio president of the SPG, for the establishment of an Anglican chaplain at the British factory in the bustling port of Leghorn.[73] The SPG member and historian White Kennett was charged with the task of procuring a suitable candidate for the post and soon lit upon his younger brother, Basil Kennett, Master of Arts and Fellow of Corpus Christi College at Oxford. The activist circles in which White Kennett traveled were enthusiastic about the prospect of another continental outpost. On 10 September 1706, Robert Nelson wrote approvingly of the design to Samuel Brewster, both of whom were close associates of Kennett and leading lights of the SPCK. Nelson cautioned circumspection: "It will be necessary he should be as careful to conceal his character in Italy, as a popish priest is to conceal his in England." And Catholic suspicion would not be the only stumbling block. Nelson reflected, "He will have work enough to bring that factory to a serious sense of religion."[74] His trepidation would be justified.

The first years of Basil Kennett's tenure as the Anglican chaplain at the British factory in Leghorn were marked by almost constant harassment and surveillance by the Inquisition and the courts at Florence and Rome. In the end, Kennett's ministry was protected only by a threat of military reprisal from Queen Anne herself, whose secretary of state the Earl of Sunderland informed the Tuscan court that "any molestation given to her chaplain, residing at Leghorn, she shall look upon it as an affront done to herself and the nation, a breach of peace, and a violation of the law of nations."[75] Shielded by a threat of confessional militancy (in an age that had supposedly expelled religion from geopolitical considerations), Basil Kennett served as an apostle of the expanding Church of England. He bid his expatriate flock rejoice "that the God of their fathers has blessed them with his ordinances in a strange land."[76]

Simmering sectarian strife also formed the backdrop for Anglican expansion efforts on the island of Minorca.[77] Shortly after the ratification of the Treaty of Utrecht in spring 1713, which formally ceded the Balearic island in the western Mediterranean to the British crown, the SPCK dispatched a large packet of Anglican devotional books to the soldiers of "Her Majesty's garrison at Port Mahon."[78] For the next several decades, Minorca would remain a perennial object of concern for Anglican activists, who served as a restless lobby for what Henry Newman, the secretary of the SPCK, deemed "the more effectual establishment of the Protestant interest in Minorca."[79]

The society found an active collaborator in the lieutenant governor of the island, Richard Kane, a northern Irish veteran of the campaigns of both William and Marlborough.[80] As lieutenant governor, Kane was charged with upholding the eleventh article of the Treaty of Utrecht, which stipulated "the free use of the Roman Catholic religion."[81] Neither Kane nor his allies in London interpreted this to exclude the establishment of Protestantism on the island. To that end, the lieutenant governor immediately requisitioned four Roman Catholic chapels for Anglican worship, an act that proved to be only the first in a series of outrages to the local population.[82] The native clergy complained to the Spanish of frequent harassment at the hands of the English soldiers.[83] In the town of Ciudadela, the English allegedly fell upon a nocturnal procession carrying the consecrated host to a sick person and extinguished the torches. They stole the clappers from the bells at the parish church in Mahon. Sailors flirted with the nuns through the grates of the convent in the city, which Kane assured the Spanish ambassador caused "more mirth in the convent than uneasiness." The friars of the convent at St. James complained of the incursion by a young English ensign, "looking and examining into the consecrated hosts." Kane attributed the intrusion to harmless curiosity, being "the first time he had been in a Roman Catholic country." He reassured the Spanish that these were isolated incidents, unfortunate yet predictable "where so many young men happen to be together," but in no way representing any systematic breach of the treaty.[84]

In London, however, the advocates of Anglican expansion bristled at this low-level confessional conflict and sought to implant the Church of England more securely on the island. In 1718, William Wake, archbishop of Canterbury, was tasked by the crown with the settlement of ecclesiastical affairs there.[85] Wake's proposal was radical indeed, preserving Catholic worship within the island, while effectively extracting it from the spiritual jurisdiction of the Roman church. All foreign clergy were to be barred from admittance into any local office or benefice. The Inquisition and all foreign spiritual courts were prohibited. Oaths of fidelity to the British crown were to be exacted from all native clergy, and all spiritual immunities such as sanctuary and the benefit of clergy were to be dissolved.[86] Most radical, however, was Wake's demand that the island be "wholly discharged from the government of the bishop of Majorca, and the archbishop of Valencia; and from all manner of dependence upon and obedience to any foreign generals and provincials."[87] Lieutenant Governor Kane concurred with the high Erastianism of Wake's proposals and contributed his own memorandum advocating separation from the diocese of Majorca. Incredibly, he demanded that the inhabitants of the island "be given a bishop of their own," whose nomination and all attendant rents and fees would be transferred to the British crown.[88]

The containment of Roman Catholicism on Minorca required the augmentation of the Church of England. Wake proposed that the crown authorize the construction of two churches in Mahon and Fort St. Philip, "for the use of your Protestant subjects," and that the daily ministry by "men of learning and prudence" be settled in each. He also argued for the foundation of a school near the garrison, modeled on the charity schools then being promoted throughout England and Wales by the SPCK. He further added that the ecclesiastical government of the island be formally annexed to the jurisdiction of "some archbishop of England." Finally, the governor of the island must be empowered to protect converts among the natives, "to secure such persons as shall embrace the Protestant religion from suffering any loss or detriment on that account."[89] To Wake's memorandum of 1718 was added a proposal to convert the military chaplains of the British garrisons into beneficed clergymen.[90]

The Whig ministry of George I never relished the prospects of confessional war on an island that had been secured for strategic and commercial purposes, and official interest in the ecclesiastical affairs of the island languished. The advocacy of the Protestant interest on Minorca fell to an informal lobby of activists, including Lieutenant Governor Kane; Archbishop Wake; the successive bishops of London, John Robinson and Edmund Gibson; and the SPCK. The society began corresponding with Kane regularly in December 1719; its secretary Henry Newman praised Kane's efforts effusively, deeming the governor "an instrument raised up by Providence to be the means of abundance of good in those parts."[91] Newman advocated that Kane divert sequestered ecclesiastical revenue from the church in Minorca toward publishing and distributing the New Testament "in Spanish or Italian or both" and pledged the support of the society in lobbying the king and the bishops for such an undertaking.[92] Newman prayed that God would soon "open the eyes of the Minorcans to see what is truly for their own interest, viz. to be entirely in the English interest, and as fast as they can to become as good Protestants as their governor."[93]

The Church of England possessed no missionary order comparable to those of the Roman Catholic Church and therefore promoted its church abroad by a grab bag of alternative methods. In December 1720, Kane's military chaplain, James Auchmooty, was chosen to be a corresponding member of the SPCK, "to assist [Kane] in civilizing and Christianizing the people under your care."[94] The society actively sought out the works of Don Felix Antonio de Alverado, a Spanish convert to the Church of England, who had translated the Book of Common Prayer and several theological dialogues in his capacity as minister to a congregation of Spanish merchants in London.[95] They dispatched hundreds of copies of Archbishop John Tillotson's discourses against popery and transubstantiation, along with a tract called *Short Refutation of the Principal Errors of the Church of Rome* to fortify Protestant soldiers in their occupation of Roman Catholic territories.[96] Even more ambitiously, the society lobbied assiduously to have a pension of £60 per year established by Queen Mary for the education of two Vaudois youths "for the service of the Protestant churches" in the Piedmont transferred to "the service of religion" in Minorca.[97] If secured, these funds would go to support Protestant schools throughout the island.[98] The schools would serve as a beachhead of Anglicanism on Minorca, and the SPCK was convinced that it would not be long before "many of the natives would send their children to be instructed, who would of course embrace our religion, and their allegiance to the British Crown be better depended on."[99]

In the absence of any mobile and international missionary orders, the Anglican societies turned to the extensive English chaplainry as a surrogate institution. Chaplains throughout the naval, military, and mercantile sectors were recruited into a correspondence with the societies. The SPCK deliberately sought out and recruited into its ranks English factory chaplains throughout Europe, claiming correspondents in Hamburg, Danzig, and Moscow.[100] Moreover, the societies offered their organizations (and their influence with the episcopate) as an ersatz chapter for the clergy abroad.[101] In 1706–1707, for instance, the SPG sought to redress "the great neglect and want of care which is aboard our Men of War relating to their chaplains." It ordered its missionaries, en route to the plantations and factories abroad, to serve as examples of piety and virtue to the ship's company; to prevail with the captain to have morning and evening prayers read daily, and preaching and catechism on the Sabbath; and "that throughout their passage they instruct, exhort, admonish and reprove, as they have occasion and opportunity," which if done with seriousness and prudence, would win them credit and authority with the crew.[102] The purpose was to strengthen the hand of the clergy with respect to their flock and habituate the English abroad to the presence of the church. In the absence of any genuinely imperial ecclesiastical establishment, the activists of the Anglican societies would consecrate parishes of the quarterdecks and garrisons, the hospitals and factories that serviced and maintained the English maritime empire.[103]

Imagining a Global Church of England

The Church of England sought to shadow English commerce beyond Europe as well. In the years 1704–1705, two Anglican chaplains in the employ of the East India Company, William Anderson and Benjamin Adams, struggled mightily to erect a proper place of worship at Fort William in Bengal. Having solicited private subscriptions from the community there and a thousand rupees from the company's account, they found themselves in a protracted battle with company merchants over the location of the proposed church and the distribution of the funds.[104] The resistance of local merchants to ecclesiastical aggrandizement in Bengal only served to reinforce the East India Company's long-standing reputation for irreligion and anticlericalism abroad.[105] From the company outpost of St. Helena in the south Atlantic, the Anglican minister Charles Masham reported to Archbishop Tenison on his flock in which "no body professes any other here than the Church of England," but the offices of the church were routinely neglected and the church's building and burial grounds remained unconsecrated. Masham frequently found himself in conflict with the governor, "who is supreme magistrate here in civil affairs, is likewise so far in ecclesiastical."[106] It was not long before Masham was in correspondence with the SPG, which began dispatching Bibles, Books of Common Prayer, and Anglican devotional literature to the island to aid in ministering to the population and catechizing their children.[107]

In 1710, the SPCK initiated what became a long relationship with the East India Company.[108] The society procured and helped support the clergy required by the company charter of 1698, which stipulated a minister in every garrison and factory and a chaplain on every ship carrying two tons or more.[109] It was the intent of the society, Henry Newman informed Josiah Woodward on 6 December 1711, "to procure the service of worthy chaplains to the Indies in the Company service, till it please God to enable them to send missionaries of their own."[110] George Lewis, the chaplain at Fort St. George, accepted a membership in the SPCK the following year. Lewis wondered "that in so many years that we have been possessed of large plantations, settlements &c. in the East and West Indies, that no such thing hath been set on foot." He supported Anglican missionary efforts in India but considered them a secondary concern. "I think we ought to begin at home," he told Newman. "For there are thousands of people, I may say some hundreds of thousands, who live in the settlements and under the jurisdiction of the R[igh]t Hon[ora]ble Company . . . and while we have so large a harvest at home, let us first gather in that, and then it will be time enough to look abroad."[111] This largely remained the policy of the SPCK during the first third of the eighteenth century. In 1718, Newman reported to one society member, "The English chaplains generally confine their care to the English congregation in the garrisons where they are, excepting a few Indian slaves who happen to become domestics among the English."[112] The ecclesiological, rather than the evangelical, logic remained predominant. The church would expand by encompassing the English abroad and their foreign dependents and economic clients. Extension beyond the English sphere of commercial and strategic interests remained a distant consideration.

Opportunity and imagination, however, occasionally induced the Anglican societies beyond the immediate sphere of English interest abroad. In 1721, the appearance of two princes from the region of Delagoa Bay in southeastern Africa (modern-day Mozambique) convinced the SPCK of the good prospects for evangelization on that continent. With the support of both the East India Company and the Royal African Company, the SPCK sought to return the two brothers, who took the Christian names James Chandos Mastoon and John Towgood Mastoon, to their native country, with two Anglican missionaries in tow.[113] Unlikely to secure ordained ministers in such a risky and unprofitable endeavor, the society contented itself with "sending thither two sober mechanics qualified at least as charity schoolmasters to make a beginning in so illustrious a design."[114] The society could enlist only a single schoolmaster, Marmaduke Penwell by name, who was to accompany the princes to southeastern Africa "to preserve and improve that knowledge they have happily imbibed since their residence in London, and even to remain in the country if he finds it practicable with safety to try what impressions may be made on the nature for the reception of Christianity."[115] The SPCK member John Perceval, Earl of Egmont, spearheaded the project. In January 1722, he told the princes "what we do is no more than Christ our master obliges us to, who bids us love our neighbors as our selves and though we are of different complexions, we yet are brethren as descending from one common parent."[116]

The instructions that Perceval sketched out for Penwell are indicative of the spirit that animated the society's designs. Penwell was to pray aloud morning and evening with his charges, and "let your prayers be short and very distinctly repeated." He was to instruct the princes in reading, writing, and numeracy and to avoid at all costs the mysteries and subtleties of religion, focusing instead on the commands of Christ. "Appear at all times to delight in their company and behave respectfully and civilly towards them," he instructed. "And if they hear the seamen swear and talk loudly, tell them you are sorry for it, for the book of God does not allow it." More importantly, Penwell was to take copious notes on the country and its inhabitants: on "whether these people have any show of religion"; on their temperament; on their form of government, "whether the king be absolute"; on the extent and demography of the king's dominions; on "their method of living," that is, their techniques for obtaining food, clothing, and shelter; on the occasions of war and commerce; and on the vagaries of weather and disease. But above all, Penwell was to proceed in the spirit of charity. He would tell the king that he came "out of love to his and his people's souls to teach them how to save them by knowing the true God and living after his own orders in a book you have brought with you." If need be, he must also be an evangel of civilization, willing to instruct the Africans "in all things useful to their living."[117]

Unfortunately, the mission was a fiasco from start to finish. Penwell was considered a fairly lackluster emissary on behalf of the church, "the best we could get," as Henry Newman charitably confessed.[118] A week after departing from Gravesend on 14 March 1722, the ship struck a rock at the mouth of the River Exe and was forced ashore for repairs. At that point, the elder brother James began to show signs of mental illness: he attacked his brother John without provocation and at another time grabbed a dagger and threatened to cut his own throat.[119] The erratic and violent behavior of the elder brother caused the ship's captain to intervene. On 1 May, while still ashore, Penwell walked in on the captain severely beating James. "As soon as he saw me, he called me a Presbyterian rogue and said he would use me like a scoundrel when he got me on board." After Penwell retired to his lodgings that night, James left the inn and hanged himself from an apple tree with his own garters.[120] John seemed untroubled by the news of his older brother's suicide but became anxious the next day and reportedly remained so until his brother was buried. The ship eventually resumed its voyage, and by the end of the year the Royal African Company had received word that "the African behaved himself to their great satisfaction."[121] Upon arriving on the southeastern coast of Africa, the English found their hopes dashed by the presence of the Dutch East India Company, which told the captain "that he had no business at Delagoa" and forbid them entrance into that country, and even from restocking their provisions.[122] By March 1723, Henry Newman advised Perceval to "put an end to their expectations from the Delagoa Mission, which like many other good designs was well intended, though the success has not answered the wishes of those that promoted it."[123]

The moral imagination of the Anglican societies was already beginning to outstrip their admittedly limited resources for direct evangelization abroad. In 1720, the SPCK entertained a curious proposal for the printing and distribution of an Arabic translation of the New Testament throughout the Ottoman Empire. Although such a project would not expand the Church of England abroad, it was deemed a "great service to the Christian religion in Judea, Palestine, Syria and other eastern countries."[124] The project required a considerable mobilization of resources. The SPCK launched a funding drive among members and at court, a difficult prospect, for the project "comes into the world when it finds many of the rich people in great distress, by reason of their late disappointments in the South Sea Project."[125] The aggressive solicitations of the society eventually won the project a bounty of £500 from the king.[126] The SPCK requested cost estimates from publishing contacts in the Netherlands and made inquiries among scholars in London and the universities on fonts and translations.[127] It was also necessary to discern by "what channel the books had best be conveyed."[128] To this end, the SPCK made contacts among the various former and current diplomatic and mercantile chaplains with experience in the Ottoman domains.[129] By summer 1721, it was found that all the Arabic translations of the New Testament available in England were largely defective; more accurate editions had to be procured from Aleppo, bearing the sanction of the Greek Orthodox Patriarch of Antioch.[130] All of these steps had to be taken without news of the project reaching Roman Catholic communities either in England or abroad, which, as Newman warned William Ayerst, "will be vigorous to make all the opposition they can to the success of anything of this nature from a Protestant country."[131]

By 1724, the SPCK had published six thousand copies of the Psalms in Arabic and labored mightily to complete the New Testament.[132] In that year, Sylvester succeeded Athanasius IV as Patriarch of Antioch; "when the Psalters sent over were presented to him as a token of the respect of the British Nation to his flock he returned a thousand benedictions to the benefactors and promised he would distribute them with his own hands."[133] The Arabic New Testament was not published until the end of the summer of 1727. In September, the SPCK shipped the first three hundred copies to Scanderoon aboard the *Amalia*, along with one hundred copies of Hugo Grotius's *De veritate religionis Christianae* in Arabic.[134] They shipped another thirteen hundred copies the following September.[135] By 1729, they had printed more than ten thousand copies and were shipping Bibles along with the society's own *Catechetical Instruction*, drawn up by James Vernon, as well as Arabic translations of the affiliated Swiss theologian Jean-Frédéric Ostervald's *History of the Bible*.[136] These materials were soon requested by the English chaplain at Narva "for the use of poor Christians in the Russian conquests of Persia."[137] Enlivened by the lengthening reach of its efforts, the SPCK inquired "whether the Patriarch of Antioch has any authority over or holds any correspondence with the St. Thomas Christians in the East Indies," that is, the Nasrani on the Malabar coast of India, who traced their conversion directly to the first-century apostle of Jesus of Nazareth.[138]

Such ventures suggest an established church undergoing something of a cognitive expansion, if not always a substantive institutional extension. The Church of England would not make Anglicans of all nations, but by the mid-eighteenth century, the moral imagination of its dedicated activists had widened perceptibly. Indeed, this expanded Anglican consciousness often blurred the line between missionary efforts in the strictest sense of confessional aggrandizement and modern humanitarianism. That clergy and gentlemen gathered in a coffee-house near St. Dunstan's-in-the-West could take cognizance of the plight of Coptic and Orthodox Christians in the Ottoman Empire neither in furtherance of a grand eschatological program of Christian reunion nor from a desire to formally convert them to the Church of England, but simply to facilitate the practice of their own religion suggests the emergence of a global sympathy previously unknown in early modern Europe.

Anglican Expansion and the British Public

The Anglican societies and their international networks of activists and correspondents equipped early-eighteenth-century English men and women with the ideological and organizational resources to reimagine commercial and territorial expansion in moral terms. Moreover, the dependence of these organizations and activists upon public engagement and benevolence effectively invited all of civil society to participate in a wide-ranging discussion of the moral obligations of empire. Such a public conversation, it is not unfair to say, could hardly proceed without an element of utopianism.

Consider the rapturous public enthusiasm that greeted one of the more quixotic schemes mooted by the advocates of Anglican expansion. In 1724, the Anglo-Irish clergyman and philosopher George Berkeley, dean of Derry, proposed the erection of a missionary college in the New World. Berkeley was aware that the SPCK had struggled for years to convert the bequest of three sugar plantations in Barbados into the imperial seminary and hospital that the donor Colonel Christopher Codrington intended. Berkeley attributed the failures of Codrington College to the "wealth and luxury" of Barbados and lit upon an ill-conceived alternative with considerably less commercial potential: Bermuda. The public response was, on the whole, quite favorable. Berkeley's sympathetic friend Jonathan Swift thought the scheme "a romantic design," while Dublin wits launched broadsides at the dean, dispatching to his door a young girl bedecked in flowers and myrtle, presumably an Eve to Berkeley's new Adam of Bermuda: "I famous for breeding, you famous for knowledge / I'll found a whole nation, you'll found a whole college."[139] More seasoned activists like Thomas Bray ridiculed the project as "crude" and riddled with errors arrived at through "want of experience," but even he could not help but notice the staggering popularity of the dean's designs. The Bermuda project, Bray confessed, was "prodigiously in vogue . . . it has captivated good people through the nation, of both sexes, and of all ranks and degrees, from the highest to the lowest, that very large grants of revenues, and moreover of voluntary contributions are made towards it; It is really become too invidious a thing, and perhaps too dangerous to one's peace and quiet to dissent from it, and not most readily to give into it."[140]

Bray's heaping derision notwithstanding, the Bermuda project found a prominent champion in the Anglican voluntary sector, Berkeley's Irish friend John Perceval.

Since 1717, Perceval had been a member of the Commission for Relieving Poor Proselytes, another of the great Anglican organizations of the age, the personnel of which had been drawn overwhelmingly from the SPCK.[141] In February 1720, the SPCK formally elected Perceval a member.[142] In January 1724, Bray named Perceval as a trustee for the legacy of William III's Dutch secretary Abel Tassin, Sieur D'Allone, who had bequeathed a tenth of his English estates to Thomas Bray "and his Associates" for the express purpose of "instructing in the Christian religion the young children of Negro slaves."[143] Citing his wife's illness, Perceval refused to get involved in yet another philanthropic endeavor.[144] He changed his mind in 1725, however, when there seemed to be a disposition among the Bray Associates that Berkeley's college would be a suitable instrument for fulfilling the intent of D'Allone's legacy.[145] Bray's personal disapproval of the Bermuda project prevented the funds from being diverted, but it did not prevent Berkeley's design from being enthusiastically received among the other activists of the Anglican voluntary sector. The SPCK heartily embraced the Bermuda project, and a few short months after the design's publication, the dean was unanimously elected a member of the society.[146]

In spite of (or perhaps on account of) the utopianism of the project, Berkeley's Bermuda College had raised some £5,000 in subscriptions within two years of its proposal—a testament to the enduring popular appeal of Anglican expansion.[147] Reservations persisted, but Perceval cheerfully suggested to Berkeley that if these may be overcome, the project "may exalt your name beyond that of St. Xavier."[148] By summer 1725, Berkeley had brought his project before the bishop of London, the Board of Trade, and the attorney and solicitor general. In June, he reported that the charter for his Bermuda College "hath passed all the seals and is now in my custody."[149] By May 1726, Berkeley had successfully lobbied Parliament to grant to his project the revenue from crown lands in St. Kitts, acquired from France in the Treaty of Utrecht. Only two members voted against the proposal, Berkeley informed his friend Thomas Prior, "none having the confidence to speak against it." Curiously, Berkeley sensed some residual opposition from the "governors and traders to America . . . who apprehended this College may produce an independency in America, or at least lessen its dependency upon England."[150] He soon after penned his famous verses on the westward course of empire in a letter to Perceval.[151] In September 1728, with charter in hand, Berkeley set out for New England.

The story of the failure of the Bermuda project is relatively well known. London newspapers periodically updated the metropolitan public on the fortunes of Berkeley's American adventure. The dean tarried two years in Newport, Rhode Island, while his funding back in London evaporated.[152] Upon his return to London in 1731, Berkeley was invited as a consolation to preach the anniversary sermon before the SPG. The sermon was laced with bitterness, particularly toward the government of Sir Robert Walpole, which had conspicuously failed to deliver the funds allocated by Parliament. In Berkeley's estimation, corruption and infidelity at home, and a "weak reliance upon human politics and power," had rendered England an unworthy instrument of the propagation of the gospel.[153] Berkeley's failures, however, did little to curb the ambitions or vision of the broader movement. In the end, the sanguine remarks of SPCK secretary Henry Newman proved prescient: "Providence may make the attempt a door to an establishment somewhere else for the same purpose."[154]

Thomas Bray had by this time befriended one of his own parishioners at St. Botolph's, Aldgate, London, the colonial shipbuilder Thomas Coram, whose reputation for benevolence would eventually rest on his establishment of the Foundling Hospital orphanage in 1739.[155] However, in the 1720s, his philanthropic vision was as decidedly imperial as his business interests, and he and Bray would frequently discuss the founding of a charitable colony between Massachusetts and Nova Scotia "for the relief of such honest poor distressed families from hence as by losses, want of employment or otherwise reduced to poverty, and such who were persecuted for their professing the Protestant religion abroad." Bray was of the opinion that Coram's projected colony was located "too far northward" and looked to warmer climes.[156] Perhaps it was the growing ferocity of anti-Catholic propaganda during the 1720s that directed the attention of the metropolitan merchant community toward the southern frontier, where settlement south of the Carolinas might serve as a barrier province against Spanish and French expansion.[157] The southern frontier had become something of an "oneiric horizon" (to borrow a phrase from Jacques Le Goff): a blank screen upon which the most ambitious military, commercial, social, and confessional policies could be projected; an imagined repository for debtors and refugees; a site for the production of foreign luxury commodities; and a bulwark against popery.[158] In 1724, the Swiss East India merchant Jean Pierre Purry petitioned the Duke of Newcastle for a grant of territory south of Carolina, "that vast space of land which formerly went by the name of Florida, but which the French have sometime since changed into that of Louisiana, tho' the English might with a much better title call it *Georgia* or *Georgina*." His colony was to be peopled with "the refugees of France, of Switzerland, or Württemberg, of the Palatinate, Holland, Saxony, and other Protestant Churches . . . all which should be faithful subjects of the king of Great Britain."[159] The mercantilist writer Joshua Gee advocated colonizing the southern Carolinas in his popular 1729 tract *The Trade and Navigation of Great-Britain Considered*, in which he argued, "the county is large enough to canton out into distinct lots all the inhabitants we shall be capable of sending."[160] The language—religious, imperial, and mercantile—echoed that of Bray and Coram and would recur in the early promotional literature for the colony of Georgia.[161]

In 1729, as Bray lay dying, he was approached by James Edward Oglethorpe, a member of Parliament for Haslemere, Surrey, who sat with John Perceval on a committee to investigate the condition of English prisons. Oglethorpe proposed that the work of the Bray Associates, the trust founded to administer the D'Allone legacy, might be expanded to include the establishment of a charitable colony for English debtors.[162] On 15 January 1730, one month before his death, Bray and the other trustees of the D'Allone legacy executed a feoffment that added twenty-eight new trustees to the bequest, mostly handpicked by Oglethorpe.[163] The reconstructed trust included not only Oglethorpe and Perceval, but Thomas Coram and several clergymen associated with the SPCK; the rest were drawn overwhelmingly from Oglethorpe's parliamentary jails committee.[164] Oglethorpe's aim was to transfer D'Allone's and other legacies, as well as the unused parliamentary grant for Berkeley's failed Bermuda project, to the establishment of a charitable colony on the southern frontier.

Interestingly, Perceval relayed the new project to George Berkeley as being promoted largely in terms of "secular interest," but this was something of an overstatement.[165] Like the SPG before it, the newly formed Georgia Trust commissioned anniversary sermons by Anglican clergymen, who sounded the now familiar notes of Anglican expansion.[166] The same rhetoric also made its way into the early promotional literature for the fledgling colony, buttressed by the SPCK's Whiggish language of the "Protestant interest," the precariousness of which had again been made manifest by the continued persecution of continental Protestants, such as the so-called Thorn massacre of 1724 in Poland or the archbishop of Salzburg's expulsion of Protestants from his domain in 1731.[167] It was not long before Henry Newman and the SPCK had embraced the project and assigned themselves the task of procuring Protestant refugees for settlement on the southern frontier.[168] The early promotional literature sublimated both worldly and explicitly religious conceptions of empire into the language of the patriotic and virtuous imperialism then gaining ground among the urban and commercial opposition to Robert Walpole.[169] "Common is the complaint we hear, that public spirit is lost among us, and that no one pursues at dictates but those of his interest. I hope this is not true," read one promotional pamphlet for the new colony; "it is time to awaken people to a love of their country, to see her welfare and to promote it."[170] The public responded exuberantly to such appeals. Between 1732 and 1735, the Georgia Trust managed to raise the staggering sum of £20,000 for the founding of a philanthropic colony on the southern frontier.[171] Such enthusiasm testifies to the widening public mandate to reimagine the British Empire as an arena for the exercise of human benevolence.

Although the trustees found it practical to draw members from across the political spectrum, it was not long before the Georgia Trust in both personnel and rhetoric had acquired a reputation as a hotbed of opposition to the ministry.[172] This is not surprising, as Oglethorpe himself had long been a sharp critic of Walpole. He was joined in the project by the London alderman and West India merchant George Heathcote; the voluble Tory Edward Digby; James Vernon, brother of the patriot Admiral Edward Vernon; the independent Whig James Lowther; Erasmus Philips, a cousin of Walpole, though a fairly consistent opponent of his administration; and auditor Edward Harley.[173] Even Perceval, who had spent the whole of his parliamentary career on excellent terms with Walpole, had broken with the ministry by 1734 over government opposition to his son's election to succeed him for Harwich.[174] In June 1736, Perceval noted Walpole's antipathy in his journal, "because some of our board vote in parliament against the ministerial measures." Walpole himself began to number the charity among his political enemies, telling Oglethorpe, "I can't say I think so well of the Trustees as I do of the design, for many of them don't think well of me."[175] Long a pillar of the Whig establishment, the institutions of the Anglican revival were suddenly rediscovering in the age of Walpole something of the oppositional potential they possessed during the reign of James II.[176] The critique of corruption at home and the promotion of virtue and religion abroad were mutually reinforcing. In describing the Georgia project to a correspondent in 1732, Henry Newman cited the decadence of imperial Greece and Rome as cautionary examples for their own empire: "If old England should ever (which God forbid) prostitute herself to the abominations of those once flourishing commonwealths, it will be happy for her patriots that there are plantations to retire to where they may mend the faults that has undone their mother country, and unite in the advancement of religion and virtue in America when [they] can no longer find protection in Europe."[177] The Anglican revival had finally found an affinity with the moral imperatives of British patriotism. And patriotism, for all its gestures toward classical republican ideas of virtue, was suffused with Anglican notions of national Protestant renewal at home and abroad.[178]

By the age of Walpole, the Anglican societies occupied the center of a great web of British endeavors, with ties to dozens of other associations, corporations, projects, and trusts operating throughout the British Isles and stretching from Bombay to the Savannah River. The SPCK and the SPG shared personnel and ideals with the Sons of the Clergy, Queen Anne's Bounty, the Commission for Relieving Poor Proselytes, the Bray Associates, the Georgia Trust, the Henry Hoare Bible Fund, and countless charity schools, workhouses, and religious and reformation societies. They maintained correspondences with emissaries of the Lutheran and reformed worlds in Europe and America, not to mention counterpart organizations in Scotland, Ireland, and Wales. The naval, military, and mercantile chaplains among their ranks maintained an Anglican presence throughout the vessels, factories, and garrisons of the British commercial and territorial empires. The societies' handful of diplomatic chaplains even gave the Church of England a scattering of outposts at the heart of Catholic Europe. Among their ranks were to be found the men who intervened most visibly in the moral life of the British nation and its empire, the early humanitarians Oglethorpe, Coram, Perceval, and Stephen Hales and the great Anglican moral philosophers George Berkeley and Joseph Butler. By 1731, the SPCK was collaborating with the great benefactress Lady Elizabeth Hastings, who was to become the godmother of English Methodism.[179] These endeavors were, by the mid-eighteenth century, imbricated in the moral fabric of Britain and its empire. Through this vast network, the Church of England—alongside commerce and war—continued to provide an ideological and institutional framework through which ordinary Britons experienced empire.

Conclusion

Anglican expansion during the early eighteenth century proceeded through a complex civic and institutional infrastructure that is sometimes obscured by top-down accounts of the postrevolutionary emergence of "imperial Anglicanism." The Anglican revival throughout the English maritime empire was no less experimental and improvisational than the Anglican revival at home. During this period, a movement emerged to adapt a stubbornly terrestrial ecclesiastical establishment to a global commercial and strategic presence abroad. Doing so required a process of de-territorializing Anglicanism, protruding the informal presence of the church where the formal structures of ecclesiastical authority could not yet reach. The movement relied upon a nascent culture of Anglican associations, projects, and publicity subsisting largely in the sphere of civil society to overcome the deficiencies of the church and the uninterest of the state. The involvement of civil society effectively transformed the work of Anglican expansion into a societal concern rather than a piece of imperial statecraft. Church activists thus invited a widening sector of the British public to participate in the moral oversight of nation and empire.[180] Denizens of the metropole became increasingly habituated to solicitations on behalf of Protestant refugees, decayed sailors and soldiers, and benighted Indians East and West. This "culture of sympathy" was becoming a common element of civic life.[181]

The Church of England thus stewarded Britain's passage into what has come to be known as the age of benevolence. The established church, in pursuit of its own agenda of confessional renewal at home and abroad, fostered much of the organizational, promotional, and ideological infrastructure by which British philanthropy throughout the eighteenth century would engage with empire and nation. Indeed, the established church continued to provide the aegis under which a whole host of entities, including the rival denominations of England, Scotland, and America subsisting within the ambit of a broader "Protestant interest," collaborated in the amelioration of human suffering.[182] Postrevolutionary Anglican contributions to the culture of sympathy that permeated British public life in the eighteenth century laid the foundations of modern British humanitarianism. And those historians who date the origins of British humanitarianism no earlier than midcentury take for granted the structures put in place by Anglican activists of the revolutionary generation and enter the story in medias res. Historians of antislavery who remain stolidly unimpressed with the early-eighteenth-century age of benevolence for its tremendous inertia in the face of African slavery might consider the achievement of the Anglican revival in developing a socially generalized framework for imagining and engaging with nation and empire in explicitly moral terms. Surely, it is not without significance that William Warburton, bishop of Gloucester, in 1766 gave voice to the growing Anglican opposition to slavery in an annual sermon before the SPG.[183] After all, it was only after nation and empire were first publicly consecrated to a higher purpose, after benevolence had been firmly enshrined in national and imperial identity, that Britain might be publicly judged and found wanting.

Conclusion

The English gentleman and erstwhile nonjuror Robert Nelson died on 16 January 1715. His many eulogists rose to point out that there had been no "great undertaking of religion" in his lifetime that proceeded without his assistance.[1] Nelson was a devotional writer; the patron of churches, charity schools, and parochial libraries; a promoter of the reformation of manners; and a member of the Society for Promoting Christian Knowledge (SPCK) and the Society for Propagating the Gospel in Foreign Parts (SPG), as well as the Commission for Building Fifty New Churches. His will, with generous bequests to a host of worthy causes, was a veritable thumbnail sketch of the Anglican revival.[2] At the Ormond Street chapel in London, the clergyman John Marshall cited Nelson's life and works as a repudiation of the principle of self-interest, which he deemed "directly opposite to the large and noble spirit of religion and utterly destructive to the great law of general benevolence."[3]

Robert Nelson's final work, *An Address to Persons of Quality and Estate*, edited and published posthumously by his friend and biographer Francis Lee, comprised a virtual blueprint for the age of benevolence in eighteenth-century Britain. In it, Nelson documented the myriad ways and methods by which a free and prosperous nation might yet remain a good and godly one. To this end, he directed his address to the wealthy and well-born in particular, the titular "persons of quality and estate," whom he prayed might, like heavenly bodies, "dispense a general light and influence, and scatter happiness and blessings among all that are below you." Nelson's *Address* then catalogued the dozens of methods by which Britons of means and influence might use their fortunes to relieve both the spiritual and temporal wants of their fellow citizens: building churches and chapels of ease; dispensing Bibles, Books of Common Prayer, and other works of piety and devotion; augmenting poor livings; patronizing religious societies and societies for the reformation of manners; erecting charity schools and workhouses; endowing parochial libraries; and sponsoring missions and founding seminaries for the training of missionaries. He pressed for the reform of prisons, the relief of debtors, and the redemption of captive Christians from the cells of the Inquisition or the bondage of the Turk. Nelson also advocated a new round of hospital foundations to exceed those of the Protestant Reformation: hospitals for the incurable; for the blind; for those stricken with gout, dropsy, consumption, and palsy; even teaching hospitals and dispensaries, "that there might be mighty improvements made in the art of curing." He proposed a "a house of charity to receive poor exposed infants," one to receive and reform penitent prostitutes, a hospital to relieve decayed gentlemen, another to house new immigrants, and still another to receive Anglican converts from Roman Catholicism and Protestant Nonconformity.[4] One can already discern in the text faint outlines of the monuments of later eighteenth-century benevolence that Nelson did not survive to see: the Foundling, Lock, and Magdalene hospitals; the Marine Society; and the great missionary organizations of the end of the century. Nelson's *Address* not only predicted, if not inspired, much of the institutional architecture of social welfare and philanthropy in mid-eighteenth century Britain and the empire, it traced the ways in which a program of Anglican confessionalization opened onto the wider horizon of national benevolence.

The Anglican revival was born of an era of ecclesiastical reconstruction. The Restoration had returned the Church of England to its place in the constitution but not in the hearts and minds of the English people. In the later seventeenth century, coercion shored up the communion of the established church, but it could not by itself inculcate a lively and popular piety. The Stuart monarchy, meanwhile, was content to accept the outsized royalism demanded by Anglican political theology, while vacillating in its affections for the established church. Uncertain of both state and populace, churchmen during the later Restoration— particularly those in the great metropolis of London—began to cultivate a vast new array of instruments of Anglican confessionalization. Schools, libraries, charities, and religious societies were founded with the intertwined objectives of promoting popular Anglicanism, reforming manners, and repelling threats from rival denominations. Churchmen were thus reasonably well prepared when one of those rival denominations, Roman Catholicism, began to advance throughout the kingdom with the connivance of the court of James II. The instruments of revival—the schools, the charities, the religious press— inadvertently became instruments of revolution. Anglican pastoral work and anti-Catholic apologetics, even where they ardently disclaimed any subversive intent, acquired the force of insurrection. To the extent that there was an Anglican Revolution of 1688, it lay in pastoral practice rather than in political theology. Ascending the throne on a wave of popular Protestantism, the revolutionary monarchs William and Mary shrewdly adopted the nascent Anglican revival as part of their own program of civil and ecclesiastical reform, promoting its advocates to positions at court and the episcopate, reissuing its imperatives with the royal imprimatur, and even recommending much of its agenda to the consideration of Parliament and the convocation. Formal ecclesiastical reform was sacrificed to the increasingly bitter civil and ecclesiastical politics of the postrevolutionary era, and the work of Anglican renewal devolved to more informal channels: royal proclamations, episcopal admonition, voluntary associations, and a host of other lay and clerical projects bubbling up in the English public sphere. The proliferation of entities such as the SPCK, the religious societies, and the societies for the reformation of manners on the margins of the ecclesiastical constitution soon provoked a backlash from conservative churchmen jealous of the independence of the church and the rights of the clergy. At the heart of the postrevolutionary Anglican high-church movement was a program to formally reground these generalized pastoral impulses within the refurbished disciplinary institutions of the established church. The failures of these efforts effectively ratified the civic and voluntaristic character of the Anglican revival and secured the place of its imperatives and institutions within the framework of eighteenth-century Whig churchmanship. By the second third of the eighteenth century, the ideals of the Anglican revival formed part of a more general rhetoric of English patriotism, with its aspirations toward national reformation and moral empire.

In the quarter century after Robert Nelson's death, the ideals and institutions outlined in his *Address*, conceived and proposed in the matrix of the Anglican revival, became part of the fabric of national life throughout Great Britain. They formed a substantial part of the increasingly self-conscious rhetoric of British national greatness. "There is not any thing," Jonathan Swift assured his readers in 1733, "that contributes more to the reputation of particular persons, or to the honor of a nation in general, than erecting and endowing proper edifices, for the reception of those who labor under different kinds of distress."[5] And as the various philanthropic institutions catalogued in the writings of Nelson and his acolytes were adopted into the civic infrastructure of the towns and the cities of the "English urban renaissance," one could hear such sentiments proclaimed from pulpits across the kingdom.[6] Wherever charity schools, workhouses, and hospitals were founded, the clergy of the established church were routinely on hand to consecrate the proceedings and to ruminate more generally on the benevolence of the age. The increasingly prosperous kingdom was also, the clergyman George Watts assured his auditors in the language of the gospel, laying up treasure in heaven, "using that wealth which Providence has put into our hands . . . in all proper offices of charity, relieving the distresses of the poor, encouraging such undertakings as are proper to advance religion, to keep up a sense of virtue and goodness amongst men."[7] The eminent theologian Samuel Clarke went further. He considered the proliferating works of benevolence in the nation as nothing less than "the establishment of the kingdom of God among men."[8] The kingdom of heaven, indeed—the work of voluntary associations and projectors and public trusts, erected there amidst the terraced red brick town-houses and the grand Palladian exchanges of the Georgian cityscape.

Not all observers were quite so sanguine. In 1723, the freethinking physician Bernard Mandeville appended a thoroughgoing assault on the entire culture of English benevolence to his already notorious work *The Fable of the Bees*. Mandeville's great theme was, of course, the indispensability of avarice and self-interest to the social and economic dynamics of a prosperous, commercial society. "No society," he wrote, "can be raised into such a rich and mighty kingdom, or so raised, subsist in wealth and power for any considerable time, without the vices of man." Thus, for Mandeville, the celebrated program of national reformation was particularly self-defeating. He condemned the new vogue for charity, and the Anglican charity schools in particular, as a mania, "a kind of distraction the nation has labored under for some time." First, Mandeville lambasted the conceit and hypocrisy of the philanthropic sector, where "diminutive patriots . . . form themselves into a society and appoint stated meetings, where everyone concealing his vices has liberty to display his talents." Such individuals, he claimed, were animated not by benevolence, but by boundless narcissism and the desire to govern others. "Pride and vanity," hissed Mandeville, "have built more hospitals than all the virtues together." More importantly, their munificence was ultimately deleterious to a commercial nation. Philanthropy transferred vast sums of potentially productive wealth to the "dead stock of the kingdom." The educational and material uplift institutionalized in charity schools and hospitals threatened to rob the nation of its most precious resource, the vast multitudes of the laboring poor—whose necessity and tractability remained the final guarantor of their compliance. "Charity, where it is too extensive, seldom fails of promoting sloth and idleness," Mandeville maintained, "and is good for little in the commonwealth but to breed drones and destroy industry." He ruthlessly exposed as irrational the premises underlying the eighteenth-century age of benevolence. Philanthropy and religious voluntarism, he concluded, were but fads, "in fashion in the same manner as hooped petticoats, by caprice."[9]

In arguing that a commercial nation could not really be a Christian one, Bernard Mandeville exposed the profound tension at the heart of eighteenth-century British national identity, and the instrumentality of the mythos of national benevolence in papering over it. Indeed, the overwhelming response to Mandeville suggests how vital the compatibility of Christianity and capitalism had become to the self-conceit of the age. In the years after the publication of the 1723 edition of *The Fable of the Bees*, a number of thinkers took to print to defend vigorously the charity schools and the broader culture of benevolence of which they were the signal example. The political and ideological diversity of the respondents, not to mention their geographical distribution throughout the British Isles, illustrates the extent to which an ideology of national benevolence had outstripped the Anglican confessional program with which it had initially been associated. In a sharp riposte to Mandeville, the London Presbyterian minister Samuel Chandler celebrated the charity schools and the philanthropic instincts behind them. "To do good," he preached to a Southwark meetinghouse, "is the noblest imitation of the best beings."[10] The English nonjuror and mystic William Law asserted that the charity schools "must be reckoned amongst our best works."[11] The high-church Anglican clergyman William Hendley deemed the schools "a blessing to the nation" and went so far as to accuse their critics of treason. "Whoever therefore speaks against these schools," he wrote, "speaks against his country, against the Established religion of his country and in fine, must be deemed an enemy to both."[12] The evangelical Sir John Thorold lamented Mandeville's "unjust censure upon public-spirited persons." If Mandeville's antipathy toward charity took root in the nation, Thorold warned, "I am afraid we should see a great many more in misery and want than we do at present."[13] Far from the charity schools being an impediment to prosperity, the Inner Temple lawyer George Blewitt hailed them as "one of the most useful and unexceptionable projects for the advancement, not only of virtue and religion, but the trade and wealth of the kingdom, that this or perhaps any better age has produced."[14] Perhaps more important than the ad hoc responses was the wave of moral philosophical treatises produced in the 1720s and 1730s that took Mandeville's *Fable* as their point of departure—the Irish churchman George Berkeley's *Alciphron*, the English divine Joseph Butler's *Dissertation Upon the Nature of Virtue*, and the Scottish philosopher Francis Hutcheson's *Inquiry into the Original of Our Ideas of Beauty and Virtue*.[15] Against Mandeville's insistence on the egoism of all social action, Butler and Hutcheson were both deeply committed to demonstrating the naturalness of altruism, a tendency to will the public good at the expense of self-interest. They deemed this disposition "benevolence." As benevolence was being nationalized, it was being simultaneously naturalized.[16]

There was something plainly secularizing about this mid-eighteenth-century discourse of benevolence, not in the sense of diminished religious significance or the shifting focus from spiritual to corporeal relief. Blatantly religious and utilitarian motives mingled freely in the literature of philanthropy throughout the eighteenth and nineteenth centuries. There was, however, an attenuated ecclesiality. Christian charity and benevolence were less imperatives of ecclesiastical communion than obligations of civic life. In 1683, John Kettlewell attributed a "tender concern and diligent care for each other's welfare" to parochial participation in the sacrament of the Lord's Supper. Half a century later, such sympathy and charitable regard were widely considered normative elements of life in a modern civil society. In 1733, Andrew Trebeck, rector of St. George's, Hanover Square, deployed explicitly eucharistic language to recommend the proliferating institutions of social welfare. "Our good and charitable works," he told his auditors, "are oblations and sacrifices with which God is well pleased." And in earning heavenly favor, such works of benevolence "will probably procure the affluence and secure the continuance of such national blessings as will make things well with us and our children forever."[17] These social sacraments were performed not in the holy offices of the church, but in what White Kennett called "the many offices of doing good," the enterprises, associations, and projects of public life. This was secularization in the sense in which the term was first posited in the introduction to this book: the unmistakable outward movement from church to world.

Eighteenth-century Britain was characterized less by the privatization of religion than by the Anglican achievement of a different mode of publicness. During this period, private individuals increasingly took it upon themselves to publicly minister to the needs of society. They undertook these endeavors on the basis of neither election nor commission nor ordination. Though these individuals may well have been members of Parliament or local magistrates or clergy, they derived their mandate to act not from an institution, but rather from something altogether more ineffable: conviction—the sense that they had correctly divined the public interest and the best methods for its pursuit. At worst, they were projectors; at best, they were good Christians or simply public-spirited men and women. Charity briefs were, of course, still read from the pulpits of parish churches, stirring parishioners to a liberal contribution for the amelioration of all sorts of distress. But such solicitations could also take place elsewhere in the public sphere, and one might be moved to action not only in the pew, but at the coffeehouse, the opera, or Change Alley. As we have seen, even the most devout churchmen might take their cherished causes before a voluntary society of gentlemen rather than the court, Parliament, or church hierarchy as the best means to bring it to public attention.

There is no reason to think of these developments, at least in the first instance, as secularization in terms of disenchantment or desacralization. Certainly, the figures that populate this book would hardly recognize themselves as any less authentically Christian than their early-seventeenth-century forebears. Indeed, as this book has strived to show, many conspicuously believed they were contributing to a *revival* of the Church of England and the moral life of the nation generally. But neither should one assume that the absence of disenchantment signals a lack of religious change altogether. This would be a dangerous error, and one that is all too common in the current historiography of the eighteenth-century Church of England. Perhaps the age of benevolence in Britain might best be understood as an alternative sacralization—the sacralization of civil society: the valorization of the space of free association, commercial enterprise, and intersubjective communication as an alternative ecology for Christian life. The Church of England, it must be emphasized, was not passive in this process. In an era of profound political and ecclesiastical crisis, the church lent its aura and its moral authority to a sphere of public life that it could neither wholly control nor comprehend—a sphere, most importantly, that outstripped even the most extensive demarcations of its communion. This transaction equipped the church with new technologies for augmenting its patrimony, ministering to mobile populations, propagating the gospel abroad, and competing with rival denominations; but it also invested civil society with an unprecedented moral legitimacy. Once the troublesome space of baleful combinations and conventicles, civil society was reimagined as the preeminent stage of public moral enterprises—not just churches, charities, and civic associations, but eventually the social movements and nongovernmental organizations that direct the modern conscience to the repair of justice and the amelioration of human suffering.

The question of whether churches or any other religious entities *belong* in civil society is today seldom asked. Their residence there—and not within the superstructure of the modern state—is, for all intents and purposes, normative in pluralistic liberal democracies. As John Locke foresaw as early as the mid-1680s, a church defined by its essentially voluntary constitution would be no less innocuous than any other voluntary association; and accordingly, he routinely compared churches to the worldlier cohort of clubs, commercial entities, and crowds into which social life was commonly apportioned. "Why," Locke wondered in his famous case for religious toleration, "are assemblies less sufferable in a church than in a theater or a market?"[18] But he did not ask whether the putatively sacred character of a church should give it more purchase on public life than any of the other decidedly mundane organizations with which it now shares the morphology of a voluntary association. Modern tax codes, such as that of the United States, are at least somewhat more discriminating, classifying churches and religious entities alongside other philanthropic, educational, and anticruelty societies ostensibly devoted to serving the public and doing good—if not always at the behest of the divine. Nascent liberal theory, no less than modern governance, elides the transcendent aspirations of the church in favor of its voluntariness or its benevolence. *Societas Christiana* resides thusly in modern civil society, one noncoercive association among many. In the modern world, the nonnegotiability of the sacred persists within a sphere of public life entirely constituted by negotiation.

One thinks, then, of the term the Edwardian literary critic T. E. Hulme coined to dismiss the spiritual wooliness of nineteenth-century romanticism: "spilt religion." Perhaps the Anglican revival of the late seventeenth and early eighteenth centuries was a great spillage of religion: the meliorative and pastoral functions of the established church overtopping their appointed channels. Even as reactionary forces pressed for a thoroughgoing reclamation and reconstruction of sacerdotal authority, a burgeoning Anglican voluntary sector moved toward continuing social engagement and institutional innovation. In doing so, it fashioned works of Anglican confessionalization into monuments of national benevolence. The result was the making of modern civil society in Britain, a spilt religion: moral rather than confessional, associational rather than parochial, benevolent rather than sacramental—a space perhaps where individuals may be improved, but not saved.

Notes

Abbreviations

Add MS	Additional manuscript, British Library
ALB	Abstract Letter Book
Atterbury Correspondence	*The Epistolary Correspondence, Visitation Charges, Speeches and Miscellanies of the Right Reverend Francis Atterbury, D.D. Lord Bishop of Rochester with Historical Notes.* Edited by J. Nichols. 5 vols. London, 1783
Ballard	Ballard manuscripts, Bodleian Library, Oxford University
BL	British Library, London
Bodl.	Bodleian Library, Oxford University
CHC	C. Hoare and Co., London
CUL	Cambridge University Library
EHR	*English Historical Review*
HJ	*Historical Journal*
HMC	Historical Manuscripts Commission
HMPEC	*Historical Magazine of the Protestant Episcopal Church*
HNL	Henry Newman Letter Books, *S.P.C.K.: Early Eighteenth Century Archives.* London: World Microfilm Publications, 1977
HOT	Gilbert Burnet, *Bishop Burnet's History of His Own Time.* 6 vols. Oxford: Oxford University Press, 1833
HRC	Harry Ransom Center, Austin, TX
JEH	*Journal of Ecclesiastical History*
LMA	London Metropolitan Archive

LPL	Lambeth Palace Library, London
Luttrell	Narcissus Luttrell, *A Brief Historical Relation of State Affairs*. 6 vols. Oxford: Oxford University Press, 1857
Morrice	*The Entring Book of Roger Morrice, 1677–1691*. Edited by Mark Goldie, John Spurr, Tim Harris, Stephen Taylor, and Mark Knights. 6 vols. Woodbridge, UK: Boydell Brewer, 2007
MS/MSS	Manuscript/manuscripts
NLW	National Library of Wales, Aberystwyth
ODNB	*Oxford Dictionary of National Biography*
OSB	Osborn Collection, Beinecke Rare Book and Manuscript Library, Yale University, New Haven, CT
SPCK	Society for the Promotion of Christian Knowledge
SPG	Society for the Propagation of the Gospel in Foreign Parts
Tanner	Tanner manuscripts, Bodleian Library, Oxford University
WMQ	*William and Mary Quarterly*

Minutes of the SPCK are found in two sources. In the notes, *SPCK Minutes* (italicized) refers to Edmund McClure, ed., *A Chapter in English Church History: Being the Minutes of the Society for Promoting Christian Knowledge for the Years 1698–1704* (London: SPCK, 1888). When not italicized, SPCK Minutes refers to the microfilmed collection *S.P.C.K.: Early Eighteenth Century Archives* (London: World Microfilm Publications, 1977).

Introduction

1. William Wake, *The Excellency and Benefits of a Religious Education, A Sermon Preach'd in the Parish-Church of St. Sepulchre, June the IXth, 1715* (London, 1715), 27–28.

2. The term "revival" is used here advisedly and perhaps somewhat confusingly, given its conventional association with the evangelical awakenings occurring throughout the Protestant world during the period covered by this book. Although these developments, particularly the rise of pietism in the German-speaking world, provide some background for the present narrative, the term "revival" is not here intended to convey the incipience of an evangelical movement within the established church. The Anglican revival of the later seventeenth and early eighteenth centuries was an ecclesiastical program of moral and religious renewal, decidedly less oriented toward the procurement of spontaneous individual conversions than the broader refurbishing of the national confession. On contemporaneous revivals in the explicitly evangelical sense of the term, see W. R. Ward, *The Protestant Evangelical Awakening* (Cambridge: Cambridge University Press, 1992); on this broader national sense of revival, see William G. McLoughlin, *Revivals, Awakenings, and Reform* (Chicago: University of Chicago Press, 1980).

3. There has been a vigorous debate on the contribution of Protestantism and Anglicanism to the creation of British nationalism; see Adrian Hastings, *The Construction of Nationhood: Ethnicity, Religion and Nationalism* (Cambridge: Cambridge University Press, 1997); Linda Colley,

Britons: Forging the Nation 1707–1837 (New Haven, CT: Yale University Press, 1992), 11–54 and passim; J. C. D. Clark, "Protestantism, Nationalism and National Identity, 1660–1832," *HJ* 43 (March 2000): 249–276; Jeremy Black, "Confessional State or Elect Nation? Religion and Identity in Eighteenth-Century England," in *Protestantism and National Identity: Britain and Ireland, c. 1650–c. 1850,* ed. Tony Claydon and Ian McBride (Cambridge: Cambridge University Press, 1998), 53–74; Steve Pincus, "'To Protect English Liberties': The English Nationalist Revolution of 1688–89," in *Protestantism and National Identity,* 75–104; Anthony D. Smith, *Chosen Peoples: Sacred Sources of National Identity* (Oxford: Oxford University Press, 2003), 115–130.

4. Geoffrey Finlayson, *Citizen, State and Social Welfare in Britain, 1830–1900* (Oxford: Oxford University Press, 1994).

5. On the twenty-first-century program of the "big society," see Phillip Blond, *Red Tory: How the Left and Right Have Broken Britain and How We Can Fix It* (London: Faber and Faber, 2010); and Matthew Hilton and James McKay, eds., *The Ages of Voluntarism: How We Got to the Big Society* (Oxford: Oxford University Press, 2011). For an overview of the concept, see Fred Powell, "Big Society," presentation to the Social Policy Conference at Lincoln, UK, 4–6 July 2011; for a critique from the left, see Mike Davis and Andy Gregg, *The Big Society: The Big Con and the Alternative* (London: Chartist, 2012).

6. Wake, *Excellency and Benefits,* 32–33.

7. Wake, *Excellency and Benefits,* 32–33.

8. Garnet V. Portus, *Caritas Anglicana, or, An Historical Inquiry into those Religious and Philanthropic Societies that Flourished in England between the years 1678 and 1740* (London: A. R. Mowbray, 1912), 46.

9. F. W. B. Bullock, *Voluntary Religious Societies, 1520–1799* (St. Leonard's on Sea, UK: Budd and Gilatt, 1963), 109.

10. Dudley Bahlmann, *The Moral Revolution of 1688* (New Haven, CT: Yale University Press, 1957), 105.

11. Mark Pattison, "Philanthropic Societies in the Reign of Queen Anne" [1860], in *Essays by the Late Mark Pattison,* 2 vols., ed. Henry Nettleship (New York: Burt Franklin, 1889), 2:309–322.

12. J. H. Overton, *Life in the English Church (1660–1714)* (London: Longmans, Green, 1885), 207–230; Charles H. Abbey and John H. Overton, *The English Church in the Eighteenth Century,* 2 vols. (London: Longmans, Green, 1878), 1:28, 106–176.

13. J. Wickham Legg, *English Church Life from the Restoration to the Tractarian Movement* (London: Longmans, Green, 1914), 281–314; William Holden Hutton, *The English Church from the Accession of Charles I to the Death of Anne, 1625–1714* (London: Macmillan, 1913), 304–319.

14. B. Kirkman Gray, *A History of English Philanthropy* (London: P. S King, 1905), 79–81; David Owen, *English Philanthropy, 1660–1960* (Cambridge, MA: Belknap, 1964), 11–68.

15. John Walsh and Stephen Taylor, "Introduction: The Church and Anglicanism in the 'Long' Eighteenth Century," in *The Church of England c. 1689–c. 1833: From Toleration to Tractarianism,* ed. John Walsh, Colin Haydon, and Stephen Taylor (Cambridge: Cambridge University Press, 1993), 17–22.

16. On ecclesiastical reform in the late seventeenth and eighteenth centuries, see Norman Sykes, *From Sheldon to Secker: Aspects of English Church History, 1660–1768* (Cambridge: Cambridge University Press, 1959), 188–224; Stephen Taylor, "Whigs, Bishops and America: The Politics of Church Reform in Mid-Eighteenth Century England," *HJ* 36 (1993): 331–356;

Stephen Taylor, "Bishop Edmund Gibson's Proposals for Church Reform," in *From Cranmer to Davidson: A Church of England Miscellany*, ed. Stephen Taylor (Woodbridge: Boydell, 1999), 169–175; Peter Virgin, *The Church in an Age of Negligence: Ecclesiastical Structure and Problems of Church Reform, 1700–1840* (Cambridge: James Clark, 1989); Robert G. Ingram, *Religion, Reform and Modernity: Thomas Secker and the Church of England* (Woodbridge, UK: Boydell, 2007); Robert E. Rodes Jr., *Law and Modernization in the Church of England: Charles II to the Welfare State* (Notre Dame, IN: University of Notre Dame Press, 1991).

17. White Kennett, *The Charity of schools for poor children recommended in a sermon preach'd in the Parish-church of St. Sepulchres, May 16, 1706* (London, 1706), 38–39.

18. White Kennett, *A sermon preach'd at the funeral of the Right Noble William Duke of Devonshire* (London, 1707), 11.

19. Samuel Bradford, *Unanimity and Charity, the Characters of Christians. A Sermon Preached in the Parish-Church of St. Sepulchre, June 16th, 1709* (London, 1709), 19.

20. Francis Lee, "A Premonition by the Editor," in Robert Nelson, *An Address to Persons of Quality and Estate* (London, 1715), ix.

21. On the debates over the nature of benevolence in the eighteenth century, see Betsy Rodgers, *Cloak of Charity: Studies in Eighteenth Century Philanthropy* (London: Methuen, 1949), 1–20; Donna T. Andrew, *Philanthropy and Police: London Charity in the Eighteenth Century* (Princeton, NJ: Princeton University Press, 1989), 11–43, 135–162; Shelley Burtt, *Virtue Transformed: Political Argument in 1688–1740* (Cambridge: Cambridge University Press, 1992); Evan Radcliffe, "Revolutionary Writing, Moral Philosophy and Universal Benevolence," *Journal of the History of Ideas* 54 (April 1993): 221–240; Carolyn D. Williams, " 'The Luxury of Doing Good': Benevolence, Sensibility, and the Royal Humane Society," in *Pleasure in the Eighteenth Century*, ed. Roy Porter and Marie Mulvey Roberts (New York: New York University Press, 1996), 77–107.

22. Jonathan Swift, *A Serious and Useful Scheme, To Make an Hospital for Incurables* (London, 1733), 3.

23. John Strype, *A Survey of the Cities of London and Westminster*, 2 vols. (London, 1720), 2:30; Andrew Gairdner, *An historical account of the old people's hospital, commonly called, the Trinity hospital in Edinburgh* (Edinburgh, 1728), 9; O. Sedgwick, *The universal masquerade*, 2 vols. (London, 1742), 2:7; John Thomas, *A sermon preach'd in the parish-church of All-Saints in Northampton* (Northampton, 1748), 5; William May, *Twenty practical sermons on several important subjects* (London, 1757), 165; *A congratulatory epistle from a reformed rake* (London, 1758?) 44; James Welton, *A sermon preached at the cathedral church at Norwich, on Thursday, Nov. 29, 1759* (Norwich, 1759), 11; *Useful and practical observations on agriculture* (London, 1783), 239; and see Basil Williams, *The Whig Supremacy, 1714–1760* (Oxford: Clarendon, 1939), 91–92, 132–133.

24. For a comparison of a (French) enlightenment and a (British) age of benevolence, see Gertrude Himmelfarb, *The Roads to Modernity: The British, French and American Enlightenments* (New York: Alfred A. Knopf, 2004); see also Gordon S. Wood, *The Radicalism of the American Revolution* (New York: Vintage, 1991), 189–225.

25. "History of the reverend Mr. Hanbury's Charitable foundations at Church-langton, in Leicestershire, Established in March 1767," *London Magazine*, June 1767.

26. Beilby Porteus, *A sermon preached before the Lords spiritual and temporal, in the abbey-church, Westminster, on Friday, January 30, 1778* (London, 1778), 18.

27. Jonas Hanway, "Letter to the Encouragers of Practical Public-Love," in *Three Letters on the Subject of the Marine Society* (London, 1758), 57.

28. In his controversial "Essay on Charity and Charity-Schools" (1723), Bernard Mandeville went out of his way to refute the increasingly prevalent English conceit of national benevolence. "There is no miraculous conversion to be perceived among us," he insisted, "no universal bent to goodness and morality that has on a sudden overspread the island." Bernard Mandeville, *The Fable of the Bees and Other Writings*, ed. E. J. Hundert (Indianapolis, IN: Hackett, 1997), 119.

29. For a definition of civil society, see Michael Walzer, "The Concept of Civil Society," in *Toward a Global Civil Society*, ed. Michael Walzer (New York: Berghahn, 1995), 27; and Charles Taylor, "Modes of Civil Society," *Public Culture* 3 (1990): 94–118. For some caution on the historical use of the term "civil society," see Jose Harris, "From Richard Hooker to Harold Laski: Changing Perceptions of Civil Society in British Political Thought, Late Sixteenth to Early Twentieth Centuries," in *Civil Society in British History*, ed. Jose Harris (Oxford: Oxford University Press, 2003), 13–37; John Dunn, "The Contemporary Political Significance of John Locke's Conception of Civil Society," in *Civil Society: History and Possibilities*, ed. Sudipta Kaviraj and Sunil Khilnani (Cambridge: Cambridge University Press, 2001), 39–57; and Frank Trentmann, "The Problem with Civil Society: Putting Modern European History Back into Contemporary European Debate," in *Exploring Civil Society: Political and Cultural Contexts*, ed. Marlies Glasius, David Lewis, and Hakan Seckinelgin (London: Routledge, 2004), 26–35.

30. For a sense of the Restoration critique of voluntary association, see John Spurr, "The Church, the Societies and the Moral Revolution of 1688," in *The Church of England c. 1689–c. 1833*, 127–142; Steve Pincus, "'Coffee Politicians Does Create': Coffee Houses and Restoration Political Culture," in *Journal of Modern History* 67, 4 (December 1995): 807–834; and R. D. Lund, "Guilt by Association: The Atheist Cabal and the Rise of the Public Sphere in Augustan England," *Albion* 34 (2002): 391–421.

31. On the origins of civil society in early modern Britain, see Marvin Becker, *The Emergence of Civil Society in the Eighteenth Century* (Bloomington: Indiana University Press, 1994); Ernest Gellner, *Conditions of Liberty* (New York: Penguin, 1994); M. C. Jacob, *Living the Enlightenment: Freemasonry and Politics in Eighteenth-Century Europe* (Oxford: Oxford University Press, 1991), 3–51; Peter Clark, *British Clubs and Societies, 1580–1800* (Oxford: Clarendon, 2000); Richard Price, *British Society, 1680–1880* (Cambridge: Cambridge University Press, 1999), 194–204; James Livesey, *Civil Society and Empire: Ireland and Scotland in the Eighteenth-Century Atlantic World* (New Haven, CT: Yale University Press, 2009); Michael McKeon, *The Secret History of Domesticity: Public, Private, and the Division of Knowledge* (Baltimore, MD: Johns Hopkins University Press, 2005), 3–48; Paul Langford, *A Polite and Commercial People: England, 1727–1783* (Oxford: Clarendon, 1989), 481–487; and Paul Langford, "Manners and the Eighteenth-Century State: The Case of the Unsociable Englishman," in *Rethinking Leviathan: The Eighteenth-Century State in Britain and Germany*, ed. John Brewer and Eckhart Hellmuth (Oxford: Oxford University Press, 1999), 281–316.

32. Paul Slack, *From Reformation to Improvement: Public Welfare in Early Modern England* (Oxford: Clarendon, 1999), 148–149.

33. Clark, *British Clubs*, 4.

34. John Brewer, "The Eighteenth Century British State: Contexts and Issues," in *An Imperial State at War: Britain from 1689 to 1815*, ed. Lawrence Stone (New York: Routledge, 1994), 52–71; and see Ernest Barker, "The Discredited State," *Political Quarterly* 2 (1916): 101–126; Kenneth Dyson, *The State Tradition in Western Europe* (New York: Oxford University Press, 1980), 36–47,

51–58; Bertrand Badie and Pierre Birnbaum, *The Sociology of the State*, trans. Arthur Goldhammer (Chicago: University of Chicago Press, 1983), 121–124. For a reconsideration, see James Meadowcroft, *Conceptualizing the State: Innovation and Dispute in British Political Thought, 1880–1914* (Oxford: Oxford University Press, 1995); and Cécile Laborde, "The Concept of the State in British and French Political Thought," *Political Studies* 48 (2000): 540–557.

35. The Church of England has not played a particularly important role in the prevailing accounts of the genesis of the English (and British) "fiscal-military state" during this period: see John Brewer, *Sinews of Power: War, Money and the English State, 1688–1783* (New York: Alfred A. Knopf, 1988); Thomas Ertman, *Birth of the Leviathan* (New York: Cambridge University Press, 1997); Michael Braddick, *State Formation in Early Modern England, c. 1550–1700* (Cambridge: Cambridge University Press, 2000); and Allan I. Macinnes, *Union and Empire: The Making of the United Kingdom in 1707* (Cambridge: Cambridge University Press, 2007).

36. Colley, *Britons*, 58–59; Kathleen Wilson, "'Empire of Virtue': The Imperial Project and Hanoverian Culture, c. 1720–1785," in *Imperial State at War*, 128–164; Kathleen Wilson, "Urban Culture and Political Activism in Hanoverian England: The Example of the Voluntary Hospitals," in *The Transformation of Political Culture*, ed. Eckhart Hellmuth (Oxford: Oxford University Press, 1990), 165–184.

37. On the concept of the "immanent frame," see Charles Taylor, *A Secular Age* (Cambridge, MA: Belknap, 2007).

38. On affinities between Christian and utilitarian agendas in eighteenth-century Britain, see Charles Wilson, "The Other Face of Mercantilism," *Transactions of the Royal Historical Society*, 5th series, 9 (1959): 81–101; Andrew, *Philanthropy and Police*, 11–43; James Stephen Taylor, *Jonas Hanway: Founder of the Marine Society: Charity and Policy in Eighteenth-Century Britain* (London: Scolar, 1985); D. G. C. Allan and R. E. Schoenfield, *Stephen Hales: Scientist and Philanthropist* (London: Scolar, 1980); Joanna Innes, "Politics and Morals: The Reformation of Manners Movement in Later Eighteenth-Century England," in *Transformation of Political Culture*, 57–118.

39. The literature on confessionalization is immense, but useful recent overviews in English may be found in Ute Lotz-Heumann, "The Concept of 'Confessionalization': A Historiographical Paradigm in Dispute," *Memoria y Civilización* 4 (2001): 93–114; Ute Lotz-Heumann, "Confessionalization," in *Reformation and Early Modern Europe: A Guide to Research*, ed. David M. Whitford (Kirksville, MO: Truman State University Press, 2008), 136–157; Thomas A. Brady Jr., "Confessionalization: The Career of a Concept," in *Confessionalization in Europe, 1555–1700*, ed. John M. Headley, Hans J. Hillerbrand, and Anthony J. Papalas (Aldershot, UK: Ashgate, 2004), 1–20; Susan Boettcher, "Confessionalization: Reformation, Religion, Absolutism and Modernity," *History Compass* 2 (2004): 1–10; and Philip S. Gorski, *The Protestant Ethic Revisited* (Philadelphia: Temple University Press, 2011), 1–38.

40. Andrew Pettegree, "Confessionalization in North Western Europe," in *Konfessionalisierung in Ostmitteleuropa: Wirkungen des religiösen Wandels im 16. und 17. Jahrhundert in Staat, Gesellschaft und Kultur*, ed. Joachim Bahlcke and Arno Strohmeyer (Stuttgart: Franz Steiner Verlag, 1999), 105–120; Peter Marshall, "(Re)Defining the English Reformation," *Journal of British Studies* 48 (July 2009): 564–586; Peter Marshall, "Confessionalization, Confessionalism and Confusion in the English Reformation," in *Reforming Reformation*, ed. Thomas F. Mayer (Farnham, UK: Ashgate, 2012).

41. Eamon Duffy, "The Long Reformation: Catholicism, Protestantism and the Multitude," in *England's Long Reformation, 1500–1800*, ed. Nicholas Tyacke (London: UCL, 1998), 33–70; and see Patrick Collinson, "Comment on Eamon Duffy's Neale Lecture and the Colloquium," in *England's Long Reformation*, 71–78.

42. Perhaps the foundational text for this approach is John Bossy, *Christianity in the West, 1400–1700* (Oxford: Oxford University Press, 1985). For treatments of the later seventeenth and early eighteenth centuries within a broader "long reformation" context, see Jeremy Gregory, "The Eighteenth Century Reformation: The Pastoral Task of Anglican Clergy after 1689," *The Church of England, c. 1689–c. 1833*, 67–85; Jeremy Gregory, *Restoration, Reformation and Reform: Archbishops of Canterbury and Their Diocese* (Oxford: Clarendon, 2000); Jeremy Gregory, "The Making of the Protestant Nation: 'Success' and 'Failure' in England's Long Reformation," in *England's Long Reformation*, 307–333; Jonathan Barry, "Bristol as a 'Reformation City,' c. 1640–1780," in *England's Long Reformation*, 261–284; Ian Green, *The Christian's ABC: Catechisms and Catechizing in England, c. 1530–1740* (Oxford: Clarendon, 1996); Ian Green, *Print and Protestantism in Early Modern England* (Oxford: Oxford University Press, 2001); Alexandra Walsham, *Charitable Hatred: Tolerance and Intolerance in England, 1500–1700* (Manchester: Manchester University Press, 2006); Ingram, *Religion, Reform and Modernity*; and Sarah Apetrei, *Women, Feminism and Religion in Early Enlightenment England* (Cambridge: Cambridge University Press, 2010).

43. J. C. D. Clark, *English Society 1660–1832*, 2nd ed. (Cambridge: Cambridge University Press, 2000); J. C. D. Clark, "England's Ancien Régime as a Confessional State," *Albion* 21 (1989): 450–474; and see William Gibson, *The Church of England, 1688–1832: Unity and Accord* (London: Routledge, 2001).

44. Collinson, "Comment on Duffy," 79.

45. Gregory, *Restoration, Reformation and Reform*, 3–4; Jeremy Gregory, ed., *The Speculum of Archbishop Secker* (Woodbridge, UK: Boydell, 1995), xiii–xiv.

46. José Casanova, *Public Religions in the Modern World* (Chicago: University of Chicago Press, 1994), 13, 21.

47. On secularization in England during this period, see C. John Sommerville, *The Secularization of Early Modern England* (New York: Oxford University Press, 1992); Blair Worden, "The Question of Secularization," in *A Nation Transformed: England after the Restoration*, ed. Alan Houston and Steve Pincus (Cambridge: Cambridge University Press, 2001), 20–40; Kaspar von Greyerz, "Secularization in Early Modern England (1660–c. 1750)," in *Säkularisierung, Dechristianisierung, Rechristianisierung im neuzeitlichen Europa*, ed. Harmut Leghmann (Göttingen: Vandenhoeck and Ruprecht, 1997), 86–100; and J. C. D. Clark, "Providence, Predestination and Progress: Or, Did the Enlightenment Fail?," *Albion* 35 (2003): 559–589.

48. Hannah More, *An estimate of the religion of the fashionable world*, 4th ed. (London, 1791), 50; Isaac Crouch, *The eternity of future punishments* (Oxford, 1786), 16; William Cobbett, *A History of the Reformation in England and Ireland* (Baltimore, 1852), iii–xxiii, 91, 217.

49. Michel Foucault, *Security, Territory, Population: Lectures at the Collège de France, 1977–1978*, trans. Graham Burchell (New York: Picador, 2004), 115–253; Michel Foucault, "Omnes et Singulatum: Towards a Criticism of 'Political Reason,'" *The Tanner Lectures on Human Values* (Salt Lake City: University of Utah Press, 1981). There is a very helpful treatment of these

themes in Ben Golder, "Foucault and the Genealogy of Pastoral Power," *Radical Philosophy Review* 10 (2007): 151–176.

1. Revival and Revolution

1. *HOT*, 1:346; Edward Carpenter, *Thomas Tenison, Archbishop of Canterbury* (London: SPCK, 1948), 35–78.

2. J. H. Overton, *Life in the English Church (1660–1714)* (London: Longmans, Green, 1885), 168.

3. 2 Tim 3:16: "All scripture is given by inspiration of God, and is profitable for doctrine, for reproof, for correction, for instruction in righteousness."

4. *Diary of John Evelyn*, ed. William Bray, 4 vols. (London: Bickers and Son, 1906), 2:55–56.

5. G. R. Cragg, *From Puritanism to the Age of Reason* (Cambridge: Cambridge University Press, 1950), 136; Norman Sykes, *Church and State in England in the XVIIIth Century* (New York: Octagon, 1973), 29.

6. W. A. Speck, *Reluctant Revolutionaries: Englishmen and the Revolution of 1688* (Oxford: Oxford University Press, 1988), 199–200.

7. Jonathan Scott, *England's Troubles* (Cambridge: Cambridge University Press, 2000), 209.

8. Tim Harris, *Revolution: The Great Crisis of the British Monarchy, 1685–1720* (London: Penguin, 2007), 242; Justin Champion, "Political Thinking between Restoration and Hanoverian Succession," in *A Companion to Stuart Britain*, ed. Barry Coward (Malden, MA: Blackwell, 2003), 485.

9. George Hilton Jones, *Convergent Forces: Immediate Causes of the Revolution of 1688 in England* (Ames: Iowa State University Press, 1990).

10. See, for instance, Sykes, *Church and State*, 21–23, 257–258, 343–346; Isabel Rivers, *Reason, Grace and Sentiment, Vol. 1: Whichcote to Wesley* (Cambridge: Cambridge University Press, 1991), 25–88; R. N. Stromberg, *Religious Liberalism in Eighteenth Century England* (Oxford: Oxford University Press, 1954); John Coffey, *Persecution and Toleration in Protestant England, 1558–1689* (Harlow: Longman, 2000), 179–182; C. R. Beechey, "The Defence of the Church of England in James II's Reign" (master's thesis, University of Lancaster, 1985), 14–20.

11. Thomas Babbington Macaulay, *The History of England from the Accession of James the Second*, ed. Charles Harding Firth, 6 vols. (London: Macmillan, 1914), 2:867; G. M. Trevelyan, *The English Revolution, 1688–1689* (London: Oxford University Press, 1950), 241–242.

12. Cragg, *From Puritanism*, 62–86.

13. Martin I. J. Griffin, *Latitudinarianism in the Seventeenth Century Church of England* (Leiden: E. J. Brill, 1992), 31.

14. Gordon Rupp, *Religion in England, 1688–1791* (Oxford: Clarendon, 1986), 33; W. M. Spellman, *The Latitudinarians and the Church of England, 1660–1700* (Athens: University of Georgia Press, 1993), 49–53, 132–155.

15. Margaret C. Jacob, *The Newtonians and the English Revolution, 1689–1720* (Ithaca, NY: Cornell University Press, 1976), 72–99.

16. Richard Ashcraft, "Latitudinarianism and Toleration: Historical Myth versus Political History," in *Philosophy, Science and Religion in England, 1640–1700*, ed. Richard Kroll, Richard

Ashcraft, and Perez Zagorin (Cambridge: Cambridge University Press, 1992), 151–177; John Marshall, "The Ecclesiology of the Latitude-men, 1660–1689: Stillingfleet, Tillotson, and 'Hobbism,'" *JEH* 36 (July 1985): 407–427; John Spurr, "'Latitudinarianism' and the Restoration Church," *HJ* 31 (1988): 61–82; John Spurr, "'Rational Religion' in Restoration England," *Journal of the History of Ideas* 49 (October–December 1988): 563–585; John Spurr, *The Restoration Church of England* (New Haven, CT: Yale University Press, 1991), 296–311; William Gibson, *The Church of England, 1688–1832: Unity and Accord* (London: Routledge, 2001), 48–61.

17. G. V. Bennett, "King William III and the Episcopate," in *Essays in Modern English Church History: In Memory of Norman Sykes*, ed. G. V. Bennett and J. D. Walsh (London: Black, 1966), 104–132; and G. V. Bennett, "Conflict in the Church," in *Britain after the Glorious Revolution, 1689–1714*, ed. Geoffrey Holmes (London: Macmillan, 1969), 155–175; Craig Rose, *England in the 1690s* (Malden, MA: Blackwell, 1999), 182–183.

18. Roger Thomas, "The Seven Bishops and Their Petition, 18 May 1688," *JEH* 12 (April 1961): 56–70.

19. Tony Claydon, *William III and the Godly Revolution* (Cambridge: Cambridge University Press, 1996); Warren Johnston, "Revelation and the Revolution of 1688–1689," *HJ* 48 (2005): 351–389.

20. Claydon, *William III and the Godly Revolution*, 159.

21. Steve Pincus, *1688: The First Modern Revolution* (New Haven, CT: Yale University Press, 2009), 400–434.

22. Mark Goldie, "The Political Thought of the Anglican Revolution," in *The Revolutions of 1688*, ed. Robert Beddard (Oxford: Clarendon, 1991), 102–136; G. V. Bennett, "The Seven Bishops: A Reconsideration," in *Studies in Church History* 15 (1978): 267–287; Harris, *Revolution*, 239–268. But see William Gibson, *James II and the Trial of the Seven Bishops* (Basingstoke: Palgrave Macmillan, 2009), who believes that conservative episcopal opposition, with its mobilization of public opinion, made possible the "popular Whig revolution of 1688."

23. Gerald M. Straka, *Anglican Reaction to the Revolution of 1688* (Madison: State Historical Society of Wisconsin, 1962), ix, 69–79, 98.

24. J. C. D. Clark, *English Society 1660–1832* (Cambridge: Cambridge University Press, 2000), 43–124; Gibson, *Church of England, 1688–1832*, 11, 28–63.

25. Spurr, *Restoration Church of England*, 163–165, 379–383; William J. Bulman, "Constantine's Enlightenment: Culture and Religious Politics in the Early British Empire, c. 1648–1710" (PhD diss., Princeton University, 2009), 216–226.

26. Bulman, "Constantine's Enlightenment," 386–388, 437.

27. Rupp, *Religion in England*, 51; Claydon, *William III and the Godly Revolution*, 66; John Spurr, "The Church, the Societies and the Moral Revolution of 1688," in *The Church of England, c. 1689–c. 1833*, ed. J. Walsh, C. Haydon, and S. Taylor (Cambridge: Cambridge University Press, 1993), 127–142; Mark Knights, "'Meer Religion' and the 'Church-State' of Restoration England: The Impact and Ideology of James II's Declarations of Indulgence," in *A Nation Transformed: England after the Restoration*, ed. Alan Houston and Steve Pincus (Cambridge: Cambridge University Press, 2001), 41–70; Beechey, "Defence of the Church of England," 51–81.

28. Overton, *Life in the English Church*, 6–15, 158–206.

29. Mark Goldie, "Restoration Political Thought," in *The Reigns of Charles II and James VII & II*, ed. L. K. J. Glassey (New York: St. Martin's, 1997), 12–35; Mark Goldie, "John Locke and Anglican Royalism," *Political Studies* 31 (1983): 61–85; R. A. Beddard, "Tory Oxford," in *The*

History of the University of Oxford: The Seventeenth Century, ed. Nicholas Tyacke (Oxford: Clarendon, 1997), 863–905.

30. Tim Harris, *Restoration: Charles II and His Kingdoms* (New York: Penguin, 2005), 300–308.

31. C. John Sommerville, *Popular Religion in Restoration England* (Gainesville: University Presses of Florida, 1977), 8.

32. J. R. Jones, *The Revolution of 1688 in England* (New York: Norton, 1972), 119.

33. Mark Goldie, "Voluntary Anglicans," *HJ* 46 (2003): 979; for an important correction, see Bulman, "Constantine's Enlightenment," 327–344, 380.

34. R. A. Beddard, "The Restoration Church," in *The Restored Monarchy, 1660–1688*, ed. J. R. Jones (Totowa, NJ: Rowman and Littlefield, 1979), 155–175; Jeffrey R. Collins, "The Restoration Bishops and the Royal Supremacy," *Church History* 68 (September 1999): 549–580; Jacqueline Rose, "Royal Ecclesiastical Supremacy and the Restoration Church," *Historical Research* 209 (June 2007): 324–345.

35. Goldie, "John Locke and Anglican Royalism," 61–85; Mark Goldie, "Priestcraft and the Birth of Whiggism," in *Political Discourse in Early Modern Britain*, ed. N. T. Phillipson and Quentin Skinner (Cambridge: Cambridge University Press, 1993), 209–231; Goldie, "Restoration Political Thought," 12–35; J. A. I. Champion, *The Pillars of Priestcraft Shaken: The Church of England and Its Enemies, 1660–1730* (Cambridge: Cambridge University Press, 1992).

36. Anthony Fletcher, "The Enforcement of the Conventicle Acts, 1664–1679," in *Persecution and Toleration*, ed. W. J. Sheils (Oxford: Basil Blackwell, 1984), 235–246; John Miller, *Popery & Politics in England, 1660–1688* (Cambridge: Cambridge University Press, 1973), 191; R. A. Beddard, "The Commission for Ecclesiastical Promotions, 1681–84: An Instrument of Tory Reaction," *HJ* 10 (1967): 11–40; Mark Goldie, "The Theory of Religious Intolerance in Restoration England," in *From Persecution to Toleration: The Glorious Revolution in England*, ed. O. P. Grell, J. I. Israel, and N. Tyacke (Oxford: Oxford University Press, 1991), 331–368; Grant Tapsell, *The Personal Rule of Charles II, 1681–85* (Woodbridge: Boydell, 2007), 64–91.

37. Rupp, *Religion in England*, 51; Claydon, *William III and the Godly Revolution*, 66; Spurr, "Church, the Societies and the Moral Revolution," 127–142.

38. R. O. Bucholz, "The Chapel Royal: Chaplains, 1660–1837," in *Office-Holders in Modern Britain: Vol. 11 (revised): Court Officers, 1660–1837* (2006), 251–278, available at http://www.british-history.ac.uk/source.aspx?pubid=316.

39. White Kennett, Materials for a History of SPG, BL Lansdowne MS 1032, ff. 211–212; Edward Carpenter, *The Protestant Bishop, Being the Life of Henry Compton 1632–1713, Bishop of London* (London: Longmans, Green, 1956), 253–254; Lawrence Brown, "Henry Compton 1632–1714," *Historical Magazine* 25 (March 1956): 7–68.

40. Sugiko Nishikawa, "Henry Compton, Bishop of London (1676–1714) and Foreign Protestants," in *From Strangers to Citizens*, ed. R. Vigne and C. Littleton (Brighton: Sussex Academic Press, 2001), 359–365; Carpenter, *Protestant Bishop*, 321–342; John M. Hintermaier, "The First Modern Refugees? Charity, Entitlement, and Persuasion in the Huguenot Immigration of the 1680s," *Albion* 32 (2000): 429–449.

41. "Diary of Dr. Edward Lake," *Camden Miscellany* 1 (London: Camden Society, 1847), 11, 17, 19–20.

42. "Diary of Lake," 21 [5 January 1678].

43. Carpenter, *Protestant Bishop*, 61–67; on informal meetings of the London clergy, see "The Autobiography of Symon Patrick," in *The Works of Simon Patrick, D.D.*, ed. Alexander Taylor, 9 vols. (Oxford: Oxford University Press, 1858), 9:454. There is evidence of such clerical conferences occurring in other dioceses at this time as well; see *The Autobiographies and Letters of Thomas Comber*, ed. C. E. Whitting, 2 vols. (Durham: Surtees Society, 1946–1947), 1:15; Francis Turner, *A Letter to the Clergy of the Diocess of Ely* (Cambridge, 1686), 7–8.

44. See also "Autobiography of Symon Patrick," 9:483.

45. *Episcopalia: or, Letters of the Right Reverend Father in God, Henry, Lord Bishop of London, to the Clergy of His Diocess* (London, 1686), 3–15, 19–29, 41–47, 63–64.

46. Arthur Bury, *The Constant Communicant* (Oxford, 1681), introduction.

47. *Episcopalia*, 8–12. As early as 1670, the Devonshire clergyman Abednego Seller noted that "among the multitude of practical divine treatises, are none more numerous than on the Lord's Supper," in Seller, *The devout communicant exemplifi'd, in his behaviour before, at, and after the sacrament of the Lords Supper* (London, 1670), sig A2r; among those written by London clergymen were Anthony Horneck, *The crucified Jesus, or, A full account of the nature, end, design & benefits of the Sacrament of the Lord's Supper* (London, 1686); Edward Lake, *Officium Eucharisticum, A Preparatory Service to a Devout and Worthy Reception of the Lords Supper*, 8th ed. (London, 1683); Simon Patrick, *A Book for Beginners, Or, a Help to Young Communicants*, 2nd ed. (London, 1680); William Smythies, *The Unworthy Non-communicant*, 2nd ed. (London, 1683); John Tillotson, *A Persuasive to Frequent Communion in the Holy Sacrament of the Lord's Supper* (London, 1683); and see "The Protestant Lady's Library," in Evelyn to Countess of Sunderland, 12 September 1686, BL Add MS 78299, f. 40. On the prominence of sacramental writings among the "religious best sellers of the Restoration," see Sommerville, *Popular Religion*, 33–59; Overton, *Life in the English Church*, 261–295.

48. *The Remains of Denis Granville, D.D.*, Surtees Society, vol. 37 (Durham, 1860), 174–177, 177–179, 183, 210–211; Denis Granville, "Advice concerning Strict Conformity," in *The compleat conformist* (London, 1684), 4; Christopher Wordsworth, *Notes on Mediaeval Services in England* (London: Thomas Baker, 1898), 64–65; Jeremy Gregory, "Canterbury and the *Ancien Régime:* The Dean and Chapter, 1660–1828," in *A History of Canterbury Cathedral*, ed. P. Collinson, N. Ramsay, and M. Sparks (Oxford: Oxford University Press, 1995), 230–232.

49. Thomas Comber, *The Memoirs of the Life and Writings of Thomas Comber, D.D.* (London, 1799), 179.

50. *Episcopalia*, 76–90; William Basset, *A discourse on my Lord Arch-Bishop of Canterbury's and my Lord Bishop of London's letters to the clergy touching catechizing, and the sacrament of the Supper* (London, 1684).

51. "Autobiography of Symon Patrick," 9:483.

52. Comber, *Memoirs*, 179.

53. [Richard Kidder], "The Life of the Reverend Anthony Horneck, D.D.," in *Several sermons upon the fifth of St. Matthew: being part of Christ's sermon on the mount*, 2nd ed. (London, 1706), v–vi.

54. *The Life of Richard Kidder, D.D., Bishop of Bath and Wells Written by Himself*, ed. Amy Edith Robinson, Somerset Record Society, vol. 37 (London: Butler and Tanner, 1924), 19–20.

55. Spurr, "Church, Societies and the Moral Revolution," 139–140.

56. Granville, "Advice concerning Strict Conformity," 11–12.

57. William Smith, *A Sermon Preached on the Fourth Sunday in Lent in the Cathedral Church of Norwich* (London, 1680), sig A2v; Joseph Glanvill, *An Earnest Invitation to the Sacrament of the Lords Supper* (London, 1673), 50; Granville, *Compleat conformist*, 15–16; and see Peter Samwaies to Denis Granville, 12 May 1681, *Remains of Granville*, 73–74. On the relative popularity of sermon and sacrament, see Donald A. Spaeth, "Common Prayer? Popular Observance of the Anglican Liturgy in Restoration Wiltshire," in *Parish, Church and People: Local Studies in Lay Religion, 1350–1750*, ed. Susan Wright (London: Hutchinson, 1988), 125–151.

58. Glanvill, *Earnest Invitation*, 36–37, 46; John Kettlewell, *A help and exhortation to worthy communicating* (London, 1683), 42–43, 79, 263–264; William Sherlock, *A Practical Discourse of Religious Assemblies* (London, 1681), 49–50, 245, 247; Seller, *The devout communicant*, 111; Lancelot Addison, *An Introduction to the Sacrament, or, A Short, Plain, and Safe Way to the Communion Table* (London, 1682), 80–82.

59. C. W. Dugmore, *Eucharistic Doctrine in England from Hooker to Waterland* (London: SPCK, 1942), 112–114.

60. Simon Patrick, *Mensa Mystica: Or, A Discourse Concerning the Sacrament of the Lord's Supper*, 5th ed. (London, 1684), 134–135.

61. On the debate over "holy living" in seventeenth-century Anglican theology, see H. R. McAdoo, *The Structure of Caroline Moral Theology* (London: Longmans, Green, 1949); C. F. Alison, *The Rise of Moralism* (New York: Seabury, 1966); Spurr, *Restoration Church of England*, 296–311; Neil Lettinga, "Covenant Theology Turned Upside Down: Henry Hammond and Caroline Anglican Moralism," *Sixteenth Century Journal* 24 (1993): 653–669; G. F. Scholtz, "Anglicanism in the Age of Johnson: The Doctrine of Conditional Salvation," *Eighteenth Century Studies* 22 (Winter 1988–1989): 182–207; Paul Cefalu, *Moral Identity in Early Modern English Literature* (Cambridge: Cambridge University Press, 2004).

62. Goldie, "Priestcraft," 209–231; Pincus, *1688*, 403; but see Bulman, "Constantine's Enlightenment," 284–293, 400–403.

63. Daniel Brevint, *The Christian sacrament and sacrifice* (Oxford, 1673), 24–25.

64. *The Diary and Autobiography of Edmund Bohun, Esq.* (privately published, 1853), 52–56; Thomas Ken, *A Manual of Prayers for the Use of the Scholars of Winchester Colledge* (London, 1677), 20–50; Patrick, *Book for Beginners*; Lake, *Officium Eucharisticum*.

65. Kettlewell, *A help and exhortation*, 175–178.

66. Tillotson, *Persuasive to Frequent Communion*, 15; Whitelocke Bulstrode, "In Recepconem Sacram[en]ti," [1 March 1688/89?], HRC Pforzheimer MS 2k.

67. Josiah Woodward, *An Account of the Rise and Progress of the Religious Societies in the City of London, &c.*, 2nd ed. (London, 1698); "Life of Horneck," viii.

68. Spurr, "Church, Societies and Moral Revolution"; G. V. Portus, *Caritas Anglicana* (London: A. R. Mowbray, 1912), 1–27; S. T. Kisker, "Anthony Horneck (1641–1697) and the Rise of Anglican Pietism" (PhD diss., Drew University, 2003), 114–126; Eamon Duffy, "Primitive Christianity Revived: Religious Renewal in Augustan England," in *Studies in Church History* 14 (1977): 287–300; M. R. Hunt, *The Middling Sort: Commerce, Gender and the Family in England, 1680–1780* (Berkeley: University of California Press, 1996), 104–114.

69. Woodward, *Account of the Rise and Progress*, 120.

70. "Life of Horneck," v–vi; Woodward, *Account of the Rise and Progress*, 19; Articles for the Society of Young Men of St. Martin's in the fields and thereabouts [1681], BL Add MS 38693, f. 137.

71. Spurr, "Church, Societies and Moral Revolution," 139.

72. Woodward, *Account of the Rise and Progress*, 125.

73. Bury, *Constant Communicant*, introduction.

74. Woodward, *Account of the Rise and Progress*, 131, 214–215; J. Wickham Legg, *English Church Life from the Restoration to the Tractarian Movement* (London: Longmans, Green, 1914), 291–297.

75. "Autobiography of Symon Patrick," 9:454.

76. For instance, Robert Grove of St. Andrew Undershaft in 1680; William Beveridge of St. Peter's, Cornhill, in 1681; and William Sherlock of St. George's, Botolph-Lane, in 1683. See Guildhall Library MS 10525, "Ordered by the President, Deans, Court of Assistants & Fellows of Sion Colledge that all the Ministers of London & the Adjacent parts bee desired to give Something towards the finishing of Sion Colledge" [26 April 1681]; E. H. Pearce, *Sion College and Library* (Cambridge: Cambridge University Press, 1913), 121–126; J. Russell, ed., *Sion College* (London: Richard Clay, 1859), 54–55.

77. *Diary of John Evelyn*, 2:428–429, 470; Carpenter, *Thomas Tenison*, 23–26; Memorandum on the library at St. Martin's [168?], BL Add MS 38693, f. 147.

78. *An abstract of the charter granted by the late Majesty King Charles II . . . for erecting a Corporation for Relief of Poor Widows and Children of Clergy-Men* (London, 1711).

79. Thomas Sprat, *A Sermon Preached at the Anniversary Meeting of the Sons of Clergy-Men in the Church of St. Mary Le Bow, Nov vii. 1678* (London, 1678), 3, 36.

80. M. G. Jones, "Two Accounts of the Welsh Trust, 1675 and 1678(?)," *Bulletin of the Board of Celtic Studies* 9 (1939): 71–80; *The Life of Mr. Thomas Firmin, Late Citizen of London* (London, 1791), 42–43.

81. Goldie, "Theory of Religious Intolerance," 331.

82. Francis Lee, *Memoirs of the Life of Mr. John Kettlewell* (London, 1718), 143–144; A Discourse of the Means to secure the Church of England, [ca. 1685–6?], BL Harleian MS 6273, ff. 16–24.

83. "A True Relation of the Late King's Death," *Somers Tracts*, 8:428–429.

84. *Diary of John Evelyn*, 2:449–450; Luttrell, 1:330; J. S. Clarke, ed., *The Life of James the Second*, 2 vols. (London: Longman, Hurst, Rees, Orme, and Brown, 1816), 2:6–7; *London Gazette*, 12 February 1685 (no. 2008); H. C. Foxcroft, ed., *A Supplement to Burnet's History of My Own Time* (Oxford: Clarendon, 1902), 143–144; *Memoirs of the Verney Family from the Restoration to the Revolution, 1660 to 1696*, ed. M. M. Verney, 4 vols. (London: Longmans, Green, 1899), 4:321; White Kennett, *A Complete History of England*, 3 vols. (London, 1706), 3:427.

85. *Diary of John Evelyn*, 2:450.

86. Clarke, ed., *Life of James*, 2:9. These were published several times as *Copies of two papers written by the Late King Charles II* (London, 1685) and the following year were published with a third paper of James's first wife, Anne Hyde, Duchess of York, detailing her private conversion to Catholicism.

87. Adrian Tinniswood, *His Invention So Fertile: A Life of Christopher Wren* (London: Jonathan Cape, 2001), 280–281.

88. *Memoirs of the Verney Family*, 4:342.

89. *Diary of John Evelyn*, 2:460; *The memoirs of Sir John Reresby of Thrybergh, Bart., MP for York, &c. 1634–1689*, ed. James J. Cartwright (London: Longmans, Green, 1875), 318–319. I am very grateful to Dr. Peter McCullogh for information regarding the usages of the Chapel Royal.

90. *Diary of John Evelyn*, 2:462; Luttrell, 1:339; *HOT*, 3:21–22; Francis Sandford, *The History of the Coronation of the Most High, Most Mighty, and Most Excellent Monarch James II* (London, 1687); Macaulay, *History of England*, 2:48–50.

91. Francis Turner to William Sancroft, April 1685, Tanner MS 31, f. 36; Francis Turner, *A Sermon Preached Before Their Majesties K. James II and Q. Mary, at their Coronation in Westminster-Abby, April 23, 1685* (London, 1685), 20–21, 25.

92. *HOT*, 3:21; John Dalrymple, *Memoirs of Great Britain and Ireland*, 3 vols. (London, 1790), 1:167; George Hickes to Arthur Charlett, 23 Jan 1710/11 in *Letters written by eminent persons in the Seventeenth and Eighteenth Centuries*, 2 vols. (London: Longman, Hurst, Rees, Orme, and Brown, 1813), 1:213–214.

93. Kennett, *Complete History*, 3:444; Miller, *Popery & Politics*, 203–205.

94. HMC *Frankland-Russell-Astley*, 59.

95. *London Gazette*, 12 February 1685 (no. 2008); *HOT*, 3:7; Carpenter, *Protestant Bishop*, 79.

96. *London Gazette*, 16 March 1685 (no. 2017); *London Gazette*, 26 March 1685 (no. 2020).

97. Leopold von Ranke, *A History of England Principally in the Seventeenth Century*, 6 vols. (Oxford: Clarendon, 1875), 4:218.

98. Earl of Sunderland to Archbishop Sancroft, Windsor, 4 September 1685, Tanner MS 31, f. 198.

99. Dalrymple, *Memoirs*, 1:163.

100. "Autobiography of Symon Patrick," 9:502.

101. Bishop Lloyd of Peterborough to Archbishop Sancroft, 2 May 1685, Tanner MS 31, f. 52; Morrice, P491; Dalrymple, *Memoirs*, 1:63; Ranke, *History of England*, 277; *The Autobiography of Sir John Bramston* (London: Camden Society, 1845), 216–217; Carpenter, *Protestant Bishop*, 83–84; Harris, *Revolution*, 97–99.

102. Miller, *Popery & Politics*, 209.

103. See Jacqueline Rose, *Godly Kingship in Restoration England: The Politics of the Royal Supremacy, 1660–1688* (Cambridge: Cambridge University Press, 2011), 229–274.

104. *Memoirs of Thomas, Earl of Ailesbury written by himself*, 2 vols. (Westminster: Nicholas and Sons, 1890), 1:159.

105. Morrice, P492; *Diary of John Evelyn*, 3:10; Luttrell, 1:362.

106. *The Ellis Correspondence*, ed. G. A. Ellis, 2 vols. (London: Henry Coburn, 1829), 1:4; Agnes Strickland, *The Lives of the Seven Bishops Committed to the Tower in 1688* (London, 1866), 178.

107. *Diary of John Evelyn*, 3:13.

108. *Ellis Correspondence*, 1:3, 6, 105–106; *The Correspondence of Henry Hyde, Earl of Clarendon*, 2 vols. (London: Henry Colburn, 1828), 1:258; *Memoirs of Reresby*, 351; HMC, 12th Report, Part VII, Le Fleming MS, 198; *Autobiography of Bramston*, 217; Morrice, P508; Luttrell, 1:368; HMC *Downshire* I, 1:83, 227.

109. "Memoirs of Nathaniel, Lord Crewe," ed. Andrew Clark, *Camden Miscellany* 9 (London: Camden Society, 1895): 20–21; Luttrell, 1:368; Kennett, *Complete History*, 3:445; on Crewe, see Foxcroft, ed., *Supplement*, 212.

110. Morrice, P563.

111. Morrice, P520, P526.

112. Ranke, *History of England*, 293–294; for Compton on the suppression of lectures, ca. early 1686, see Tanner MS 31, f. 268; Morrice, P623; for a list of the roughly fifty London lectureships, see Tanner MS 31, f. 269.

113. HRC Bulstrode Newsletters, 26 February, 8 March, 12 March 1685/86; HMC *Downshire* I, 1:130–131; *Memoirs of Reresby*, 359; Luttrell, 1:374; *Diary of John Evelyn*, 3:8–10, 19; *Letters of Lady Rachel Russell*, 7th ed. (London, 1809), 85–87; *James the Second . . . whereas it is the highest prerogative and most desirable advantage of kings and soveraign princes to have it in their power and will to do acts of publick clemency and beneficience* (London, 1686).

114. Chancellor Jeffreys to Archbishop Sancroft, 1 March 1685/86, Tanner MS 31, f. 279.

115. *To the most Reverend Fathers in God, William Lord Archbishop of Canterbury, Primate of all England and Metropolitan, and John Lord Archbishop of York, Primate of England and Metropolitan* (London, 1686); HRC Bulstrode Newsletters, 15 March 1685/86; Luttrell, 1:373; *Autobiography of Bramston*, 222.

116. *Diary of John Evelyn*, 3:18; Robert Frampton to William Sancroft, 27 March 1686, Tanner MS 30, f. 7; T. S. Evans, ed., *The Life of Robert Frampton Bishop of Gloucester* (London: Longmans, Green, 1876), 144–146; E. H. Plumptre, *The Life of Thomas Ken, D.D.*, 2 vols. (London: Wm. Isbister, 1890), 1:242–243.

117. The anonymous translation of Jean Claude's *An Account of the Persecutions and Oppressions of the Protestants in France* (1686) has been attributed to both Rayner and Tenison; Morrice, P533, P535; HRC Bulstrode Newsletters, 7 May 1686; Luttrell, 1:377; *Autobiography of Bramston*, 228; Carpenter, *Thomas Tenison*, 323.

118. *Ellis Correspondence*, 1:90–91.

119. HRC Bulstrode Newsletters, 8 March 1685/86; Luttrell, 1:371; Morrice, P526.

120. Luttrell, 1:378.

121. *Autobiography of Bramston*, 231; HMC *Rutland*, 2:109; *Diary of John Evelyn*, 3:24.

122. *Ellis Correspondence*, 1:83–84, 111–112, 118–119; HRC Bulstrode Newsletters, 29 March, 19 April 1686; Morrice, P530, P532; Luttrell, 1:373, 375; HMC *Downshire* I, 1:172–173; HMC *Kenyon*, 184; Miller, *Popery & Politics*, 245–246; Harris, *Revolution*, 200–201.

123. HRC Bulstrode Newsletters, 31 May, 4 June 1686; *Diary of John Evelyn*, 3:96.

124. John Gother, *A Papist Misrepresented and Represented: Or, a Twofold Character of Popery* (1685), 19–21; HMC *Frankland-Russell-Astley*, 63; William Sherlock to ————, Temple, 2 September 1685, Tanner MS 31, f. 190; and see James Blake, *A Sermon on the blessed Sacrament preach'd in the chapel of his Excellency the Spanish embassador on Corpus Christi Day, June 3, 1686* (London, 1686); *A Dialogue between a new Catholic convert and a Protestant shewing the doctrin of transubstantiation to be as reasonable to be believed as the great mystery of the trinity by all good Catholicks* (London, 1686); and see Dugmore, *Eucharistic Doctrine*, 124–134.

125. *HOT*, 3:104–106; "Autobiography of Symon Patrick," 9:490; *Diary of John Evelyn*, 3:11; *Life of Richard Kidder*, 37; William Sherlock to ————, 2 September 1685, Tanner MS 31, f. 190; HMC *Downshire* I, 1:175; William Nichols, *A defence of the doctrine and discipline of the Church of England*, 3rd ed. (London, 1730), 100; Charles Dodd, *The Church History of England from the year 1500, to the year 1688*, 3 vols. (Brussels [London], 1737–1742), 3:418–419.

126. *Copies of two papers written by the late King Charles II* (Dublin, 1686); HMC *Downshire* I, 1:95–96; Luttrell, 1:368; *Memoirs of Reresby*, 359.

127. [Edward Stillingfleet], *An Answer to some Papers Lately Printed* (Dublin, 1686); Gilbert Burnet, *A letter, containing some remarks on the two papers, writ by His late Majesty King Charles the Second* (London, 1686); HRC Bulstrode Newsletters, 16 April, 12 July 1686; *Diary and Letters of Philip Henry, M.A.*, ed. Matthew Henry Lee (London: Kegan, Paul, Trench, 1882), 353.

128. John Dryden, *A Defense of the Papers written by the Late King* (London, 1686), preface; Kennett, *Complete History*, 3:453–454; *HOT*, 3:106.

129. John Gother, *Good Advice to the Pulpits, Deliver'd in a few Cautions* (London, 1687), 69–70.

130. John Sharp, "Sermon V," in *Sermons against Popery, Preach'd In the Reign of James II* (London, 1735), 111–112.

131. Thomas Sharp, *The Life of John Sharp, D.D. Lord Archbishop of York*, ed. Thomas Newcome, 2 vols. (London: C. and J. Rivington, 1825), 1:70–71.

132. John Sharp, "Sermon VI," in *Sermons against Popery*, 7:128–132, 147.

133. Sharp, *Life of John Sharp*, 1:74–78; *HOT*, 3:106–107; Morrice, P556; Kennett, *Complete History*, 3:457; Dalrymple, *Memoirs of Great Britain*, 2:78–79.

134. Sharp, *Life of John Sharp*, 1:80–86; Luttrell, 1:381; HRC Bulstrode Newsletters, 25 June, 2 July, 5 July, 9 July 1686; *Autobiography of Bramston*, 232–233; Morrice, P556, P581; *Ellis Correspondence*, 1:136–137; HMC *Downshire* I, 1:185–186; *Memoirs of Ailesbury*, 159; Kennett, *Complete History*, 3:456.

135. HRC Bulstrode Newsletters, 18 July, 19 July, 30 July 1686; *Diary of John Evelyn*, 3:25; *Ellis Correspondence*, 1:144–150, 157; H. C. Foxcroft, *The Life and Letters of Sir George Saville, First Marquis of Halifax*, 2 vols. (London: Longmans, Green, 1898), 1:466–467; James Welwood, *Memoirs of the Most Material Transactions in England* (London, 1820), 179–180; Morrice, P573, P577, P587, P595; Kennett, *Complete History*, 3:454–456; Luttrell, 1:383; *Autobiography of Bramston*, 234; *Memoirs of Reresby*, 364; "Memoirs of Lord Crewe," 21; HMC *Downshire* I, 1:197; and see J. P. Kenyon, "The Commission for Ecclesiastical Causes 1686–1688: A Reconsideration," *HJ* 34 (1991): 727–736.

136. Kennett, *Complete History*, 3:457–460; HRC Bulstrode Newsletters, 9 August, 20 August, 31 August, 6 September 1686; Morrice, P601, P602, P603, P608, P609, P610, P613, P619, P620, P621, P622, P642; *Autobiography of Bramston*, 239–245; John Lowther, *Memoirs of the Reign of James II* (York: T. Wilson and R. Spence, 1808), 19–20; HMC *Downshire* I, 1:207, 210–211, 216–217; Henry Compton, *An exact account of the whole proceedings against the Right Reverend Father in God, Henry, Lord Bishop of London, before the Lord Chancellor and the other ecclesiastical commissioners* (London, 1688); An Account of the proceedings in the case of my Lord of London, BL Egerton MS 3882, ff. 182–187; Carpenter, *Protestant Bishop*, 109.

137. Luttrell, 1:386; HRC Bulstrode Newsletters, 8 October 1686.

138. Morrice, P623.

139. Pincus, *1688*, 170–171.

140. Morrice, P627; HRC Bulstrode Newsletters, 6 September 1686; HMC *Downshire* I, 1:217.

141. Tanner MS 30, f. 93; George D'Oyly, *The Life of William Sancroft, Archbishop of Canterbury*, 2 vols. (London: John Murray, 1821), 1:234–239; HRC Bulstrode Newsletters, 23 August 1686; Morrice, P598, P618; *The Diary of Dr. Thomas Cartwright, Bishop of Chester*, ed. Rev. Joseph Hunter (London: Camden Society, 1843), 1; Thomas Cartwright, *A Sermon preached upon the Anniversary Solemnity of the happy Inauguration of Our Dread Soveraign Lord King James II in the Collegiate Church at Ripon, February the 6th 1685/6* (London, 1686); *Ellis Correspondence*, 1:98, 141; Kennett, *Complete History*, 3:462; *HOT*, 3:146–147; on Parker, see Gordon Schochet, "Samuel Parker, Religious Diversity and the Ideology of Persecution," in *The Margins of Orthodoxy: Heterodox Writing and Cultural Response, 1660–1750*, ed. Roger D. Lund (Cambridge: Cambridge University Press, 1995), 119–148; Gordon Schochet, "Between Lambeth and Leviathan: Samuel Parker on the Church of England and Political Order," in *Political Discourse in Early Modern Britain*, 189–208; on Cartwright, see R. A. Beddard, "Bishop Cartwright's Death-Bed," *Bodleian Library Record* 11 (1984): 220–230.

142. HRC Bulstrode Newsletters, 11 October 1686; *Autobiography of Bramston*, 247–248; Morrice, P633.

143. Luttrell, 1:384–386; HRC Bulstrode Newsletters, 18 October, 22 October 1686; Morrice, P636.

144. HRC Bulstrode Newsletters, 5 November 1686; *Diary of John Evelyn*, 3:29; Morrice, Q42; Harris, *Revolution*, 209–210; Francis Turner to William Sancroft, 6 June 1687, Tanner MS 29, f. 36.

145. On Edward Sclater, see Morrice, P533; John Gutch, *Collectanea Curiosa*, 2 vols. (Oxford: Clarendon, 1781), 1:290–293; James Mackintosh, *History of the Revolution in England in 1688* (Philadelphia: Cary, Lea and Blanchard, 1835), 260; Edward Sclater, *Consensus Veterum: Or, The Reasons of Edward Sclater Minister of Putney For His Conversion to the Catholic Faith and Communion* (London, 1686); Anthony Horneck, *An Account of Mr. Edward Sclater's return to the communion of the Church of England* (London, 1689).

146. "The Proceedings against Mr. Samuel Johnson," in *A Complete Collection of State Trials*, ed. T. B. Howell, 34 vols. (London: Longman, Hurst, Rees, Orme, and Brown, 1816), 11:1339–1354; "Some Memorials of Reverend Samuel Johnson," in *The works of the late Reverend Samuel Johnson* (London, 1710), iv–xii; Morrice, Q10, Q31, Q32; HRC Bulstrode Newsletters, 21 June 1686; *Autobiography of Bramston*, 248–250; HMC *Downshire* I, 1:172–173; on Johnson, see M. Zook, "Early Whig Ideology, Ancient Constitutionalism, and the Reverend Samuel Johnson," *Journal of British Studies* 32 (April 1993): 139–165; J. A. I. Champion, "'To Govern Is to Make Subjects Believe': Anticlericalism, Politics and Power, c. 1680–1717," in *Anticlericalism in Britain*, ed. N. Aston and M. Cragoe (Stroud: Sutton, 2000), 42–66.

147. N. Salmon, *The Life of the Right Honourable and Right Reverend Dr. Henry Compton the Lord Bishop of London* (London, [1713?]), 40; Tanner MS 30, f. 146; Morrice, Q12, Q13, Q14, Q32, Q33; "Proceedings against Samuel Johnson," 1351; "Some Memorials of Johnson," xii; *Autobiography of Bramston*, 248–250; Kennett, *Complete History*, 3:452; J. Wickham Legg, "The Degradation in 1686 of the Rev. Samuel Johnson," *EHR* 29 (1914): 723–742.

148. Morrice, Q43, Q46, Q73, Q80; Foxcroft, ed., *Supplement*, 213; Carpenter, *Protestant Bishop*, 87–88, 108–115.

149. Henry Compton, *The Bishop of London's Seventh Letter of the Conference with his Clergy Held in the Year 1686* (London, 1690).

150. Miller, *Popery & Politics*, 210–213; Harris, *Revolution*, 211.

151. Bulman, "Constantine's Enlightenment," 394–395.

152. Lee, *Memoirs of the Life of Kettlewell*, 97–98, 153; Morrice, Q88; *Diary of John Evelyn*, 4:33; Foxcroft, ed., *Life and Letters of Halifax*, 467; Clarke, ed., *Life of James*, 2:80.

153. Lee, *Memoirs of the Life of Kettlewell*, 97–98, 153; Morrice, Q44, Q45, Q46, Q73, Q80, Q94; Sharp, *Life of John Sharp*, 88–89; *Correspondence of the Family of Hatton*, ed. E. M. Thompson, 2 vols. (London: Camden Society, 1878), 2:65–66; *Autobiography of Bramston*, 266; Lutrell, 1:392, 397–398; *Diary of John Evelyn*, 4:33, 35; Plumptre, *Life of Ken*, 1:269–270, 397; Mackintosh, *History of the Revolution*, 268; John Tillotson, "Sermon LVII," in *The Works of John Tillotson*, ed. Thomas Birch, 10 vols. (London: J. Dove, 1820), 4:51–72; *Diary of Cartwright*, 44, 91; [Simon Patrick], *A Sermon Preached Upon St. Peter's Day* (London, 1687); *Memoirs of Ailesbury*, 1:160–161; Evans, ed., *Life of Frampton*, 145–146; *Life of Richard Kidder*, 38–39, 45; Richard Kidder, *The judgment of private discretion in matters of religion defended* (London, 1687); Gilbert Burnet, *The Ill Effects of Animosities among Protestants in England Detected* (1688), 15.

154. "Autobiography of Symon Patrick," 9:490; *The Notes of the Church As Laid Down by Cardinal Bellarmin Examined and Confuted* (London, 1688); William Wake, *A Collection of Several Discourses against Popery* (London, 1688); William Wake to Arthur Charlett, 6 March 1687, Ballard MS 3, f. 11; Norman Sykes, *William Wake, Archbishop of Canterbury, 1657–1737*, 2 vols. (Cambridge: Cambridge University Press, 1957), 1:17–43; *Autobiography of Bramston*, 301; William Lloyd, Bishop of St. Asaph to Archbishop William Sancroft, 8 December 1687, Tanner MS 29, f. 118; Autobiography of William Wake, LPL MS 2932, f. 29: *The present state of the controversie between the Church of England and the Church of Rome* (London, 1687); *A Continuation of the Present State of the Controversy*, 2nd ed. (London, 1688); Edward Gee, *The Catalogue of all the discourses published against popery, during the reign of King James II by the members of the Church of England* (London, 1689); Francis Peck, *A Complete Catalogue of all the Discourses written, both for and against popery, in the time of King James II* (London, [1735]); HMC *Downshire* I, 1:286; Jones, *Revolution of 1688*, 87–91.

155. HMC *Downshire* I, 1:237–238.

156. Henry Dove, et al., To the Rectors, Vicars Lecturers & Curates of the City and Liberties of London Brethren [Sion College, 30 May 1687]; The Names of Several Benefactors to Sion-College in the Year 1687, Guildhall Library MS 10525.

157. Herbert Croft to Adam Ottley, 18 March 1686, NLW Ottley MS 1634; Herbert Croft to Adam Ottley, 16 April 1687, NLW Ottley MS 1727.

158. HMC *Downshire* I, 1:246–247, 272, 282, 286; "Autobiography of Symon Patrick," 9:505–506; "The Life of Dr. Thomas Ken, Late Lord Bishop of Bath and Wells," in Ken, *A Manual of Prayers for the use of scholars of Winchester College*, 27th ed. (London, 1748), vi; William Hawkins, *A short account of the life of the Right Reverend Father in God Thomas Ken, D.D.* (London, 1713), 13; Morrice, Q150; Luttrell, 1:424, 437; *Memoirs of Reresby*, 374; Miller, *Popery & Politics*, 239–249; Pincus, *1688*, 164–166.

159. Thomas Tenison, *A true account of a Conference Held about Religion at London, September 29, 1687 Between A. Pulton, Jesuit, and Tho. Tenison, D.D.* (London, 1687); HMC *Downshire* I, 1:269–270; Nichols, *Defence of the doctrine*, 100; Carpenter, *Thomas Tenison*, 49–66, contains the fullest account of the conference and subsequent pamphlet controversy; Morrice, Q209.

160. "Life of Horneck," xii; Woodward, *Account of the Rise and Progress*, 38–42; Kisker, "Horneck and the Rise of Anglican Pietism," 148–157; Wickham Legg, *English Church Life*, 291–301.

161. *His Majesties Gracious Declaration to All His Loving Subjects for Liberty of Conscience* (London, 1687); Harris, *Revolution*, 216–224; Welwood, *Memoirs*, 173; *Memoirs of Reresby*, 374, 377; HRC Bulstrode Newsletters, 2 April 1687; Luttrell, 1:402–420, 427, 429; *Autobiography of Bramston*, 271, 275.

162. Edward Stillingfleet, *The Mischief of Separation, A Sermon preached at Guild-Hall Chappel, May 11, 1680* (London, 1680); John Tillotson, *The Protestant Religion Vindicated From the Charge of Singularity & Novelty in a Sermon Preached before the King at White-hall, April the 2d 1680* (London, 1680); on the controversy, see Marshall, "Ecclesiology of the Latitude-men," and Martin P. Sutherland, "Protestant Divergence in the Restoration Crisis," *Journal of Religious History* 21 (2002): 285–301.

163. Morrice, Q107, Q114, Q127, Q132, Q137; The Address of 4 BB (D[urham], R[ochester], O[xford] & Ch[ester]) to ye Kg, Tanner MS 29, f. 13; The Reasons agst Subscription, Tanner MS 29, f. 13; *Remains of Granville*, 1:226; *Autobiographies and Letters of Thomas Comber*, 18; Francis Turner to Sancroft, Ely, 25 August 1687, Tanner MS 29, f. 64; Jonathan Trelawney, Bp of Bristol to Sancroft, 20 March 1687/88, Tanner MS 29, f. 141; H. Aubrey to Ellis, 2 August 1687, BL Add MS 28876, f. 23; HMC *Downshire* I, 1:246–247; [George Saville, marquis of Halifax], *A letter to a Dissenter upon His Majesties late Gracious Declaration of Indulgence* [1687], 3.

164. Francis Turner to William Sancroft, 6 June 1687, Tanner MS 29, f. 36; The Reasons agst Subscription, Tanner MS 29, f. 13; Morrice, Q216, Q233; *Remains of Granville*, 1:228–229; "Diary of Henry Earl of Clarendon, for part of the year 1687; the years 1688 and 1689; and part of the year 1690," in *Clarendon Correspondence*, 2:156, 163–164.

165. See William J. Bulman, "Enlightenment and Religious Politics in Restoration England," *History Compass* 10, 10 (2012): 752–764.

166. Roger Thomas, "Comprehension and Indulgence," in *From Uniformity to Unity, 1662–1962*, ed. Owen Chadwick and G. F. Nuttall (London: SPCK, 1962), 225–231; and see John Spurr, "The Church of England, Comprehension and the Toleration Act of 1689," *EHR* 413 (October 1989): 927–946; Mark Goldie and John Spurr, "Politics and the Restoration Parish: Edward Fowler and the Struggle for St. Giles Cripplegate," *EHR* 432 (June 1994): 572–596; Morrice, Q89, Q90; *Memoirs of Reresby*, 372; on the varieties of Nonconformist addresses, see Harris, *Revolution*, 217–219.

167. Morrice, Q86, Q116, Q120, Q128, Q214; Burnet, *Ill Effects of Animosities*, 23; Plumptre, *Life of Ken*, 1:280; [Halifax], *Letter to a Dissenter*, 5; J. R. Western, *Monarchy and Revolution: The English State in the 1680s* (London: Blandford, 1972), 225–229; on the popularity of Halifax's pamphlet, see Pincus, *1688*, 194–196.

168. Thomas, "Seven Bishops," 56–70; Bennett, "Seven Bishops," 267–287; Western, *Monarchy and Revolution*, 230–235; Gibson, *James II and the Trial*; Jones, *Convergent Forces*,

9–13; Morrice, Q255–260; "Autobiography of Symon Patrick," 9:509–512; *Clarendon Correspondence*, 2:171–172; HRC Bulstrode Newsletters, 17 May, 22 May 1688; D'Oyly, *Life of Sancroft*, 155–156; *HOT*, 3:223–226.

169. Tanner MS 28, ff. 38–39; "Autobiography of Symon Patrick," 9:509–512; Morrice, Q260–262; *Clarendon Correspondence*, 2:172; HRC Bulstrode Newsletters, 17 May, 22 May 1688; Gutch, *Collectanea Curiosa*, 1:335–341; *Diary of John Evelyn*, 3:46–47; HMC *Downshire* I, 1:292–293; *Memoirs of Reresby*, 394; D'Oyly, *Life of Sancroft*, 156–157; *HOT*, 3:227–228; HMC *Kenyon*, 190.

170. Western, *Monarchy and Revolution*, 233; Thomas, "Seven Bishops," 56–70; *Diary of John Evelyn*, 3:47–48; HRC Bulstrode Newsletters, 17 May, 25 May 1688; "Autobiography of Symon Patrick," 9:511; Adam Ottley, Acct of the reading of the Dec[laration]n [of Indulgence] in London, ca. 1688, NLW Ottley Correspondence MS 1467; [William Sherlock], A letter from a Clergyman in the City of London to his Friend in ye Country containing his reasons for not reading the Declaration [22 May 1688], Tanner MS 29, ff. 4–6; *Memoirs of Reresby*, 394; Morrice, Q261, Q265; Signed copies of the petition, May 1688, Tanner MS 29, ff. 34–36; William Stanley to Sancroft, 31 May/10 June 1688, Tanner MS 29, f. 40; Bishop Herbert Croft to Adam Ottley, 8 August 1688, NLW MS 1723; Copy of Bishop Herbert Croft to James II, 6 June 1688, NLW MS 1725; Bishop Herbert Croft to Adam Ottley, 22 August 1688, NLW MS 1726; William Hopkins to Arthur Charlett, Lindbridge, 11 June 1688, Ballard MS 13, f. 3; Considerations on ye Bp of Hereford's Discourse conc. ye Reading his Majties late Declaracon, Tanner MS 29, f. 72; *Autobiographies and Letters of Thomas Comber*, 19–20; *HOT*, 3:229; HMC *Kenyon*, 191.

171. *An Answer to a Letter from a Clergyman in the City to his Friend in the Country, containing his Reasons for Reading the Declaration* (1688), 11; William Wake to Arthur Charlett, 19 June 1688, Ballard MS 3, f. 14; *Diary of John Evelyn*, 3:48; *Clarendon Correspondence*, 2:174–177; HRC Bulstrode Newsletters, 8 June, 18 June 1688; *Hatton Correspondence*, 2:81; *Memoirs of Reresby*, 395–396; Morrice, Q267–268, Q274; *Ellis Correspondence*, 2:2; Nichols, *Defense of the doctrine*, 105–106; HMC *Kenyon*, 192.

172. Pincus, *1688*, 198; *Memoirs of Reresby*, 396–397; *Ellis Correspondence*, 2:11–12; Nichols, *Defense of the doctrine*, 106; Commonplace Book of Whitelocke Bulstrode, 30 June 1688, HRC Pforzheimer MS 2k; *Diary of John Evelyn*, 3:49–50; HRC Bulstrode Newsletters, 2 July 1688; HMC *Kenyon*, 191; Newsletter to Dean Jones, NLW Plas Gwyn (Vivian) Papers MS 78.

173. Bishop Lloyd to Archbishop Sancroft, 2 July 1688, Tanner MS 28, f. 114; *Ellis Correspondence*, 61, 163; Draft address to bishops and clergy, Tanner MS 28, ff. 125–127; Some Heads of Things to be more fully insisted upon by ye Bps in ye Addresses to ye Clergy, Tanner MS 28, ff. 121–122; Circular letters, Tanner MS 28, f. 129; Things to be endeavourd after, Tanner MS 28, f. 130; D'Oyly, *Life of Sancroft*, 194–196; Bulman, "Constantine's Enlightenment," 395–397.

174. *Ellis Correspondence*, 2:63; Lee, *Life of Kettlewell*, 392–395; Autobiography of William Wake, LPL MS 2932, f. 31; "The Bishop of Lincoln's Speech to the House of Lords, March 17th, At the Opening of the Second Article of Impeachment against Dr. Sacheverell," in *Complete Collection of State Trials*, 15:503–516; George Every, *The High Church Party, 1688–1718* (London: SPCK, 1956), 22–25; Timothy J. Fawcett, *The Liturgy of Comprehension 1689*, Alcuin Club Collections 54 (Southend-on-Sea: Mahew-McCrimmon, 1973), 16–22; for Sancroft's earlier concern about augmenting poor livings, see Sancroft to Compton, 2 February 1680, CHC MS RN/8/5.

175. James II, *By the King, a Proclamation* [29 June 1688] (London, 1688); *Ellis Correspondence*, 2:61–62; *A Pastoral Letter from the Four Catholic Bishops to the Lay-Catholics of England* (London: Henry Hills, 1688), 2; Dr. Maurice's Draught of an Answer to ye 4 tit. Bps, Tanner MS 29, ff. 147–152.

176. Tanner MS 28, ff. 181–187.

177. Gilbert Burnet to the Prince of Orange, ND, in *Diary of the Times of Charles the Second by the Honourable Henry Sidney*, ed. R. W. Blencowe (London: Henry Coburn, 1843), 281–288; Gilbert Burnet, *A sermon preached in the Chapel of St. James's before his highness the Prince of Orange, the 23rd of December 1688*, 2nd ed. (London, 1689); Claydon, *William III and the Godly Revolution*, 177; Wake Diary, LPL MS 2932, f. 31.

2. The Church in an Age of Projects

1. *Diary of John Evelyn*, ed. William Bray, 4 vols. (London: Bickers and Son, 1906), 3:96–97; John Evelyn to Thomas Tenison, 4 August 1690, BL Add MS 78299, f. 69; on Trinity Chapel, see James Patterson, *Pietas Londinensis* (London, 1714), 277–278; John Strype, ed., *A Survey of the Cities of London and Westminster by John Stow*, 2 vols. (London, 1720), 2, Book 6:73; Thomas Pennant, *Some Account of London*, 5th ed. (London, 1813), 169–170; *The Gentleman's Magazine Library*, ed. George Laurence Gomme (London: Elliot Stock, 1905), Part 16, 283–284; "Hanover Square and neighbourhood," *Old and New London* (1878), 4:314–326, online at British History Online, http://www.british-history.ac.uk/report.aspx?compid=45200.

2. Daniel Defoe, *An Essay upon Projects* (London, 1697), 1–2.

3. Tony Claydon, *William III and the Godly Revolution* (Cambridge: Cambridge University Press, 1996), 177.

4. T. B. Macaulay, *The History of England from the Accession of James the Second* (London: Macmillan, 1914), 5:2274–2282.

5. Steve Pincus, *1688: The First Modern Revolution* (New Haven, CT: Yale University Press, 2009).

6. See Chapter 1.

7. *Memoirs of Mary, Queen of England (1689–1693)*, ed. R. Doebner (Leipzig: Veit and Comp, 1886), 12–13, 15–16; Morrice, Q476; Claydon, *William III and the Godly Revolution*, 94–95.

8. "Memoirs of Nathaniel, Lord Crewe," ed. Andrew Clark, *Camden Miscellany* 9 (London: Camden Society, 1895), 27–29; Thomas Sprat, *A letter from the Bishop of Rochester, to the right honourable the Earl of Dorset and Middlesex* ([London] 1688 [1689]); Thomas Sprat, *The Bishop of Rochester's Second Letter to the Right Honourable the Earl of Dorset and Middlesex*, 2nd ed. (London, 1689); note how in the *Second Letter*, 14–15, Sprat places the London clergy, which he called "the most learned and pious clergy in the world," at the forefront of the crisis, recalling "the terrible aspect of things from court upon the London clergy."

9. Morrice, Q476; compare Edward Chamberlayne, *Angliae Notitia: or, The Present State of England* (London, 1687), 157–158, with Guy Miege, *The New State of England* (London, 1691), Part 3, 162–163; R. O. Bucholz, "The Chapel Royal: Chaplains, 1660–1837," *Office-Holders in Modern Britain: Vol. 11 (revised): Court Officers, 1660–1837* (2006), 251–278. I am very grateful to Dr. Bucholz for his help in tracking changes in the personnel of the Chapel Royal.

10. "A letter written by Dr. Fr. Turner, Bp of Ely to unknown Friend, Dated Febry 17 88 [1689]" BL Add MS 29546.

11. Morrice, Q476.

12. Thomas Birch, *The life of the most reverend Dr. John Tillotson, Lord Archbishop of Canterbury* (London, 1752), 151; Luttrell, 1:546; Morrice, R31.

13. Wake Diary, LPL MS 2932, f. 70.

14. "Life of Stanley," in William Stanley, *The Faith and Practice of a Church of England Man*, ed. Robert Eden (London: William Pickering, 1848), xxii–xxiv.

15. On the centrality of providence in the Anglican defense of the Revolution, see Gerald M. Straka, *Anglican Reaction to the Revolution of 1688* (Madison: State Historical Society of Wisconsin, 1962), 69–79; Gerald M. Straka, "The Final Phase of Divine Right Theory in England, 1688–1702," *EHR* 305 (October 1962): 638–658; J. P. Kenyon, *Revolution Principles: The Politics of Party, 1689–1720* (Cambridge: Cambridge University Press, 1977), 24–29; Claydon, *William III and the Godly Revolution*, 28–52, 231.

16. Luttrell, 1:548; Morrice, Q575; Donald MacLean, ed., *London at Worship, 1689–1690* (Manchester: Presbyterian Historical Society of England, 1928), 7.

17. Abel Campion to Arthur Charlett, 5 February 1688 [1689], Ballard MS 30, f. 18; Morrice, Q430–431, pp. 483–484.

18. George D'Oyly, *The Life of William Sancroft, Archbishop of Canterbury*, 2 vols. (London: John Murray, 1821), 1:438–439; Morrice, Q521; *HOT*, 4:13–14; Birch, *Life of Tillotson*, 329–332.

19. The eleven were Gilbert Burnet, chaplain at the Rolls Chapel (Salisbury, 1689); Edward Fowler, St. Giles's, Cripplegate (Gloucester, 1691); Robert Grove, St. Andrew's, Underhill (Chichester, 1691); Richard Kidder, St. Martin's, Outwich (Bath and Wells, 1691); John Moore, St. Augustine's by St. Paul's (Norwich, 1691); Simon Patrick, St. Paul's, Covent Garden (Chichester, 1689, and Ely, 1691); John Sharp, St. Giles-in-the-Fields (York, 1691); Edward Stillingfleet, dean of St. Paul's (Worcester, 1689); Nicholas Stratford, St. Mary Aldermanbury (Chester, 1689); Thomas Tenison, St. Martin's-in-the-Fields (Lincoln, 1691); and John Tillotson, dean of St. Paul's (Canterbury, 1691).

20. *Letters of Humphrey Prideaux*, ed. E. M. Thompson (London: Camden Society, 1875), 148–149.

21. *A Just censure to the answerer to Vox Cleri* (London, 1690), 8.

22. *Advice to English Protestants, being a sermon preached November the Fifth* (London, 1689), 30.

23. William Wake, *An exhortation to mutual charity and union among Protestants in a sermon preach'd before the King and Queen at Hampton-Court, May 21, 1689* (London, 1689), 33; Wake Diary, LPL MS 2932, f. 67.

24. Gilbert Burnet, *A Sermon Preach'd at the Coronation of William III and Mary II* (London, 1689), 19.

25. John Scott, *A Sermon Preached at Fulham, on Sunday Oct. 13, 1689* (London, 1689), 2–3, 32–33; Anthony Horneck, *A Sermon Preached at Fulham in the Chapel of the Palace, Upon Easter-Day MDCLXXXIX* (London, 1689), 31–32.

26. Robert Brograve, *A Sermon Preach'd before the King and Queen at Hampton Court, May the 12th 1689* (London, 1689), 31; Edmund Hickeringill, *A speech without-doors, or, Some*

modest inquiries humbly proposed to the right honourable the Convention of Estates (London, 1689), 4.

27. "The Autobiography of Symon Patrick," in *The Works of Simon Patrick, D.D.*, ed. Alexander Taylor, 9 vols. (Oxford: Oxford University Press, 1858), 9:516–517; *The Correspondence of Henry Hyde, Earl of Clarendon*, 2 vols. (London: Henry Colburn, 1828), 2:240.

28. *An Address of the Dissenting Ministers (in and about the City of London) to the King and Queen upon their Accession to the Crown* (London, 1689); Morrice, Q488; Edmund Calamy, *An Abridgement of Mr. Baxter's History of His Life and Times*, 2 vols. (London, 1713), 1:423–425.

29. *Clarendon Correspondence*, 2:240.

30. *Several Arguments for Concessions and Alterations in the Common Prayer, and in the Rites and Ceremonies of the Church of England in order to a Comprehension* (London, 1689), 1, 13; John Humphreys, *The Healing Attempt* (London, 1689), 2; [Gilbert Burnet?], *A Letter from a Minister in the Country to a Member of the Convocation* (London, 1689), 18; Gilbert Burnet, *An Exhortation to Peace and Union*, 2nd ed. (London, 1689), 10–11.

31. *The Grievances of the Church of England, which are not in the Power of the Governours of it to Remedy* (London, 1689); *Proposals Tender'd to the Consideration of Both Houses of Parliament, for Uniting the Protestant Interest* (London, 1689), 10–11.

32. "Reasons for an Union Between the Church and the Dissenters," in *The Works of the Right Honourable Henry late L. Delamer and Earl of Warrington* (London, 1694), 463–466.

33. Campion to Charlett, 2 April 1689, Ballard MS 30, f. 26.

34. Edward Stephens, *A Specimen of a Declaration against Debauchery Tendered to the Consideration of his Highness the Prince of Orange, and of the Present Convention of the Nation* (London, 1689).

35. John Evelyn to [Sidney Godolphin?], November 1688, BL Add MS 78299, f. 53; on these proposals, see Steve Pincus, "John Evelyn: Revolutionary," in *John Evelyn and His Milieu*, ed. Frances Harris and Michael Hunter (London: British Library, 2003), 185–219.

36. *Diary of John Evelyn*, 3:73–74.

37. Edmund Hickeringill, *The Ceremony-monger, his character* (London, 1689), sig A4r.

38. *An Expedient for Peace among Christians, the Second Part* (London, 1689), 30–31.

39. *The Amicable Reconciliation of the Dissenters to the Church of England* (London, 1689); Edmund Elys to William Sancroft, 6 April 1689, Tanner MS 27, f. 5; *King William's Toleration: Being, An Explanation of that Liberty of Religion, Which May be Expected from His Majesty's Declaration, with a Bill for Comprehension and Indulgence* (London, 1689), 16.

40. Francis Bacon, *Certain Considerations for the better Establishment of the Church of England* (London, 1689), preface.

41. Herbert Croft, *The Naked Truth, or, The True State of the Primitive Church* (London, 1689); John Spurr, "The Church of England, Comprehension and the Toleration Act of 1689," *EHR* 413 (October 1989): 943.

42. "The Reverend Dean of Pauls His Proposals or Terms of Union, betwixt the Church of England and the Dissenters," in *Proposals Tender'd*, 25–31.

43. Edward Chamberlayne, *England's Wants; or, Several Proposals Very Advantageous for England* (London, 1689); Sir Richard Bulkeley, one of the founders of the reformation of manners movement, was also at this time urging the new monarchs to divert funds toward

a variety of social welfare institutions, including schools, workhouses, and relief funds for decayed tradesmen and young women in need of marriage portions; see A. G. Craig, "The Movement for the Reformation of Manners, 1688–1715" (PhD diss., University of Edinburgh, 1980), 10–11.

44. HMC *Finch*, 2:194; Henry Horwitz, *Revolution Politicks: The Career of Daniel Finch, Second Earl of Nottingham* (Cambridge: Cambridge University Press, 1968), 86–95.

45. Henry Compton to William Sancroft, n.d. [April 1689], Tanner MS 27, f. 50; "An Act for the Uniting their Majesties Protestant Subjects," BL Harleian MS 1237, ff. 1–2.

46. Morrice, Q527.

47. Lady Mary Kemeys to Sir Charles Kemeys, 3 December 1689, NLW Kemeys-Tynte 2 C162; Commonplace Book of Whitelocke Bulstrode, 16 April 1689, HRC Pforzheimer MS 2k.

48. Morrice, Q504; HMC *Portland* 3:434.

49. On the parliamentary negotiations over the oaths, see John Findon, "The Nonjurors and the Church of England, 1689–1714" (PhD diss., Oxford University, 1978), 4–17.

50. *Diary of John Evelyn*, 3:76.

51. Daniel Whitby to Arthur Charlett, 9 April 1689, Ballard MS 34, f. 16.

52. Craig Rose, *England in the 1690s* (Malden, MA: Blackwell, 1999), 214–215; Tim Harris, *Revolution: The Great Crisis of the British Monarchy, 1685–1720* (London: Penguin, 2007), 350–351; A. Campion to Arthur Charlett, 14 May 1689, Ballard MS 30, f. 20; [William Cade], "The Close of a Sermon preach't at Christ Church Cant. March 9, 1689 on 2 Cor VI.4," BL Harleian MS 5790, ff. 169–170.

53. A. Campion to Arthur Charlett, 2 April 1689, Ballard MS 30, f. 26; Earl of Clarendon to Tenison, 9 April 1689, BL Add MS 3512, f. 38; William Nichols, *A Defense of the Doctrine and Discipline of the Church of England*, 3rd ed. (London, 1730), 109–110; Birch, *Life of Tillotson*, 179–180.

54. *Journal of the House of Commons* 10 (1688–1693), 86–87; Morrice, Q539, Q540; HMC *Downshire* I, 1:308; *Journal of the Very Rev. Rowland Davies, LL.D. Dean of Ross (and afterward Dean of Cork)* (London: Camden Society, 1857), 6; Edward Calamy, *An Historical Account of My Own Life with some Reflections on the Times I have Lived in*, ed. John Towill Rutt, 2nd ed., 2 vols. (London: Henry Coburn and Richard Bentley, 1830), 1:202–203.

55. *The memoirs of the Honorable Sir John Reresby, Baronet* (London, 1734), 195; *HOT*, 4:20–21; and see John Hampden to Rev. Mr. Tallents, 27 May 1693, BL Stowe 747, f. 16.

56. Keith Feling, *A History of the Tory Party, 1640–1714* (Oxford: Clarendon, 1924), 263–266.

57. Morrice, Q558.

58. *HOT*, 4:54.

59. Morrice, Q601.

60. Commission printed in Timothy J. Fawcett, *The Liturgy of Comprehension 1689*, Alcuin Club Collections 54 (Southend-on-Sea: Mahew-McCrimmon, 1973), 26–27; HMC *Downshire* I, 1:328; *A glance on the Ecclesiastical Commission* (London, 1690), 12.

61. Morrice, Q635; Burnet reportedly attributed the withdrawal of Jane and Aldrich to the influence of the Earl of Clarendon, who denied it; see "Diary of Henry Earl of Clarendon," *Clarendon Correspondence*, 2:295.

62. Fawcett, *Liturgy of Comprehension*, 26–30, has a very useful prosopographical analysis of the composition of the ecclesiastical commission; see also George Every, *The High Church Party, 1688–1718* (London: SPCK, 1956), 43–44.

63. John Tillotson to Lady Russell, 19 September 1689, BL Add MS 4236, ff. 21–22.

64. HMC *Portland*, 3:466; *Diary of John Evelyn*, 3:94.

65. Thomas Tenison, *A discourse concerning the Ecclesiastical Commission, open'd in the Jerusalem-Chamber, October the 10th, 1689* (London, 1689); and see Thomas Comber to Simon Patrick, 19 October 1689, Tanner MS 27, f. 93; Morrice, Q635; on John Locke's opinion of the commission, see Mark Goldie, "John Locke, Jonas Proast and Religious Toleration, 1688–1692," in *The Church of England, c. 1689–c. 1833*, ed. John Walsh, Colin Haydon, and Stephen Taylor (Cambridge: Cambridge University Press, 1993), 157.

66. *A Just censure*, 8; Thomas Long, *Vox cleri, or, the sense of the clergy concerning the making of alterations in the established liturgy* (London, 1690), 16.

67. William Jane, *A Letter to a Friend, containing some quaeries about the new commission for making alterations in the liturgy, canons, &c. of the Church of England* (London, 1689), 4.

68. William Payne, *An Answer to Vox Cleri* (London, 1690), 4.

69. MacLean, *London at Worship*, 13; Jane, *Letter to a Friend*, 6.

70. "Autobiography of Symon Patrick," 9:522–523; George Royce to Robert Nelson, 1 April 1690, BL Add MS 45511, f. 39.

71. Every, *High Church Party*, 46–47.

72. Richard Kidder included a schema of his new translations of the psalms in his autobiography, *The Life of Richard Kidder, D.D., Bishop of Bath and Wells Written by Himself*, ed. Amy Edith Robinson, Somerset Record Society, vol. 37 (London: Butler and Tanner, 1924), 50–59.

73. [Burnet?], *A Letter from a Minister in the Country*, 25. Timothy Fawcett (*Liturgy of Comprehension*, 32) has persuasively suggested that the author of this pamphlet was Gilbert Burnet, or at the very least one of the bishops involved in the commission, although some suspected that John Tillotson was the author of this work; Ralph Bridges to William Trumbull, 16 January 1711, BL Add MS 72495, f. 42.

74. As Fawcett notes (*Liturgy of Comprehension*, 245 n. 60), several of the commissioners were strong advocates for weekly communions, already established in at least ten churches in London.

75. "Concessions which will probably be made by the Church of England for the union of Protestants, which I sent to the Earl of Portland by Dr. Stillingfleet, Sept 13, 1689," BL Add MS 4236, f. 19.

76. Morrice, Q601, Q611, Q622.

77. Fawcett, *Liturgy of Comprehension*, 58.

78. Morrice, Q647, Q648.

79. "Diary of John Williams," in Fawcett, *Liturgy of Comprehension*, 176.

80. "Diary of John Williams," in Fawcett, *Liturgy of Comprehension*, 170.

81. "Diary of John Williams," in Fawcett, *Liturgy of Comprehension*, 176.

82. This did not stop Richard Baxter from praying for "a blessed effect of convocation," see MacLean, *London at Worship*, 16.

83. *HOT*, 4:57–58; Morrice, Q647; the names of the members of the 1689 convocation are listed in Long, *Vox cleri*, 60–62.

84. William Wake to Arthur Charlett, 9 November [1689], Ballard MS 3, f. 53.

85. HMC *Portland*, 3:441.

86. Jane, *Letter to a Friend*, 6; Henry Maurice, *Remarks from the country, upon the two letters relating to the convocation and alterations in the liturgy* (London, 1690), 16.

87. Morrice, Q673; and see *Diary of John Evelyn*, 3:81.

88. MacLean, *London at Worship*, 24.

89. Morrice, Q674; Luttrell, 1:607; Long, *Vox cleri*, 7.

90. James Newton to Arthur Charlett, 21 November 1689, Ballard MS 22, f. 50; HMC *Downshire* 1:328; White Kennett, *A Complete History of England*, 3 vols. (London, 1706), 3:552; Luttrell, 1:607; Long, *Vox cleri*, 62–63.

91. George Royce to Robert Nelson, 18 January 1689/90, BL Add MS 45511, f. 34; also see White Kennett's memorandum in BL Lansdowne MS 1039, f. 7.

92. Payne, *Answer to Vox Cleri*, 5.

93. HMC *Seventh Report*, Part 2, Ormonde MSS, 759; John Hutton to Arthur Charlett, 28 November 1689, Ballard MS 35, f. 85; Morrice, R10; "Diary of Clarendon," 295; Birch, *Life of Tillotson*, 202.

94. Kennett, *Complete History*, 3:552.

95. Thomas Tenison, *A Discourse concerning the Ecclesiastical Commission* (London, 1689), 21; William Wake to Arthur Charlett, 7 November [1689], Ballard MS 3, f. 53.

96. [Burnet?], *Letter from a Minister in the Country*, 18, 26–27.

97. [Humphrey Prideaux], *A Letter to a Friend Relating to the present Convocation at Westminster* (London, 1690), 17–18.

98. W. Heyler to Arthur Charlett, 7[?] December 1689, Ballard MS 38, f. 123; "Diary of Clarendon," 297; the commission and message are printed in Long, *Vox cleri*, 63–67; Kennett, *Complete History*, 3:552–554; also see the summary in Morrice, R29.

99. Long, *Vox cleri*, 67–68; Kennett, *Complete History*, 3:554.

100. Morrice, R29, R30; "Autobiography of Symon Patrick," 9:527–529.

101. "Loyal address by both Houses of Convocation to William III, 1689," LPL Gibson MS 934, §42; Long, *Vox cleri*, 67–69; Kennett, *Complete History*, 3:554–555; Morrice, R29, R30, R38, R41; Birch, *Life of Tillotson*, 204–206.

102. Long, *Vox cleri*, 72.

103. Brent S. Sirota, "The Trinitarian Crisis in Church and State: Religious Controversy and the Making of the Postrevolutionary Church of England, 1687–1702," *Journal of British Studies* 52, 1 (January 2013): 26–54.

104. Morrice, R48; Long, *Vox cleri*, 69, 72; Kennett, *Complete History*, 3:555.

105. "I am now convinced," noted Burnet in his "Autobiography," "that if ever our Church is to be set right, it must be by some such method, and not by a majority in Convocation, for little good is to be expected from the Sinodicall Meetings of the clergy"; H. C. Foxcroft, ed., *A Supplement to Burnet's History of My Own Time* (Oxford: Clarendon, 1902), 498.

106. *Diary of John Evelyn*, 3:82; White Kennett to Samuel Blackwell, 21 December 1689, BL Lansdowne MS 1013, f. 21; Long, *Vox cleri*, 56; "Diary of Clarendon," 297; *The life of the Reverend Humphrey Prideaux* (London, 1748), 57–58; Maurice, *Remarks from the country*; William Bassett, *A Vindication of the Two Letters concerning Alterations in the Liturgy* (London, 1690); Payne, *Answer to Vox Cleri* (London, 1690); *A just censure; Vox Populi; or, the Sense of the Sober Lay-Men of the Church of England* (London, 1690); *The Judgment of Foreign Divines Concerning the Liturgy and Ceremonies of the Church of England* (London, 1690); as late as

September 1690, the nonjuror George Hickes was advocating circulating anticomprehension literature "to some of the London divines who are not of the latitudinarian party," George Hickes to Arthur Charlett, 6 September 1690, Ballard MS 12, f. 65.

107. "Diary of Clarendon," 299; Morrice, R87; and see Dr. Hollings to Arthur Charlett, 18 January 1690, Ballard MS 34, f. 46.

108. Kennett to Blackwell, 8 February 1689 [1690], BL Lansdowne MS 1013, f. 18; Morrice, R111; "Diary of Clarendon," 304; on the continued meetings of the deprived bishops at Lambeth, see White Kennett's ecclesiastical diary, BL Lansdowne MS 1024, f. 71.

109. Morrice, Q662.

110. Sirota, "Trinitarian Crisis," 36–48.

111. James Harrington to Arthur Charlett, 18 March [1690], Ballard MS 22, f. 15; Morrice, R129.

112. *His Majesties Letter to the Lord Bishop of London. To be Communicated to the Two Provinces of Canterbury and York* (London, 1690); *Diary of John Evelyn*, 3:83; Morrice, R117. Dudley Bahlmann's crucial misdating of these injunctions to February 1689 strengthens his case for a "moral revolution" immediately consequent upon the political revolution, when in fact the injunctions appeared only after the failure of the ecclesiastical settlement in early 1690 (Bahlmann, *The Moral Revolution of 1688* [New Haven, CT: Yale University Press, 1957], 22. This error is repeated in Tina Isaacs, "Moral Crime, Moral Reform and the State in Early Eighteenth Century England: A Study of Piety and Politics" (PhD diss., University of Rochester, 1979), 66.

113. On this point, see Craig, "Movement for the Reformation of Manners," 262–263.

114. *Life of Prideaux*, 67–71; Jeremy Gregory, "The Eighteenth Century Reformation: The Pastoral Task of Anglican Clergy after 1689," in *The Church of England, c. 1689–c. 1833*, 83–85; for the reverberations of these efforts in Ireland, see T. C. Barnard, "Reforming Irish Manners: The Religious Societies in Dublin during the 1690s," *HJ* 35 (December 1992): 805–838.

115. Gilbert Burnet, *Injunctions for the Arch-Deacons of the Diocess of Sarum* (London, 1690); Burnet later claimed that his vigorous efforts in his diocese stemmed directly from the failure of the 1689 convocation, Foxcroft, ed., *Supplement*, 504.

116. Burnet, *Injunctions*, 3; on contemporary concerns over abuses of the Toleration Act, see Humphrey Prideaux, "A Circular Letter to the Clergy of the Arch-Deaconry of Suffolk" [17 August 1692], appended to Humphrey Prideaux, *Directions to Church-Wardens for the Faithful Discharge of their Office*, 3rd ed. (London, 1713), 104–119; Edward Bowerman to Thomas Tenison, 17 December 1692, LPL Gibson MS 933, §9.

117. Simon Patrick, *A Letter of the Bishop of Chester to His Clergy* (London, 1690).

118. Nicholas Stratford, *The Bishop of Chester's Charge in his Primary Visitation at Chester, May 5, 1691* (London, 1692).

119. Richard Kidder, *The Charge of Richard, Lord Bishop of Bath and Wells to the Clergy of his Diocese at his Primary Visitation, Begun at Axebridge, June 2, 1692* (London, 1693); on the details of this visitation, see *Life of Kidder*, 64–72.

120. Edward Stillingfleet, *The Bishop of Worcester's Charge to the Clergy of his Diocese in His Primary Visitation, Begun at Worcester Sept. 11, 1690* (London, 1691).

121. Henry Compton, *The Bishop of London's Eighth Letter to his Clergy, Upon a Conference How they Ought to behave Themselves under the Toleration* (London, 1692), 10–13; and see

Compton's "Instructions for a Rural Dean" issued at this time, Bodl. Rawlinson C 984, ff. 123–124.

122. Birch, *Life of Tillotson*, 287–288; Foxcroft, ed., *Supplement*, 506.

123. Gilbert Burnet, *A Discourse of the Pastoral Care* (London, 1692), sig A4, xiv–xvi, 184–191, 193–194, 205; and see T. E. S. Clarke and H. C. Foxcroft, *A Life of Gilbert Burnet, Bishop of Salisbury* (Cambridge: Cambridge University Press, 1907), 309–314.

124. John Tillotson to Gilbert Burnet, 12 April 1692, in Birch, *Life of Tillotson*, 290–292.

125. *Memoirs of Mary*, 31, 41.

126. Tillotson to Nelson, 15 June 1691, CHC MS RN/1/8.

127. George Hickes to Arthur Charlett, 19 September 1691, Ballard MS 12, f. 70; Henry Horwitz, "Comprehension in the Later Seventeenth Century: A Postscript," *Church History* 34 (September 1965): 342–348; in a sermon of October 1692, Robert South warned about "some projectors amongst us" laboring "to transform, mangle and degrade [the Church's] noble constitution to the homely, mechanic model of those Republican, imperfect churches abroad"; Robert South, *Sermons Preached Upon Several Occasions*, 6 vols. (London, 1737), 2:448.

128. HMC *Portland*, 3:486; Craig, "Movement for the Reformation of Manners," 58–59; *A proclamation against vitious, debauched, and profane persons* (London, 1692).

129. Archbishop Tillotson, "The Heads of a Circular Letter to ye Suffragan Bishops of ye province of Canterbury" [1692], Tanner MS 25, ff. 15–16.

130. John Tillotson to Gilbert Burnet, 12 April 1692, in Birch, *Life of Tillotson*, 291.

131. See "Injunctions given by the king's majesty to the archbishops of this realm, to be communicated by them to the bishops and the rest of the clergy" [15 February 1695]; and "The archbishop's letter to the bishops of his province" [16 July 1695], in Edward Cardwell, ed. *Documentary Annals of the Reformed Church of England* (Oxford: Oxford University Press, 1844), 2:380–388.

132. Sirota, "Trinitarian Crisis," 44–50.

133. Horwitz, "Comprehension," 342–348; and see Atterbury to Trelawny, 20 February 1701, Atterbury Correspondence, 3:27.

134. On fast days, see Claydon, *William III and the Godly Revolution*, 100–110; Rose, *England in the 1690s*, 201–205.

135. J. Wickham Legg, *English Church Life from the Restoration to the Tractarian Movement* (London: Longmans, Green, 1914); Walter Besant, *London in the Eighteenth Century* (London: Adam and Charles Black, 1925), 622–624.

136. The October 1692 list of religious societies is printed in Craig, "Movement for the Reformation of Manners," 82–83; Josiah Woodward, *An Account of the Rise and Progress of the Religious Societies in the City of London, &c.*, 2nd ed. (London, 1698), 65; *A Short account of the several kinds of societies, set up of late years, for carrying on reformation of manners, and propagation of Christian Knowledge* (London, 1700), 1–2; on the spread of religious societies outside the capital, see W. M. Jacob, *Lay People and Religion in the Early Eighteenth Century* (Cambridge: Cambridge University Press, 1996), 77–92.

137. Thomas Zouch, "Memoir of Sir George Wheler," in *The Works of the Rev. Thomas Zouch*, 2 vols. (York: F. C. and J. Rivington, 1820), 2:179–182; E. G. Wheler, ed., *Autobiography of Sir George Wheler* (Birmingham: Cornish Brothers, 1911), 5–6.

138. MacLean, *London at Worship*, 8.

139. [Edward Stephens], *The Beginning and Progress of a Needful and Hopeful Reformation in England* (London, 1691), 4–5; Craig, "Movement for the Reformation of Manners," 23, 25–26.

140. HMC *Portland*, 3:471.

141. Edward Fowler, *A Vindication of a Late Undertaking of Certain Gentlemen, In Order to the Suppressing of Debauchery and Profaneness* (London, 1692), 7–8, 13.

142. Craig, "Movement for the Reformation of Manners," 40–66; Bahlmann, *The Moral Revolution*, 17–22.

143. Woodward, *Account of the Rise and Progress*, 83–85.

144. On the secularity of the societies, see Isaacs, "Moral Crime," 19–20; for a useful corrective, see Jeremy Gregory, "The Making of a Protestant Nation: 'Success' and 'Failure' in England's Long Reformation," in *England's Long Reformation 1500–1800*, ed. Nicholas Tyacke (London: UCL Press, 1998), 322–324.

145. *Proposals for a National Reformation of Manners* (London, 1694), 4.

146. The first society for the reformation of manners began to commission quarterly sermons around 1697; their frequency was reduced to twice a year in 1699, and annually in 1705. For a complete list of preachers, see Craig, "Movement for Reformation of Manners," 217–222; for an overview of sermon themes, see Karen Sonnelitter, "The Reformation of Manners Societies, the Monarchy, and the English State, 1696–1714," *Historian* 72 (Fall 2010), 517–542.

147. *Proposals for a National Reformation of Manners*, 22–23.

148. [Stephens], *Beginning and Progress*, 4; Edward Stephens, *A Plain Relation of the Late Action at Sea Between the English & Dutch and the French Fleets* (London, 1690), 31, 40; Edward Stephens, *A Seasonable and Necessary Admonition to the Gentlemen of the First Society for Reformation of Manners concerning reforming of themselves, of the bishops, and of the House of Commons* (London, 1700), 6; White Kennett to Samuel Blackwell, n.d. [ca. 1691], BL Lansdowne MS 1013, f. 19.

149. [Stephens], *Beginning and Progress*, 10.

150. Craig, "Movement for the Reformation of Manners," 83–88, transcribes the lengthy 11 October 1692 letter to the religious societies in full; and see T. C. Curtis and W. A. Speck, "The Societies for the Reformation of Manners: A Case Study in the Theory and Practice of Moral Reform," *Literature and History* 3 (1976): 45–64.

151. Stephens, *Plain Relation of the Late Action*, 32–36; *Proposals for a National Reformation of Manners*, 18.

152. Craig Rose, "Providence, Protestant Union and Godly Reformation in the 1690s," *Transactions of the Royal Historical Society* 3, 6th series (1993): 151–169; for the limitations on ecumenical sentiment, see T. Isaacs, "The Anglican Hierarchy and the Reformation of Manners, 1688–1738," *JEH* 33 (1982): 391–411.

153. Daniel Chadwick, *A Sermon preach'd at St. Mary in Nottingham to the Society for the Reformation of Manners on July the 6th* (London, 1698), 47–48.

154. Woodward, *Account of the Rise and Progress*, 53–55; on the broader Restoration critique of associational life, see the Introduction.

155. Samuel Wesley, *A Sermon concerning reformation of manners preach'd at St. James Church, Westminster* (London, 1698), 1, 15.

156. Samuel Bradford, *A Sermon preach'd at the Church of St. Mary le Bow to the Societies for the Reformation of Manners, Octob. 4, 1697* (London, 1697), 17; John Russell, *A Sermon preach'd at St. Mary-le-Bow to the Societies for the Reformation of Manners, June 28, 1697* (London, 1697), 38; Josiah Woodward, *The Duty of Compassion to the souls of others endeavoring their Reformation* (London, 1697), viii.

157. *Short account of the several kinds of societies*, 1; White Kennett to Samuel Blackwell, 16 September 1707, BL Lansdowne MS 1013, f. 111.

158. Francis Grant Cullen, *A brief account of the nature, rise and progress of the societies for reformation of manners, &c. in England and Ireland* (Edinburgh, 1700), 13; Gilbert Burnet, *Charitable reproof, a sermon preached at the Church of St. Mary-le-Bow to the Societies for the Reformation of Manners, the 25th of March 1700* (London, 1700), 27.

159. See John Spurr, " 'Virtue, Religion, and Government': The Anglican Uses of Providence," in *The Politics of Religion in Restoration England*, ed. Tim Harris, Paul Seaward, and Mark Goldie (Oxford: Basil Blackwell, 1990), 29–47.

160. Although Faramerz Dabhoiwala has illuminated the paradoxical ways in which the reformation of manners movement accelerated the professionalization of policing, see Dabhoiwala, "Sex and Societies for Moral Reform, 1688–1800," *Journal of British Studies* 46, 2 (April 2007): 290–319.

161. Wesley, *Sermon concerning reformation of manners*, 13–14; Woodward, *Duty of Compassion*, vii.

162. Chadwick, *Sermon preach'd at St. Mary*, 46.

163. Bradford, *Sermon preach'd at the Church of St. Mary le Bow*, 17–18; Strype, *Survey of London and Westminster*, 2:30; and see the Huguenot internationalist Pierre Jurieu's response to the societies reported in Woodward, *Account of the Rise and Progress*, 8.

164. Frank J. Klingberg, "Evolution of the Humanitarian Spirit in Eighteenth Century England," *Pennsylvania Magazine of History & Biography* 66 (July 1942): 260–278.

165. Geoffrey Nuttall, "Assembly and Association in Dissent, 1689–1831," in *Studies in Church History*, ed. G. J. Cumming and D. Baker (Cambridge: Cambridge University Press, 1971), 7:289–309.

166. J. M. Cramp, *Baptist History* (London: Elliot Stock, 1868), 462–463.

167. Nuttall, "Assembly and Association," 304–305.

168. Alexander Gordon, ed., *Freedom after Ejection* (Manchester: Manchester University Press, 1917), 155–156; and see the "Bristol Articles" for "a general correspondence of all the united ministers throughout the kingdom," among Robert Nelson's papers, CHC MS RN/8/39.

169. R. Thomas, "The Break-up of Nonconformity," in *The Beginnings of Nonconformity*, Hibbert Lectures for 1962 (London: James Clarke, 1964), 33–60; Richard Taylor, *A History of the Union between the Presbyterian and Congregational Ministers, in and about London, and the causes of the breach of it* (London, 1698).

170. Michael Watts, *The Dissenters: From the Reformation to the French Revolution*, 2 vols. (Oxford: Clarendon, 1978), 1:289–297.

171. William C. Braithwaite, *The Second Period of Quakerism* (York: William Sessions, 1979), 274–286; N. C. Hunt, *Two Early Political Associations* (Oxford: Clarendon, 1961), 14; Watts, *The Dissenters*, 300–303.

172. John Kettlewell to Bishop William Lloyd, 20 December 1694, OSB MSS File 8348; John Kettlewell, About settling a fund of charity for relief of the needy suffering Clergy & ye regular collection and distribution thereof [January 1694/95], CHC MS RN/4/1.

173. John Kettlewell, "Model of a Fund of Charity for the Needy, Suffering Clergy," in *A compleat collection of the works of the Reverend and learned John Kettlewell*, 2 vols. (London, 1719), 2: appendix, xxv–xxvi; "The Answer of Thomas Bath and Wells to certain Interrogatories proposed to him by the Lords of the Privy Council," in *Compleat collection of works of Kettlewell*, 2: appendix, xxviii–xxix; *The Life of Thomas Firmin, Late Citizen of London* (London, 1791), 19–22, 44–46, 55–56; *Journal of Rowland Davies*, 9–10, 18, 20, 21, 25, 26; Francis Lee, *Memoirs of the Life of Mr. John Kettlewell* (London, 1718), 130, 417–422; and see Thomas Lathbury, *A History of the Nonjurors: their controversies and writings* (London: William Pickering, 1845), 163–167; C. F. Secretan, *Memoirs of the Life and Times of the Pious Robert Nelson* (London: John Murray, 1860), 53–55.

174. *The Charitable Samaritan: Or, A Short and Impartial Account of that Eminent and Publick-Spirited Sermon Citizen, Mr. Tho. Firmin* (London, 1698); Stephen Nye, *An Account of Mr. Firmin's religion, and the present state of the Unitarian controversy* (London, 1698), 50.

175. Thomas Watts, *The Christian indeed, and faithful pastor: impartially represented in a practical essay, and historical account of the exemplary life and works of the late eminent William Assheton, D.D.* (London, 1714), 191–192; William Assheton, *A full account of the rise, progress & advantages of Dr. Assheton's proposal* (London, 1708); Robert Bishop to Robert Nelson, 3 May 1708, CHC MS RN/1/19; and see White Kennett's 1698 proposal for a college of clergymen's sons, Tanner MS 22, ff. 1–2.

176. Mary Ransome, "The Parliamentary Career of Sir Humphrey Mackworth, 1701–1713," *Birmingham Journal of History* 1 (1947–1948): 232–254; SPCK memo on Mine Adventurers, n.d., BL Harleian MS 7190, f. 93; for Robert Nelson's Mine Adventurers material, see CHC RN/6.

177. Diary of Humphrey Mackworth, NLW MS 14362E (D. Rhys Phillips MS 1), 113.

178. Charles Gildon, "A Proposal of a Method of Restoring the Clergy the Long Alienated Impropriations Made to His Grace the Lord Archbishop of Canterbury" [ca. 1700], LPL Gibson MS 933, §51; Charles Leslie, *An Essay concerning the Divine Right of Tythes* (London, 1700), 229; Mackworth Diary [March 1703], NLW MS 14362E, 146.

179. Wickham Legg, *English Church Life*, 281–314; Paul Slack, *From Reformation to Improvement: Public Welfare in Early Modern England* (Oxford: Clarendon, 1999), 148–149; Bridget Hill, "A Refuge from Men: The Idea of a Protestant Nunnery," *Past and Present* 117 (November 1987): 107–130.

180. Thomas Tanner, *Notitia Monastica, Or, A Short History of the Religious Houses in England and Wales* (Oxford, 1695), preface; Edward Stephens, *The Life of St. Antony* (London, 1697), preface; Tanner was careful to pay tribute to the vast sums "that Protestants have given, or laid out for the public good since the Reformation in works of piety and charity, for the promotion of learning, the relief of the poor, and the honor of the nation." See also Francis Atterbury, "The Power of Charity to Cover Sin, A Sermon Preach'd before the President and Governors of Bridewell and Bethlehem, in Bridewell-Chapel, August xvi, 1694," in *Sermons and Discourses on Several Subjects*, 2 vols. (London, 1723), 1:74–84; John Evelyn, *Numismata, or, A Discourse of Medals Ancient and Modern* (London, 1697), 265.

181. Maurice Wheeler to Archbishop Thomas Tenison, 11 February 1698/99, LPL Gibson MS 929, §49.

182. Edward Stephens, *The More Excellent Way, Or, A Proposal for a Compleat Work of Charity* (1696); Samuel Brewster to Thomas Tanner, 10 July 1697, Tanner MS 23, f. 69; Edward Stephens to Thomas Tanner, September 1697, Tanner 23, f. 70; Eamon Duffy, "Primitive Christianity Revived: Religious Renewal in Augustan England," in *Studies in Church History* 14 (1977): 297–298.

183. George Wheler, *The Protestant Monastery: Or, Christian Oeconomicks, Containing Directions for the Religious Conduct of a Family* (1698), 13–19.

184. Wheler cited both the *Serious Proposal* by "an ingenious lady" and "proposals of the same nature by Mr. Stevens [*sic*]" in *Protestant Monastery*, 18; Mary Astell, *A Serious Proposal to the Ladies for the Advancement of their True and Greatest Interest*, 2 parts (London, 1697), 36, 43, 45–46, 51, 53–54, 90–91; and see Hannah Smith, "Mary Astell, *A Serious Proposal to the Ladies* (1694), and the Anglican Reformation of Manners in Late-Seventeenth-Century England," in *Mary Astell: Reason, Gender, Faith*, ed. William Kolbrenner and Michal Michelson (Aldershot: Ashgate, 2007), 31–48; Sarah Apetrei, *Women, Feminism and Religion in Early Enlightenment England* (Cambridge: Cambridge University Press, 2010).

185. Defoe, *Essay upon Projects*, 282–286; Hill, "Idea of a Protestant Nunnery," 118.

186. Lewis Maidwell, *A Scheme for a Publick Academy, some Reasons for its Institution, the Common Objections answer'd, with the Easie Method of its Support* (London, 1700).

187. C. Roderick to Arthur Charlett, 29 January 1700, Ballard MS 23, f. 45; Thomas Greene to Arthur Charlett, 27 February 1699/1700, Ballard MS 9, f. 106; Thomas Greene to Arthur Charlett, 11 April 1700, Ballard MS 9, f. 108; William Finch to Arthur Charlett, 28 February 1699/1700, Ballard MS 20, f. 10; Matthew Hutton to Arthur Charlett, 23 January 1704, Ballard MS 35, f. 127; William Bromley to Arthur Charlett, 23 December 1704, Ballard MS 38, f. 142; Lewis Maidwell to Robert Harley, 28 July 1705, BL Add MS 70276; and see the collected reports on Maidwell's project in BL Add MS 70324, ff. 91, 126–129.

188. "Dr. Wallis' Letter against Mr. Maidwell, 1700," is transcribed with commentary in C. R. L. Fletcher, ed., *Collectanea*, 1st series (Oxford, 1885): 269–337.

189. Bahlmann, *Moral Revolution*, 83–97; Isaacs, "Anglican Hierarchy," 391–411; Isaacs, "Moral Crime," 265–307.

190. Josiah Woodward, *Account of the societies for reformation of manners in London and Westminster, and other parts of the kingdom* (London, 1699); Bishop Nicholas Stratford to William Gilpin, 6 April 1700, BL Add MS 34265, f. 57.

191. A. Tindal Hart, *The Life and Times of John Sharp, Archbishop of York* (London: SPCK, 1949), 179.

192. Thomas Sharp, *The Life of John Sharp, D.D.*, 2 vols. (London: C. and J. Rivington, 1825), 1:170–189.

193. William Nicolson to Mr. Wootton, 13 April 1700, BL Add MS 34265, f. 59.

194. William Nicolson to Archbishop John Sharp, 15 February 1699, BL Add MS 34265, f. 47.

195. William Nicolson to Mr. Gilpin, 26 April 1700, BL Add MS 34265, f. 60; William Nicolson to Francis Yates, 15 March 1699, BL Add MS 34265, f. 55; Gilpin to Chamberlayne, 18 April 1700, CUL SPCK MS D2/2, §87.

196. Archbishop Thomas Tenison to Archbishop John Sharp, 7 April 1699; quoted in Craig, "Movement for Reformation of Manners," 267–268.

197. Archbishop Sharp to William Nicolson, 27 February 1700, in Sharp, *Life of John Sharp*, 182–186; Hart, *Life and Times of John Sharp*, 183–184; compare with the attitude of the Tory George Bull, who vigorously supported the societies as archdeacon of Llandaff and after becoming bishop of St. David's in 1705 recommended them to his own clergy, George Bull, circular letter to the archdeacons and clergy of St. David's [c. 1709], NLW MS 1484E, ff. 43–45; and see Robert Nelson, *The life of Dr. George Bull, late lord Bishop of St. David's* (London, 1713), 366–369, 441–452.

198. When White Kennett contemplated precedents for these modern organizations, he lit upon two failed enterprises, the Elizabethan Society of Antiquaries (1586–1607) and the pre-Civil War Feoffees for Impropriations (1626–1633), "two excellent and great designs both nipped in the bud, one for raising the jealousy of the state, the other of the Church"; White Kennett to Thomas Tanner, 26 August 1699, Tanner MS 21, f. 148.

199. *Angliae Tutamen: or, The Safety of England* (London, 1695), 23; on the failure of "projects," see *The Poor Man's Petition to the Lords and Gentlemen of the Kingdom: Or, England's Cry for Peace* (London, 1693), 4.

200. George Meriton, *Immorality, debauchery and profaneness exposed to the reproof of Scripture, and the censure of the law* (London, 1698), sig. A4; Chadwick, *Sermon preach'd at St. Mary*, 20–21; Matthew Hole, *The true reformation of manners, or, The nature and qualifications of true zeal in a sermon preach'd in the parish Church at Bridgewater* (Oxford, 1699), 25–26; George Stanhope, *The duty of rebuking. A sermon preach'd at Bow-Church, December the 28th. 1702. Before the Right Honourable the Lord-Mayor and aldermen of London, And the Societies for Reformation of manners* (London, 1703), 23–24; Curtis and Speck, "Societies for the Reformation of Manners," 60–61.

201. Henry Gandy, A Letter to a Gentleman of the Society for the Reformation of Manners, Westminster, 30 January 1701, BL Add MS 40160, ff. 142–143.

202. Thomas Bray, "A General Plan of the Constitution of a Protestant Congregation, or Society for the Propagation of Christian Knowledge [1697]," Sion College Library, Bray MSS, Box 1; see also Francis Atterbury, *The Rights, Powers, and Priviledges of an English Convocation* (London, 1700), sig. A2, 464–465; and the appended letter dated 7 June 1698 from William Taylor intended for one "Mr. Saunders, Minister of the Gospel," and apparently miscarried to "Mr. Saunders, chaplain of All Souls College, Oxford," which also appears in BL Add MS 34265, f. 39; Thomas Curgenven to Henry Shute, 1 May 1700, CUL SPCK MS D2/2, §99; on the models for these forms of organization, see Jon Butler, *Power, Authority, and the Origins of American Denominational Order: The English Churches in the Delaware Valley, 1680–1730* (Philadelphia: American Philosophical Society, 1978), 25–27.

203. Quoted in H. P. Thompson, *Thomas Bray* (London: SPCK, 1954), 103.

204. Samuel Smith, *Publick Spirit Illustrated in the Life and Designs of Reverend Thomas Bray, D.D.* (London, 1746), 6; John Wolfe Lydekker, "Thomas Bray (1658–1730), Founder of Missionary Enterprises," *HMPEC* 12 (September 1943): 188–189; Thompson, *Thomas Bray*, 6–12; Thomas Bray, "A Brief Account of the Life of the Reverend Mr. John Rawlet, Author of the Christian Monitor," in *Two select and exemplary lives, of two parochial ministers* (London, 1728).

205. Thomas Bray, "A Memorial Representing the Rise Progress and Issue of Dr. Bray's Missionary Undertaking," Sion College Library, Bray MSS, Box 1.

206. Thomas Bray, "A General Plan of a Penitential Hospital for the Employing and Reforming Lewd Women," [1698], Sion College Library, Bray MSS, Box 1; and see Samuel Clyde McCulloch, "Dr. Thomas Bray's Commissary Work in London, 1696–1699," *WMQ*, 3rd series, 2 (October 1945): 347–348.

207. Thomas Bray, "A Memorial Representing the Rise Progress and Issue of Dr. Bray's Missionary Undertaking," Sion College Library, Bray MSS, Box 1.

208. [Thomas Bray], *Proposals for the Incouragement and Promoting of Religion and Learning in the Foreign Plantations* (London, 1697); Bray, "A Memorial Representing the Rise Progress and Issue"; McCulloch, "Bray's Commissary Work in London," 335–342; Charles T. Laugher, *Thomas Bray's Grand Design: Libraries of the Church of England in America, 1695–1785* (Chicago: American Library Association, 1973).

209. Thomas Bray, *An Essay Toward Promoting All Necessary and Useful Knowledge, Both Divine and Human in all the Parts of His Majesty's Dominions, Both at Home and Abroad* (London, 1697); Thomas Bray, *Bibliotheca Parochialis* (London, 1697), xv–xvi; [Thomas Bray], *An Essay to shew the Incompetent Provision there is in many Parishes* (London, 1703); Bray, "A Memorial Representing the Rise Progress and Issue"; on the decay of the rural deaneries, see William Dansey, *Horae Decanicae Rurales*, 2 vols. (London: Bohn, Rivington, 1835), 2:101–108, 120–127.

210. Thomas Bray, "A Memorial Wherein, is Established, I. A View of ye Original Institution & Jurisdiction of Rural Deanes, &c.," Sion College Library, Bray MSS, Box 1; Thompson, *Thomas Bray*, 22–24.

211. Court Book of the Corporation of the Sons of the Clergy, LMA A/CSC/007A, 11 November 1700, f. 146v; 8 April 1701, f. 148; 16 September 1701, ff. 150–151; Nicholas Stratford, bishop of Chester and the clergy of the archdeaconry of Chester, petition to Archbishop Tenison [1700], LPL Gibson MS 933, §20; see also ———— to Tanner, n.d., Tanner MS 24, f. 141.

212. Samuel Wesley, "A Letter Concerning Religious Societies" [1699], *The holy communicant rightly prepar'd*, 2nd ed. (London, 1716).

213. [Thomas Frank], *A Letter from a Minister in the Country to a Minister in London Giving an Account of the Original, Nature and Design of the Societies of the Clergy in Bedford and Buckingham Shires* (London, 1699); on Frank's authorship, see BL Lansdowne MS 1024, f. 127; Nicolson to Wootton, 26 February 1699 [1700], BL Add MS 34265, f. 49.

214. Bray, "General Plan of the Constitution of a Protestant Congregation," Sion College Library, Bray MSS, Box 1; this draft differs somewhat from the "General Plan" printed in Lydekker, "Thomas Bray," 194–195.

215. Smith, *Publick Spirit Illustrated*, 15; Thompson, *Thomas Bray*, 37.

216. Sometimes known in its early years as the Society for the Propagation of Christian Knowledge.

217. Lydekker, "Thomas Bray," 193–198; Thompson, *Thomas Bray*, 37–38; Samuel Clyde McCulloch, "The Foundation and Early Work of the Society for Promoting Christian Knowledge," *HMPEC* 18 (1949): 3–22; William A. and Phyllis W. Bultmann, "The Roots of Anglican Humanitarianism: A Study of the Membership of the S.P.C.K. and the S.P.G., 1699–1720," *HMPEC* 33 (March 1964): 3–48; *SPCK Minutes*, 1–18; M. G. Jones, *The Charity School Movement: A Study of Eighteenth Century Puritanism in Action* (Hamden, CT: Archon, 1964), 36–41; Craig Rose, "Politics, Religion and Charity in Augustan London, c. 1680–c. 1720" (PhD

diss., University of Cambridge, 1989), 64–95; Craig Rose, "The Origins and Ideals of the SPCK, 1699–1716," in *The Church of England c. 1689–c. 1833*, 172–190; David Hayton, "Moral Reform and Country Politics in the Late-Seventeenth-Century House of Commons," *Past and Present* 128 (August 1990), 48–91.

218. Jeremy Gregory, *Restoration, Reformation and Reform: Archbishops of Canterbury and Their Diocese* (Oxford: Clarendon, 2000), 245–246.

219. An Essay towards ye Reformation of Newgate and ye other Prisons in and about London, LPL Gibson MS 933, §11; A Proposal for Regulating of the Stage & Stage-Plays, LPL Gibson MS 933, §57; The Memorial of Thomas Bray, Relating to ye Libraries sent into America, LPL Gibson MS 941, §71; Means for Raising a Fund for Purchasing of the foresaid General and Parochial Libraries, LPL Gibson MS 933, §36; Nicholas Stratford, bishop of Chester and the clergy of the archdeaconry of Chester, petition to Archbishop Tenison [1700], LPL Gibson MS 933, §20; 12 March 1698/99, McClure, *SPCK Minutes*, 19; Stratford to William Gilpin, 6 April 1700, BL Add MS 34265, f. 57; Craig, "Movement for the Reformation of Manners," 264–269.

220. See also Burnet, *Discourse of the Pastoral Care*, 209–210.

221. Thomas Tenison, *His Grace the Lord Archbishop of Canterbury's letter to the Right Reverend the Lords Bishops of his Province* (London, 1699), 1–7.

222. 26 October 1699, 2 November 1699, McClure, *SPCK Minutes*, 33, 35.

223. "The Second Circular Letter to the Clergy Correspondents" [approved on 8 February 1700]; on 8 August 1700, the society resolved to apply to the archbishop for leave to print and disperse his circular letter, McClure, *SPCK Minutes*, 45–46, 75–76, 154; BL Harleian MS 7190, ff. 4–5; *A Second Letter From a Member of the Society for the Propagation of Christian Knowledge, to a Friend in the Country* (London, 1705), 2.

224. Cornelius Yeate to Henry Shute, 28 November 1699, CUL SPCK MS D2/2, §3; on clerical organization in Wiltshire, see Donald Spaeth, *The Church in an Age of Danger: Parsons and Parishioners, 1660–1740* (Cambridge: Cambridge University Press, 2000), 55–56, 225–232.

225. [Frank], *Letter from a Minister in the Country*, 1.

226. Willett to Chamberlayne, 15 April 1700, CUL SPCK MS D2/2, §79.

227. Vincent Edwards to [Chamberlayne], 24 February 1701, CUL SPCK MS D2/2, §250.

228. "Recommendations by the Bishop of Bangor to the clergy of Anglesey, circa 1700," NLW Plas Gwyn (Vivian) MS 24; Robert Wynne to Dr. Evans, 14 December 1699, CUL SPCK MS D2/2, §10.

229. Minutes, 5 March 1699/1700, 17 April 1700, 20 June 1700, Plas Gwyn (Vivian) MSS 19, 24, 21; the minutes from the 21 May 1700 meeting at Penmynydd do not seem to be extant; Robert Wynne to John Chamberlayne, 15 April 1700, CUL SPCK MS D2/2, §84; John Jones to [Chamberlayne?], 23 May 1700, CUL SPCK MS D2/2, §109.

230. Jonathan Barry, ed., "The Society for the Reformation of Manners 1700–5," in *Reformation and Revival in Eighteenth-Century Bristol*, ed. Jonathan Barry and Kenneth Morgan (Bristol: Bristol Record Society, 1994), 46; 19 October 1699, McClure, *SPCK Minutes*, 33.

231. Scot to Chamberlayne, 21 October 1700, CUL SPCK MS D2/2, §192.

232. John Adamson to Chamberlayne, 22 January 1701, CUL SPCK MS D2/2, §242.

233. John Tatam to Chamberlayne, 12 June 1700, CUL SPCK MS D2/2, §118.

234. W. Bernard to [Chamberlayne?], 19 April 1700, CUL SPCK MS D2/2, §85.

235. Lewis to Chamberlayne, 28 February 1700, CUL SPCK MS D2/2, §54.

236. John Tatam to Chamberlayne, 12 June 1700, CUL SPCK MS D2/2, §118; the clergy there suspected that the association was instigated by a local society for the reformation of manners founded by Dissenters.

237. Henry Gilbert to Aylmer, 20 January 1699; Gilbert to Chamberlayne, 8 May 1700; Frank to Chamberlayne, 27 May 1700; Nicholas Kendal to Chamberlayne, 3 June 1700; John Tatam to Chamberlayne, 12 June 1700, CUL SPCK MS D2/2, §19, §101, §110, §113, §118; Lloyd to Chamberlayne, 1 Aug 1700, CUL SPCK MS D2/2, §146; Lloyd further added that some of the clergy, "cavil at the word association," a reference to the fallout from the 1696 assassination plot against William.

238. Lewis to Chamberlayne, 28 February 1700, CUL SPCK MS D2/2, §54.

239. Harris to Chamberlayne, 21 June 1700, CUL SPCK MS D2/2, §123.

240. John Osmond to Chamberlayne, 24 March 1701, CUL SPCK MS D2/2, §267.

241. George Wheler to Chamberlayne, 28 March 1701, CUL SPCK MS D2/2, §272; Samuel Wesley of Epworth also conceived of the objective of the society as "the union of the clergy in several parts of the kingdom under their rural deans," Wesley to Hooke, 10 July 1700, CUL SPCK MS D2/2, §135.

242. Again in August 1703, Tenison reaffirmed this policy in his *Letter to the Reverend the Arch-Deacons, And the rest of the Clergy Of the Diocese of St. David* (London, 1703); a few months later, two thousand copies of this circular letter were printed for distribution by the SPCK; 28 October 1703, McClure, *SPCK Minutes*, 241; Humphrey Wanley to Bp of Worcester, 20 October 1705 (draft), BL Harleian MS 7190, f. 37.

243. Gilbert to Chamberlayne, 20 June 1700; W. Bernard to Chamberlayne, 19 April 1700; CUL SPCK MS D2/2, §122, §85.

244. Newman to Mr. Gordon, Governor of Ft. William in North Britain, 29 June 1714, HNL vol. 4, f. 54.

245. Newman to Colman, 20 October 1722, SPCK New England Letters, vol. 1, f. 42.

3. The Antinomies of the Society for Promoting Christian Knowledge, 1699–1720

1. 3 February 1700, McClure, *SPCK Minutes*, 44, 46; [John Hooke], *A Short Account of the Several Kinds of Societies, Set Up of Late Years, for carrying on reformation of manners, and propagation of Christian Knowledge* (London, 1700); Henry Newman to Emerson, 29 March 1715, HNL vol. 5, f. 21; Craig Rose, "Politics, Religion and Charity in Augustan London, c. 1680–c. 1720" (PhD diss., University of Cambridge, 1989), 52.

2. White Kennett to Arthur Charlett, 11 July 1703, Ballard MS 7, f. 113.

3. "The Third Circular Letter to the Clergy Correspondents" [6 June 1700], McClure, *SPCK Minutes*, 67–68.

4. "The Second Circular Letter to the Clergy Correspondents" [8 February 1700], McClure, *SPCK Minutes*, 45–46.

5. See Andrew C. Thompson, *Britain, Hanover and the Protestant Interest, 1688–1756* (Woodbridge: Boydell, 2006), esp. 25–60.

6. Craig Rose, "The Origins and Ideals of the SPCK, 1699–1716," in *The Church of England, c. 1689–c. 1833: From Toleration to Tractarianism*, ed. John Walsh, Colin Haydon, and Stephen Taylor (Cambridge: Cambridge University Press, 1993), 179–180.

7. W. K. Lowther Clarke, *A History of the SPCK* (London: SPCK, 1959), 82; W. K. Lowther Clarke, *Eighteenth Century Piety* (London: SPCK, 1944), 3.

8. T. C. Curtis and W. A. Speck, "The Societies for the Reformation of Manners: A Case Study in the Theory and Practice of Moral Reform," *Literature and History* 3 (1976): 59.

9. Tina Isaacs, "Moral Crime, Moral Reform and the State in Early Eighteenth Century England: A Study of Piety and Politics" (PhD diss., University of Rochester, 1979), 169.

10. Andrew Porter, *Religion versus Empire? British Protestant Missionaries and Overseas Expansion, 1700–1914* (Manchester: Manchester University Press, 2004), 17; and see Linda Colley, *In Defiance of Oligarchy: The Tory Party, 1714–60* (Cambridge: Cambridge University Press, 1982), 104–117.

11. Donald Gray, "Manningham, Thomas (d. 1722)," *ODNB*.

12. Dudley Bahlmann, *The Moral Revolution of 1688* (New Haven, CT: Yale University Press, 1957).

13. Garnet V. Portus, *Caritas Anglicana* (London: A. R. Mowbray, 1912), 67.

14. G. V. Bennett, *The Tory Crisis in Church and State, 1688–1730* (Oxford: Clarendon, 1975), 22; G. V. Bennett, "Conflict in the Church," in *Britain after the Glorious Revolution, 1689–1714*, ed. Geoffrey Holmes (London: Macmillan, 1969), 155–175; and see John Spurr, *The Post-Reformation: Religion, Politics and Society in Britain, 1603–1714* (Harlow: Pearson, 2006), 211–221.

15. John Gascoigne, "Politics, Patronage and Newtonianism: The Cambridge Example," *HJ* 27, 1 (March 1984): 7.

16. M. G. Jones, *The Charity School Movement: A Study of Eighteenth Century Puritanism in Action* (Hamden, CT: Archon, 1964), 6–14, 36–41; and see Samuel Clyde McCulloch, "The Foundation and Early Work of the Society for Promoting Christian Knowledge," *HMPEC* 18 (1949): 3–22.

17. Eamon Duffy, "The Long Reformation: Catholicism, Protestantism and the Multitude," in *England's Long Reformation, 1500–1800*, ed. Nicholas Tyacke (London: UCL, 1998), 33–70; and see also Eamon Duffy, "Primitive Christianity Revived: Religious Renewal in Augustan England," in *Renaissance and Renewal in Christian History*, ed. Derek Baker (Oxford: Basil Blackwell, 1977), 287–300; Eamon Duffy, "Correspondence Fraternelle: The SPCK, the SPG and the Churches of Switzerland in the War of the Spanish Succession," in *Reform and Reformation in England and the Continent, c. 1500–c. 1750*, ed. Derek Baker (Oxford: Basil Blackwell, 1979), 251–280; Eamon Duffy, "The Society of Promoting Christian Knowledge and Europe: The Background to the Founding of the *Christentumsgesellschaft*," *Pietismus und Neuzeit* 7 (1981): 28–42.

18. David Hayton, "Moral Reform and Country Politics in the Late Seventeenth-Century House of Commons," *Past and Present* 128 (August 1990): 48–91.

19. Jeremy Gregory, "The Eighteenth Century Reformation: The Pastoral Task of Anglican Clergy after 1689," in *Church of England, c. 1689–c. 1833*, 67–85; Jeremy Gregory, *Restoration, Reformation and Reform: Archbishops of Canterbury and Their Diocese* (Oxford: Clarendon, 2000), 237–254; Daniel L. Brunner, *Halle Pietists in England: Anthony Wilhelm Boehm and the Society for Promoting Christian Knowledge* (Gottingen: Vandenhoeck and Ruprecht, 1993), 27–28.

20. Rose, "Origins and Ideals," 172–190; Rose, "Politics, Religion and Charity," 64–95; this judgment has been wholeheartedly accepted by Travis Glasson, *Mastering Christianity: Missionary Anglicanism and Slavery in the Atlantic World* (New York: Oxford University Press, 2011), 23–24.

21. Rose, "Origins and Ideals," 177.

22. On church Whiggery, see Norman Sykes, "Archbishop Wake and the Whig Party, 1716–1723," *Cambridge Historical Journal* 8 (1945): 93–112; Stephen Taylor, "Sir Robert Walpole, the Church of England, and the Quaker Tithes Bill of 1736," *HJ* 28 (March 1985): 51–77; Stephen Taylor, "The Character of a Church Whig," lecture, Dr. Williams's Library, London, November 24, 2007. I am grateful to Dr. Taylor for making a copy of his lecture available to me.

23. Both Duffy, "The Society of Promoting Christian Knowledge and Europe," and Brunner, *Halle Pietists in England*, 107–112, address the tensions generated by ecumenical engagement with continental Protestants.

24. This trend is directly opposed to that which David Hayton discerns in the increasingly Tory complexion of "country interest" moral reform; Hayton, "Moral Reform and Country Politics," 77–78.

25. "Mackworth, Sir Humphrey (1657–1727)," in *The House Commons, 1690–1715*, ed. Eveline Cruickshanks, Stuart Handley, and D. W. Hayton, 5 vols. (Cambridge: Cambridge University Press, 2002), 4:724–734; Mary Ransome, "The Parliamentary Career of Sir Humphrey Mackworth, 1701–1713," *Birmingham Journal of History* 1 (1947–1948): 232–254; Roger North, *The Lives of the Right Hon. Francis North, Baron Guilford, the Hon. Sir Dudley North and the Hon. And Rev. Dr. John North*, ed. Augustus Jessop, 3 vols. (London: George Bell and Sons, 1890), 3:294.

26. "Colchester, Maynard (1665–1715)," in *House of Commons*, 3:645–647.

27. Stuart Handley, "Hooke, John (1655–1712)," *ODNB*; Hayton, "Moral Reform and Country Politics," 76.

28. John Hooke, *Catholicism with Popery, an essay to render the Church of England a means and a pattern of union to the Christian world* (London, 1704); Humphrey Mackworth, *Peace at Home: Or, a Vindication of the Proceedings of the Honourable House of Commons on the Bill for Preventing Danger from Occasional Conformity*, 4th ed. (London, 1703); Philip Stubbs, *For God or for Baal; or, No Neutrality in Religion. A Sermon against Occasional Conformity, Preach'd on Sunday Oct. 4th 1702* (London, 1702); during the debates over occasional conformity, Daniel Defoe listed Philip Stubbs with Henry Sacheverell as "my more direct antagonists," Defoe to Harley, April 1703, BL Add MS 70291, unfoliated.

29. John Wolfe Lydekker, "Thomas Bray (1658–1730), Founder of Missionary Enterprises," *HMPEC* 12 (September 1943): 188–189, 211; H. P. Thompson, *Thomas Bray* (London: SPCK, 1954), 5–13, 86–87; Leonard W. Cowie, "Bray, Thomas (bap. 1658, d. 1730)," *ODNB*; on Samuel Brewster, see Rose, "Origins and Ideals," 176; G. V. Bennett, *White Kennett, 1660–1728, Bishop of Peterborough* (London: SPCK, 1957), 24, 179–180; Paul K. Monod, *Jacobitism and the English People, 1688–1788* (Cambridge: Cambridge University Press, 1989), 40.

30. 19 April 1699, McClure, *SPCK Minutes*, 21; Chamberlayne to Earl of Sunderland, 13 March 1707, BL Add MS 61649, f. 34; Reavley Gair, "Chamberlayne, John (1668/69–1723)," *ODNB*.

31. "Philipps, John (c. 1666–1737)," in *House of Commons*, 5:138–141; John Chamberlayne to Sir John Philipps, 30 January 1699, NLW Picton Castle MS 1593; Thomas Shankland, "Sir

John Philipps; the Society for Promoting Christian Knowledge and the Charity-School Movement in Wales, 1699–1738," *Transactions of the Honourable Society of Cymmrodorion* (1904–1905): 74–215.

32. "Comyns, John (c. 1667–1740)," in *House of Commons*, 3:669–671; William Melmoth [the younger], *Memoirs of a Late Eminent Advocate and Member of the Honourable Society of Lincoln's Inn* (London, 1796); Emma Major and Nicole Pohl, "Melmoth, William, the elder (1665/66–1743)," *ODNB*; William Melmoth, *The Great Importance of a Religious Life Consider'd* (London, 1711), 54–56.

33. For SPCK links with Tory MPs, see Mackworth Diary, 22 December 1701, NLW MS 14362E, p. 129.

34. John Spurr, "Woodward, Josiah (1657–1712)," *ODNB; A Copy of a Letter to Mr. Shute, by the present Lord Bishop of Worcester, some time after the Death of our late gracious Queen Mary*, BL Lansdowne MS 1039, f. 190.

35. See Francis Lee's heads for a biography of Nelson, BL Add MS 45511, f. 174.

36. John Tillotson to Robert Nelson, 20 December 1690, CHC MS RN/1/6; George Bull was close with a number of early SPCK members, including Bray, Colchester, and the anti-Quaker missionary George Keith, see John Philipps to Robert Nelson, 9 October 1712, BL Add MS 45511, ff. 93–94.

37. Nelson's connections are traced at length throughout C. F. Secretan, *Memoirs of the Life and Times of the Pious Robert Nelson* (London: John Murray, 1860); and Charles J. Abbey and John H. Overton, *The English Church in the Eighteenth Century* (Teddington: Echo Library, 2006), 35–76; and see Lee notes on Nelson, BL Add MS 45512, ff. 2–7; and the extracts from Nelson's will in Tenison's papers, LPL Gibson MS 933, §77.

38. Nicholas Kendal to John Chamberlayne, 3 June 1700; Robert Booth to John Chamberlayne, 22 July 1700, CUL SPCK MS D2/2, §113, §141.

39. 2 May 1700, McClure, *SPCK Minutes*, 63; Fowler and Burnet were subsequently listed as "resident members who have been chosen, but have not subscribed to the Society," BL Harleian MS 7190, f. 97.

40. The SPCK had two levels of membership, corresponding and residing. Both types required invitation from residing members in London, although the latter required a monetary subscription and entailed a somewhat more rigorous screening process.

41. All were signatories of the 15 December 1705 protest of the lower house of convocation against the innovations of Francis Atterbury and his allies, BL Add MS 61612, ff. 140–141; BL Harleian MS 6848, ff. 194–195.

42. On Manningham, a Hanoverian Tory, see Norman Sykes, "Queen Anne and the Episcopate," *EHR* 50 (July 1935): 433–464; on Wheler, see Thomas Zouch, "Memoir of Sir George Wheler," in *The Works of the Rev. Thomas Zouch*, 2 vols. (York: F. C. and J. Rivington, 1820), 2:179–182; E. G. Wheler, ed., *Autobiography of Sir George Wheler* (Birmingham: Cornish Brothers, 1911).

43. Subscriptions of the Fellows of Sion College, London, 13 May 1690, Guildhall Library MS 10525; Subscription List, 1704–1705, Guildhall Library MS 10538, File 1; Persons in Nomination for Governors of Sion College for ye year 1711, Guildhall Library MS 10538, File 2; for governors of Sion College, see John Chamberlayne, *Magnae Britanniae Notitia: Or, The Present State Of Great-Britain* (London, 1710), 639–641; and John Chamberlayne, *Magnae Britanniae Notitia: Or, The Present State Of Great-Britain* (London, 1716), 651–653; 29 March 1716, SPCK Minutes, vol. 7, 1715–1716, §7.

44. A Proposal for Incorporating ye Society in Order to Receive Charitable Donations, &c, in McClure, *SPCK Minutes*, 61–63.

45. Court Book of the Corporation of the Sons of the Clergy 1678–1708, LMA A/CSC/007A, ff. 75, 79–80, 90, 105, 157, 162; William Lancaster to Arthur Charlett, n.d. [1694?], Ballard MS 21, f. 99.

46. Robert Booth to William Hodges, 3 May 1700, CUL SPCK MS D2/2, §96; 21 November 1700, McClure, *SPCK Minutes*, 92; Court Book of the Corporation of the Sons of the Clergy, LMA A/CSC/007A, 11 November 1700, f. 146v; 8 April 1701, f. 148; 16 September 1701, ff. 150–151; Nicholas Stratford, bishop of Chester and the clergy of the archdeaconry of Chester, petition to Archbishop Tenison, [1700], LPL Gibson MS 933, §20; 10 June 1714, SPCK Minutes, vol. 6, 1712–1715, §8.

47. White Kennett, *The Case of Impropriations and of the Augmentation of Vicarages* (London, 1704), 319–321.

48. On the establishment of Queen Anne's Bounty, see Alan Savidge, *The Foundation and Early Years of Queen Anne's Bounty* (London: SPCK, 1955); G. F. A Best, *Temporal Pillars: Queen Anne's Bounty, the Ecclesiastical Commissioners and the Church of England* (Cambridge: Cambridge University Press, 1964); I. M. Green, "The First Five Years of Queen Anne's Bounty," in *Princes and Paupers in the English Church, 1500–1800*, ed. F. Heal and R. O'Day (Totowa, NJ: Barnes and Noble, 1981), 231–254.

49. 2 & 3 Anne c. 11; Edmund Gibson to Arthur Charlett, 9 February 1704, Ballard MS 6, f. 91.

50. White Kennett to Arthur Charlett, 21 October 1704, Ballard MS 7, f. 114.

51. William Dawes, *A sermon preach'd before the Society for the Propagation of the gospel in foreign parts at the parish-church of St. Mary-le-Bow on Friday February 18, 1708/9* (London, 1709), 16.

52. John Mapletoft was also reportedly close with the anti-Trinitarian Thomas Firmin, himself an intimate of the Williamite London clergy; see White Kennett to Arthur Charlett, 13 October 1716, Ballard MS 7, f. 139.

53. Philip Stubbs to Thomas Tenison, 11 March 1705, LPL Gibson MS 941, §8; Canon Scott Robertson, *Archdeacon Philip Stubbs (1665–1735)* (London: Mitchell and Hughes, 1889); William A. and Phyllis W. Bultmann, "The Roots of Anglican Humanitarianism: A Study of the Membership of the S.P.C.K. and the S.P.G., 1699–1720," *HMPEC* 33 (March 1964): 46; on Stubbs and the Greenwich Hospital, see Brent S. Sirota, "Anglicanism and the Nationalization of Maritime Space," in *Mercantilism Reimagined: Political Economy in Early Modern Britain and Its Empire*, ed. Philip J. Stern and Carl Wennerlind (New York: Oxford University Press, forthcoming).

54. John Spurr, "Woodward, Josiah (1657–1712)," *ODNB*.

55. Henry Newman to Rowland Cotton, 27 April 1717, HNL vol. 6, 1716–1717, f. 41; Chamberlayne, *Magnae Britanniae Notitia* (1716), 661.

56. Bahlmann, *Moral Revolution*, 70–80; John Chamberlayne to Wanley, 4 February 1702, BL Add MS 70475; although see the SPCK secretary Humphrey Wanley's note which sharply differentiates the SPCK from "that for reformation of manners, which I would never concern myself withal," at Robert Nelson to Humphrey Wanley, 11 December 1705, BL Harleian MS 3780, f. 223.

57. Thomas Bray, "A Memorial Representing the Rise Progress and Issue of Dr. Bray's Missionary Undertaking," Sion College Library, Bray MSS, Box 1.

58. A. G. Craig, "The Movement for the Reformation of Manners, 1688–1715" (PhD diss., University of Edinburgh, 1980), 26, 61–66; Bulkeley was first proposed for membership on 31 October 1699, McClure, *SPCK Minutes*, 34; Richard Bulkeley to Humphrey Wanley, 1 December 1704, BL Harleian MS 3777, f. 283.

59. Edward Fowler, *A Vindication of a Late Undertaking of Certain Gentlemen, In Order to the Suppressing of Debauchery and Profaneness* (London, 1692).

60. "A List of the Correspondents in England & Wales," [ca. 1705], BL Harleian MS 7190, ff. 102–105; Jonathan Barry, ed. "The Society for the Reformation of Manners 1700–5," in *Reformation and Revival in Eighteenth-Century Bristol*, ed. Jonathan Barry and Kenneth Morgan (Bristol: Bristol Record Society, 1994), 3–62; on Yate, see *House of Commons*, 5:949–953.

61. *The charge of Whitlocke Bulstrode, Esq; to the Grand-Jury, and other juries, of the county of Middlesex* (London, 1718).

62. John Disney, *An essay upon the execution of the laws against immorality and prophaneness* (London, 1710); John Disney, *A second essay upon the execution of the laws against immorality and prophaneness* (London, 1710); John Disney, *A view of ancient laws, against immorality and profaneness* (Cambridge, 1729); Robert Watts to Henry Newman, 30 June 1709, CUL SPCK ALB 1708–1709, §1654; Peter Lavigne to Henry Newman, 2 April 1710, Bodl. Rawlinson D 839, f. 89; William Nicolson to Humphrey Wanley, 3 June 1714, BL Harleian MS 3780, f. 286; Henry Newman to John Percival, 2 December 1728, BL Add MS 47032, f. 89; Henry Newman to John Disney, 18 May 1728, HNL vol. 19, f. 38; Henry Newman to John Disney, 25 June 1728, HNL vol. 19, f. 44; Newman to Sir Thomas Lowther, 15 October 1728, HNL vol. 19, f. 62; Newman to Disney, 28 November 1728, HNL vol. 19, f. 67; and see the 1728 list of subscribers to Disney's book at HNL vol. 19, ff. 73–75.

63. 2 May 1700, McClure, *SPCK Minutes*, 63.

64. 25 January 1700, McClure, *SPCK Minutes*, 43.

65. The Reverend Mr. Thomas Frank's Proposals to the Honble Society for Propagating Christian Knowledge, McClure, *SPCK Minutes*, 53–54.

66. 11 July 1700, McClure, *SPCK Minutes*, 71.

67. Frank's Proposals to SPCK, 14 July 1701 and 3 July 1703, McClure, *SPCK Minutes*, 53–54, 141–142, 231; Robert Hales to Chamberlayne, 15 January 1700, CUL SPCK MS D2/2, §239; Humphrey Wanley to Robert Nelson, 11 January 1704, CHC MS RN/1/13; Robert Watts to Newman, 20 March 1709, CUL SPCK ALB 1708–1709.

68. *A Second Letter From a Member of the Society for the Propagation of Christian Knowledge, to a Friend in the Country* (London, 1705), 1.

69. On Newman, see Leonard W. Cowie, *Henry Newman: An American in London* (London: SPCK, 1956).

70. Thomas Kelly, *Early Public Libraries: A History of Libraries in Great Britain before 1850* (London: Library Association, 1966), 104–110; William D. Houlette, "Parish Libraries and the Work of the Reverend Thomas Bray," *Library Quarterly* 4 (October 1934): 588–609; Sarah Gray and Chris Baggs, "The English Parish Library: A Celebration of Diversity," *Libraries and Culture* 35 (Summer 2000): 414–433; I. M. Green, *Print and Protestantism in Early Modern England* (Oxford: Oxford University Press, 2000), 29–30.

71. Rose, "Politics, Religion and Charity," 89–135; Jones, *Charity School Movement*, 36–72.

72. Gilbert Burnet, *Of the propagation of the gospel in foreign parts. A sermon preach'd at St. Mary-le-Bow, Feb 18. 1703/4* (London, 1704), 22–23.

73. Act for the Encouragement of Charitable Gifts and Dispositions, 7 & 8 William III c. 37; A Proposal for Incorporating ye Society, 61–62; White Kennett to Arthur Charlett, 28 June 1701, Ballard MS 7, f. 100.

74. 9 June 1701, McClure, *SPCK Minutes*, 137.

75. Humphrey Wanley to Arthur Charlett, 9 December 1700, Ballard MS 13, f. 92; on the circumstances of Wanley's hiring, see Chamberlayne to Wanley, 17 December 1700, BL Add MS 70474; and 2 December 1700, McClure, *SPCK Minutes*, 93–94.

76. Second Circular Letter to the Clergy Correspondents, [8 February 1700], McClure, *SPCK Minutes*, 45–46.

77. John Bradshaw to Chamberlayne, 12 February 1700; Theophilus Dorrington to Chamberlayne, 8 January 1701, CUL SPCK MS D2/2, §29, §244.

78. Thomas Bray, *Bibliotecha Parochialis: Or, A Scheme of Such Theological Heads Both General and Particular, as are More peculiarly Requisite to be well studied by every Pastor of a Parish* (London, 1697), 73; Allen to Hodges, 2 March 1700; George Parkhall to Hodges, 16 March 1700; Knight to Broughton, 1 June 1700; Hugh Mapletoft to Chamberlayne, 8 October 1700; Hales to Hodges, 8 February 1701, CUL SPCK D2/2, §67, §72, §112, §179, §258; 19 September 1700, McClure, *SPCK Minutes*, 80; Henry Shute, An Essay towards ye Reformation of Newgate and ye other Prisons in and about London, LPL Gibson MS 933, §11; Catalogue of the small Tracts allowed the Missionaries to Distribute among, &c., [1705], LPL Gibson MS 941, §73; 3 September 1713, SPCK Minutes, §1; 21 March 1716/17, SPCK Minutes, vol. 8, 1717–1719 §3.

79. John Rawlet, *The Christian Monitor, Containing an Earnest Exhortation to an Holy Life* (London, 1686), 3, 31, 47; Green, *Print and Protestantism*, 92, 357–358.

80. Lowther Clarke (*Eighteenth Century Piety*, 2) asserts "the Society's literature during the eighteenth century is uniformly High Church," while Eamon Duffy ("The Long Reformation," 53–65) suggests that the SPCK evinced "a devotional root in the Puritan tradition."

81. Duffy, "The Long Reformation," 53–65.

82. Thomas Curgenven to Henry Shute, 1 May 1700, CUL SPCK MS D2/2, §99; Thomas Morrison to John Jones, 3 August 1706, NLW Plas Gwyn (Vivian) MS 94; Joseph Stephens to Robert Nelson, 8 August 1712, NLW MS 1484E, f. 45.

83. On the society's distribution of these tracts and others by the same authors, see Kendall to Chamberlayne, 14 March 1699, Ellis to Chamberlayne, 15 January 1700, CUL SPCK D2/2, §68, §235; Fox to [Newman], 9 August 1708, Nelson to Hoare, 10 August 1708, John Bradshaw to [Newman], 13 December 1708, CUL SPCK ALB, §1366, §1367, §1524; 23 July, 30 July, 27 July 1713, SPCK Minutes, vol. 6, 1712–1715; Bodl. Rawlinson D 839, f. 63.

84. Hugh Todd to Chamberlayne, 8 September 1701, CUL SPCK MS D2/2, §342.

85. Jones, *Charity School Movement*, 24.

86. Rose, "Politics, Religion and Charity," 96–134.

87. *An Account of Charity-Schools Lately Erected in England, Wales and Ireland* (London, 1706), 4–6; and see James Talbot, *The Christian School-Master, Or, The Duty of those who are Employ'd in the Publick Instruction of Children Especially in Charity-Schools* (London, 1707), 4–16.

88. [White Kennett], *The Christian Scholar: In Rules and Directions for Children and Youth Sent to Charity Schools*, 3rd ed. (London, 1704), 32; Hewetson to Nelson, n.d., BL Add MS 45511, ff. 140–141.

89. William Wake, *The Excellency and Benefits of a Religious Education, A Sermon Preach'd in the Parish-Church of St. Sepulchre, June the IXth, 1715* (London, 1715), 41; William Dawes, *The Excellency of the Charity Schools; in a Sermon Preach'd in the Parish-Church of St. Sepulcher, May 28, MDCCXIII* (London, 1713), 14; William Whiston, *A Sermon Preach'd at Trinity-Church in Cambridge, January the 25th 1704/5* (Cambridge, 1705), 19–20; John Jackson, *The Blessedness of Communicating to Charity Schools. A Sermon Preach'd at Dursely in Gloucester-Shire, February 18, 1710* (London, 1710), 10.

90. Dawes, *Excellency of Charity Schools*, 14.

91. Booth to Hodges, 16 March 1700; Booth to Hodges, 3 May 1700, CUL SPCK MS D2/2, §63, §96.

92. John Bradshaw [to Newman], 13 December 1708, CUL SPCK ALB, §1524; interestingly enough, Bradshaw believed the professors of believers' baptism were "supported by a Fund from London."

93. Henry Newman to Thomas Mangey, 10 March 1719/20, HNL vol. 9, f. 40.

94. On Keith's associations, see E. W. Kirby, *George Keith (1638–1716)* (New York: D. Appleton, 1942), 107–109; George Keith to Wanley, 12 March 1696, BL Harleian MS 3780, f. 18; White Kennett to Arthur Charlett, 11 May 1700, Ballard MS 7, f. 86; John Philipps to Robert Nelson, 9 October 1712, BL Add MS 45511, ff. 93–94.

95. 8–10 March 1699, McClure, *SPCK Minutes*, 18.

96. Kirby, *George Keith*, 113–124.

97. Bedford to Chamberlayne, 8 January 1701, CUL SPCK MS D2/2, §229.

98. Booth to Chamberlayne, 8 October 1700; Archdeacon Entwistle to Chamberlayne, 15 November 1700; Laugharne to Chamberlayne, 4 April 1701; Harris to Chamberlayne, 8 April 1701; Bedford to Chamberlayne, 3 May 1701, CUL SPCK MS D2/2, §182, §207, §274, §276, §293.

99. 12 February 1702, McClure, *SPCK Minutes*, 170.

100. George Keith, *A journal of travels from New-Hampshire to Caratuck, On the Continent of North-America* (London, 1706); A Plan propos'd to ye Society for the propagation of the Gospel in foreign Parts relating to ye furnishing out of Mr. Keith with books, Sion College Library, Bray MSS, Box 1; 27 February 1701 [1702], LPL SPG Papers, vol. 1, f. 1; Compton to Tenison, 27 March 1702, LPL SPG Papers vol. 7, f. 14; White Kennett to Arthur Charlett, 28 March 1702, Ballard MS 7, f. 106; Lewis Morris to George Keith, 4 April 1704, LPL SPG Papers, vol. 13, f. 42; White Kennett to Samuel Blackwell, 21 October 1704, BL Lansdowne MS 1013, f. 71; for Keith's effect on American Protestantism, see Jon Butler, *Power, Authority, and the Origins of American Denominational Order: The English Churches in the Delaware Valley, 1680–1730* (Philadelphia: American Philosophical Society, 1978).

101. C. M. Haydon, "The Anti-Catholic Activity of the S.P.C.K., c. 1698–1740," *Recusant History* 18 (1986–1987): 418–421.

102. Booth to Hodges, 16 March 1700; Frank to Chamberlayne, 23 September 1700, CUL SPCK MS D2/2, §63, §165.

103. White Kennett, *The Charity of schools for poor children recommended in a sermon preach'd in the Parish-church of St. Sepulchres, May 16, 1706* (London, 1706), 37.

104. 12 February 1713, §12, SPCK Minutes, vol. 6, 1712–1715; 10 September 1713, §5–6, SPCK Minutes, vol. 6, 1712–1715.

105. *William the Third, by the grace of God . . . Whereas we are credibly informed, That in many of Our Plantations, Colonies and Factories beyond the Sea (13 June 1701)* (London, 1701).

106. *A Second Letter From a Member of the Society for the Propagation of Christian Knowledge*, 2.

107. On the context of early seamen's missions, see Roald Kverndal, *Seamen's Missions: Their Origin and Early Growth* (Pasadena, CA: William Carey Library, 1986), 23–52.

108. Thomas Bray, "A Memorial Representing the Rise Progress and Issue of Dr. Bray's Missionary Undertaking," Sion College Library, Bray MSS, Box 1; Thomas Bray, "To the Rt Honble and Rt. Reverend Together with others, the Excellent Members of the Society for propagating Christian Knowledge," [March 1700], Sion College Library, Bray MSS, Box 1.

109. 21 April 1701; the next meeting on 28 April saw "a debate arising about a lending library for the fleet," and the project seems to have been dropped; McClure, *SPCK Minutes*, 130–131.

110. 16 December 1700, 23 December 1700, 27 February 1701, McClure, *SPCK Minutes*, 98, 100, 109; Lowther Clarke, *Eighteenth Century Piety*, 91–95.

111. 24 March 1701, McClure, *SPCK Minutes*, 125; Thomas Shewell to Chamberlayne, 4 April 1701; Shewell to Chamberlayne, 28 April 1701, CUL SPCK MS D2/2, §271, §291.

112. A copy of the appointment may be found in Philip Stubs [Stubbs], *God's Dominion over the Seas, and the Seaman's Duty Consider'd* (London, 1701), 32–33; William Hodges to Chamberlayne, 16 August 1701, CUL SPCK MS D2/2, §396; 14 July 1701, McClure, *SPCK Minutes*, 142; White Kennett to Arthur Charlett, 8 July 1701, Ballard MS 7, f. 51.

113. 2 December 1701, McClure, *SPCK Minutes*, 156; and see Gordon [to Chamberlayne], 24 May 1701, CUL SPCK MS D2/2, §304, where he promised to consult with Shewell and Stubbs in pursuance of the society's designs.

114. See the partial membership list at BL Harleian MS 7190, f. 8, dated March 7, 1702; on Stanhope's liaison with the navy, see 16 April 1701, McClure, *SPCK Minutes*, 137.

115. 28 May 1702, McClure, *SPCK Minutes*, 191–192; Prince George's death in 1708 would be the occasion of Philip Stubbs's maritime-themed sermon *The Sea-Assize; Or, Sea-faring Persons to be judged according to their Works* (London, 1708); Stubbs donated a packet of these sermons for distribution, Stubbs to [Newman], 27 January 1709, CUL SPCK ALB, §1547.

116. 25 June 1702, McClure, *SPCK Minutes*, 195.

117. This might be contrasted with the more concrete steps undertaken by the SPG to reform the chaplainry; see White Kennett's materials for the history of the SPG, BL Lansdowne MS 1032, ff. 46–48.

118. Gordon to Wanley, 10 April 1701; Hodges to Chamberlayne, 16 August 1701, CUL SPCK MS D2/2, §280, §336.

119. 28 June 1701, McClure, *SPCK Minutes*, 138; Memoranda Book of Sir John Philipps, 3 May 1701, NLW Picton Castle MS 579, p. 11.

120. 2, 8 December 1701, McClure, *SPCK Minutes*, 157–158.

121. 13 August, 1 October 1702, McClure, *SPCK Minutes*, 198, 201.

122. McClure, *SPCK Minutes*, 119–120, 199–200, 203, 204, 231, 249, 271.

123. Sirota, "Anglicanism and the Nationalization of Maritime Space."

124. Josiah Woodward, *The Seaman's Monitor* (London: Joseph Downing, 1705), preface, 1–2, 16, 23, 26, 30–31, 34, 35–37.

125. 22 December 1701, McClure, *SPCK Minutes*, 159.

126. On the logistics of this project, see Copy of the Letter Sent along with the Seaman's Monitor, 31 May 1723; Henry Newman to Josiah Burkett, Esq. Secretary to the Lords Commissioners of the Admiralty, 1 June 1723; Henry Newman to Sir Jacob Ackworth, Commissioner of the Navy in Colchester, 18 July 1723; Newman to Ackworth, 12 August 1723, HNL vol. 13, ff. 7–8, 8, 28, 38; Newman to [J. Downing], 15 September 1725, Bodl. Rawlinson D 839, f. 23, in which he tallied the total number of copies at 10,694.

127. Kverndal, *Seamen's Missions*, 101.

128. Hales to Chamberlayne, 19 May 1701, CUL SPCK MS D2/2, §308.

129. 21 July, 12 August 1701, McClure, *SPCK Minutes*, 142, 144.

130. 14 October 1701, McClure, *SPCK Minutes*, 148.

131. 4, 11 November 1701, McClure, *SPCK Minutes*, 152–153.

132. 12 January 1702, McClure, *SPCK Minutes*, 162.

133. 25 November 1701, McClure, *SPCK Minutes*, 155.

134. 9 April 1702, McClure, *SPCK Minutes*, 177.

135. Henry Newman to Col. Richard Kane at Port Mahon, 27 June 1713, HNL vol. 3, f. 38; Henry Newman to William Gordon, 29 June 1714, HNL vol. 4, f. 54; and for SPG involvement, see 11 March, 15 March, 12 June 1705, LPL, SPG Minutes vol. 1, ff. 43, 46, 105; The Copy of a Letter from an English Chaplain in Portugal to John Chamberlayne, Esq., [1 November 1711], BL Lansdowne MS 1024, ff. 355–356.

136. 26 July 1716, §8, §9; August 1716 §1–2, SPCK Minutes, vol. 7, 1715–1716.

137. Newman to Lord Carpenter, 26 July 1722; Newman to Mr. Arnold at the War Office, 10 August 1622; "Copy of a Letter sent to the Commanding Officers of the Several Camps of Great Britain, 2 Aug 1722"; Newman to Col. Richard Kane, 24 October 1722, HNL vol. 7, ff. 33, 34, 44.

138. 25 January 1700, McClure, *SPCK Minutes*, 43; it is possible that Compton's initiative might have been provoked by the first stirrings of scandal that would lead to the dismissal of John Allen as ordinary of Newgate for corrupt practices; see *An Account of a new and strange discovery that was made by John Sheirly, alias Davis, & Joseph Fisher, the same day of their execution relating to the ordinary of Newgate* (London, 1700); and *Mr. Allen's vindication, or, Remarks upon a late scandalous pamphlet, entituled, A strange and new discovery* (London, 1700).

139. [Henry Shute], An Essay towards ye Reformation of Newgate, LPL Gibson MS 933, §11; Hepworth Dixon misidentified these proposals as the work of Thomas Bray, *John Howard and the Prison-World of Europe*, 2nd ed. (London: Jackson and Wolford, 1850), 1–11; and see Laurie Throness, *A Protestant Purgatory: Theological Origins of the Penitentiary Act, 1779* (Aldershot: Ashgate, 2008), 186–187.

140. 19 January 1702, 2 February 1702, McClure, *SPCK Minutes*, 163, 169.

141. On Lorraine, see L. B. Faller, "In Contrast to Defoe: The Rev. Paul Lorrain, Historian of Crime," *Huntington Library Quarterly* 60 (1976): 59–78; Peter Linebaugh, "The Ordinary of Newgate and His Account," in *Crime in England, 1550–1800*, ed. J. S. Cockburn (Princeton, NJ: Princeton University Press, 1977), 246–269.

142. 26 February 1702, McClure, *SPCK Minutes*, 172.

143. Letter draft (in Humphrey Wanley's hand), March 1702, BL Harleian MS 7190, f. 19.

144. McClure, *SPCK Minutes*, 177, 182, 193, 196.

145. A. W. Boehm to Henry Newman, 3 March 1709, Bodl. Rawlinson C 743, ff. 13–14; Boehm was probably commenting on the devotional tract *A Charitable Visit to the prisons containing suitable and proper advice or counsel to those who are confined there* (London, 1709), published by the SPCK printer Joseph Downing, which largely offered prayers and meditations for inmates. Society member Sir George Wheler authored a "treatise concerning abuses in prisons," although it is unclear whether it was ever published; Henry Newman to George Wheler, 26 October 1712, HNL vol. 2, f. 86. Wheler's "letter . . . touching the abuses in prisons in general" was discussed at an SPCK meeting on 23 June 1715, SPCK Minutes, vol. 7, 1715–1716.

146. 19 November 1713, SPCK Minutes, vol. 6, 1712–1715.

147. Newman to Jennings, 17 October 1711, HNL vol. 2, f. 15; Newman to Chamberlayne, 23 November 1713, HNL vol. 3, f. 79; Newman to Davies, 1 October 1714, HNL vol. 4, f. 68; Newman to Robert Nelson, 19 November 1714, HNL vol. 4, f. 76; 11 December 1712, 1 January 1713, 15 January 1713, 15 October 1713, 29 October 1713, 7 January 1714, 21 January 1714, 30 September 1714, 7 October 1714, SPCK Minutes, vol. 6, 1712–1715.

148. 19 May 1715, *Journals of the House of Commons (1714–1718)* (London: H.M. Stationery Office, 1803), 125; Newman to Chamberlayne, 20 June 1715, HNL vol. 5, f. 80.

149. Tim Hitchcock, "Paupers and Preachers: The SPCK and the Parochial Workhouse Movement," in *Stilling the Grumbling Hive: The Response to Social and Economic Problems in England, 1689-1750*, ed. Lee Davison, Tim Hitchcock, Tim Keirn, and Robert B. Shoemaker (New York: St. Martin's, 1992), 145–165; Joan Simon, "From Charity School to Workhouse in the 1720s: The SPCK and Mr. Marriott's Solution," *History of Education* 17 (1988): 113–129; Jeremy Schmidt, "Charity and the Government of the Poor in the English Charity-School Movement circa 1700-1730," *Journal of British Studies* 49, 4 (October 2010): 774–800.

150. *London Post*, 10–13 November 1699 (no. 69); *London Gazette*, 29 April–2 May 1700 (no. 3597); *Post-Boy*, 27–30 April 1700 (no. 789); *Flying Post or The Post Master*, 18 April 1701 (no. 994); and see HMC *Fitzherbert*, 189; [B.M.], *A Letter from a Gentleman to the Right Reverend Father in God, Henry, Lord Bishop of London* (London, 1701).

151. White Kennett's ecclesiastical diary, BL Lansdowne MS 1024, ff. 133, 140; Thomas Tanner to Arthur Charlett, 4 June 1700, Ballard MS 4, f. 44; *London Gazette*, 22 August 1700 (no. 3630); *New State of Europe or A True Account of Publick Transactions and Learning*, 9 December 1701 (no. 36); and see William Sherlock, *An exhortation to those redeemed slaves, who came in a solemn procession to St. Pauls Cathedral, on the 11th of March 1701/02* (London, 1702).

152. 31 October 1700, McClure, *SPCK Minutes*, 88.

153. James Kirkwood to Newman, 11 May 1709; James Kirkwood to Newman, 6 June 1709; CUL SPCK ALB, §1635, §1639; Mrs. M. Kynaird to [Henry Newman?], n.d., Bodl. Rawlinson D 839, f. 64.

154. Chamberlayne to ————, 17 July 1709, BL Add MS 61649, f. 46.

155. Newman to William Gordon, 29 June 1714, HNL vol. 4, f. 54.

156. Gelieu, Dean & Minister of Neuchâtel in the Name of the whole Body of Divines of that Government, to the Society, 12 June 1701, CUL SPCK MS D2/2, §329; Duffy,

"Correspondence Fraternelle," 252; W. R. Ward, *The Protestant Evangelical Awakening* (Cambridge: Cambridge University Press, 1992).

157. May 1699, McClure, *SPCK Minutes*, 24; on Francke's own efforts, see August Hermann Francke, *Pietas Hallensis: or a publick demonstration of the foot-steps of a divine being yet in the world* (London, 1705), translated into English by SPCK member A. W. Boehm and frequently included in the society's book packets.

158. Ostervald to Society, 11 March 1701, McClure, *SPCK Minutes*, 326.

159. Chamberlayne to De Beringhen, 3 December 1700, McClure, *SPCK Minutes*, 94–96; De Beringhen to Chamberlayne, 11 January 1701, NS, CUL SPCK MS D2/2, §230; interestingly, de Beringhen's proposal for a Protestant international sounds very similar to one that Gilbert Burnet attributed to Oliver Cromwell, *HOT*, 1:142–143.

160. J.-F. Ostervald, *The grounds and principles of the Christian religion* (London, 1704), vii.

161. Francke to Society, 21 January 1701, CUL SPCK MS D2/2, §241.

162. *The Remains of John Locke, Esq.* (London, 1714), 15–16.

163. A Letter from a Learned Divine proposing the forming a Society of Divines and others for promoting the Interest of the Protestant Religion and the weakening of popery, [*temp.* Anne], BL Add MS 4474, ff. 14–21; Samuel Brewster to Robert Nelson, 5 May 1714, BL Add MS 45511, f. 114; Edmund Gibson to Lewis Atterbury, 31 July 1701, OSB MS 26, Box 1, Folder 9.

164. Duffy, "Correspondence Fraternelle," 256–257; Linda Kirk, "Eighteenth-Century Geneva and a Changing Calvinism," in *Religion and National Identity*, ed. Stewart Mews (Oxford: Studies in Church History, 1982), 367–379; Philip Benedict, *Christ's Churches Purely Reformed: A Social History of Calvinism* (New Haven, CT: Yale University Press, 2002), 348–352.

165. William Bultmann, "A Layman Proposes Protestant Union: Robert Hales and the Helvetic Churches, 1700–1705," *Church History* 27 (March 1958): 32–45.

166. Hales's own ideological convictions seem somewhat nebulous, but he was a firm supporter of the Protestant succession and the house of Hanover. Theophilus Dorrington to Arthur Charlett, 12 May 1711, Ballard MS 30, f. 56; Newman to Hales, 23 February 1713/14, HNL vol. 4, f. 7; and see Hales's lengthy correspondence with the nonjuror George Harbin in 1712–1713, BL Add MS 29545, ff. 6, 8, 12–13, 14, 17; and BL Add MS 32096, ff. 105–106, 108–109.

167. Robert Hales to Chamberlayne, 12 January 1701; Hales to John Hodges, 8 February 1701; Ostervald to Masson, 6 April 1701, CUL SPCK MS D2/2, §239, §258, §292.

168. Hales to Chamberlayne, 12 January 1701; Hales to Hodges, 8 February 1701; Scherer to Chamberlayne, 18 February 1701; Hales to Chamberlayne, 19 May 1701, CUL SPCK MS D2/2, §239, §258, §259, §308.

169. Chamberlayne to Wanley, 19 April 1703, BL Add MS 70475 (unfoliated); Nelson to Wanley, 22 December 1703, BL Harleian MS 3780, f. 213; Catalogue of the small Tracts allowed the Missionaries to Distribute among, &c., [1705], LPL Gibson MS 941, §73; Newman to Whitfield, 14 December 1710, HNL vol. 1; Newman to de la Mothe, 21 June 1712, HNL vol. 2, f. 64; A Catalogue of Books given by the Society for Promoting Xtian Knowledge to the Hon. Governor Pitt, [1716], HNL vol. 6, f. 18.

170. Bruno Bürki, "Reformed Worship in Continental Europe Since the Seventeenth Century," *Christian Worship in Reformed Churches Past and Present*, ed. Lukas Vischer (Grand Rapids, MI: Wm. B. Eerdmans, 2003), 37–39.

171. William Finch to Arthur Charlett, n.d. [ca. 1701], Ballard MS 20, f. 8; Gilbert Burnet to Archbishop Tenison, 15 August 1702, LPL Gibson MS 930, §31; 21 September 1705, LPL, SPG Minutes vol. 1, f. 66; Robert Watts to Arthur Charlett, 23 August 1708, Ballard MS 25, f. 84; Robert Watts to Henry Shute, 23 May 1709, CUL SPCK ALB, §1620; Newman to Wood, 31 March 1711; Newman to Wood, 7 August 1711, HNL vol. 1; Newman to Wood, 15 September 177, HNL vol. 2, ff. 8–9; De la Mothe to Henry Newman, 20 May [1712?]; De la Mothe to Newman, 4 September [1712?], Bodl. Rawlinson D 839, ff. 65, 134–135; White Kennett memorandum, 27 February 1712, BL Lansdowne MS 1024, f. 368; 8 January 1713, SPCK Minutes, vol. 6, 1712–1715; Newman to Dean & Pastors of the Church of Neuchâtel, 16 June 1714, HNL Special Letters, f. 120; 28 July 1715, SPCK Minutes, vol. 7, 1715–1716; Newman to Colman, 20 October 1722, HNL New England Letters vol. 1, ff. 41–45.

172. *The liturgy used in the churches of the principality of Neufchatel* (London, 1712), iv; De la Mothe to Newman, 4 September [1712?], Bodl. Rawlinson D 839, ff. 134–135; on de la Mothe, see P. Bultmann and W. A. Bultmann, "Claude Groteste de la Mothe and the Church of England, 1685 to 1713," *Proceedings of the Huguenot Society of London* 20 (1956–1964): 89–101; Charles Leslie, *The Wolf Stript of His Shepherd's Cloathing* (London, 1704), appendix 4, 16; George Every, *The High Church Party, 1688–1718* (London: SPCK, 1956), 123–124; Duffy, "Correspondence Fraternelle," 267–273; Bishop John Williams to Arthur Charlett, 8 May 1707, Ballard MS 9, f. 86.

173. Hales to Hodges, 8 February 1701, CUL SPCK MS D2/2, §258.

174. Scherer to Chamberlayne, 18 February 1701, CUL SPCK MS D2/2, §259; John Leonhardi, *A true and faithful representation of the miserable state of the church of Christ in the country of the Grisons* (London, 1704), 3, 5; Duffy, "Correspondence Fraternelle," 259.

175. Bultmann, "A Layman Proposes Union," 42; HMC *Portland*, 4:109, 115, 170, 177, 196.

176. Notes as to Mr. Hales being appointed Commissioner to Investigate the position & grievances of Protestants in various States [ca. 1706], CHC MS RN/8/40.

177. White Kennett, *The Charity of schools for poor children recommended in a sermon preach'd in the Parish-church of St. Sepulchers, May 16, 1706* (London, 1706), 32; and see White Kennett to Arthur Charlett, 27 March 1707, Ballard MS 7, f. 115.

178. Sugiko Nishikawa, "The SPCK in defence of protestant minorities in Early Eighteenth-Century Europe," *JEH* 56 (October 2005): 730–748; Thompson, *Britain, Hanover and the Protestant Interest*, 159–167; Robert Ingram, "Archbishop Thomas Secker (1693–1768), Anglican Identity and Relations with Foreign Protestants in the Mid-18th Century," in *From Strangers to Citizens*, ed. R. Vigne and C. Littleton (Brighton: Sussex Academic Press, 2001), 527–538.

179. 28 November 1700, 11 March 1703, 28 October 1703, McClure, *SPCK Minutes*, 94, 218, 241–242.

180. Humphrey Wanley Letter Draft, 12 September 1705, BL Harleian MS 7190, f. 33; Chamberlayne to Arthur Charlett, 3 June 1707, Ballard MS 17, f. 117; Newman to Chamberlayne, 12 Dec 1713, HNL vol. 3, f. 82; on the broader campaign for the emancipation of Protestants on the French galleys, see Laurence Huey Boles Jr., *The Huguenots, the Protestant Interest and the War of the Spanish Succession, 1702–1714* (New York: Peter Lang, 1997), 202–209.

181. See the comments of A. W. Boehm, quoted in Brunner, *Halle Pietists in England*, 55; and Newman to Chamberlayne, 12 December 1713, HNL vol. 3, f. 82.

182. White Kennett's materials for the history of the SPG, BL Lansdowne MS 1032, ff. 79–80.

183. H. T. Dickinson, "The Poor Palatines and the Parties," *EHR* 324 (July 1967): 464–485; Daniel Statt, *Foreigners and Englishmen: The Controversy over Immigration and Population, 1660–1760* (Newark, NJ: University of Delaware Press, 1995); William O'Reilly, "The Naturalization Act of 1709 and the Settlement of Germans in Britain, Ireland and the Colonies," in *From Strangers to Citizens*, 492–502; Phillip Otterness, *Becoming German: The 1709 Palatine Migration to New York* (Ithaca, NY: Cornell University Press, 2004), 41–56.

184. Ralph Bridges to William Trumbull, 30 March 1709, BL Add MS 72494, f. 107; *A View of the Queen and Kingdom's Enemies, In the Case of the Poor Palatines* (London, 1711?).

185. Extracts of the Palatine Commission Minutes, 12 June 1709, BL Add MS 61649, f. 82; also present was the London banker and SPCK member Henry Hoare, a solid Tory, though a veteran of other Protestant relief efforts.

186. White Kennett's materials for the history of the SPG, BL Lansdowne MS 1032, ff. 79–80.

187. Chamberlayne to Sunderland, 20 September 1709, BL Add MS 61649, f. 50.

188. Brunner, *Halle Pietists in England*, 49–70.

189. 26 March 1702, 9 April 1702, McClure, *SPCK Minutes*, 175–176.

190. Ludolf to Arthur Charlett, 17 February 1698; 10 July 1699; 14 August 1700, Ballard MS 26, ff. 81–96; Mr. Wilhelm Henry Ludolf's Proposals for Relating to Instruction of Greek Christians, 23 December 1700; Mr. Wilhelm Henry Ludolf's Scheme About a Catechism To Be Compos'd For the Use of the Greek Christians, McClure, *SPCK Minutes*, 101–103, 113–115; Chamberlayne to Wanley, 26 December 1700, 11 February 1701, BL Add MS 70474, unfoliated; Samuel Hayward to James Hoare, 2 June 1708, CUL SPCK ALB, §1470; and see Brunner, *Halle Pietists in England*, 42–46.

191. On Boehm, see Brunner, *Halle Pietists in England;* Newman to Cotton Mather, 31 August 1722, in W. O. B. Allen and Edmund McClure, *Two Hundred Years: The History of the Society for Promoting Christian Knowledge* (London: SPCK, 1898), 231–233.

192. Graham Jefcoate, "Joseph Downing and the Publication of Pietist Literature in England, 1705–1734," in *The German Book, 1450–1750*, ed. John L. Flood and William A. Kelly (London: British Library, 1995), 319–332.

193. *Propagation of the Gospel in the East* (London, 1709), i–xxxi.

194. Robert Watts to Arthur Charlett, 8 January 1711, Ballard MS 25, f. 86; Robert Nelson to Arthur Charlett, 20 January 177, Ballard MS 23, f. 86; White Kennett's materials for the history of the SPG, BL Lansdowne MS 1032, ff. 67–71; Newman to Ayerst, 27 January 1713, HNL vol. 3, ff. 5–6.

195. Lowther-Clarke, *History of the S.P.C.K*, 61; the committee members are listed in a letter "To the Governor and Council of Fort St. George, 2 Feb 1713," HNL Special Letters, 1708–1736, ff. 90–92.

196. Ziegenbalg to a friend in London, 17 January 1710 [1711], in *Propagation of the Gospel in the East*, 3rd ed. (London, 1718), Part 2: 45.

197. Draft of an appeal for subscriptions toward printing 8000 Copies of the NT & Psalter in Arabic, Bodl. Rawlinson D 839, f. 121.

198. The Charitable Subscriptions upon the Proposal for Encouraging the Protestant Missionaries and Erecting Charity Schools in the East Indies, [1711], LPL Fulham Papers, Compton MS 2, f. 98; Newman to Wood, 15 September 1711, HNL vol. 2, ff. 8–9.

199. Newman to Woodward, 18 December 1710, HNL vol. 1; To the Honble the Court of Directors of the United East India Company of England, 8 December 1710, HNL Special Letters, 1708–1736, f. 36.

200. Newman to Archbishop Tenison, 17 May 1712, HNL vol. 2, f. 51; Newman to Ayerst at Utrecht, 27 January 1712/13, HNL vol. 3, ff. 5–6; Newman to William Lewis, 21 April 1712, HNL vol. 2, f. 47; Newman to Boehm, 19 May 1712, HNL vol. 2, f. 50; The East India frigate *Jane*, on which Fincke had set sail, was taken by a French admiral at Rio de Janeiro and eventually ransomed for £3,500, £150 of which covered the supplies for the mission. Fincke died at sea shortly after the release of the *Jane*.

201. "Heads which may be used in answering Mons. Du Mont's letter," n.d., Bodl. Rawlinson D 839, f. 202; Boehm to Newman, 1 January 1711, BL Add MS 4277, f, 32.

202. *Propagation of the Gospel in the East*, Part 2: 50; E. Benz, "Pietist and Puritan Sources of Early Protestant World Missions (Cotton Mather and A. H. Francke)," *Church History* 20 (June 1951): 30.

203. Newman to Postlethwayte, 12 November 1712, HNL vol. 2, f. 87.

204. Newman to Chamberlayne, 19 December 1713, HNL vol. 3, f. 84.

205. Quoted in Brunner, *Halle Pietists in England*, 109; I have largely followed Brunner's in-depth analysis of this controversy, 107–112.

206. Unsurprisingly, the house of Hanover was an enthusiastic supporter of the mission; see George I's letter to the Danish missionaries, 3 August 1717, Bodl. Rawlinson D 839, f. 171.

207. Robert Booth to Hodges, 16 March 1700, CUL SPCK MS D2/2, §63.

208. Samuel Brewster and Vigerus Edwards, *Account of a design to erect libraries in the Highlands of Scotland* (1703); 18 November 1703, McClure, *SPCK Minutes*, 245–246; Humphrey Wanley Letter Draft, BL Harleian MS 7190, f. 20.

209. *Acts of the General Assembly of the Church of Scotland, 1648–1832* (Edinburgh: Edinburgh Printing and Publishing, 1843), 332, 388–389.

210. Sir John Philipps to Society, 17 December 1708, CUL SPCK ALB, §1529.

211. The first genll Lettr sent to N. Btish Correspondents, Nov 1708; Newman to Carstares, Stirling and Baillie, 28 December 1708, HNL Special Letters, ff. 5–7, 7–8; William Carstares to Society, 27 November 1708; Robert Baillie to Chamberlayne, 24 December 1708, CUL SPCK ALB, §1519, §1542.

212. Sir John Philipps to Society, 17 December 1708; Bishop Lloyd to Society, 16 November 1708, CUL SPCK ALB, §1529, §1497.

213. John Chamberlayne to ————, 23 June 1709; BL Add MS 61649, f. 38; Newman to Carstares, [December 1710?], HNL vol. 1.

214. Newman to Baillie, 25 January 1709, HNL Special Letters, f. 9.

215. William Carstares to Newman, 12 May 1709, CUL SPCK ALB, §1626; *An Account of the Rise, Constitution, and Management of the Society in Scotland for Propagating Christian Knowledge* (London, 1714), 8–17; on the Society in Scotland for Propagating Christian Knowledge, see Ryan K. Frace, "The Foundations of Enlightenment: Transformations in Religious Toleration, Orthodoxy, and Pluralism in Early Modern Scotland, 1660–1752" (PhD diss., University of Chicago, 2005), 390–435.

216. John Dundas to John Chamberlayne, 10 December 1709; Chamberlayne to Dundas, 31 December 1709 [copy], Bodl. Rawlinson D 839, f. 32, 144c.

217. Ralph Bridges to William Trumbull, 23 January 1710, BL Add MS 72494, f. 153; Every, *High Church Party*, 111–116, 120–121.

218. "The Reverend Mr. [Benjamin] Wood's reasons against writing a congratulatory letter to the Corporation Society established in Scotland, addrest to the Society for Promoting Christian Knowledge in England, 10 Nov 1709," CHC MS RN/1/22.

219. Newman to Carstares, 9 February 1710, HNL Special Letters, f. 18.

220. As exemplified in the lay baptism debate, for which, see Chapter 4.

221. John Toland, *The State Anatomy of Great Britain* (London, 1717), 55; "The King to the Soldiers att the Battle of Mons, A Song," BL Add MS 3677, f. 7.

222. All attendance statistics are from attendance records in SPCK Minutes, Part A: Minutes and Reports, reel no. 2, vols. 6–8, 1712–1719.

223. Craig Rose, " 'Seminarys of Faction and Rebellion': Jacobites, Whigs and the London Charity Schools, 1716–1724," *HJ* 34 (December 1991): 831–855.

224. Robert Watts to Newman, 8 March 1709, CUL SPCK ALB, §1580.

225. Newman to William Lloyd, 26 May 1713, HNL vol. 2, ff. 29–30.

226. Newman to John Evans, Bishop of Bangor, 19 May 1715, HNL vol. 5, f. 29.

227. Newman to Nelson, 2 December 1713, HNL vol. 3, f. 81.

228. 29 January, 12 February 1713, SPCK Minutes, vol. 6, 1712–1715.

229. Newman to Archbishop Wake, 11 June 1716, Wake MS 15, f. 440, *The Papers of Archbishop Wake* (London: World Microfilm Publications, 1999); Newman to Hales, 23 February 1714, HNL vol. 4, f. 7; Thomas Bray to Robert Hales, 8 October 1714, Bodl. Rawlinson C 743, ff. 29–30; Newman to Dolins, 19 February 1715, HNL vol. 5, f. 7; and on Bray's anti-Jacobite activities, see John Findon, "The Nonjurors and the Church of England, 1689–1714" (PhD diss., Oxford University, 1978), 89–90.

230. 16 April 1713, SPCK Minutes, vol. 6, 1712–1715; Newman to Holling, 23 February 1714, HNL vol. 4, f. 9; Newman to Bishop John Robinson, 8 November 1715; Newman to Philip Stubbs, 2 May 1716, HNL vol. 5, ff. 56–57, 74.

231. Newman to the Princess Sophia, 3 August 1713, HNL vol. 3, f. 47.

232. William Ayerst to Newman, 16 August 1713, Bodl. Rawlinson D 839, f. 57; 14 January 1714, SPCK Minutes, vol. 6, 1712–1715; Newman to Hales, 17 August 1714; Newman to Hales, 27 August 1714, HNL vol. 4, ff. 58–59, 60–62; Thomas Bray to Robert Hales, 8 October 1714, Bodl. Rawlinson C 743, f. 29.

233. Newman to Hales, 23 February 1714, HNL vol. 4, f. 6.

234. Newman to Hales, 27 August 1714, HNL vol. 4, f. 62.

235. Thomas Bray to Robert Hales, 8 October 1714, Bodl. Rawlinson C 743, f. 29.

236. Newman to Hales, 17 August 1714, HNL vol. 4, f. 58–59.

237. Newman to Dolins, 19 February 1715, HNL vol. 5, f. 7.

238. 28 June, 19 July, 26 July, 30 August, 6 September 1716, SPCK Minutes, vol. 7, 1715–1716; Newman to Wake, 8 September 1716, HNL vol. 5, ff. 84–85.

239. Newman to Harvey, 1 November 1716, HNL vol. 6, f. 15; 22 November 1716, SPCK Minutes, vol. 7, 1715–1716.

240. Kennett, *Charity schools for poor children*, 38–39.

241. Stephen John Charles Taylor, "Church and State in England in the Mid-Eighteenth Century: The Newcastle Years 1742–1762" (PhD diss., University of Cambridge, 1987).

4. Sacerdotalism and Civil Society

1. "Minutes on the Church in Danger debates, 6 Dec 1705," BL Lansdowne 1034, ff. 4–5; "The Church in Danger Debates, 1705," BL Add MS 28252, ff. 82–88; Abel Boyer, *The History of the reign of Queen Anne . . . Year the fourth* (London, 1706), 203–212; Clyve Jones, "Debates in the House of Lords on 'The Church in Danger,' 1705 and Dr. Sacheverell's Impeachment, 1710," *HJ* 19 (September 1976): 759–771.

2. Leonard J. Trinterud, "A.D. 1689: The End of the Clerical World," in *Theology in Sixteenth and Seventeenth Century England: Papers Read at Clark Library Seminar, February 6, 1971*, ed. Winthrop S. Hudson and Leonard J. Trinterud (Los Angeles: William Andrews Clark Memorial Library, 1971), 25–51.

3. John Neville Figgis, *Churches in the Modern State*, 2nd ed. (London: Longmans, Green, 1914) remains one of the most thoughtful considerations of this subject available. Useful examinations may also be found in Adrian Hastings, *Church and State: The English Experience* (Exeter: University of Exeter Press, 1991); David Fergusson, *Church, State and Civil Society* (Cambridge: Cambridge University Press, 2004); William T. Cavanaugh, *The Theopolitical Imagination: Christian Practices of Space and Time* (London: T & T Clark, 2002); and Rupert Graf Strachwitz, "The Churches and Civil Society," in *Church and Civil Society: The Role of Christian Churches in the Emerging Countries of Argentina, Mexico, Nigeria and South Africa*, ed. Gerhard Kruip and Helmut Reifeld (Sankt Augustin/Berlin: Konrad Adenauer Foundation, 2007), 29–33.

4. J. A. I. Champion, *The Pillars of Priestcraft Shaken* (Cambridge: Cambridge University Press, 1992); Nigel Aston, "Anglican Responses to Anticlericalism in the 'Long' Eighteenth Century, c. 1689–1830," in *Anticlericalism in Britain, c. 1500–1914*, ed. Nigel Aston and Matthew Cragoe (Stroud: Sutton, 2001), 115–137; S. J. Barnett, *Idol Temples and Crafty Priests: The Origins of Enlightenment Anticlericalism* (New York: St. Martin's Press, 1999); Jeffrey R. Wigelsworth, *Deism in Enlightenment England: Theology, Politics and Newtonian Public Science* (Manchester: Manchester University Press, 2009).

5. Mark Goldie, "The Revolution of 1689 and the Structure of Political Argument," *Bulletin for Research in the Humanities* 83 (1980): 473–564; Harold Laski, *Political Thought in England from Locke to Bentham* (New York: Henry Holt, 1920), 77–94; L. M. Hawkins, *Allegiance in Church and State: The Problem of the Nonjurors in the English Revolution* (London: Routledge and Sons, 1928); Charles Mullett, "A Case of Allegiance: William Sherlock and the Revolution of 1688," *Huntington Library Quarterly* 10 (1946): 83–103; Kenneth Padley, "Rendering unto Caesar in the Age of Revolution: William Sherlock and William of Orange," *JEH* 59 (October 2008): 680–696; John Findon, "The Nonjurors and the Church of England, 1689–1714" (PhD diss., Oxford University, 1978), 126–151.

6. See, for instance, Dr. [Thomas] "Togry" Smith, A Just Complaint against the Degenerous Clergie of the Church of England, April 1690, BL Add MS 40160, ff. 123–137; or Thomas Cartwright, "Bishop of Chester's Dying Declaration, 27 August 1689," BL Stowe MS 746, f. 116.

7. George Hickes, *An Apology for the New Separation in a letter to Dr. John Sharpe, Archbishop of York* (London, 1691), 8–9.

8. On the crucial shift in nonjuring polemic from Tory "state point" to Cyprianic "church point," see Findon, "The Nonjurors," 152–173.

9. Edward Stillingfleet, *A Discourse concerning the unreasonableness of a new separation* (London, 1689), 2–3.

10. *Anglicani novi schismatis redargutio, seu, Tractatus ex historiis ecclesiasticis* (Oxford, 1691); Humphrey Hody, *The unreasonableness of a separation from the new bishops, or, A treatise out of ecclesiastical history* (London, 1691); Humphrey Hody, *The Case of Sees vacant by an unjust or uncanonical deprivation stated* (London, 1693); John Willes to Arthur Charlett, 15 October [1691?], Ballard MS 25, f. 27; for an overview of this debate, see Findon, "The Nonjurors," 164–168; Mark Goldie, "The Nonjurors, Episcopacy, and the Origins of the Convocation Controversy," in *Ideology and Conspiracy: Aspects of Jacobitism, 1689–1759*, ed. E. Cruickshanks (Edinburgh: J. Donalds, 1982), 20–24.

11. Francis Brokesby, *The life of Mr. Henry Dodwell*, 2 vols. (London, 1715), 2:223; Thomas Lathbury, *A History of the Nonjurors: Their Controversies and Writings* (London: William Pickering, 1845), 201–203, 260–263; Hawkins, *Allegiance in Church and State*, 11–118.

12. George Every, *The High Church Party, 1688–1718* (London: SPCK, 1956), 61–74; Andrew Starkie, "Contested Histories of the English Church: Gilbert Burnet and Jeremy Collier," *Huntington Library Quarterly* 68 (2005): 335–351.

13. Thomas Ken to George Hickes, 17 March 1700, LPL MS 3171, p. 150; Dodwell to an unnamed bookseller, 28 May 1694, BL Harleian MS 6210, f. 62.

14. Hawkins, *Allegiance in Church and State*, 118–130; R. D. Cornwall, *Visible and Apostolic: The Constitution of the Church in High Church Anglican and Non-Juror Thought* (Newark: University of Delaware Press, 1993), 73–93.

15. George Hickes, A Letter to a Clergyman on occasion of the New Separation [ca. 1691], LPL MS 3171, p. 165.

16. J. H. Overton, *The Nonjurors: Their Lives, Principles and Writings* (London: Smith, Elder, 1902), 14; Paul Kléber Monod, *Jacobitism and the English People, 1688–1788* (Cambridge: Cambridge University Press, 1989), 138–145.

17. Charles Leslie, *The Case of the regale and of the pontificat stated.*, 2nd ed. (London, 1701), 75.

18. On these ambiguities and their intolerability in the postrevolutionary climate, see the illuminating analysis in John Spurr, *The Restoration Church of England, 1646–1689* (New Haven, CT: Yale University Press, 1991), 132–165; Kenneth Locke, *The Church in Anglican Theology* (Farnham, UK: Ashgate, 2009), 26–27, 62–66, 72–73.

19. Jean-Louis Quantin, *The Church of England and Christian Antiquity* (Oxford: Oxford University Press, 2009), 389–392, makes very clear the relative eccentricity of Cyprianic theories of episcopacy from the mainstream of Restoration Anglican ecclesiology; Jean-Louis Quantin, "Anglican Scholarship Gone Mad? Henry Dodwell (1641–1711) and Christian Antiquity," in *History of Scholarship: A Selection of Papers from the Seminar on the History of Scholarship held annually at the Warburg Institute* (Oxford: Oxford University Press, 2006), 331–332; Spurr, *Restoration Church of England*, 129–130, 157–158; Findon, "The Nonjurors," 169.

20. Nathaniel Bisbie, *Unity of Priesthood Necessary to the Unity of Communion in a Church* (London, 1692), 6; John Kettlewell, *Of Christian Communion* (1693), Part 3, 7.

21. Charles Leslie, *A Discourse shewing who they are that are now qualify'd to administer baptism and the Lord's Supper* (London, 1698), 4.

22. Henry Dodwell, *A Vindication of the deprived bishops* (London, 1692), 17.

23. Dodwell, *A Vindication*, 29; Kettlewell, it should be noted, was decidedly less uncompromising on this question, see *Of Christian Communion*, Part 3, 34–43; Edward Stephens, *An Abstract of Common Principles of a Just Vindication of the Rights of the Kingdom of God upon Earth* (London, 1700), 3.

24. On the counter-Enlightenment thrust of nonjuring thought, see C. D. A. Leighton, "The Religion of the Non-Jurors and the Early British Enlightenment: A Study of Henry Dodwell," *History of European Ideas* 28 (2002): 247–262; and C. D. A. Leighton, "Ancienneté among the Non-Jurors: A Study of Henry Dodwell," *History of European Ideas* 31 (2005): 1–16.

25. Kettlewell, *Of Christian Communion*, Part 3, 11; The Controversy betwixt Dr. Hickes and Mrs. Mary Astel, [1705], LPL MS 3171, p. 172.

26. Jeremy Collier, *A Brief Essay concerning the independency of church-power* (1692), 2.

27. George Hickes, *Two Treatises, One of the Christian Priesthood, The Other of the Dignity of the Episcopal Order*, 2nd ed. (London, 1707), 62–63; George Hickes to an unnamed clergymen, 25 May 1714, LPL MS 3171, p. 218.

28. Henry Dodwell, *An Epistolary Discourse Proving, from the Scriptures and the First Fathers, that the Soul is a Principle Naturally Mortal* (London, 1707), x.

29. Leslie, *Case of the regale*, 215–216.

30. Goldie, "Origins of the Convocation Controversy," 18–19.

31. But see the nonjurors' opponent Edward Welchman, *A Second Defense of the Church of England from the Charge of Schism and Heresy* (London, 1698), 12.

32. Leslie, *Case of the regale*, 17; *No-Church Establish'd: Or, The Schismatical Unmasked* (London, 1706), 4.

33. Henry Dodwell, *The Doctrine of the Church of England concerning the independency of the Clergy on the lay-power* (London, 1694), xiv.

34. Collier, *Brief Essay*, 6; Henry Dodwell, *A defence of the vindication of the deprived bishops* (London, 1695), 84–85; also cf. Matthew Tindal, *Rights of the Christian Church asserted, against the Romish and all other priests who claim an independent power over it*, 3rd ed. (London, 1707), 83–84.

35. Leslie, *Case of the regale*, 10–11; and see Welchman, *Second Defense*, 7.

36. "Mr. Dodwell's Letter to the Dean of Canterbury, 12 May 1691," BL Stowe MS 746, f. 141; Henry Dodwell, "To the Right Revd ye Ld Bp of St. Asaph now Elect of Coventry & Lichfield," [1692?], BL Stowe MS 746, f. 143.

37. Hickes, Letter to a Clergyman, LPL MS 3171, p. 165.

38. Bisbie, *Unity of Priesthood*, 28; Leslie, *Case of the regale*, 19; *No-Church Establish'd*, 12.

39. Bisbie, *Unity of Priesthood*, 27.

40. Leslie, *Case of the regale*, 19.

41. Kettlewell, *Of Christian Communion*, Part 1, 45; Stephens, *Abstract of Common Principles*, 7.

42. Dodwell, *Epistolary Discourse*, xlvi–xlvii; for a reply, see John Turner, *Justice Done to Human Souls, In a Short View of Mr. Dodwell's late Book* (London, 1706), 109.

43. Michael Heyd, *Be Sober and Reasonable: The Critique of Enthusiasm in the Seventeenth and Early Eighteenth Centuries* (New York: E. J. Brill, 1995); a much wider survey may be found in R. A. Knox, *Enthusiasm: A Chapter in the History of Religion with Special Reference to XVII and XVIII Centuries* (Oxford: Clarendon, 1951).

44. Charles Leslie, *The snake in the grass* (London, 1696), v–viii.

45. Charles Leslie, *A Discourse Proving the Divine Institution of Water-Baptism* (London, 1697), 30; and see George Hickes, "The Spirit of Enthusiasm Exorcised," in *Sermons on several subjects* (London, 1715), 102–105.

46. Charles Leslie, *A Short and Easie Method with the Deists* (London, 1698), 26–27.

47. John Locke, *A Letter concerning toleration, humbly submitted* (London, 1689), 7; for a discussion of this distinction, see J. G. A. Pocock, "Within the Margins: The Definition of Orthodoxy," in *The Margins of Orthodoxy: Heterodox Writing and Cultural Response, 1660–1750*, ed. R. D. Lund (Cambridge: Cambridge University Press, 1995), 33–53.

48. Leslie, *Snake in the grass*, 209–210; Leslie, *A Discourse Proving*, 35–36; and on the anti-individualism of the nonjurors, see C. D. A Leighton, "The Non-Jurors and Their History," *Journal of Religious History* 29 (October 2005): 247–249.

49. Controversy betwixt Hickes and Astel, 1705, LPL MS 3171, p. 173; George Hickes to Scandret, 11 August 1697, BL Add MS 40160, f. 94; Roger Laurence, *Lay Baptism Invalid* (London, 1708), 32; for a critical evaluation of these claims, see Tindal, *Rights of the Christian Church*, xliii.

50. Hickes, *Two Treatises*, 62–63, 86–91.

51. Cornwall, *Visible and Apostolic*, 116–141.

52. Dodwell, *Defence of the vindication*, 84; Henry Dodwell, "An Hypothesis concerning Sacerdotal Remission of Sins," in *Epistolary Discourse*, lxiv; see also Tindal, *Rights of the Christian Church*, 87.

53. George Hickes to Scandret, 11 August 1697, BL Add MS 40160, f. 95.

54. Dodwell, *Defence of the Vindication*, 84; Dodwell to an unnamed bookseller, 28 May 1694, BL Harleian MS 6210, ff. 58–59.

55. Leslie, *A Discourse Proving*, 7–8.

56. Cornwall, *Visible and Apostolic*, 133–136.

57. On Dodwell's *Epistolary Discourse*, see Quantin, "Anglican Scholarship Gone Mad?," 308–309, 333, 353; Philip C. Almond, *Heaven and Hell in Enlightenment England* (Cambridge: Cambridge University Press, 1994), 60–67; Roy Porter, *Flesh in the Age of Reason* (London: Allen Lane, 2003), 98–99; Justin Champion, "'The Men of Matter': Spirits, Matter and the Politics of Priestcraft, 1701–1709," in *Scepticisme, clandestinité et libre pensée*, ed. Gianni Paganini, Miguel Benítez, and James Dybikowski (Paris: Honore Champion, 2002), 115–150; Ann Thomason, *Bodies of Thought: Science, Religion, and the Soul in the Early Enlightenment* (Oxford: Oxford University Press, 2008), 97–134.

58. Dodwell, *Epistolary Discourse*, 50, 115, 281.

59. On the actual mortality of the soul, see Anthony Collins, *A Letter to the Learned Mr. Dodwell*, 2nd ed. (London, 1709); Jeffrey R. Wigelsworth, "Samuel Clarke's Newtonian Soul," *Journal of the History of Ideas* 70 (January 2009): 45–68; Turner, *Justice Done to Human Souls*, 110–112.

60. Richard Smalbroke, *The doctrine of an universal judgment asserted* (London, 1706), 20; Edmund Chishull, *A Charge of Heresy, Maintain'd against Mr. Dodwel's late Epistolary Discourse* (London, 1706), 157; John Hutton to Arthur Charlett, 7 February 1706, Ballard MS 35, f. 104.

61. *Observator* 6, 61 (27 September–1 October 1707).

62. See Leslie's rather feeble defense in *Rehearsal* 2, 36 (11 February 1707); John Davys, *A sort of answer to a piece of a book entituled A battle royal* (Oxford, 1710), 25–26.

63. Overton, *Nonjurors*, 291–292; Alfred G. Mortimer, *The Eucharistic Sacrifice* (London: Longmans, Green, 1901), 363–393.

64. Hickes, *Two Treatises*, 57; George Hickes to Arthur Charlett, 11 October 1707, Ballard MS 12, f. 160; John Johnson to Arthur Charlett, 15 September 1710, Ballard MS 15, ff. 95–96; and see Cornwall, *Visible and Apostolic*, 136–141; C. W. Dugmore, *Eucharistic Doctrine in England from Hooker to Waterland* (London: SPCK, 1942), 140–154; Kenneth Hylson-Smith, *High Churchmanship in the Church of England* (Edinburgh: T & T Clark, 1993), 54–65; Findon, "The Nonjurors," 93–94.

65. The restoration of these older liturgical forms stood at the center of the so-called usages controversy that divided the nonjuring Church of England from 1717 to 1733; see Overton, *Nonjurors*, 290–308; Henry Broxap, *The Later Nonjurors* (Cambridge: Cambridge University Press, 1924); James David Smith, *The Eucharistic Doctrine of the Later Nonjurors: A Revisionist View of the Eighteenth-Century Usages Controversy* (Cambridge: Grove Books, 2000).

66. John Johnson, *The propitiatory oblation in the Holy Eucharist truly stated, and defended* (London, 1710), 27–29, 32, 68, 95, 97–98, 99–100.

67. Charles Trimnell, *A charge deliver'd to the clergy of the diocess of Norwich* (London, 1710), 13; John Turner, *A defence of the doctrine and practice of the Church of England against some modern innovations* (London, 1712), 9; Gilbert Burnet, *A Discourse of the Pastoral Care*, 4th ed. (London, 1713), preface; John Hancocke, *An answer to some things contain'd in Dr. Hicks's Christian priesthood asserted* (London, 1709).

68. John Clutterbuck, *A plain and rational vindication and explanation of the liturgy of the Church of England* (London, 1702), 7–8.

69. Dodwell, "An Hypothesis," lxii–lxix; Henry Dodwell, "The Sacerdotal Absolution is necessary for the remission of Sins, even of those who are truly Penitent," LPL MS 2522, pp. vi–xi; Brokesby, *Life of Dodwell*, 2:72–74.

70. See Thomas Brett, *A Sermon on Remission of Sins* (London, 1711); [Roger Laurence], *Sacerdotal Powers: Or the Necessity of Confession, Penance and Absolution* (London: Henry Clements, 1711); Edmund Gibson to William Nicolson, 5 August 1713, Bodl. Add MS A 269, ff. 23–24.

71. White Kennett's ecclesiastical diary, BL Lansdowne MS 1024, f. 374; and see William Newton, *The principles of the low-church-men fairly represented and defended* (London, 1714), 20; William Quarles to Tenison, London, 5 September 1711, LPL Gibson MS 941, §30; Burnet, *Pastoral Care*, 4th ed., preface.

72. Monod, *Jacobitism and the English People*, 99–100.

73. *A true copy of papers delivered by Sir John Friend and Sir William Parkyns* (London, 1696).

74. *Diary of John Evelyn*, ed. William Bray, 6 vols. (London: Bickers and Son, 1906), 3:324–325; and see Lathbury, *History of the Nonjurors*, 168–177; Overton, *Nonjurors*, 124–127; Leighton, "Non-Jurors and Their History," 251–252.

75. Declaration by Tenison and the Bishops attending Parliament condemning the absolution of Sir John Friend and Sir William Perkins at Tyburn, 10 April 1696, LPL Gibson MS 934, §73.

76. Jeremy Collier, *A Defence of the Absolution given to Sr William Perkins* (1696); Humphrey Hody, *Animadversions on two pamphlets lately publish'd by Mr. Collier* (London, 1696); P. H. J., *The Absolution of a Penitent* (London, 1696); and see Leighton, "Non-Jurors and Their History," 251–252.

77. Jeremy Collier, *The great question in the case of the absolution of Sir John Friend and Sir William Parkens* (London, 1696), 1–2; Jeremy Collier, *The Case of the Two Absolvers* (London, 1696), 2.

78. Collier, *A Defence of the Absolution*, 4.

79. Jeremy Collier, *A reply to The absolution of a penitent* (London, 1696), 11.

80. Collier, *A reply*, 11.

81. Hylson-Smith, *High Churchmanship in the Church of England*, 71–78.

82. See, for instance, Charles Leslie's ingenious appeal, *Querela Temporum* (London, 1694); *A Brief answer to several popular objections against the present established clergy of the Church of England* (London, 1694).

83. As I have tried to show elsewhere, Mark Goldie dramatically overstates the case in Goldie, "Origins of the Convocation Controversy," 15–35; see Brent S. Sirota, " 'The Leviathan Is Not Safely to be Angered': The Convocation Controversy, Country Ideology and Anglican High Churchmanship," in *Religion and the State: Europe and North America in the Seventeenth and Eighteenth Centuries*, ed. Joshua B. Stein and Sargon G. Donabed (Lanham, MD: Lexington Books, 2012), 41–61.

84. Charles Allestree to Humphrey Henchman, 9 July 1702, BL Add MS 27440, f. 99.

85. For an overview, see John Brewer, *The Sinews of Power: War, Money and the English State, 1688–1783* (Cambridge, MA: Harvard University Press, 1988), 155–161; H. T. Dickinson, *Liberty and Property: Political Ideology in Eighteenth Century Britain* (New York: Holmes and Meier, 1977), 163–192.

86. Francis Atterbury, *The Rights, Powers, and Privileges of an English Convocation* (London, 1700), sig. A6r.

87. Atterbury, *Rights, Powers, and Privileges*, 148.

88. R. J. Smith, *The Gothic Bequest: Medieval Institutions in British Thought, 1688–1813* (Cambridge: Cambridge University Press, 1987), 28–38; G. V. Bennett, *The Tory Crisis in Church and State, 1688–1730* (Oxford: Clarendon, 1975), 48–56; David Douglass, *English Scholars, 1660–1730*, 2nd ed. (London: Eyre and Spottiswoode, 1951), 195–221; Isaac Kramnick, "Augustan Politics and English Historiography: The Debate on the English Past, 1730–35," *History and Theory* 6 (1967): 33–56.

89. This was perfectly clear to George Hickes, who said "they are not the rights of the Church but the legal, parliamentary rights on an English convocation," for which the juring clergymen contend; Thomas Ken to George Hickes, 17 March 1700; Hickes to Ken, 9 June 1700, LPL MS 3171, pp. 150–152.

90. Francis Atterbury, *A Letter to a Convocation-Man, Concerning the Rights, Powers and Privileges of that Body* (London, 1697), 16, 50.

91. Samuel Hill, *Municipium Ecclesiasticum, or, The Rights, Liberties, and Authorities of the Christian Church* (London, 1697), 119.

92. William Nicolson to William Wake, 3 March 1697, f. 1 in *The copy correspondence of Bishop William Nicolson & Archbishop Wake, 1697–1725*, Victoria and Albert Museum, Forster Collection, microfilm.

93. Edmund Gibson to Arthur Charlett, 12 December 1699, Ballard MS 6, f. 5; White Kennett to Arthur Charlett, 3 October 1702, Ballard MS 7, f. 109; Henry Sacheverell, *The Character of a Low-Churchman* (London, 1702), 14; Francis Atterbury to Bishop Trelawny, 17 June 1703, Atterbury Correspondence, 4:411–412; Robert Ferguson, *The extraordinary case of the Bp. of St. David's* (1703); Robert Ferguson, *The Bishop of St. David's Vindicated* (London, 1705); A Letter from the Borders of Scotland concerning a Defence of the late Bishop of St. David's made and published by Mr. Ferguson, 4 Oct 1702," BL Lansdowne MS 940, ff. 22–36; and see Ruth Paley, "A Matter of Judgement: Politics, Law and the Trial of Bishop Thomas Watson," *Parliamentary History* (forthcoming); my thanks to Dr. Paley for making a copy of this essay available to me.

94. Account of the Lower House of Convocation, 20 January 1701, LPL Gibson MS 934, §8; *A Letter to the Reverend Mr. Jonathan Kimberly* (London, 1702); Charles Allestree, note, March 1702, BL Add MS 27440, f. 85; Atterbury to Trelawny, 17 March 1703, Atterbury Correspondence, 4:397.

95. Findon, "The Nonjurors," 174–175.

96. George Hickes to Arthur Charlett, 7 September 1710, Ballard MS 12, f. 180; Monod, *Jacobitism and the English People*, 147–148.

97. Henry Dodwell, *A case in view consider'd* (London, 1705); Brokesby, *Life of Dodwell*, 2:453–490; there is an excellent collection of letters regarding the reunion in John Leake's notebook, LPL MS 2522; and see Overton, *Nonjurors*, 247–237; Findon, "The Nonjurors," 178–179; Sarah Apetrei, *Women, Feminism and Religion in Early Enlightenment England* (Cambridge: Cambridge University Press, 2010), 139–147.

98. Keith Feiling, *A History of the Tory Party, 1640–1714* (Oxford: Clarendon, 1924), 368–378; Geoffrey Holmes, *British Politics in the Age of Anne*, 2nd ed. (London: Hambleden, 1987), 98–104.

99. *The Proceedings of Both Houses of Parliament in the Years 1702, 1703, 1704 upon the Bill to Prevent Occasional Conformity* (London, 1710), 11.

100. Henry Sacheverell, *The Political Union* (Oxford, 1702), 61; William Bromley to Arthur Charlett, 22 October 1702, Ballard MS 38, f. 137; "The Autobiography of Symon Patrick," in *The Works of Simon Patrick, D.D.*, ed. Alexander Taylor, 9 vols. (Oxford: Oxford University Press, 1858), 9:554–555; Peter Birch to Arthur Charlett, 14 November 1702, Ballard MS 34, f. 58; William Moore to Arthur Charlett, 24 November 1702; William Moore to Arthur Charlett, 2 December [1702], Ballard MS 32, ff. 179–180; John Wallis to Archbishop Tenison, 22 December 1702, LPL Gibson MS 930, §52.

101. Charles Davenant, *Essays upon peace at home, and war abroad* (London, 1704), 217–264; Atterbury to Bishop Trelawny, 8 and 20 November 1703, Atterbury Correspondence, 3:132–133, 135–136; Feiling, *History of the Tory Party*, 371.

102. Atterbury to Bishop Trelawny, 23 and 26 November, 9 December 1703, Atterbury Correspondence, 3:138, 140–141, 146–147; Sir John Packington's speech on occasional conformity, [1703], Ballard MS 11, ff. 78–79.

103. J. Cockburn to Nottingham, 1 January 1704, BL Add MS 29589, f. 339; Atterbury to Bishop Trelawny, 18 October 1704, Atterbury Correspondence, 3:254; Defoe to Harley, 2 November 1704, BL Add MS 70291; George Smalridge to Arthur Charlett, 23 December 1704, Ballard MS 7, f. 5; Feiling, *History of the Tory Party*, 377.

104. Holmes, *British Politics in the Age of Anne*, 100; John Flaningham, "The Occasional Conformity Controversy: Ideology and Party Politics, 1697–1711," *Journal of British Studies* 17 (Autumn 1977): 38–62; Martin Greig, "Bishop Gilbert Burnet and Latitudinarian Episcopal Opposition to the Occasional Conformity Bills, 1702–1704," *Canadian Journal of History* 41 (Autumn 2006): 247–262; Sandra J. Sarkela, "Moderation, Religion and Public Discourse: The Rhetoric of Occasional Conformity in England, 1697–1711," *Rhetorica* 15 (Winter 1997): 53–79.

105. *Proceedings of Both Houses*, 39, 53; James Owen, *Moderation a Virtue* (London, 1703), 20–21; *Review* 33 (19 May 1705).

106. *Rehearsal* 65 (11–17 October 1705); and see Mary Astell, *Moderation truly stated* (London, 1704), 100–104.

107. Henry Dodwell, *Occasional communion fundamentally destructive to the discipline of the primitive Catholick Church* (London, 1705), 8, 141.

108. Thomas Wagstaffe, *The Case of Moderation and Occasional Communion Represented* (London, 1705), 27.

109. [William Higden?], *Occasional Conformity a most unjustifiable practice* (London, 1704), 36.

110. Wagstaffe, *The Case of Moderation*, 26.

111. Samuel Grascome, *Schism Triumphant* (London, 1707), 50.

112. Dodwell, *Occasional communion fundamentally destructive*, 5–6.

113. On the ambivalent rhetorical deployment of the concept of moderation, see Ethan Shagan, "Beyond Good and Evil: Thinking with Moderates in Early Modern England," *Journal of British Studies* 49 (July 2010): 488–513; Ethan Shagan, *The Rule of Moderation: Violence, Religion and the Politics of Restraint in Early Modern England* (Cambridge: Cambridge University Press, 2011).

114. Owen, *Moderation a Virtue*, 11–12.

115. John Hooke, *Catholicism with Popery*, 2 vols. (London, 1704), 2:5.

116. Hickes, *Two Treatises*, xx.

117. *The Principle of the Protestant Reformation Explain'd* (London, 1704), 14.

118. *The Distinction of High-Church and Low-Church* (London, 1705), 38–39; *The Devil upon Dun: Or, Moderation in Masquerade* (London, 1705); William Shippen, *Moderation Display'd. A Poem* (London, 1705).

119. Astell, *Moderation truly stated*, 5; *Distinction of High-Church and Low-Church*, 44.

120. *The Establishment of the Church, the Preservation of the State* (London, 1702), 4, 13–14.

121. Wagstaffe, *The Case of Moderation*, 32–33.

122. Grascome, *Schism Triumphant*, 3.

123. Charles Leslie, *The Wolf Stript of His Shepherd's Cloathing* (London, 1704), 6, 79–80, 82.

124. Robert Nelson, *The Necessity of Church Communion Vindicated* (London, 1705), 9; *A Letter from a Dissenter in the City to his Country-Friend* (London, 1705), 6.

125. *An English Monster, Or, the Character of an Occasional Conformist* (London, 1703), 4.

126. Sir Humphrey Mackworth, *Peace at Home*, 4th ed. (London, 1703), 11; Leslie, *The Wolf stript*, 79–80; *No-Church Establish'd*, 30.

127. James Drake, *The Memorial of the Church of England* (London, 1705), 12, 13, 14–15, 26–27; on the circulation of the *Memorial*, see White Kennett's ecclesiastical diary, BL MS Lansdowne 1024, f. 164; John Hutton to Arthur Charlett, 7 August 1705, Ballard MS 35, f. 102; John White to Arthur Charlett, 22 January 1706, Ballard MS 24, f. 141; HMC *Portland* 4:190–191.

128. Daniel Defoe to Robert Harley, [July], 9 July, 10 July, 1705, BL Add MS 70291; John White to Arthur Charlett, 22 January 1706, Ballard MS 34, f. 141; it probably did not help that Charles Leslie immediately published a defense of *The Memorial*, see Charles Leslie, *The Case of the Church of England's Memorial Fairly Stated* (London, 1705).

129. Daniel Defoe, *The High-Church Legeon* (London, 1705), 9; Elkanah Settle, *Fears and Dangers, Fairly Display'd* (London, 1706), 20.

130. *Some considerations on the present danger of the Religion of the Church of England* (London, 1706), 28, 5; *A Review of the Dangers of the Church* (London, 1706), 3, 9.

131. John Toland, *The Memorial of the State of England* (London, 1705), 10, 13–15.

132. White Kennett's ecclesiastical diary, BL Lansdowne MS 1024, ff. 165, 167; William Bromley to Arthur Charlett, 8 September 1705, Ballard MS 38, f. 144; *An Elegy on the Burning of the Church Memorial* (London, 1705).

133. Boyer, *History of the reign of Queen Anne*, 203–212; Jones, "Debates in the House of Lords," 759–771; Bennett, *Tory Crisis in Church and State*, 81–82.

134. "The Church in Danger Debates, 1705," BL Add MS 28252, ff. 82–88; "Minutes on the Church in Danger Debates, 6 Dec 1705," BL Lansdowne 1034, ff. 4–5.

135. "The Church in Danger Debates, 1705," BL Add MS 28252, ff. 82–88; "Minutes on the Church in Danger Debates," BL Lansdowne 1034, ff. 4–5.

136. "The Church in Danger Debates, 1705," BL Add MS 28252, ff. 82–88; "Minutes on the Church in Danger Debates," BL Lansdowne 1034, ff. 4–5.

137. "Minutes on the Church in Danger Debates," BL Lansdowne 1034, f. 5; William Wake Diary, LPL MS 1770, f. 8.

138. White Kennett's ecclesiastical diary, BL Lansdowne MS 1024, f. 167.

139. Bennett, *Tory Crisis in Church and State*, 81; G. V. Bennett, "Robert Harley, the Godolphin Ministry, and the Bishoprics Crisis of 1707," *EHR* 82 (October 1967): 726–746; Feiling, *History of the Tory Party*, 377–385.

140. White Kennett's ecclesiastical diary, BL Lansdowne MS 1024, f. 365; Turner, *Justice Done to Human Souls*, 114; Burnet, *Pastoral Care*, 4th ed., preface.

141. Although to just what extent was arguably not obvious until the Bangorian controversy of 1717–1721, when the mass of Anglican churchmen found themselves caught between more or less equally unpalatable ecclesiologies; see Andrew Starkie, *The Church of England and the Bangorian Controversy, 1716–1721* (Woodbridge: Boydell, 2007).

142. On Tindal, see Stephen Lalor, *Matthew Tindal, Freethinker* (London: Continuum Books, 2006), 54–90; Jonathan I. Israel, *Radical Enlightenment: Philosophy and the Making of Modernity, 1650–1750* (Oxford: Oxford University Press, 2001), 619–622; William J. Bulman, "Constantine's Enlightenment: Culture and Religious Politics in the Early British Empire, c. 1648–1710" (PhD diss., Princeton University, 2009), 428–431; Dmitri Levitin, "Matthew Tindal's *Rights of the Christian Church* (1706) and the Church-State Relationship," *HJ* 54 (2011): 714–740.

143. Tindal, *Rights of the Christian Church*, lxxxiv–lxxxv.

144. Tindal, *Rights of the Christian Church*, 19.

145. Champion, *Pillars of Priestcraft*, 97–98; J. A. I. Champion, " 'Le culte privé est libre quand il est rendu dans le secret': Hobbes, Locke et les limites de la tolérance, l'athéisme et l'hétérodoxie," in *Les fondements philosophiques de la tolerance*, ed. Yves Charles Zarka, Franck Lessay, and John Rogers (Paris: Presses Universitaires Paris, 2002), 221–253; Levitin, "Tindal's *Rights of The Christian Church*," 719–720.

146. And see Matthew Tindal, *An Essay Concerning the Power of the Magistrate and the Rights of Mankind in Matters of Religion* (London, 1697).

147. Tindal, *Rights of the Christian Church*, 12–19.

148. Tindal, *Rights of the Christian Church*, 26.

149. Tindal, *Rights of the Christian Church*, 64–69, 73.

150. Tindal, *Rights of the Christian Church*, 83–84, 88, 92, 94–95, 246–247.

151. Tindal, *Rights of the Christian Church*, 24, 78, 80, 163.

152. William Lloyd to Archbishop Tenison, 9 October 1706, LPL Gibson MS 931, §18.

153. George Hickes to Arthur Charlett, 10 August 1708, Ballard MS 12, f. 168; *Remarks and Collections of Thomas Hearne*, ed. C. E. Doble, D. W. Rannie, and H. E. Salter, 11 vols. (Oxford: Clarendon, 1886), 2:5, 12, 72, 179; Samuel Pratt to Thomas Brett, 9 May 1706, Bodl. MS Eng Th c 24, f. 281; and see Propositions contain'd in a Book entitul'd The Rights of the Christian Church Asserted, 28 October 1710, BL Add MS 22083, ff. 3–4.

154. White Kennett to Arthur Charlett, 29 January 1709, Ballard MS 7, f. 122; Ralph Bridges to William Trumbull, 25 August 1710, BL Add MS 72495, f. 17.

155. William Wotton, *The rights of the clergy in the Christian Church asserted* (London, 1706[?]).

156. Peter Nourse, *A Vindication of the Christian Priesthood* (London, 1708), 9; and see Robert Moss, *A Sermon preach'd at the parish church at St. Lawrence-Jewry, London, October 5, 1708* (London, 1708); William Whitfield, *The Kingdom of Jesus Christ* (London, 1708); William Beveridge, *The Dignity, Office and Authority of the Priesthood* (London, 1708).

157. Hickes, *Two Treatises*, xxiv–xxv; and see Charles Leslie, *The Second Part of The Wolf Stript of His Shepherd's Cloathing* (London, 1707).

158. *No-Church Establish'd*, 56; *The Villainous Principles of the Rights of the Christian Church Asserted* (London, 1708); *Dangerous Positions; or blasphemous, profane immoral and Jesuitical assertions faithfully discover'd* (London, 1708); Abel Evans, *The Apparation, A Poem*, 2nd ed. (London, 1710).

159. Geoffrey Holmes, *The Trial of Doctor Sacheverell* (London: Eyre Methuen, 1973); Brian Cowan, "The Spin Doctor: Sacheverell's Trial Speech and Political Performance in the Divided Society," *Parliamentary History* 31, 1 (February 2012): 28–46; Brian Cowan, ed., *The State Trial of Dr. Sacheverell*, Parliamentary History: Texts and Studies, vol. 6 (Hoboken, NJ: Wiley-Blackwell, 2012).

160. Bennett, *Tory Crisis in Church and State*, 152; Findon, "The Nonjurors," 175–176.

161. The Humble Representation by the Lower House to the Upper House, 11 February 1703/04, LPL Gibson MS 934, §38.

162. On Laurence, see Every, *High Church Party*, 128–132; Robert D. Cornwall, "Politics and the Lay Baptism Controversy in England, 1708–15," in *Religion, Politics and Dissent, 1660–1832: Essays in Honor of James E. Bradley*, ed. Robert D. Cornwall and William Gibson (Farnham, UK: Ashgate, 2010), 147–163.

163. [Roger Laurence], *Lay Baptism Invalid* (London, 1708), 31–32, 59, 66, 68, 83.

164. William Roberts, *The Divine Institution of the Gospel Ministry* (London, 1712), 25; White Kennett's ecclesiastical diary, BL Lansdowne MS 1024, ff. 371; and see Samuel Asplin, *The Divine Rights and Duties of the Christian Priesthood* (London, 1711).

165. Gilbert Burnet, *Two sermons, preached in the Cathedral church of Salisbury; the first, on the fifth of November, . . . the second, on the seventh of November* (London, 1710), 22.

166. Thomas Brett, *A Letter to the Author of Lay-Baptism Invalid* (London, 1711), 15.

167. Thomas Brett, *A Sermon on Remission of Sins* (London, 1711).

168. William Quarles to Tenison, 5 December 1711, LPL Gibson MS 941, §30; but see John Johnson of Cranbrook commending Brett for preaching "in vindication of the rights of the priesthood," Johnson to Arthur Charlett, 15 September 1711, Ballard MS 15, f. 105.

169. White Kennett's ecclesiastical diary, BL Lansdowne MS 1024, f. 345; Theophilus Dorrington to Arthur Charlett, 13 June 1712, Ballard MS 30, f. 62.

170. *A letter about a motion in convocation, to the Reverend Dr. Thomas Brett* (London, 1712).

171. White Kennett's ecclesiastical diary, BL Lansdowne MS 1024, ff. 364–365; John Johnson to Arthur Charlett, 17 February 1712, Ballard MS 15, f. 106.

172. White Kennett's ecclesiastical diary, BL Lansdowne MS 1024, ff. 366; Bennett, *Tory Crisis in Church and State*, 153.

173. Kennett to Blackwell, 26 April 1712, BL Lansdowne 1013, f. 175.

174. Tenison to Sharp, 27 April 1712, LPL Gibson MS 941, §33.

175. Declaration issued by the Upper House of Convocation respecting the validity of Baptism by unauthorized persons, with a reply from the lower house, 1712, Bodl. Rawlinson MS C 743, f. 74; White Kennett's ecclesiastical diary, BL Lansdowne MS 1024, f. 375; Bps Paper abt Baptism sent to Lowr H. of Conv. 14 May 1712, BL Add MS 72495, f. 145.

176. White Kennett's ecclesiastical diary, f. 375.

177. Sharp to Tenison, 28 April 1712, LPL MS 941, §32.

178. Ralph Bridges to William Trumbull, Fulham, 25 April, 14 May 1712, BL Add MS 72495, ff. 138–139, 143; Edmund Gibson to William Nicolson, 8 May 1712, Bodl. Add MS A 269, f. 10; Atterbury to Trelawny, 9 May 1712, Atterbury Correspondence, 3:301–302; Declaration issued by the Upper House of Convocation respecting the validity of Baptism, Bodl. Rawlinson C 743, f. 74.

179. White Kennett's ecclesiastical diary, BL Lansdowne MS 1024, f. 378.

180. White Kennett's ecclesiastical diary, BL Lansdowne MS 1024, f. 378; Edmund Gibson to William Nicolson, 15 May 1712, Bodl. Add MS A 269, f. 12; William Nicolson to William Wake, 9 June 1712, *Copy correspondence of Nicolson & Wake*, f. 97.

181. Atterbury to Trelawny, 30 December 1712, Atterbury Correspondence, 3:311; Atterbury to Trelawny, 10 February 1713, Atterbury Correspondence, 4:446–447; Kennett to Blackwell, 2 August 1713, BL Lansdowne 1013, f. 197; De La Croze to Arthur Charlett, 1 December 1713, Ballard MS 26, f. 100; John Johnson to Arthur Charlett, 5 September 1714, Ballard MS 15, f. 107; Theophilus Dorrington to Arthur Charlett, 10 September 1714, Ballard MS 30, f. 64; Bennett, *Tory Crisis in Church and State*, 160.

182. Cornwall, "Lay Baptism Controversy," 147–149, 163; on Brett's defection, see John Johnson to Arthur Charlett, 22 April, 11 May, 29 May 1715 and 24 November 1716, Ballard MS 15, ff. 115, 116, 118, 132; and on the new nonabjurors, see White Kennett to Arthur Charlett, 13 October 1716, Ballard MS 7, f. 139.

183. Turner, *Defence of the doctrine and practice;* William Talbot, *The Bishop of Oxford's Charge to the Clergy of his Diocese in the Year 1712* (London, 1712), 10–19; White Kennett, *The wisdom of looking backward* (London, 1715).

184. Starkie, *Church of England and the Bangorian Controversy*, 73–77; William Bradford Gardner, "George Hickes and the Origin of the Bangorian Controversy," *Studies in Philology* 39 (January 1942): 65–78.

185. Burnet, *Discourse of the Pastoral Care*, 4th ed., preface.

186. Robert Nelson, *A Companion for the festivals and fasts of the Church of England* (London, 1704), ii–iii, xviii–xiv; William Lloyd, Bishop of Norwich, to Nelson, 24 March 1703, CHC RN/1/12; Humphrey Wanley to Nelson, 11 January 1704, CHC RN/1/13; Thomas Rogerson to Nelson, 11 February 1705, CHC RN/1/15.

187. See Richard Sharp, "New Perspectives on High Church Tradition: Historical Background 1730–1780," in *Tradition Renewed: The Oxford Movement Conference Papers*, ed. Geoffrey Rowell (Allison Park, PA: Pickwick, 1986), 4–23; F. C. Mather, "Georgian Churchmanship Reconsidered: Some Variations in Anglican Public Worship, 1714–1830," *JEH* 36 (April 1985): 255–283; F. C. Mather, *High Church Prophet: Bishop Samuel Horsley (1733–1806) and the Caroline Tradition in the Later Georgian Church* (Oxford: Oxford University Press, 1992); Peter B. Nockles, *The Oxford Movement in Context* (Cambridge: Cambridge University Press, 1994), 44–103.

188. Nelson's book was still being distributed gratis at midcentury, Henry Hoare Bible Fund Minutes, 14 October 1740, CHC BF/1.

189. Dodwell, *Occasional communion fundamentally destructive*, 137–138.

190. Commonplace book of Francis Cherry, BL Add MS 39314, f. 68.

5. The Moral Counterrevolution

1. Lewis to Chamberlayne, 28 February 1700, CUL SPCK MS D2/2, §54; Harris to Chamberlayne, 21 June 1700, CUL SPCK MS D2/2, §123.

2. Henry Sacheverell, *The Character of a Low-Churchman* (London, 1702), 10–11.

3. On "laicization," see Norman Sykes, *Church and State in England in the XVIIIth Century* (New York: Octagon, 1979), 379; W. M. Jacob, *Lay People and Religion in the Early Eighteenth Century* (Cambridge: Cambridge University Press, 1996).

4. Dudley Bahlmann, *The Moral Revolution of 1688* (New Haven, CT: Yale University Press, 1957); G. V. Bennett, "The Convocation of 1710: An Anglican Attempt at Counter-Revolution," in *Studies in Church History* 7 (1971): 311–319.

5. See also G. V. Bennett, "Conflict in the Church," in *Britain after the Glorious Revolution, 1689–1714*, ed. Geoffrey Holmes (London: Macmillan, 1969), 155–175.

6. White Kennett's ecclesiastical diary, BL Lansdowne MS 1024, ff. 266, 277.

7. "Representation of the State of Religion, March 1710–11," Atterbury Correspondence, 2:319.

8. Francis Atterbury, *A Letter to a Convocation-Man, Concerning the Rights, Powers and Privileges of that Body* (London, 1697), 2.

9. Brent S. Sirota, "The Trinitarian Crisis in Church and State: Religious Controversy and the Making of the Post-Revolutionary Church of England, 1687–1701," *Journal of British Studies* 52, 1 (January 2013): 26–54.

10. Brent S. Sirota, "'The Leviathan Is Not Safely to Be Angered': The Convocation Controversy, Country Ideology and Anglican High Churchmanship," in *Religion and the State: Europe and North America in the Seventeenth and Eighteenth Centuries*, ed. Joshua B. Stein and Sargon G. Donabed (Lanham, MD: Lexington Books, 2012), 41–61.

11. R. J. Smith, *The Gothic Bequest: Medieval Institutions in British Thought, 1688–1813* (Cambridge: Cambridge University Press, 1987), 28–38; David Douglass, *English Scholars, 1660–1730*, 2nd ed. (London: Eyre and Spottiswoode, 1951), 195–221; Isaac Kramnick, "Augustan Politics and English Historiography: The Debate on the English Past, 1730–35," *History and Theory* 6 (1967): 33–56.

12. Atterbury, *Letter to a Convocation-Man*, 38.

13. Atterbury, *Letter to a Convocation-Man*, 22–23, 31–33, 50, 61, 66–67; on the rights of the inferior clergy, see [Gilbert Burnet], *Reflections on a Book Entituled, The Rights, Powers and Privileges of an English Convocation, Stated and Vindicated* (London, 1700), 9.

14. William Nicolson to William Wake, 3 March 1697, f. 1 in *The copy correspondence of Bishop William Nicolson & Archbishop Wake, 1697–1725*, Victoria and Albert Museum, Forster Collection, microfilm.

15. Most notably, William Wake's "official" court rejoinder, William Wake, *The Authority of Christian princes over the ecclesiastical synods* (London, 1697); William Wake Diary, LPL MS 2932, f. 80; William Nicolson to Arthur Charlett, 6 May 1700, Ballard MS 4, f. 12.

16. Francis Atterbury, *The Rights, Powers, and Priviledges of an English Convocation* (London, 1700), sig. A3v, A6r, 132, 148; William Nicolson to William Wake, 2 January 1701, BL Add MS 34265, f. 65; Sacheverell, *Character of a Low-Churchman*, 13, 16.

17. G. V. Bennett, *The Tory Crisis in Church and State, 1688–1730* (Oxford: Clarendon, 1975), 55; Henry Horwitz, *Parliament, Policy and Politics in the Reign of William III* (Newark, NJ: University of Delaware Press, 1977), 278–279; Julian Hoppit, *Land of Liberty? England 1689–1727* (Oxford: Oxford University Press, 2000), 156–162.

18. Geoffrey Holmes, *British Politics in the Age of Anne*, rev. ed. (London: Hambleden, 1987), 98.

19. White Kennett, *The present state of Convocation* (London, 1702), 33–34.

20. A large portion of the records of the post-Reformation convocation of the province Canterbury were burned in the Great Fire of London in 1666.

21. Francis Atterbury, *A Faithful Account of some Transactions in the Three Last Sessions of the Present Convocation* (London, 1702), 5–6; Kennett, *The present state of Convocation*, 33.

22. *A Narrative of the Proceedings of the Lower House of Convocation Relating to Prorogations and Adjournments* (London, 1701), 4.

23. *Narrative of the Proceedings*, xiii.

24. John Moore to Tenison, 8 January 1701, LPL Gibson MS 934, §41; Atterbury to Trelawny, 15 February 1701, Atterbury Correspondence, 3:24–25.

25. *Narrative of the Proceedings*, 9; White Kennett to Arthur Charlett, 1 March 1701, Ballard MS 7, f. 92.

26. *Narrative of the Proceedings*, 13.

27. *Narrative of the Proceedings*, 41.

28. White Kennett to Arthur Charlett, 2 April 1701, Ballard MS 7, f. 96; Edmund Gibson to Arthur Charlett, 3 April 1701, Ballard MS 6, f. 49; Edmund Gibson, *A Letter to a Friend in the country concerning the proceedings of the present Convocation* (London, 1701), 2.

29. *Narrative of the Proceedings*, 46–47; Edmund Gibson to Smith, 8 April 1701, Ballard MS 6, f. 51.

30. Peter Birch to Arthur Charlett, 1 April 1701, Ballard MS 34, f. 53; White Kennett to Arthur Charlett, 10 April 1701, Ballard MS 7, f. 98; Edmund Gibson to Arthur Charlett, 10 April 1701, Ballard MS 6, f. 53; Peter Birch to Arthur Charlett, 26 April 1701, Ballard MS 34, f. 54.

31. White Kennett to Arthur Charlett, 10 April 1701, Ballard MS 7, f. 98; Gibson to Charlett, 3 June 1701, Ballard MS 6, f. 57.

32. White Kennett to Arthur Charlett, 28 June 1701, Ballard MS 7, f. 100; Cooke to Brett, 19 July 1701, Bodl. MS Eng Th c 24, f. 153; Atterbury to Trelawny, 6 September 1701, Atterbury Correspondence, 3:49.

33. Atterbury to Charlett, 8 March 1701, Ballard MS 9, f. 91; Atterbury to Trelawny, 8 March 1701, Atterbury Correspondence, 3:36.

34. Atterbury to Trelawny, 11 March 1701, Atterbury Correspondence, 3:38.

35. Atterbury to Trelawny, 15 and 18 March 1701, Atterbury Correspondence, 3:41–43; Travis Glasson, *Mastering Christianity: Missionary Anglicanism and Slavery in the Atlantic World* (New York: Oxford University Press, 2011), 20.

36. George Harbin to Arthur Charlett, 17 May 1701, Ballard MS 36, ff. 5–6.

37. White Kennett to Arthur Charlett, 1 March 1701, Ballard MS 7, f. 92.

38. Advice to the Lower House of Convocation in a Letter from a Gentleman, 22 December 1701, BL Lansdowne MS 940, ff. 2–12; see also John Toland, *The art of governing by partys* (London, 1701), 29.

39. Sirota, "Trinitarian Crisis in Church and State."

40. Atterbury, *Letter to a Convocation-Man*, 7.

41. William Nicolson to William Wake, 2 January 1701, BL Add MS 34265, f. 65; Atterbury to Trelawny, 8 March 1701, Atterbury Correspondence, 3:36.

42. Atterbury to Trelawny, 11 March 1701, Atterbury Correspondence, 3:39; Atterbury had cited Toland's *Christianity not Mysterious* by name in *Letter to a Convocation-Man*, 5; and see J. A. I. Champion, "Making Authority: Belief, Conviction and Reason in the Public Sphere in Late Seventeenth Century England," *Libertinage et philosophie au XVIIe siècle* 3 (1999): 143–190.

43. Atterbury to Trelawny, 18 March 1701, Atterbury Correspondence, 3:46; *Narrative of the Proceedings*, 51–52.

44. "The report of the committee of the lower house of convocation for the examination of books," in Edward Cardwell, *Synodalia*, 2 vols. (Oxford: Oxford University Press, 1842), 2:701–705; White Kennett, *A Complete History of England*, 3 vols. (London, 1706), 3:798–799.

45. Account of the Upper House of Convocation, 20 March 1701, LPL MS 934, §82; *Narrative of the Proceedings*, 51–52.

46. Gibson, *Letter to a friend*, 7.

47. Edward Thistlewayte, Account of the Lower House of Convocation, 5 April 1701, LPL Gibson MS 934, §21; Edmund Gibson to Smith, 8 April 1701, Ballard MS 6, f. 51; *Narrative of the Proceedings*, 51–52.

48. Answer by the Lower House of Convocation to Tenison and the bishops concerning two papers read to them in the Jerusalem Chamber, 8 April 1701, LPL Gibson MS 934, §22.

49. Charles Leslie, *The Case of the regale and of the pontificat stated*, 2nd ed. (London, 1701), xxx.

50. Gibson, *Letter to a friend*, 7.

51. *Narrative of the Proceedings*, xvi.

52. Peter Birch to Arthur Charlett, 17 May 1701, Ballard MS 34, f. 56; George Harbin to Arthur Charlett, 17 May 1701, Ballard MS 36, ff. 5–6.

53. Edmund Gibson to Arthur Charlett, 10 June 1701, Ballard MS 6, f. 59; Robert Lloyd to Arthur Charlett, 14 June 1701, Ballard MS 23, f. 109; Thomas Lathbury, *A History of the Convocation of the Church of England* (London: John W. Parker, 1842), 296–297.

54. Martin Greig, "Heresy Hunt: Gilbert Burnet and the Convocation Controversy of 1701," *HJ* 37 (September 1994): 569–592.

55. Francis Atterbury, *A Letter to a Clergyman in the Country* (London, 1701), 5.

56. Atterbury to Trelawny, 17 November 1701, Atterbury Correspondence, 3:57–58; Edmund Gibson to ————, 30 January 1701 [1702], BL Lansdowne MS 940, f. 51; To the Right Revd Father in God Richard Lord Bishop of Bath & Wells, 23 December 1701, LPL Gibson MS 934, §1; and see A True Coppy of a Paper Introduced by some hand Unknowne, at the Election of Convocation Members for the Diocese of Bristoll, [1701?], LPL Gibson MS 934, §3; Robert Loggan to Gilbert Burnet, 8 February 1702; Edward Thistlewayte to Gilbert Burnet, 14 February 1702, LPL Gibson MS 934, §§26–27; The Grievances of ye Church as presented by Dr. Birch in ye Lower House of Convocation answered, [ca. late 1701], LPL Gibson MS 934, §33.

57. Atterbury, *Letter to a Clergyman*, 1.

58. Maurice Wheeler to William Wake, 15 December 1701, quoted in Bennett, *Tory Crisis in Church and State*, 61–62.

59. [William Hallifax], To the Revd Mr. Ja. Stillingfleet, M.A. Rectr of Hartlebury & Wm Lloyd A.M.V. of Blockley Proctors of ye Clergy of ye Diocese of Wor[ceste]r for ye ensuing Convocation, LPL Gibson MS 934, §2; *Letter to a Clergyman in the City* (London, 1702).

60. *Letter to a Clergyman in the City*, 7; William Hallifax, *A Sermon preach'd at Old Swinford in Worcester-shire. January 30, 1701* (London, 1702), 17.

61. White Kennett to Arthur Charlett, 31 December 1701, Ballard MS 7, f. 103; Atterbury to Trelawny, 8 January 1702, Atterbury Correspondence, 3:62.

62. [White Kennett], Account of the Lower House of Convocation, 13 January 1702, LPL Gibson MS 934, §5.

63. "Draft of petition from the Lower House to the Upper House of Convocation of the Lower House's right of conferences," [1702], LPL Gibson MS 934, §30.

64. [White Kennett], Account of the Lower House of Convocation, 13 January 1701/02, and Acts of the Lower House of Convocation, 13 January 1701/02, LPL Gibson MS 934, §§5–6.

65. White Kennett to George Verney, 21 January 1702, LPL Gibson MS 934, §79. On the controversial thirtieth of January sermon that William Binckes, prebendary of Lichfield, preached before the lower house that year, see William Binckes, *A Sermon Preach'd on January the 30th, 1701/2 in King Henry VII's Chapel Before the Reverend Clergy of the Lower House of Convocation* (London, 1702); *Animadversions on the two last 30th of January sermons. The one preached to the Honourable House of Commons, the other to the Lower House of Convocation* (London, 1702).

66. Account of the Lower House of Convocation, 28 January 1701/02, LPL Gibson MS 934, §10.

67. The Protestation of some Members of ye Lower House of Convocation made in ye Lower house Feb 9 1701 [1702], LPL Gibson MS 934, §13; Some Misrepresentations having

been made concerning the three Articles agreed to in a committee of the Lower House of Convocation, 10 February 1702, LPL Gibson MS 934, §15; Atterbury, *A Faithful Account*, 5; Kennett, *The present state of Convocation*, 7.

68. [White Kennett], Account of the Lower House of Convocation, 12 February 1702, LPL Gibson MS 934, §18; Kennett, *Present State of Convocation*, 19–27; Atterbury to Trelawny, 17 February 1702, Atterbury Correspondence, 3:75–76; cf. Atterbury, *A Faithful Account*.

69. This speech is printed in Kennett, *Present State of Convocation*, 35–37; and see William Sherlock, *The New Danger of Presbytery* (London, 1703), 2.

70. Atterbury to Trelawny, 21 February 1702, Atterbury Correspondence, 3:78, where he describes their meeting "as a private company."

71. John Hutton to Arthur Charlett, 9 March 1702, Ballard MS 35, f. 91; White Kennett to Arthur Charlett, 17 March 1702, Ballard MS 7, f. 105.

72. "Speech of Dr. Atterbury to the Clergy of the Archdeaconry of Totnes, 1702," Atterbury Correspondence, 2:216–217; emphasis added.

73. Thomas Ken to George Hickes, 17 March 1700 [1701]; significantly, Hickes poured cold water on the suggestion, informing the bishop "that they are not the rights of the Church, but the legal parliamentary which your friend the prolocutor and our other old brethren of the lower house of convocation so zealously contend for," Hickes to Ken, 9 June [1701?], LPL MS 3171, 150–152.

74. Account of the Lower House of Convocation, 20 January 1701/02, LPL Gibson MS 934, §8; *A Letter to the Reverend Mr. Jonathan Kimberly* (London, 1702), 7–8, 2.

75. Advice to the Lower House of Convocation in a Letter from a Gentleman, 22 December 1701, BL Lansdowne MS 940, ff. 5–6; John Hutton to Arthur Charlett, 9 March 1702, Ballard MS 35, f. 91.

76. Queen Anne to Archbishop Tenison, 25 February 1706, BL Add MS 61612, f. 144; and see Lathbury, *History of the Convocation*, 328–329, 331–332.

77. Jonas Proast, The Due way to Ending the Controversie between the Two Houses of Convocation. In a Letter to a Friend, 28 September 1706, LPL Gibson MS 934, §34; Hare to Watkins, 22 April 1707, BL Add MS 33225, f. 5; Ralph Bridges to William Trumbull, 2 May 1707, 22 November 1708, 25 February 1709, BL Add MS 72494, ff. 21, 90, 101.

78. Ralph Bridges to William Trumbull, 15 December 1710, BL Add MS 72495, f. 35.

79. Sykes, *Church and State*, 292–296.

80. "To the most Reverend his Grace the Lord Archbishop of Canterbury, and the Right Reverend Bishops his suffragans in Convocation assembled, December 8, 1703," in *A Collection of Papers concerning what hath been transacted in the Convocation summon'd A.D. 1702 and dissolv'd A.D. 1705* (London, 1705), 15–16.

81. Atterbury to Trelawny, 6 and 22 January, 5 and 12 February 1704, Atterbury Correspondence, 3:161–168, 174–175.

82. The Humble Representation by the Lower House to the Upper House, 11 February 1704, LPL Gibson MS 934, §38; see also BL Harleian MS 6848, ff. 199–203; *A Collection of Papers*, 17–22.

83. Atterbury to Trelawny, 7 November 1704, Atterbury Correspondence, 3:253.

84. Lathbury, *History of the Convocation*, 321–322.

85. Reasons to induce the Queen's Majesty to intrust some of ye Clergy in ye Several Parts of this Kingdom with Commissions for ye Peace, LPL MS 933, §34: *temp.* Anne; *An essay towards advancing the interest of the establish'd church and state* (London, 1708), 64–72, 107–108; Jonathan Swift, *A project for the advancement of religion and the reformation of manners* (London, 1709), 39; Thomas Penn to Robert Watts, 23 March 1714, Ballard MS 25, f. 110.

86. *A Representation made by the Lower House of Convocation to the Archbishop and Bishops Anno 1703* (London, 1704), 3; emphasis added.

87. *Reflections upon a late scandalous and malicious pamphlet entitul'd, The shortest way with the dissenters* (London, 1703), 19; *Visits from the Shades: or dialogues serious, comical and political* (London, 1704), 130; *The politicks of high-church* (London, 1705), 29; *Cuckoe: or, the distinction of High-Church and Low-Church rehearsed* (London, 1706), 22; William Smithies, *The coffee-house preachers; or, high church divinity corrected* (London, 1706), 3; Henry Sacheverell, *The communication of sin: a sermon preach'd at the assizes held at Derby* (London, 1709), 15–17; John Dunton, *The bull-baiting: or, Sach—ll dress'd up in fireworks* (London, 1709), 13–16; *An Answer to Dr. Sacheverell's sermon* (London, 1710), 9; *A short essay toward promoting of love and unity among Christians of different persuasions* (London, 1710), 23; *The true church-man, and loyal subject* (London, 1710), 20–21.

88. Isaac Sharpe, *Plain-dealing: in answer to Plain-English, a sermon preached at St. Mary-le-Bow, March 27, 1704* (London, 1704), 52.

89. John Gilbert, *The Church of England's wish for the restoring of primitive discipline* (London, 1703), 244–245; Samuel Wesley, *A reply to Mr. Palmer's vindication of the learning, loyalty, morals and most Christian behavior of the dissenters toward the Church of England* (London, 1707), 142.

90. Edmund Gibson, *Codex juris ecclesiastici Anglicani*, 2 vols. (London, 1713), 2:1011; on the institution of the rural deaneries, see William Dansey, *Horae Decanicae Rurales* (London: Bohn, Rivington et al., 1835); for an illuminating comparison, see John Locke's outline of the office of the "tithingman," a local officer of social and moral regulation often associated with the rural dean, in his "Atlantis" fragments, *Locke: Political Essays*, ed. Mark Goldie (Cambridge: Cambridge University Press, 1997), 257–258; White Kennett, *Parochial Antiquities Attempted in the History of Ambrosden and Burchester*, 2 vols. (Oxford: University Press, 1818), 2:339.

91. Gilbert Burnet, *Bishop Burnet's History of His Own Time*, 2 vols. (London, 1724–1734), 2:635; James Gardiner, *Advice to the clergy of the diocese of Lincoln* (London, 1697), 6–7; White Kennett's ecclesiastical diary, BL Lansdowne MS 1024, f. 128.

92. Thomas Brett, *An account of church-government and governors* (London, 1701), 126–132.

93. James Metford, *A Humble Proposal for Parochial Reformation by restoring rural deans and chapters* (London, 1706), 2, 38–39, 120; and see Wheeler to John Chamberlayne, 28 March 1701, CUL SPCK MS D2/2, §272.

94. "Speech of Dr. Atterbury to the Clergy of the Archdeaconry of Totnes, 1708," Atterbury Correspondence, 2:234–252.

95. On the procurement of the royal license, see Bennett, *Tory Crisis in Church and State*, 120–132; White Kennett to Samuel Blackwell, 13 January 1711, BL Lansdowne MS 1013, f. 142; Robert Nelson to Arthur Charlett, 20 January 1711, Ballard MS 23, f. 86; Thomas Gawdon to

Mr. Warley, 9 February 1711, BL Add MS 27997, f. 102; James Harris to Arthur Charlett, 22 February 1711, Ballard MS 39, f. 36; White Kennett's ecclesiastical diary, ff. 259–260.

96. The letter is copied in White Kennett's ecclesiastical diary, BL Lansdowne MS 1024, ff. 283–285, but Trelawny did not convey and Kennett did not record the name of the author.

97. White Kennett's ecclesiastical diary, BL Lansdowne MS 1024, ff. 281–283.

98. Francis Atterbury, *Fourteen sermons preach'd on several occasions* (London, 1708), epistle dedicatory.

99. Commission printed in Timothy J. Fawcett, *The Liturgy of Comprehension 1689*, Alcuin Club Collections 54 (Southend-on-Sea: Mahew-McCrimmon, 1973), 26–27.

100. The Humble Representation by the Lower House to the Upper House, 11 February 1704, LPL Gibson MS 934, §38.

101. John Johnson, *The Clergy-man's Vade mecum*, 2nd ed. (London, 1707), 246.

102. Philip Stubbs to Arthur Charlett, 11 February 1711, Ballard MS 34, f. 198.

103. White Kennett ecclesiastical diary, ff. 367, 376; James Harris to Arthur Charlett, 2 April 1712, Ballard MS 39, f. 37.

104. White Kennett ecclesiastical diary, BL Lansdowne MS 1024 f. 367; Bennett, *Tory Crisis in Church and State*, 132.

105. Atterbury, *Fourteen sermons*, epistle dedicatory; and see also Peter Lancaster, An Ecclesia sit libera? A New Question about ancient Rights of ye Church, BL Lansdowne MS 422, ff. 2–31.

106. Sirota, "Trinitarian Crisis"; and see Atterbury to Trelawny, 25 March 1702, Atterbury Correspondence, 4:351–352.

107. "To the most Reverend Bishops," December 8, 1703, in *A Collection of Papers*, 15.

108. Number XX, December 1, 1704, in *A Collection of Papers*, 26–30; Lathbury, *History of the Convocation*, 329–330.

109. Francis Atterbury, *The axe laid to the root of Christianity* (London, 1706), 1.

110. George Hickes, *Two Treatises, One of the Christian Priesthood, The Other of the Dignity of the Episcopal Order*, 2nd ed. (London, 1707), xix.

111. Francis Higgins, *A Sermon Preach'd at the Royal Chappel at White-Hall on Wednesday, Febr. 26, 1706/7* (London, 1707), 2, 7.

112. Charles Leslie, *A Postscript to Mr. Higgin's Sermon, very necessary for the better understanding of it*, [Dublin, 1707], 4.

113. Anthony Collins, *Priestcraft in Perfection*, 3rd ed. (London, 1710), 12, 20.

114. Ralph Bridges to William Trumbull, 23 January, 25 February 1710, BL Add MS 72494, ff. 153, 157–158; N. Clagett to Cox Macro, 26 March 1710, BL Add MS 32556; Green to George Harbin, 21 January 1710; Hilkiah Bedford to George Harbin, 5 March 1710; Isaac Walton to Harbin, 22 April 1710; and an undated series of letters from Atterbury to Harbin from spring 1710; BL Add MS 32096, ff. 76, 83, 84, 86, 88, 92, 95, 97, 100; George Hickes to Arthur Charlett, 9 March 1710, Ballard MS 12, f. 177.

115. Atterbury to Harbin, n.d., BL Add MS 32096, f. 88.

116. Hilkiah Bedford, *A Vindication of the Church of England from the aspersions of a late libel intituled, Priestcraft in Perfection* (London, 1710), 16–17, 213–214.

117. William Pittis, *The history of the present Parliament. And Convocation* (London, 1711), 115–116, 127; Ralph Bridges to William Trumbull, 3 January 1710/11, BL Add MS 72495, f. 39.

118. On Whiston, see Eamon Duffy, "'Whiston's Affair': The Trials of a Primitive Christian, 1709–1714," *JEH* 27 (April 1976): 129–150; James E. Force, *William Whiston, Honest Newtonian* (Cambridge: Cambridge University Press, 1985), 90–120; Stephen D. Snobelen, "'To Us There Is But One God, the Father': Antitrinitarian Textual Criticism in Seventeenth- and Early Eighteenth-Century England," in *Scripture and Scholarship in Early Modern England*, ed. Ariel Hessayon and Nicholas Keene (Aldershot, UK: Ashgate, 2006), 116–136; Stephen D. Snobelen, "William Whiston, Isaac Newton and the Crisis of Publicity," *Studies in History and Philosophy of Science* 35 (2004): 573–603.

119. Kennett to Blackwell, 13 January 1711, BL Lansdowne MS 1013, f. 142.

120. See Whiston's own letter to Francis Atterbury, March 1711, printed in William Whiston, *An account of the Convocation's proceedings with relation to Mr. Whiston* (London, 1711), 2–5.

121. Kennett's speech is recorded in his ecclesiastical diary, BL Lansdowne MS 1024, ff. 280–281; Whiston, *Account of the Convocation's proceedings*, 6; White Kennett, Draft of a letter to the prolocutor, 25 April 1711, BL Lansdowne MS 1039, ff. 74–75; Materials on proceedings in Convocation against William Whiston, LPL Edmund Gibson Papers 2, ff. 223–232.

122. Whiston, *Account of the Convocation's proceedings*, 9.

123. Tenison's letter was transcribed in White Kennett's ecclesiastical diary, BL Lansdowne MS 1024, ff. 298–299, and reproduced in Whiston, *Account of the Convocation's proceedings*, 15–18.

124. Whiston, *Account of the Convocation's proceedings*, 20–22; White Kennett's ecclesiastical diary, BL Lansdowne MS 1024, ff. 299–301; Ralph Bridges to William Trumbull, 16 and 25 April 1711, BL Add MS 72494, ff. 60–61, 64.

125. Both findings are transcribed in White Kennett's ecclesiastical diary, BL Lansdowne MS 1024, ff. 312–313; Kennett to Blackwell, 5 May 1711, BL Lansdowne MS 1013, f. 152; John Johnson to Arthur Charlett, 9 May 1711, Ballard MS 15, f. 101; Jonathan Edwards to Arthur Charlett, 12 May 1711, Ballard MS 21, f. 164; Samuel Wesley to Arthur Charlett, 12 May 1711, Ballard MS 34, f. 99; Ralph Bridges to William Trumbull, 9 May 1711, BL Add MS 72495, ff. 66–67.

126. Anne's letter is reproduced in Whiston, *Account of the Convocation's proceedings*, 26–27.

127. John Johnson to Arthur Charlett, 9 May 1711, Ballard MS 15, f. 101; Jonathan Edwards to Arthur Charlett, 12 May 1711, Ballard MS 21, f. 164; White Kennett's ecclesiastical diary, f. 315.

128. Whiston, *Account of the Convocation's proceedings*, 33.

129. Ralph Bridges to William Trumbull, 14 May 1711, BL Add MS 72495, f. 69; White Kennett's ecclesiastical diary, BL Lansdowne MS 1024, f. 328; Kennett to Blackwell, 11 July 1711, BL Lansdowne MS 1013, f. 179.

130. Ralph Bridges to William Trumbull, Fulham, 19 March 1710, BL Add MS 72494, ff. 169–170; see Geoffrey Holmes, "The Sacheverell Riots: The Crowd and the Church of England in Early-Eighteenth Century London," *Past and Present* 72 (August 1976): 55–85; and Geoffrey Holmes, *The Trial of Doctor Sacheverell* (London: Eyre Methuen, 1973); Brian Cowan, "The Spin Doctor: Sacheverell's Trial Speech and Political Performance in the Divided Society," *Parliamentary History* 31 (2012): 28–46.

131. John Gascoigne, "Clarke, Samuel (1675–1729)," in *ODNB*.

132. Atterbury to Trelawny, 10 and 24 February 1713, Atterbury Correspondence, 3:312–313, 317; George Hickes to Arthur Charlett, 24 December 1713, Ballard MS 12, f. 206.

133. William Whiston, *A Proposal for Erecting Societies for Promoting Primitive Christianity* (1712).

134. White Kennett ecclesiastical diary, BL Lansdowne MS 1024, ff. 259–260.

135. Ralph Bridges to William Trumbull, 19 February 1711, BL Add MS 72495, f. 45; for the membership of this committee, see Philip Stubbs to Arthur Charlett, 11 February 1711, Ballard MS 34, f. 198.

136. "Representation of the State of Religion; drawn up by a joint Committee of both Houses of Convocation, in March 1710–11," Atterbury Correspondence, 2:317–318.

137. "Representation of the State of Religion," 2:318–319.

138. "Representation of the State of Religion," 2:321, 325, 341, 335–336; Whiston, *Account of the Convocation's proceedings*, 60–61.

139. "Representation of the State of Religion," 2:326, 330, 347–348.

140. White Kennett's ecclesiastical diary, BL Lansdowne MS 1024, f. 291.

141. Pittis, *History of the present Parliament*, 273–275.

142. The representation of the archbishop and bishops is printed in Pittis, *History of the present Parliament*, 275–288.

143. White Kennett's ecclesiastical diary, BL Lansdowne MS 1024, f. 318.

144. See Matthew Tindal, *The Nation Vindicated from the aspersions cast on it in a late pamphlet intitled, Representation of the Present State of Religion* (London, 1711), 14.

145. Kennett's notes from his speech are in BL Lansdowne MS 927, ff. 39–43.

146. White Kennett's ecclesiastical diary, BL Lansdowne MS 1024, f. 318; Atterbury denied knowing anything of their publication.

147. See William Wotton, *The Case of the present Convocation consider'd; in answer to the Examiner's unfair representation of it, and unjust reflections upon it* (London, 1711), 5—a response to one of Swift's previous assaults on the episcopate.

148. *Examiner*, 21 June 1711 (no. 46), in *The works of the Reverend Dr. Jonathan Swift*, 20 vols. (Dublin, 1772), 5:445.

149. Tindal, *The Nation Vindicated*, 5; *The laity's remonstrance to the late representation of the lower H. of C—n. with a turn of the tables* (London, 1711); *Some thoughts on the representation of the lower House of Convocation* (London, 1711).

150. Daniel Defoe, *The Representation of the Lower House of Convocation of the English Clergy Examined: being remarks on the present state of religion now in England* (London, 1711), 20–22.

151. Tindal, *The Nation Vindicated*, 5, 14.

152. White Kennett, Speech at convocation, 1711, BL Lansdowne MS 927, ff. 39–43.

153. White Kennett to Samuel Blackwell, 7 July 1711, BL Lansdowne MS 1013, f. 158.

154. On the synodical origins of the Queen Anne churches, see "Message from the Lower House of Convocation to the Speaker of the House of Commons, 28 Feb 1711," Atterbury Correspondence, 2:312–313; White Kennett ecclesiastical diary, BL Lansdowne MS 1024, f. 275; Ralph Bridges to William Trumbull, 18 November 1710, BL Add MS 72495, f. 30; on the Schism Act, see Ralph Bridges to William Trumbull, 14 May, 14 June 1713, BL Add MS 72496, ff. 141, 143.

155. Sherlock, *New Danger of Presbytery*, 5, 8; *A Letter to the Reverend Mr. Jonathan Kimberly*, 7–8; White Kennett, Convocation Papers, BL Lansdowne MS 940, f. 73; Collins, *Priestcraft in Perfection*, 20; Wotton, *The Case of the present Convocation*, 5–6.

156. Jonathan Swift, "Examiner XXI, 28 December 1710," 78.

157. Anne R. to Tenison, 25 February 1706, BL Add MS 61612, f. 144.

158. *A Representation made By the Lower House of Convocation to the Archbishops and Bishops* (London, 1705).

159. *A Review of the Dangers of the Church* (London, 1705), 18.

160. White Kennett's ecclesiastical diary, BL Lansdowne MS 1024, ff. 211–212, 376.

161. On the notion of a "weak state" in Whig historiography, see John Brewer, "The Eighteenth Century British State: Contexts and Issues," in *An Imperial State at War: Britain from 1689 to 1815*, ed. Lawrence Stone (New York: Routledge, 1994), 54–55.

6. The Blue Water Policy of the Church of England

1. Boehme to Newman, 15 July 1715, Bodl. Rawlinson MC C 743, f. 34; Newman to Pye, 16 September 1710, HNL Special Letters; Newman to Chamberlayne, 15 December 1722, HNL vol. 12, f. 48; Thomas Lynford, *Charity-Schools Recommended* (London, 1712), 22; Edward Waddington, *A Sermon Preached before the Incorporated Society for the Propagation of the Gospel in Foreign Parts* (London, 1721), 34; William Berriman, *The Great Blessing of Redemption from Captivity* (London, 1722), 3.

2. David Armitage, *The Ideological Origins of the British Empire* (Cambridge: Cambridge University Press, 2000), 100–124.

3. Elizabeth Macke, "Empire and State," in *The British Atlantic World, 1500–1800*, ed. David Armitage and Michael J. Braddick (Basingstoke, UK: Palgrave Macmillan, 2002), 175–195; Jorge Cañizares-Esguerra, *Puritan Conquistadors: Iberianizing the Atlantic, 1500–1700* (Stanford, CA: Stanford University Press, 2007); J. A. De Jong, *As the Waters Cover the Sea: Millennial Expectations in the Rise of Anglo-American Missions, 1640–1810* (Laurel, MS: Audubon Press, 2006).

4. Patrick Gordon, *Geography Anatomiz'd: Or, The Compleat Geographical Grammar* (London, 1699); on Gordon, see W. K. Lowther Clarke, *Eighteenth Century Piety* (London: SPCK, 1944), 91–95.

5. For the original geopolitical significance of the British "blue water policy," see Daniel A. Baugh, "Great Britain's 'Blue-Water' Policy, 1689–1815," *International History Review* 10 (February 1988): 33–58; Daniel A. Baugh, "Maritime Strength and Atlantic Commerce: The Uses of 'A Grand Marine Empire,'" in *An Imperial State at War: Britain from 1689 to 1815*, ed. Lawrence Stone (New York: Routledge, 1994), 185–223.

6. John Frederick Woolverton, *Colonial Anglicanism in North America* (Detroit, MI: Wayne State University Press, 1984), 107–135; J. C. D. Clark, *The Language of Liberty, 1660–1832: Political Discourse and Social Dynamics in the Anglo-American World* (Cambridge: Cambridge University Press, 1994), 141–217; B. S. Schlenther, "Religious Faith and Commercial Empire," in *The Oxford History of the British Empire, Vol. 2: The Eighteenth Century*, ed. P. J. Marshall (Oxford University Press, 1998), 128–150; James B. Bell, *The Imperial Origins of the King's Church in America, 1607–1783* (New York: Palgrave Macmillan, 2004); Rowan Strong, *Anglicanism and the British Empire, c. 1700–1850* (Oxford: Oxford University Press, 2007), 41–117.

7. Schlenther, "Religious Faith," 131; and see Travis Glasson, *Mastering Christianity: Missionary Anglicanism and Slavery in the Atlantic World* (New York: Oxford University Press, 2011), 33.

8. Steve Pincus, "Rethinking Mercantilism: Political Economy, the British Empire and the Atlantic World in the Seventeenth and Eighteenth Centuries," *WMQ*, 3rd series, 69 (January 2012): 3–34.

9. The phrase is that of Maurice Parmlee, "The Rise of Modern Humanitarianism," *American Journal of Sociology* 21 (November 1915): 345–359; see more recently, Thomas W. Laqueur, "Bodies, Details and the Humanitarian Narrative," in *The New Cultural History*, ed. Lynn Hunt (Berkeley: University of California Press, 1989), 176–204; Lynn Hunt, *Inventing Human Rights: A History* (New York: W. W. Norton, 2007), 35–69.

10. The most forceful argument for global market relations as the precondition of modern humanitarianism is that of Thomas Haskell, "Capitalism and the Origins of the Humanitarian Sensibility, Part 1," *American Historical Review* 90 (April 1985): 339–361; and "Capitalism and the Origins of the Humanitarian Sensibility, Part 2," *American Historical Review* 90 (June 1985): 547–566. Haskell rather arbitrarily posits 1750 as his starting point for the modern humanitarian sensibility.

11. Andrew F. Walls, "The Eighteenth Century Protestant Missionary Awakening in Its European Context," in *Christian Missions and the Enlightenment*, ed. Brian Stanley (Grand Rapids, MI: William B. Eerdmans, 2001), 22–44; Jeffrey Cox, *The British Missionary Enterprise since 1700* (New York: Routledge, 2008), 3–75; on the ideological origins of European humanitarianism, see D. B. Davis, *The Problem of Slavery in Western Culture* (Ithaca, NY: Cornell University Press, 1966), 291–445.

12. Philip S. Haffenden, "The Anglican Church in Restoration Colonial Policy," in *Seventeenth Century America*, ed. James Morton Smith (Chapel Hill: University of North Carolina Press, 1959), 166–191.

13. A. L. Cross, *The Anglican Episcopate and American Colonies* (New York: Longmans, Green, 1902) 9–21; Peter Heylyn, *Cyprianus anglicus, or, The history of the life and death of the Most Reverend and renowned prelate William, by divine providence Lord Archbishop of Canterbury* (London, 1668), 231–233, 275–276, 369.

14. Papers related to the appointment of Alexander Moray as Bishop of Virginia, BL Harleian MS 5790, ff. 1–4; Francis L. Hawks, "Efforts to obtain the Episcopate before the Revolution," in *Collections of the Protestant Episcopal Historical Society for the Year 1851* (New York: Stanford and Swords, 1851); James S. M. Anderson, *The History of the Church of England in the Colonies and Foreign Dependencies of the British Empire*, 3 vols. (London: Francis and John Rivington, 1845–1856), 2:569; Mary Francis Goodwin, "The Reverend Alexander Moray, M.A., D.D., The First Bishop-Designate of Virginia, 1672–3," *HMPEC* 12 (1943): 59–68.

15. J. H. Bennett, "English Bishops and Imperial Jurisdiction, 1660–1725," *HMPEC* 32 (September 1963): 175–188; Geoffrey Yeo, "A Case without Parallel: The Bishops of London and the Anglican Church Overseas, 1660–1748," *JEH* 44 (1993): 450–475.

16. Bell, *Imperial Origins*, 10–26; Stephen Saunders Webb, *1676: The End of American Independence* (New York: Knopf, 1984), 192–193.

17. Julian S. Corbett, *England in the Mediterranean*, 2 vols. (London: Longmans, Green, 1904), 2:106.

18. Edward Carpenter, *The Protestant Bishop, Being the Life of Henry Compton, 1632–1713, Bishop of London* (London: Longmans, Green, 1956), 253–254; Lawrence Brown, "Henry Compton, 1632–1714," *Historical Magazine* 25 (March 1956): 7–68; White Kennett, Materials for a history of the SPG, BL Lansdowne MS 1032, ff. 211–212.

19. Report on Barbados Petition, 17 October 1717, BL Add MS 61623, ff. 82–86; J. H Bennett, "The S.P.G. and Barbadian Politics, 1710–1720," *HMPEC* 20 (June 1951): 190–206.

20. Prideaux to Ellis, 25 June 1681, in *Letters of Humphrey Prideaux sometime Dean of Norwich to John Ellis, sometime Secretary of State, 1674–1722,* ed. E. M. Thompson (Westminster: Camden Society, 1875), 86.

21. Kennett, Materials for a history of the SPG, BL Lansdowne MS 1032, ff. 206–208; Anderson, *History of the Church of England in the Colonies,* 2:571–674; Oley's trust would eventually settle a £5 per year pension upon the SPG.

22. *The Diary and Autobiography of Edmund Bohun, Esq.* (privately published, 1853), 72.

23. Betty Wood, "Godwyn, Morgan (bap. 1640, d. 1685x1709)," in *ODNB.*

24. Francis Brokesby, *Some Proposals Towards Promoting the Propagation of the Gospel in Our American Plantations, Humbly Offered in a Letter to Mr. Nelson* (London: G. Sawbridge, 1708), 1.

25. Morgan Godwyn, *Trade preferred before religion, and Christ made to give place to Mammon* (London, 1685), epistle dedicatory; Kennett, Materials for a history of the SPG, Lansdowne MS 1032, f. 217.

26. Davis, *Problem of Slavery,* 204–206; Christopher L. Brown, *Moral Capital: Foundations of British Abolitionism* (Chapel Hill: University of North Carolina Press, 2006), 69–71; for a useful overview of the historiography concerning Godwyn, see John M. Fout, "The Explosive Cleric: Morgan Godwyn, Slavery and Colonial Elites in Virginia and Barbados, 1665–1685" (master's thesis, Virginia Commonwealth University, 2005), 1–19.

27. Morgan Godwyn, *The Negro's & Indians advocate, suing for their admission to the church* (London, 1680), sig. A3.

28. Godwyn, *Negro's & Indians advocate,* preface, 99–100.

29. Godwyn, *Trade preferred before religion,* 11.

30. Godwyn, *Trade preferred before religion,* 8, 9, 16; by "remoter places," Godwyn was referring to the East Indies.

31. Benedict Anderson, *Imagined Communities: Reflections on the Origin and Spread of Nationalism* (New York: Verso, 1983).

32. Godwyn, *Negro's & Indians advocate,* 130–131.

33. C. F. Secretan, *Memoirs of the Life and Times of the Pious Robert Nelson* (London: John Murray, 1860), 70–72.

34. Kennett to Blackwell, 29 January 1698, BL Lansdowne MS 1013, f. 62.

35. Henry Dodwell to Tenison, 29 August 1700, LPL Gibson MS 930, §38; George Every, *The High Church Party, 1688–1718* (London: SPCK, 1956), 88. Every believes that Robert Nelson was lobbying Tenison in person at Lambeth in August 1700 in favor of efforts in the American plantations.

36. "A Short Account of the Author," in Francis Lee, *Apoleipomena. Or, dissertations theological, mathematical, and physical* (London, 1752), xvii.

37. 31 January, 16 December 1706, LPL, SPG Minutes vol. 1, ff. 83, 137.

38. Kennett, Materials for a history of the SPG, BL Lansdowne MS 1032, ff. 3, 10, 214–215, 217.

39. C. M. Andrews, "The Colonies after the Restoration, 1660–1713," in *The Cambridge History of the British Empire*, 8 vols. (Cambridge: Cambridge University Press, 1929), 2:252; Webb, *1676*, 192–193.

40. Ned C. Landsman, "The Middle Colonies: New Opportunities for Settlement, 1660–1700," in *Oxford History of the British Empire*, 5 vols. (Oxford: Oxford University Press, 2001), 1:351–374; and see John Locke, "The Fundamental Constitutions of Carolina," in *Locke: Political Essays*, ed. Mark Goldie (Cambridge: Cambridge University Press, 1997), 177–178.

41. Carla Gardina Pestana, *Protestant Empire: Religion and the Making of the British Atlantic World* (Philadelphia: University of Pennsylvania Press, 2009), 100–158.

42. Pestana, *Protestant Empire*, 168–172; Bell, *Imperial Origins*, 26–40, 58–73; Jon Butler, *Awash in a Sea of Faith: Christianizing the American People* (Cambridge, MA: Harvard University Press, 1990), 98–128; on Blair, see Parker Rouse Jr., *James Blair of Virginia* (Chapel Hill: University of North Carolina Press, 1971); Samuel Clyde McCulloch, "James Blair's Plan of 1699 to Reform the Clergy of Virginia," *WMQ*, 3rd series, 4 (1947): 70–86.

43. Thomas Bray, "A General View of the English Colonies in America with Respect to Religion," in *Apostolick charity, its nature and excellence considered* (London, 1698), unpaginated appendix; on the weakness of the church in the East Indies, see Humphrey Prideaux to Archbishop Tenison, 27 March 1695, LPL Gibson MS 933, §§1–2, and the enclosed report; Prideaux's report was circulated among the members of the SPCK, see Henry Newman to W. Lewis at Fort St. George, 21 April 1712, HNL vol. 2, f. 47.

44. Bray, *Apostolick charity*, 15; H. P. Thompson, *Thomas Bray* (London: SPCK, 1954), 71.

45. Richard Willis, *A sermon preach'd before the Society for the Propagation of the Gospel in Foreign Parts* (London, 1702), 21.

46. Gordon, *Geography Anatomiz'd*, unpaginated.

47. On the cultural and political contributions of imperialism to eighteenth-century urban life, see Kathleen Wilson, *The Sense of the People: Politics, Culture and Imperialism in England, 1715–1785* (New York: Cambridge University Press, 1998).

48. Rowan Strong, "A Vision of an Anglican Imperialism: The Annual Sermons of the Society for the Propagation of the Gospel in Foreign Parts, 1701–1714," *Journal of Religious History* 30 (2006): 175–198.

49. 27 February 1701/2, LPL, SPG Minutes vol. 1, f. 34

50. Willis, *Sermon before the SPG*, 20; Gilbert Burnet to John Chamberlayne, Salisbury, 5 April 1703, LPL SPG Papers 7, f. 55.

51. "An abstract of the most material Proceedings and Occurrences within the last year's Endeavours of the Society for the Propagation of the Gospel in Foreign Parts, from February 16, 1710 to February 15, 1711–1712," in White Kennett, *The Lets and Impediments in Planting and Propagating the Gospel of Christ* (London, 1712), 37–38.

52. Queen Anne to Archbishop Tenison, 18 May 1714, LPL Gibson MS 941, §39.

53. "The Bishop of Man's Proposal for Propagating the Gospel, &c.," 12 May 1707, in *The Life of the Right Reverend Father in God Thomas Wilson, D.D.*, ed. John Keble, 2 vols. (Oxford: John Henry Parker, 1863), 1:248–249; 12 May 1707, LPL, SPG Minutes vol. 1, f. 176.

54. Robert Nelson, *An Address to Persons of Quality and Estate* (London, 1715), 122–126.

55. Frank Klingberg, ed., *Codrington Chronicle: An Experiment in Anglican Altruism on a Barbados Plantation, 1710–1834* (Berkeley: University of California Press, 1949), 16; George Stanhope, *The early Conversion of Islanders a wise Expedient for propagating Christianity* (London: J. Downing, 1714), 21.

56. William Gordon, *A sermon preach'd at the funeral of the Honourable Colonel Christopher Codrington* (London, 1710), epistle dedicatory; both Bishop Wilson and Colonel Codrington's plans were highlighted in Robert Nelson's widely circulated primer of Anglican philanthropy *An Address to Persons of Quality and Estate*, 124–126. The vicissitudes of Codrington's legacy were occasionally covered in metropolitan newspapers: *Weekly Packet*, 16 June 1716; *Post Man and the Historical Account*, 12 May, 22 December 1719; *Daily Post*, 29 December 1719; and see Glasson, *Mastering Christianity*, 141–170.

57. Kennett, *Lets and Impediments*, 8.

58. Stanhope, *The early Conversion of Islanders*, 5.

59. William Stanley, *A Sermon preach'd before the Society for the Propagation of the Gospel in Foreign Parts* (London, 1708), 22; Stanhope, *The early Conversion of Islanders*, 16. The text of 1 Cor 9:11 is "If we have sown unto you spiritual things, is it a great thing if we shall reap your carnal things?"

60. John Williams, *A Sermon preached before the Society for the Propagation of the Gospel in Foreign Parts* (London, 1706), 32; Gilbert Burnet, *Of the propagation of the gospel in foreign parts* (London, 1704), 27; Willis, *Sermon preach'd before the Society*, 20.

61. George Stanhope used the explicitly commercial language of debt and entitlement to make this point; Stanhope, *The early Conversion of Islanders*, 16.

62. Stanhope, *The early Conversion of Islanders*, 9.

63. Anthony Marie de la Croze to Thomas Tenison, 8 March 1715, LPL Gibson MS 930, §28.

64. Nelson, *Address to Persons of Quality*, 130–131.

65. White Kennett's ecclesiastical diary, Lansdowne MS 1024, f. 174, where Kennett mentions the publication of two broadsides soliciting for the Rotterdam church.

66. In 1703, the trustees for building an English church at Rotterdam opened an account at the bank of Henry Hoare, a prominent and active member of the SPCK. The ledger shows contributions from, among others, SPCK affiliates Edward Colston and Robert Yate, CHC Ledger 5, ff. 370–371. See also Sugiko Nishikawa, "English Attitudes toward Continental Protestants with Particular Reference to Church Briefs, c. 1680–1740" (PhD diss., University of London, 1998), 163–171.

67. Trustees of the English Church at Rotterdam to Duke of Marlborough, 6 February 1703/04, BL Add M 61300, f. 56.

68. Memorandum on English Church at Rotterdam, n.d., BL Add MS 61300, f. 66.

69. Thorold to Hodges, 14 July 1701, CUL SPCK MS D2/2, §334.

70. Nelson to Pepys, 2 March 1702/03, printed in Secretan, *Life of Nelson*, 68; Francis Lee, Notes on Nelson, BL Add MS 45512, f. 5.

71. A List of what Regimts have already subscrib'd to the Church at Roterdam, n.d., BL Add MS 61300, f. 68.

72. Trustees to Marlborough, 6 February 1703/04, BL Add MS 61300, f. 56; on controversies surrounding Marlborough's involvement in the project, see Brown, "Henry Compton," 42; HMC *Portland* 4:377.

73. Henry Newton to Earl of Sunderland, 16 January 1707, NS, BL Add MS 61518, f. 23; there is some evidence to suggest that the idea originated with Messrs. Tronchin and Turrentin, Swiss Protestant correspondents of the SPG, and came to Tenison only via that organization, LPL SPG MS 1, ff. 58–59.

74. Robert Nelson to Samuel Brewster, 10 September 1706, BL Add MS 45511, f. 79.

75. Sunderland to Newton, 4 February 1706/07, BL Add MS 25277, f. 108.

76. Basil Kennett, *Sermons preached on several occasions, to a society of British merchants, in foreign parts* (London, 1715), 2.

77. For Anglican encounters with the Inquisition in the Canary Islands, see Smith to Compton, Teneriffe (Canary Island), 19 June 1699, LPL Fulham Papers: Compton Papers vol. 2, f. 88.

78. SPCK Minutes, 4 June 1713, §5.

79. Newman to John Robinson, bishop of London, 23 June 1722, HNL vol. 7, ff. 26–28.

80. On Richard Kane's military career, see his autobiographical *Campaigns of King William and the Duke of Marlborough*, 2nd ed. (London, 1747).

81. On the Ecclesiastical Affairs of Minorca, LPL Fulham Papers: Edmund Gibson Papers 2, f. 24.

82. Petition of Don Manuel Merceder, son of the Marquis de la Vega, formerly Archdeacon of Valencia, Vicar General of Minorca, etc. to Robert Walpole, n.d. (ca. 1717), Bodl. Rawlinson C 743, f. 88.

83. George Bubb to Paul Methuen, 19 April 1717, NS, BL Egerton 2174, f. 161.

84. The 28 Articles part of the Complaint delivered by the Spanish Ambassador against Lt. Governour Kane with the Lt. Governour's Answer to them, [1717], Center for Kentish Studies U1590/0152, ff. 8–15; Marquis de Grimaldo, Memorial on Richard Kane, April 1717, BL Egerton MS 2174, ff. 153–157; Richard Kane to Bishop of Majorca, 8 April 1717, BL Egerton MS 2174, ff. 115–116; and see *A Vindication of Colonel Kane, Governor of Minorca* (London, 1720).

85. A fine account of Wake's involvement in Minorca can be found in Norman Sykes, *William Wake, Archbishop of Canterbury, 1657–1737*, 2 vols. (Cambridge: Cambridge University Press, 1957), 2:214–219. Interestingly, the chapter that contains this account provides ample evidence of Wake's involvement with a variety of SPCK projects but fails to mention SPCK involvement in Minorca.

86. On the operations of the Inquisition in Minorca, see Kane's remarks at Centre for Kentish Studies MS U1590/0152, f. 21, where the British freed one Cezar Moncade, "a native Sicilian turned Protestant," from captivity in the Franciscan convent in Mahon, "otherwise he would have been sent privately to Majorca, or put to death where he was."

87. On the Ecclesiastical Affairs of Minorca, LPL Fulham Papers: Edmund Gibson Papers 2, f. 31.

88. Reasons for Separating the Island of Minorca from the Diocess of Majorca and from a Dependence on any Ecclesiastical Power in the Dominion of Spain, LPL Fulham Papers: Edmund Gibson 2, f. 30.

89. On the Ecclesiastical Affairs of Minorca, LPL Fulham Papers: Edmund Gibson Papers 2 f. 42.

90. Scheme for Establishing four Clergymen in the Island of Minorca in stead of the five Chaplains that are now established there; form'd upon the Report that was made to the late King by his Grace the Arch-Bishop of Canterbury, LPL Fulham Papers: Edmund Gibson 2, f. 44.

91. Henry Newman to Richard Kane, 28 December 1719, HNL vol. 9, ff. 4–5; the society's support of Kane generally fit with the SPCK modus operandi of recruiting British military governors into its ranks and promoting society programming in the garrison under their command. See, for instance, Newman's correspondence with William Gordon at Fort William in Scotland, begun at Henry Newman to Mr. Gordon, Governor of Ft. William in North Britain, 29 June 1714, HNL vol. 4, f. 54; on SPCK outreach to the garrisons in India, see Henry Newman to Mr. Jennings at Ft. St. George, 4 January 1714/15, HNL vol. 5, f. 1.

92. Newman to Kane, 28 December 1719, 3 September 1720, HNL vol. 9, ff. 4–5, 76.

93. Newman to Kane, 7 March 1719/20, HNL vol. 9, ff. 37–38.

94. Newman to Kane, 9 December 1720, HNL vol. 10, f. 23.

95. Newman to Kane, 1 June 1721, HNL vol. 10, f. 88; Newman to Kane, 11 August 1722, HNL vol. 12, f. 36.

96. Newman to John Robinson, Bishop of London, 23 June 1722, HNL vol. 12, ff. 26–27; Newman to Lord Carpenter, 27 June 1722, HNL vol. 12, ff. 29–30.

97. Newman to Bishop Robinson, 23 June 1722, HNL vol. 12, ff. 26–27; To the King's Most Excellt Majesty, The Memorial of John Lord Bishop of London, HNL vol. 12, f. 28; Newman to Edmund Gibson, bishop of London, 31 August 1723, HNL vol. 13, f. 43; and A Memorial concerning the Pension of Sixty pounds P Annum granted by the Crown in favour of the Protestants of Piedmont, HNL vol. 13, ff. 44–45.

98. The Memorial of John Lord Bishop of London, HNL vol. 12, f. 28.

99. A Memorial concerning the Pension of Sixty pounds P Annum granted by the Crown in favour of the Protestants of Piedmont, HNL vol. 13, ff. 44–45.

100. 3 and 17 February 1704, McClure, *SPCK Minutes*, 262–263; SPCK Minutes, 2 April 1713, §1, 9 April 1713, §1; Newman to Dr. Thomas, 20 July 1731, HNL vol. 23, f. 9; for a lengthy treatment of the lot of Anglican factory chaplains, see John Colbatch, chaplain to the factory at Lisbon, to Bishop [Compton], 27 October 1606, BL Add MS 22908, ff. 12–24.

101. The Copy of a Letter from an English Chaplain in Portugal to John Chamberlayne, Esq., [1 November 1711], BL Lansdowne MS 1024, ff. 355–356.

102. Materials for a history of the SPG, BL Lansdowne MS 1032, ff. 46–48; on the state of the naval chaplaincy, see John Hext to Henry Compton, Queen, Cadiz Bay, 13 January 1695/96, Bodl. Rawlinson C 984, f. 113.

103. Philip Stubbs to Archbishop Tenison, 11 March 1705, LPL Gibson MS 941, §9.

104. William Anderson, A Narrative of the Proceedings relating to the Building of a Church in the English Settlement at Fort William in the Kingdom of Bengall, 12 March 1707, LPL Gibson MS 935, §7.

105. P. J. Marshall, "The Moral Swing to the East: British Humanitarianism, India and the West Indies," in *East India Company Studies: Papers Presented to Sir Cyril Philips*, ed. K. Ballhatchet and J. Harrison (Hong Kong: Asian Research Service, 1986), 69–95.

106. Charles Masham to Archbishop Thomas Tenison, St. Helena, 29 November 1703, LPL Gibson MS 929, §52.

107. 21 May 1706, LPL SPG Minutes vol. 1, f. 100.

108. See Philip J. Stern, *The Company-State: Corporate Sovereignty and the Early Modern Foundations of British Empire in India* (New York: Oxford University Press, 2011), 100–119.

109. Kennett, Materials for a history of the SPG, f. 173.

110. Newman to Woodward, 6 December 1711, HNL vol. 2, ff. 31–32. The SPCK struggled to find English missionaries for India, "the Gent[lemen] of our universities being bred too delicately to undertake so hardy a service," Newman told Bishop Compton in November 1714. Consequently, the society was forced to concentrate its support on the chaplains of the East India Company and the Danish missionaries at Tranquebar; Newman to Bp of London, 13 November 1714, HNL vol. 3, f. 74.

111. George Lewis to Henry Newman, Fort St. George, 1 February 1712/13, LPL Gibson MS 933, §115.

112. Newman to Revd Mr. Walton at Carlisle, 11 December 1718, HNL vol. 7, f. 89; and see Kennett, Materials for a history of the SPG, f. 165.

113. Newman to Revd Dr. Wilkins, 18 August 1721; Newman to William Wake, 9 September 1721; Newman to Mr. Woolsey, Secretary of East India Company, 13 November 1721, HNL vol. 11, ff. 18–20, 25; John Perceval to Charles Dering, December 1721; Perceval to Thomas Bray, 27 January 1721/22, BL Add MS 47029, ff. 93, 99.

114. Circular Letter to the Members in London about ye African Affair, HNL vol. 11, f. 65; John Perceval to Thomas Bray, 26 January 1721/22, BL Add MS 47029, f. 97.

115. Newman to Rev. Mr. King, 29 March 1722, HNL vol. 12, f. 11.

116. Perceval to the African Princes, 27 January 1721, BL Add MS 47029, f. 99.

117. Instructions for Marmaduke Penwell, BL Add MS 47029, ff. 99–101.

118. Newman to Rev. King at Topsham, 16 June 1722, HNL vol. 12, f. 23.

119. Marmaduke Penwell to Perceval, 31 March 1722, BL Add MS 47029, f. 112.

120. Penwell to Perceval, 21 May 1722, BL Add MS 47029, f. 122.

121. Newman to Perceval, 1 December 1722, BL Add MS 47029, f. 141.

122. Penwell to Perceval, 30 November 1722, BL Add MS 47029, f. 155.

123. Newman to Perceval, 30 March 1723, BL Add MS 47030, f. 1.

124. Newman to Chamberlayne, 2 April 1720; Newman to Prideaux, 22 April 1720, HNL vol. 9, ff. 48, 51.

125. Newman to Rev. Mr. Fox, 22 October 1720, HNL vol. 10, f. 9.

126. Newman to Wake, 15 October 1726, HNL vol. 17, f. 37.

127. Newman to Robert de Neville, 26 April 1720; Newman to Mr. Cranfield, 28 April 1720, HNL vol. 11, ff. 52–53, 53–54; Newman to Dr. Williams, 28 November 1720; Newman to Wake, 12 January 1720/21; Newman to Spencer Compton, 5 April 1721; Newman to Mr. De Robethon, 14 June 1721, HNL vol. 10, ff. 17, 34, 55, 79.

128. Newman to Chamberlayne, 2 April 1720, HNL vol. 9, f. 48.

129. Newman to Rev'd Mr. Lile at Oxford, 3 May 1720; Newman to Rev. Dr. Bridges, 12 September 1720, HNL vol. 11, ff. 55, 83; Newman to Rev. Mr. Soley, Chaplain at Aleppo, 6 December 1720, HNL vol. 10, ff. 19–20.

130. Newman to Archbishop Wake, 21 August 1721, HNL vol. 11, ff. 16–17.

131. Newman to Ayerst, 3 August 1721; Newman to Rowland Sherman, Merchant at Aleppo, 21 June 1723; Newman to the Rev. Mr. Bedford, 2 January 1723/24, HNL vol. 11, ff. 13–14, 16–17, 25.

132. Newman to Townshend, 20 November 1724, HNL vol. 11, ff. 20–21.

133. Newman to Rev. Mr. Soley at Chelsea, 27 May 1726, HNL vol. 27, f. 3.

134. Newman to Rowland Sherman, Merchant at Aleppo, 21 September 1727, HNL vol. 18, f. 49.

135. Newman to Rowland Sherman at Aleppo, 27 September 1728, HNL vol. 19, f. 60.

136. Newman to Rowland Sherman at Aleppo, 28 September 1728, HNL vol. 19, f. 61; Newman to John Meller, Esq., 31 July 1729, HNL vol. 20, f. 42.

137. Newman to Honble Major General Hockmuth, one of the Commissioners of War at Petersburg in Russia, 9 August 1729, HNL vol. 20, f. 43.

138. Newman to Rowland Sherman, 23 December 1724, HNL vol. 15, f. 29.

139. Philip Perceval to John Perceval, Dublin, 9 November 1723, BL Add MS 47030, ff. 35–36.

140. Thomas Bray, *Missionalia: or, a collection of missionary pieces relating to the conversion of the heathen; both the African negroes and American Indians* (London, 1727), 65–73.

141. George Berkeley to John Perceval, 4 March 1722, BL Add MS 47029, f. 156; *An Account of the establishment for relieving poor proselytes; with an abstract of the proceedings of the Commission for that purpose from the 30th of April 1719 to the 3d of February, 1719–1720* (London, 1720); a list of commissioners is printed on pp. 27–30.

142. John Chamberlayne to John Perceval, 24 February 1719/20, BL Add MS 47029, f. 19.

143. *Religious Philanthropy and Colonial Slavery: The American Correspondence of the Associates of Dr. Bray, 1717–1777*, ed. John C. Van Horne (Urbana: University of Illinois Press, 1985), 5; it is a testament to the complexity of the early-eighteenth-century Anglican voluntary sector that the SPG claimed with good cause that it alone comprised the "Associates" of Thomas Bray referred to in D'Allone's will.

144. John Perceval to David Humphreys, Charlton, 23 February 1724/25, BL Add MS 47030, f. 274.

145. George Berkeley to John Perceval, 10 February 1725/26; John Perceval to Daniel Dering, 12 February 1725/26, BL Add MS 47031, ff. 104–106.

146. In the year before Berkeley published his proposal, Newman noted, "There are sevll persons of Honour and Substance in Ireland who have projected to go and end their Days at Bermudas for the sake of Tranquility and innocent pleasures that are to be enjoyed there"; Henry Newman to Governor Phenny, 3 August 1723, HNL vol. 13, f. 35; Henry Newman to John Perceval, 8 January 1724/25, HNL vol. 15, f. 36.

147. CHC Ledger 27, f. 107 shows £3,124 17s 6d on hand by the end 1729. Perceval told his cousin Daniel Dering: "You will be surpris'd when you hear the Company he has engaged to go with him. Young & old, learned & rich, all desirous of retiring to enjoy peace of mind & health of body & of restoring the golden age in that corner of the World." John Perceval to Daniel Dering, 5 March 1722/23, BL Add MS 47029, f. 158; and see E. S. Gaustad, "George Berkeley and New World Community," *Church History* 48 (March 1979): 5–17; Scott Breuninger, "Planting an Asylum for Religion: Berkeley's Bermuda Scheme and the Transmission of Virtue

in the Eighteenth-Century Atlantic World," *Journal of Religious History* 34 (December 2010): 414–429.

148. John Perceval to George Berkeley, 30 June 1723, BL Add MS 47030, f. 7.

149. Edwin S. Gustaud, *George Berkeley in America* (New Haven, CT: Yale University Press, 1979), 36; and see Philip Perceval to John Perceval, Dublin, 25 May 1725, BL Add MS 47030, f. 143.

150. George Berkeley to Thomas Prior, 12 May 1726, quoted in Gustaud, *Berkeley in America*, 39–40.

151. America or the Muses a Refuge of Prophecy, BL Add MS 47031, f. 105.

152. The best account remains that of Gustaud, *Berkeley in America;* see also Anderson, *History of the Church of England in the Colonies*, 3:337–379; John Wild, *George Berkeley: A Study of His Life and Philosophy* (New York: Russell and Russell, 1962), 280–330.

153. George Berkeley, *A sermon preached before the Incorporated Society for the Propagation of the Gospel in Foreign Parts; at the parish-church of St. Mary-le-Bow, on Friday the 18th of February, 1731* (London, 1732), 29, 33.

154. Henry Newman to Rev. Mr. King, 8 February 1725/26, HNL vol. 15, f. 47; in a draft letter to Henry Robinson, Newman elaborated on the objections to the project but then crossed them out; Newman to Robinson, 4 November 1725, HNL vol. 15, f. 27.

155. H. B. Fant, "Picturesque Thomas Coram, Projector of Two Georgias, Father of the London Foundling Hospital," *Georgia Historical Quarterly* 22 (1948): 77–104; Ruth K. McClure, *Coram's Children: The London Foundling Hospital in the Eighteenth Century* (New Haven, CT: Yale University Press, 1981); Gillian Wagner, *Thomas Coram, Gent.: 1668–1751* (London: Boydell, 2004).

156. Thomas Coram to Benjamin Colman, London, 20 April 1734, "Letters of Thomas Coram," ed. Worthington C. Ford, *Proceedings of the Massachusetts Historical Society* 56 (1922–1923): 19–24.

157. On popular anti-Catholicism and foreign policy in the age of Walpole, see Jeremy Black, "The Catholic Threat and the British Press in the 1720s and 1730s," *Journal of Religious History* 12 (December 1983): 364–381.

158. See the introduction to Trevor R. Reese, ed., *The Most Delightful Country of the Universe: Promotional Literature of the Colony of Georgia, 1717–1734* (Savannah, GA: Beehive, 1972), vii–xxi.

159. Jean Pierre Purry, *A memorial presented to His Grace the Duke of Newcastle* (London, 1724), 6, 8.

160. Joshua Gee, *The trade and navigation of Great-Britain considered* (London, 1729), 22–23.

161. Verner W. Crane, "Projects for Colonizing the South, 1684–1732," *Mississippi Valley Historical Review* 12 (June 1925): 23–35.

162. Rodney M. Baine, ed., *Creating Georgia: Minutes of the Bray Associates, 1730–1732* (Athens: University of Georgia Press, 1995), xv.

163. "Assignment of Trustees for Mr. D'Allone's Bequest," in *The American Correspondence of the Associates of Dr. Bray, 1717–1777* [London, 15 January 1729/30], 62–67.

164. Verner W. Crane, *The Southern Frontier, 1670–1732* (Ann Arbor: University of Michigan Press, 1928), 303–325; Verner W. Crane, "Dr. Thomas Bray and the Charitable Colony Project, 1730," *WMQ*, 3rd series (January 1962): 49–63.

165. Perceval to Berkeley, Bath, 23 December 1730, BL Add MS 47032, f. 256; at the second meeting of the reconstituted Bray Associates under Oglethorpe, on 1 July 1730, the trustees agreed "that this Society will endeavour to cultivate a good Understanding with the Society for the Propagating of the Gospel in foreign parts, and that such Members of this Society as are Members of the other Society do acquaint them therewith." The trustees agreed to do the same with the SPCK immediately after; Baine, *Creating Georgia*, 15.

166. See, for instance, Samuel Smith, *A sermon preach'd before the trustees for establishing the colony of Georgia in America, and before the associates of the late Rev. Dr. Thomas Bray* (London, 1733); John Burton, *The duty and reward of propagating principles of religion and virtue exemplified in the history of Abraham. A sermon preach'd before the trustees for Establishing the Colony of Georgia in America. And before the Associates of the late Rev. Dr. Thomas Bray* (London, 1733).

167. *Reasons for establishing the Colony of Georgia*, 2nd ed. (London, 1733), 20; Perceval to Edward Southwell, 1 December 1725, BL Add MS 47031, f. 40; Newman to Bishop of Dromore, 19 August 1732, HNL vol. 23, f. 64; Newman to Rowland Cotton, 21 September 1732, HNL vol. 25, f. 6; on renewed threats to the Protestant interest on the Continent, see Andrew C. Thompson, *Britain, Hanover and the Protestant Interest, 1688–1756* (Rochester, NY: Boydell, 2006).

168. For SPCK involvement in the Georgia project, see *Henry Newman's Salzburger Letterbooks*, ed. George Fenwick Jones (Athens: University of Georgia Press, 1966).

169. On the patriot opposition to Walpole, see Nicholas Rogers, *Whigs and Cities: Popular Politics in the Age of Walpole and Pitt* (Oxford: Clarendon, 1989); Wilson, *Sense of the People*; Linda Colley, "Radical Patriotism in Eighteenth-Century England," in *Patriotism: The Making and Unmaking of British National Identity*, ed. Raphael Samuel, 3 vols. (London: Routledge, 1989), 1:168–187.

170. *Reasons for establishing the Colony of Georgia*, 40.

171. P. J. Marshall, "Who Cared about the Thirteen Colonies? Some Evidence from Philanthropy," *Journal of Imperial and Commonwealth History* 27 (1999): 53.

172. Richard S. Dunn, "The Trustees of Georgia and the House of Commons, 1732–1752," *WMQ*, 3rd series, 11 (October 1954): 551–565; Kathleen Wilson locates the Georgia Trust among the opposition at a slightly later date, see Wilson, *Sense of the People*, 163.

173. On George Heathcote, see Rogers, *Whigs and Cities*, 62–65; "Digby, Hon. Edward (c. 1693–1746)," in *The House of Commons, 1715–1754*, ed. Romney Sedgwick, 2 vols. (New York: History of Parliament Trust, 1970), 1:612; on Admiral Edward Vernon, see Kathleen Wilson, "Empire, Trade and Popular Politics in Mid-Hanoverian Britain: The Case of Admiral Vernon," *Past and Present* 121 (1988): 74–109, and Wilson, *Sense of the People*, 140–165; "Philips, Erasmus (1699–1743)," in *House of Commons, 1714–1754*, 2:343.

174. "Perceval, John, Visct. Perceval (1683–17148)," in *House of Commons, 1714–1754*, 2:336–338.

175. *The Journal of the Earl of Egmont: Abstract of the Trustees Proceedings for Establishing the Colony of Georgia, 1732–1738*, ed. Robert G. McPherson (Athens: University of Georgia Press, 1962), 273–274.

176. On the ecclesiastical politics of the Walpolean Church of England, see Jeffrey S. Chamberlain, *Accommodating High Churchmen: The Clergy of Sussex, 1700–1745* (Urbana: University of Illinois Press, 1997).

177. Henry Newman to Rowland Cotton, Esq., 21 September 1732, HNL vol. 25, f. 6.

178. Bob Harris, *Politics and the Nation: Britain in the Mid-Eighteenth Century* (Oxford: Oxford University Press, 2002), 321–322.

179. Newman to Lady Elizabeth Hastings, 1 February 1731/32, HNL vol. 23, f. 63; Newman to Henry Lowther, Esq. Principal at Surrat, 7 March 1731/32, HNL vol. 24, f. 4.

180. On middle-class participation in moral oversight, see Margaret Hunt, *The Middling Sort: Commerce, Gender and the Family in England, 1680–1780* (Berkeley: University of California Press, 1996), 101–124; Richard Price, *British Society, 1680–1880* (Cambridge: Cambridge University Press, 1999), 194–204.

181. The phrase belongs to Brown, *Moral Capital*, 48; Linda Colley, *Britons: Forging the Nation, 1707–1837* (New Haven, CT: Yale University Press, 1992), 85–98; Harris, *Politics and the Nation*, 278–323; Kathleen Wilson, "Urban Culture and Political Activism in Hanoverian England: The Example of Voluntary Hospitals," in *The Transformation of Political Culture: England and Germany in the Late Eighteenth Century*, ed. E. Hellmuth (Oxford: Oxford University Press, 1990), 165–184.

182. Marshall, "Who Cared about the Thirteen Colonies?," 55; Robert Ingram, *Religion, Reform and Modernity in the Eighteenth Century: Thomas Secker and the Church of England* (Woodbridge: Boydell, 2007), 209–259.

183. William Warburton, *A Sermon Preached before the Incorporated Society for the Propagation of the Gospel* (London, 1766); see Brown, *Moral Capital*, 197, 401; Glasson, *Mastering Christianity*, 199–232.

Conclusion

1. [Francis Lee], Heads for a biography of Robert Nelson, BL Add MS 45511, f. 174.

2. Extracts from the will of Robert Nelson, LPL Gibson MS 933, §77.

3. John Marshall, *A Sermon Preach'd in the Chappell of Ormond-Street on Sunday the 6th of February 1714* (London, 1715), 11.

4. Robert Nelson, *An Address to Persons of Quality and Estate* (London, 1715), 88, 105–122, 130–131, 139, 142–148, 149–150, 158, 169, 190–199, 200–215.

5. Jonathan Swift, *A Serious and Useful Scheme, To Make an Hospital for Incurables, Of Universal Benefit to all His Majesty's Subjects* (London and Dublin, 1733), 3; see also Daniel Defoe, *Augusta Triumphans: or, The Way to Make London the Most Flourishing City in the Universe* (London, 1728).

6. Peter Borsay, *The English Urban Renaissance: Culture and Society in the Provincial Town, 1660–1770* (Oxford: Clarendon, 1989), 109–111, 296–300.

7. George Watts, *A Sermon Preach'd at St. Bartholomew's Church Before the Governors and Stewards of St. Bartholomew's Hospital, July 26, 1733* (London, 1733), 7.

8. Samuel Clarke, *A Sermon Preach'd at the Parish Church of St. James Westminster, on Sunday April 18, 1725* (London, 1725), 10.

9. Bernard Mandeville, *The Fable of the Bees and Other Writings*, ed. E. J. Hundert (Indianapolis: Hackett, 1997), 101, 109–130.

10. Samuel Chandler, *Doing Good recommended from the Example of Christ* (London, 1728), 2, 31–32.

11. William Law, *Remarks upon a Late Book, Entituled, The Fable of the Bees* (London, 1724), 97–98.

12. William Hendley, *A Defence of the Charity-Schools* (London, 1725), 109, 118.

13. Sir John Thorold, *A short examination of the notions advanc'd in a (late) book, intitul'd The fable of the bees or private vices, publick benefits* (London, 1726), 27–28.

14. George Blewitt, *An enquiry whether a general practice of virtue tends to the wealth or poverty, benefit or disadvantage of a people?* (London, 1725), 179.

15. M. M. Goldsmith, *Private Vices, Public Benefits: Bernard Mandeville's Social and Political Thought* (Cambridge: Cambridge University Press, 1985), 121–123; Donna T. Andrew, *Philanthropy and Police: London Charity in the Eighteenth Century* (Princeton, NJ: Princeton University Press, 1989), 30–43.

16. Stephen Darwall, *The British Moralists and the Internal "Ought," 1640–1740* (Cambridge: Cambridge University Press, 1995).

17. Andrew Trebeck, *A Sermon Preached at the Parish Church at St. George, Hanover-Square, December 30, 1733* (London, 1733), 35–36.

18. John Locke, *A Letter Concerning Toleration* (Amherst: Prometheus Books, 1990), 22–23, 27–28, 65; Harold J. Laski, *Political Thought in England from Locke to Bentham* (New York: Henry Holt, 1920), 78–79; John Bossy, "Some Elementary Forms of Durkheim," *Past and Present* 95 (May 1982): 3–18.

Index

absolution, 161–163, 180–183

Act of Settlement (1701), 172

Africa, 240–242

African slaves, 75, 227, 228, 245, 251

age of benevolence, 3, 6–9, 13, 225, 250–260; defenses of, 256–258; first signs of, 150, 209; Mandeville's critique of, 255–256; Nelson's blueprint for, 252–253; origins of, 147, 148, 221–222, 250–251; projects of, 190

Ailesbury, Earl of (Thomas Bruce), 51

Aldrich, Henry, dean of Christ Church, 80, 190, 194, 195, 198, 201, 202

Allen, William, 122

American colonies, 7, 75, 102–103, 105, 196, 224–230, 250; charitable colony plan for, 246–248; established church in, 230; first Anglican seminary in, 230

Anglican overseas expansion, 2, 7, 15, 27, 102–103, 105, 109, 125, 126, 147, 149, 223–251; commercial orientation of, 233; diocesan jurisdiction over, 226–227; in Europe, 138–142, 234–239; global aim of, 239–244; methods of, 238–239; moral obligations of, 227–229, 244–246; opponents of, 229–230; Protestant interest and, 138–142; public reaction to, 244–251. *See also* American colonies; missionaries

(Anglican); Society for the Propagation of the Gospel in Foreign Parts

Anglican revival, 16, 18–23, 25, 31–32; accomplishments of, 149–150; ad hoc nature of, 70–71; agenda of, 3, 4, 5, 10, 11, 62–68, 70; characterization of, 150; enduring programs of, 71; instruments of, 254; moral consciousness effect of, 225; origins of, 2–3, 253; polarization of, 115, 185–186, 187–188, 203, 205–216; Whig celebration of, 173

Anne, queen of Great Britain, 16, 117, 127, 141, 164, 235; charity and, 77, 118, 231; Church of England and, 150, 172, 173, 204, 221; convocations of, 189, 193, 194, 203–220; final years of reign of, 142–148; high churchmen and, 165–166, 173–174, 179, 186; moderation policy of, 169, 170; occasional conformity bills and, 166–167, 169; policing of heresy and, 213, 214; Protestantism and, 32, 36, 38–39, 46, 51, 112, 114, 132, 137, 142, 218

anticlericalism, 174, 177, 209, 216, 217

antislavery movement, 250–251

anti-Trinitarianism. *See* Trinitarian controversy

apostolic succession, 156, 158, 177

Arianism, 69, 211–212, 215

Church of Rome. *See* Roman Catholic
Church
Church of Scotland, 140, 141, 172. *See also*
Presbyterianism
civil society, 1–2, 3, 6, 7, 8, 16, 23, 70;
Anglican investment in, 13–14; Anglican
overseas expansion and, 231–233,
244–249, 244–252, 250; church's position
in (*see* church and state); high churchmen's
fears about, 151–152, 186, 209; moral
ascendancy of, 8, 175, 215, 222; para-
ecclesial endeavors and, 31, 186; religious
obligations of, 175; sacralization of,
258–259; voluntarism and, 71, 100–101,
148, 190, 222
Clagett, William, 52
Clarendon, Earl of (Henry Hyde), 36, 58
Clarke, Samuel, 215, 255
clerical reform proposals, 75, 87–88, 196,
202–204, 217–221
clerical societies, 105–107, 110, 189, 206
Codrington, Christopher, 224, 232, 244
Colchester, Maynard, 93, 115, 118–119, 143
Collier, Jeremy, 156, 162–163
Collins, Anthony, 212; *Priestcraft in
Perfection*, 211
Comber, Thomas, dean of Durham, 122
commerce, 11, 12, 95, 97, 100, 109, 111, 118,
126, 147, 223; Anglican overseas
expansion and, 231–235, 246, 249; British
global trade and, 224, 225, 232–233, 239,
247; critique of philanthropy and, 255–256
Commission for Building Fifty New
Churches, 252
Commission for Relieving Poor Proselytes,
245, 249
Common Fund, 96, 161
communion (sacrament). *See* Lord's Supper
Compton, Henry, bishop of London, 32, 34,
35, 37, 39, 41, 47, 52, 63, 102, 171, 172,
179, 213; anti-Catholicism of, 27–28;
bishops' conflict with James II and, 59–60,
68; Chapel Royal deanery and, 72; as de
facto primate of all England, 73;

ecclesiastical commission (1686)
suspension of, 42–45, 48–49, 50, 51,
55; *Episcopalia*, 45; jurisdiction over
foreign plantations and, 102, 226–227,
229, 230; Lambeth meeting (1692) and,
90; prayer book commission (1689) and,
79–80, 83, 86; reformation of manners
and, 89, 172; royal injunction for
ecclesiastical reform and, 87–88, 93; SPCK
and, 105, 116, 129
Comyns, John, 115–116
confessionalization, 9–12, 15, 16, 123, 142;
meaning of, 9–10; new instruments of,
253–254
confirmation, 28, 63, 65, 88, 160
Congregational Fund, 95
Congregationalism, 95–96
constitutionalism, 59, 60, 62, 164–165, 185,
187, 189, 191–192; *praemunientes* clause,
191, 199, 220–221
Convention Parliament (1689), 76, 86, 87
convocation (Canterbury), 11, 79, 101, 108,
147, 165, 189, 190, 191–220; assembly of
1701, 193–199, 208; assembly of *1702*,
200–203; assessment of, 219–220;
bicameral structure of, 193, 220; lower
house discontent and, 194–195; royal
license (1711) for, 206, 208; "state of
religion" competing versions and,
215–219
Cook, Shadrach, 162–163
Coram, Thomas, 246, 247, 249
corporate institutions, 1, 6, 27, 118,
120–121, 173
Corporation Act (1661), 78
Corporation for Relief of Poor Widows and
Clergymen. *See* Sons of the Clergy
country ideology, 164–165, 191–192
Crewe, Nathaniel, bishop of Durham, 33, 37,
42, 45, 47–48, 54, 60, 72
Croft, Herbert, bishop of Hereford, 53, 60;
The Naked Truth, 76
Cyprian, St., bishop of Carthage, 155, 156,
160, 163